VOYAGES

FROM

MONTREAL

THROUGH THE

CONTINENT OF NORTH AMERICA

ALEXANDER MACKENZIE Esq.

VOYAGES

FROM

MONTREAL

ON THE RIVER ST. LAURENCE

THROUGH THE

CONTINENT OF NORTH AMERICA

TO THE

FROZEN AND PACIFIC OCEANS

In the Years 1789 and 1793

WITH A PRELIMINARY ACCOUNT

OF THE RISE, PROGRESS, AND PRESENT STATE OF

THE FUR TRADE

OF THAT COUNTRY

ILLUSTRATED WITH MAPS

BY ALEXANDER MACKENZIE, ESQ.

M. G. HURTIG LTD.
Booksellers & Publishers
EDMONTON

PRINTED IN JAPAN

TO

HIS MOST SACRED MAJESTY

GEORGE THE THIRD,

THIS VOLUME

IS INSCRIBED,

BY *HIS MAJESTY'S*

MOST FAITHFUL SUBJECT,

AND

DEVOTED SERVANT,

ALEXANDER MACKENZIE.

INTRODUCTION TO THE NEW EDITION

IN November of 1801 there appeared in London a book entitled *Voyages from Montreal through the Continent of North America to the Frozen and Pacific Oceans in 1789 and 1793*. It was intended for a public familiar with accounts of travel and avid for more. William Combe, the unacknowledged editor of the text, was a popular writer; he had already done a similar job on the voyages of John Meares, who had established a trading post in Nootka Sound. Combe did not tamper with Mackenzie's journals. A copy of the one covering the Arctic trip has survived and it is apparent that Combe formalized the style somewhat and incorporated a few notes supplied by Mackenzie, but was otherwise remarkably faithful to the original. The book was supplied with large and beautifully executed maps and Mackenzie expressed his hope that it would "not be thought unworthy the attention of the scientific geographer; and . . . will be received as a faithful tribute to the prosperity of my country."

A point of interest in the *Voyages* is the lengthy introduction, believed to be the work of Roderick Mackenzie, Alexander's cousin, describing the fur trade in North America. It reflects Alexander's role as he himself conceives it. He sees himself as a trader. He regards his voyages of exploration as interludes in his trading career and as serving the ends of the trade, a matter for honest pride; he is conscious that he is, by his discoveries, adding to "the British dominions" which he thinks of as providing scope for commerce rather than settlement. He could not anticipate the later concept of massive British emigration.

Alexander Mackenzie was born at Stornoway, Scotland, in 1764. When he was about aged ten, his mother died and his father brought him to New York. After war broke out between Britain and the American colonies, he was sent to Canada. By the age of twenty, he had had five years of experience in the fur trade and was being given positions of trust. In 1789, he was in the employ of the North West Company, which posted him to Fort Athabasca, near the lake now known by that name. He arrived there in October and settled in for the winter with Peter Pond, the trader in charge, whom he had come to replace.

He was typical of the many Scots, from the Highlands and the Islands, who took advantage of the closer association between Scotland and England brought about by the Act of Union, to make careers for themselves in Britain's far-flung domains. The Scotland from which his father carried him was at that time undergoing severe economic hardship.

Mackenzie died in 1820 and the century and a half separating us from him is just time enough to let his accomplishment recede into a new perspective. The glamour emanating from the history of the fur trade has faded. Washington Irving's "lords of the lakes and the forest" were in fact engaged in an extractive industry so ruthless that, within Mackenzie's lifetime, the beaver population was dwindling even on the last reaches of the Pacific slope. Competition among the fur trading companies was intense and bitter; only the imminence of collapse thrust the North West Company into a disadvantageous union with its stronger and older rival based on Hudson's Bay. The motto "Pro pelle cutem," which today connotes a fair trade, must have had certain additional overtones when it was first adopted, as a wry and ingenious piece of seventeenth-century wit, based on a phrase in the Vulgate spoken by the Tempter of Mankind.

The North West Company had no sense of the future of the enormous territory it exploited. Mackenzie's trip to the Arctic aroused no interest among the partners to whom, at their annual meeting, he reported it. When settlement of the Red River was attempted by Lord Selkirk, it was the North Westers and their Métis followers who opposed it and were responsible for the Seven Oaks massacre. Traders with Indian wives often abandoned them to someone else when they left the West. Those who, like Alexander Ross, remained in the country and secured education and recognition for their families were rare.

The history of the North West Company is that of a single fierce pulsation in the blood stream of economic life. The western web of canoe routes, anchored by trading posts, was no sooner completed than it proved too great a strain on the company's organization.

The fur trade was not only insecurely based on a dwindling resource; it was also precariously supported by demand. Furs, except for hunters themselves, have always been an article of luxury and largely associated with the changing fashions of affluent classes. The enormous expansion of the fur trade between the mid-seventeenth and early nineteenth centuries was made possible, in terms of supply, by the opening up of Siberian and North American wildernesses replete with fur-bearing animals, but in terms of demand, by the rapid rise of the middle classes of Europe into a degree of wealth that encouraged luxuries. A good beaver hat, after being several times renovated and being stiffened with gum in its last stages was still capable of turning up in Portugal as a desirable headgear. The advent of the silk top hat, the revival of caps and soft felts, the appearance of the Panama straw, all demonstrated how easily fashion, improvements in textiles and changes in life style can render an established article like the beaver hat quite obsolete. (It is probable that railway travel made lighter hats more practical, as the closed automobile was later to reduce the size and weight of both male and female headgear.)

The importance of the fur trade in the history of Canada is not, however, primarily economic. What it did was to establish the boundaries and settle the style of administration for the whole region west of Lake Superior. The North Westers were pioneers in the Athabasca area and in the valley of the Mackenzie River, as the account of the first voyage foreshadows. They were also first across the Rockies and into the coast region, which was the whole intention of the second voyage.

The style of administration might be termed the subjection of individual enterprise to monopoly control, by force of circumstances. It is customary to think of the Northwest as the home of the independent homesteader, the reckless cowboy, the footloose goldminer. In fact, the enormous distances, the climatic rigour, the dependence on world trade rather than local markets, all combined to erode haphazard personal endeavour. From the beginning, the fur trade cried out for monopoly control and never more clearly than when Mackenzie's company of North Westers was obliged to merge with the Hudson's Bay Company. The sale of grain, the drilling of oil wells, the construction or railroads, the mining of coal or potash, the operation of airlines: the West has seen each of these operations pass into the control of large corporations, often enjoying government support and protection. It is of interest to note that proposals made by Mackenzie in 1802 to Lord Hobart, the Colonial Secretary, called for a merging of the fur-trading companies into a single large organization, the establishment of Pacific stations by the Royal Navy, and the setting up of lines of trade to China and, via Cape Horn, to Britain.

For various reasons, an enterprise seeking to engross the whole or as much as possible of a commercial operation is likely to be preoccupied with problems of transport. The life blood of the fur trade was its movement of goods and supplies along the narrow arteries of the western waterways. The voyageurs followed *le fil d'eau* and where it tangled itself into falls and impassable rapids they made a *décharge* and carried canoes and ninety-pound packs on their strong shoulders. Half a dozen such portages might, in very bad country, be required in a single day. At vital intersections of this network, posts were established. They were nominally strongholds as well as storehouses and places of barter but the amount of physical violence they either provoked or repelled was, in the aggregate, negligible.

Mackenzie and his fellow Scots in the fur trade enjoyed peculiar advantages, in that they did not have to adapt themselves to unaccustomed rigours. The Highlands after the battle of Culloden in 1746 were not a comfortable place to live and they had never been a safe place to live. The Assiniboine region, with its abundance of fish, of fuel and of furs, with its peaceable Indians and obliging voyageurs, must have seemed positively hospitable to the two cousins Alexander and Roderick. To a Lewisman, hazards of travel in rough water and over rocky hillsides, sustained exertions on a varying diet and self-reliance in all the affairs of daily life would be nothing new or unusual. Although he had, in actuality, left Lewis when only a boy, Alexander had inherited a physique and a temperament that perfectly fitted his new surroundings.

The drainage systems of the West are such that only the Red River and the Columbia system flow north or south so as to connect Canadian and American territory. In each instance, the danger of American penetration was very real. It was a simple stroke of good luck for the future Dominion that Louis Riel did not desire an American connection or invite assistance from that quarter. It was another piece of good fortune that President Polk, faced with Earl Cathcart's vigorous preparations for the defence of British territory, did not decide to fight for "Fifty-four forty." The hook-and-eye connection between the extended line of the fur trade and the land-falls of Meares, Cook and Vancouver gave a continental continuum to British (and subsequent Canadian) claims. The outposts of the occupation were driven in by American aggressiveness. The Oregon territory and the Alaskan panhandle were not to be part of Canada's territory. But enough remained to give Canada a four hundred mile outlet on the Pacific. It makes one shudder to think how narrowly the Northwest escaped being wholly incorporated into America's "manifest destiny."

The reader who thinks over the account of Mackenzie and his two voyages and lets it slowly assume its own function in his imagination is likely to find that it is a catalyst or precipitating agent, clarifying his view of Canada. Every aspect of the great adventure ultimately composes into a view in depth of the Canadian terrain. Given the postulate of European enterprise and technology, as they existed even as early as the seventeenth century, the rest is in a sense inevitable. To put it another way, the special quality of free will apparent in Britain after the Puritan Revolution found a magnificently suitable challenge and field of action in northern North America. The Faustian problem of envisaging, estimating and conquering distances, has been uppermost everywhere in Canada at all times in Canadian history. The reader of the following pages, coming upon the incident in Friendly Village, on July 26th, 1793, where Mackenzie presents the chief with two yards of blue cloth, might take the map and consider how much muscular effort had been expended on that bit of fabric since it left the sheep's back in Britain.

No reader of the *Voyages* can escape the impression of monotony, of long successions of days unvaried except in the incidence of greater or less hazard from natural obstructions. What this signifies is that, as the history of Canada is underlain by its geography, so the geographic pattern in turn rests on the geology of the northern half of the continent. It is not surprising that geology was the first science to take flourishing root in Canada. Unlike the upended strata of England, producing a great variety of terrain within a few miles, the natural features of Canada—Great Lakes, Shield, Prairies, Rockies, coastal fijords—are all immense and outstretched to a degree that staggers the imagination.

It is this Canadian terrain which determined Mackenzie's tactics and the tactics of all who have followed him. As a trader, moving lightly armed in unfamiliar territory, he had every incentive to be cautious, careful and conciliatory in his dealings with the Indians. Without their goodwill there could be no trade. Without their acquiescence, the long, hazardous, unprotected canoe routes could not be maintained.

Mackenzie's story may be taken, as he presents it, as a story of discovery arising out of the necessities of the northern fur trade. Or, in greater depth, it can be seen as the tale of how Canada's western boundaries were roughly determined. Or, in the context of Canada's whole history, it can be seen as a paradigm of inevitable attitudes, understood aims and persisting preoccupations, all enforced, exacted and perpetuated by the inexorable demands of the land. With this backdrop and lighting, one can appreciate dramatic and even epic elements in Mackenzie's story which he himself could not foresee but which, could he have done so, would clearly have afforded him immense gratification.

ROY DANIELLS

University of British Columbia
Vancouver
July 1970

PREFACE.

ON prefenting this Volume to my Country, it is not neceffary to enter into a particular account of thofe voyages whofe journals form the principal part of it, as they will be found, I truft, to explain themfelves. It appears, however, to be a duty, which the Public have a right to expect from me, to ftate the reafons which have influenced me in delaying the publication of them.

It has been afferted, that a mifunderftanding between a perfon high in office and myfelf, was the caufe of this procraftination. It has alfo been propagated, that it was occafioned by that precaution which the policy of commerce will fometimes fuggeft; but they are both equally devoid of foundation. The one is an idle tale; and there could be no folid reafon for concealing the circumftances of difcoveries, whofe arrangements and profecution were fo honourable to my affociates and myfelf, at whofe expence they were undertaken. The delay actually arofe from the very active and bufy mode of life in which I was engaged fince the voyages have been completed; and when, at length, the opportunity arrived, the apprehenfion of prefenting myfelf to the Public in the character of an Author, for which the courfe and occupations of

my

my life have by no means qualified me, made me hefitate in committing my papers to the Prefs; being much better calculated to perform the voyages, arduous as they might be, than to write an account of them. However, they are now offered to the Public with the fubmiffion that becomes me.

I was led, at an early period of life, by commercial views, to the country North-Weft of Lake Superior, in North America, and being endowed by Nature with an inquifitive mind and enterprifing fpirit; poffeffing alfo a conftitution and frame of body equal to the moft arduous undertakings, and being familiar with toilfome exertions in the profecution of mercantile purfuits, I not only contemplated the practi- cability of penetrating acrofs the continent of America, but was con- fident in the qualifications, as I was animated by the defire, to undertake the perilous enterprize.

The general utility of fuch a difcovery, has been univerfally ac- knowledged; while the wifhes of my particular friends and commercial affociates, that I fhould proceed in the purfuit of it, contributed to quicken the execution of this favourite project of my own ambition: and as the completion of it extends the boundaries of geographic fcience, and adds new countries to the realms of Britifh commerce, the danger I have encountered, and the toils I have fuffered, have found their recompence; nor will the many tedious and weary days, or the gloomy and inclement nights which I have paffed, have been paffed in vain.

The

The firſt voyage has ſettled the dubious point of a practicable North-Weſt paſſage; and I truſt, that it has ſet that long agitated queſtion at reſt, and extinguiſhed the diſputes reſpecting it for ever. An enlarged diſcuſſion of that ſubject will be found to occupy the concluding pagec of this volume.

In this voyage, I was not only without the neceſſary books and inſtruments, but alſo felt myſelf deficient in the ſciences of aſtronomy and navigation: I did not heſitate, therefore, to undertake a winter's voyage to this country, in order to procure the one and acquire the other. Theſe objects being accompliſhed, I returned, to determine the practicability of a commercial communication through the continent of North America, between the Atlantic and Pacific Oceans, which is proved by my ſecond journal. Nor do I heſitate to declare my decided opinion, that very great and eſſential advantages may be derived by extending our trade from one ſea to the other.

Some account of the fur trade of Canada from that country, of the native inhabitants, and of the extenſive diſtricts connected with it, forms a preliminary diſcourſe, which will, I truſt, prove intereſting to a nation whoſe general policy is blended with, and whoſe proſperity is ſupported by, the purſuits of commerce. It will alſo qualify the reader to purſue the ſucceeding voyages with ſuperior intelligence and ſatisfaction.

Theſe voyages will not, I fear, afford the variety that may be expected from them; and that which they offered to the eye, is not of a

nature

nature to be effectually transferred to the page. Mountains and vallies, the dreary waste, and wide-spreading forests, the lakes and rivers succeed each other in general description; and, except on the coasts of the Pacific Ocean, where the villages were permanent, and the inhabitants in a great measure stationary, small bands of wandering Indians are the only people whom I shall introduce to the acquaintance of my readers.

The beaver and the buffalo, the moose-deer and the elk, which are the principal animals to be found in these countries, are already so familiar to the naturalists of Europe, and have been so often as well as correctly described in their works, that the bare mention of them, as they enlivened the landscape, or were hunted for food; with a cursory account of the soil, the course and navigation of lakes and rivers, and their various produce, is all that can be reasonably expected from me.

I do not possess the science of the naturalist; and even if the qualifications of that character had been attained by me, its curious spirit would not have been gratified. I could not stop to dig into the earth, over whose surface I was compelled to pass with rapid steps; nor could I turn aside to collect the plants which nature might have scattered on the way, when my thoughts were anxiously employed in making provision for the day that was passing over me. I had to encounter perils by land and perils by water; to watch the savage who was our guide, or to guard against those of his tribe who might meditate our destruction. I had, also, the passions and

fears

fears of others to control and fubdue. To day I had to affuage the rifing difcontents, and on the morrow to cheer the fainting fpirits, of the people who accompanied me. The toil of our navigation was inceffant, and oftentimes extreme; and in our progrefs over land we had no protection from the feverity of the elements, and poffeffed no accommodations or conveniences but fuch as could be contained in the burden on our fhoulders, which aggravated the toils of our march, and added to the wearifomenefs of our way.

Though the events which compofe my journals may have little in themfelves to ftrike the imagination of thofe who love to be aftonifhed, or to gratify the curiofity of fuch as are enamoured of romantic adventures; neverthelefs, when it is confidered that I explored thofe waters which had never before borne any other veffel than the canoe of the favage; and traverfed thofe deferts where an European had never before prefented himfelf to the eye of its fwarthy natives; when to thefe confiderations are added the important objects which were purfued, with the dangers that were encountered, and the difficulties that were furmounted to attain them, this work will, I flatter myfelf, be found to excite an intereft, and conciliate regard, in the minds of thofe who perufe it.

The general map which illuftrates this volume, is reduced by Mr. Arrowfmith from his three-fheet map of North-America, with the lateft difcoveries, which he is about to republifh. His profeffional abilites are well known, and no encomium of mine will advance the general and merited opinion of them.

Before

Before I conclude, I muſt beg leave to inform my readers, that they are not to expeᴄt the charms of embelliſhed narrative, or animated deſcription; the approbation due to ſimplicity and to truth is all I preſume to claim; and I am not without the hope that this claim will be allowed me. I have deſcribed whatever I ſaw with the impreſſions of the moment which preſented it to me. The ſucceſſive circumſtances of my progreſs are related without exaggeration or diſplay. I have ſeldom allowed myſelf to wander into conjeᴄture; and whenever conjeᴄture has been in dulged, it will be found, I truſt, to be accompanied with the temper of a man who is not diſpoſed to think too highly of himſelf: and if at any time I have delivered myſelf with confidence, it will appear, I hope, to be on thoſe ſubjeᴄts which, from the habits and experience of my life, will juſtify an unreſerved communication of my opinions. I am not a candidate for literary fame: at the ſame time, I cannot but indulge the hope that this volume, with all its imperfeᴄtions, will not be thought unworthy the attention of the ſcientific geographer; and that, by unfolding countries hitherto unexplored, and which, I preſume, may now be conſidered as a part of the Britiſh dominions, it will be received as a faithful tribute to the proſperity of my country.

ALEXANDER MACKENZIE.

LONDON,
November 30, 1801.

A

GENERAL HISTORY

OF THE

FUR TRADE

FROM

CANADA TO THE NORTH-WEST.

THE fur trade, from the earlieſt ſettlement of Canada, was conſidered of the firſt importance to that colony. The country was then ſo populous, that, in the vicinity of the eſtabliſhments, the animals whoſe ſkins were precious, in a commercial view, ſoon became very ſcarce, if not altogether extinct. They were, it is true, hunted at former periods, but merely for food and clothing. The Indians, there-fore, to procure the neceſſary ſupply, were encouraged to penetrate into the country, and were generally accompanied by ſome of the Cana-dians, who found means to induce the remoteſt tribes of natives to bring the ſkins which were moſt in demand, to their ſettlements, in the way of trade.

It is not neceſſary for me to examine the cauſe, but experience proves that it requires much leſs time for a civilized people to deviate into
the

the manners and cuſtoms of ſavage life, than for ſavages to riſe into a ſtate of civilization.   Such was the event with thoſe who thus accompanied the natives on their hunting and trading excurſions; for they became ſo attached to the Indian mode of life, that they loſt all reliſh for their former habits and native homes.   Hence they derived the title of *Coureurs des Bois*, became a kind of pedlars, and were extremely uſeful to the merchants engaged in the fur trade; who gave them the neceſſary credit to proceed on their commercial undertakings. Three or four of theſe people would join their ſtock, put their property into a birch-bark canoe, which they worked themſelves, and either accompanied the natives in their excurſions, or went at once to the country where they knew they were to hunt.   At length, theſe voyages extended to twelve or fifteen months, when they returned with rich cargoes of furs, and followed by great numbers of the natives. During the ſhort time requiſite to ſettle their accounts with the merchants, and procure freſh credit, they generally contrived to ſquander away all their gains, when they returned to renew their favourite mode of life: their views being anſwered, and their labour ſufficiently rewarded, by indulging themſelves in extravagance and diſſipation during the ſhort ſpace of one month in twelve or fifteen.

This indifference about amaſſing property, and the pleaſure of living free from all reſtraint, ſoon brought on a licentiouſneſs of manners which could not long eſcape the vigilant obſervation of the miſſionaries, who had much reaſon to complain of their being a diſgrace to the Chriſtian religion ; by not only ſwerving from its duties themſelves, but by

thus

thus bringing it into difrepute with thofe of the natives who had become converts to it; and, confequently, obftructing the great object to which thofe pious men had devoted their lives. They, therefore, exerted their influence to procure the fuppreffion of thefe people, and accordingly, no one was allowed to go up the country to traffic with the Indians, without a licence from the government.

At firft thefe permiffions were, of courfe, granted only to thofe whofe character was fuch as could give no alarm to the zeal of the miffionaries: but they were afterwards beftowed as rewards for fervices, on officers, and their widows; and they, who were not willing or able to make ufe of them, (which may be fuppofed to be always the cafe with thofe of the latter defcription) were allowed to fell them to the merchants, who neceffarily employed the Coureurs des bois, in quality of their agents; and thefe people, as may be imagined, gave fufficient caufe for the renewal of former complaints; fo that the remedy proved, in fact, worfe than the difeafe.

At length, military pofts were eftablifhed at the confluence of the dif- ferent large lakes of Canada, which, in a great meafure, checked the evil confequences that followed from the improper conduct of thefe forefters, and, at the fame time, protected the trade. Befides, a number of able and refpectable men retired from the army, profecuted the trade in perfon, under their refpective licences, with great order and regu- larity, and extended it to fuch a diftance, as, in thofe days, was confi- dered to be an aftonifhing effort of commercial enterprize. Thefe per- fons and the miffionaries having combined their views at the fame

time,

time, secured the respect of the natives, and the obedience of the people necessarily employed in the laborious parts of this undertaking. These gentlemen denominated themselves commanders, and not traders, though they were intitled to both those characters: and, as for the missionaries, if sufferings and hardships in the prosecution of the great work which they had undertaken, deserved applause and admiration, they had an undoubted claim to be admired and applauded: they spared no labour and avoided no danger in the execution of their important office; and it is to be seriously lamented, that their pious endeavours did not meet with the success which they deserved: for there is hardly a trace to be found beyond the cultivated parts, of their meritorious functions.

The cause of this failure must be attributed to a want of due consideration in the mode employed by the missionaries to propagate the religion of which they were the zealous ministers. They habituated themselves to the savage life, and naturalised themselves to the savage manners, and, by thus becoming dependant, as it were, on the natives, they acquired their contempt rather than their veneration. If they had been as well acquainted with human nature, as they were with the articles of their faith, they would have known, that the uncultivated mind of an Indian must be disposed by much preparatory method and instruction to receive the revealed truths of Christianity, to act under its sanctions, and be impelled to good by the hope of its reward, or turned from evil by the fear of its punishments. They should have began their work by teaching some of those useful arts which are the inlets of knowledge, and lead the mind by degrees to objects of higher comprehension. Agriculture so formed to fix and combine society, and so preparatory to

objects

objects of superior confideration, fhould have been the firft thing introduced among a favage people: it attaches the wandering tribe to that
fpot where it adds fo much to their comforts; while it gives them a fenfe
of property, and of lafting poffeffion, inftead of the uncertain hopes
of the chafe, and the fugitive produce of uncultivated wilds. Such
were the means by which the forefts of Paraguay were converted into a
fcene of abundant cultivation, and its favage inhabitants introduced to
all the advantages of a civilized life.

The Canadian miffionaries fhould have been contented to improve the
morals of their own countrymen, fo that by meliorating their character
and conduct, they would have given a ftriking example of the effect of
religion in promoting the comforts of life to the furrounding favages;
and might by degrees have extended its benign influence to the remoteft
regions of that country, which was the object, and intended to be the
fcene, of their evangelic labours. But by bearing the light of the
Gofpel at once to the diftance of two thoufand five hundred miles from
the civilized part of the colonies, it was foon obfcured by the cloud of
ignorance that darkened the human mind in thofe diftant regions.

The whole of their long route I have often travelled, and the recollection of fuch a people as the miffionaries having been there, was confined to a few fuperannuated Canadians, who had not left that country
fince the ceffion to the Englifh, in 1763, and who particularly mentioned
the death of fome, and the diftreffing fituation of them all. But if thefe
religious men did not attain the objects of their perfevering piety, they
were, during their miffion, of great fervice to the commanders who
engaged

engaged in thofe diftant expeditions, and fpread the fur trade as far Weft as the banks of the Safkatchiwine river, in 53. North latitude, and longitude 102 Weft.

At an early period of their intercourfe with the favages, a cuftom was introduced of a very excellent tendency, but is now unfortunately dif-continued, of not felling any fpirituous liquor to the natives. This admirable regulation was for fome time obferved, with all the refpe&t due to the religion by which it was fan&tioned, and whofe fevereft cen-fures followed the violation of it. A painful penance could alone reftore the offender to the fufpended rites of the facrament. The cafuiftry of trade, however, difcovered a way to gratify the Indians with their favour-ite cordial, without incurring the ecclefiaftical penalties, by giving, inftead of felling it to them.

But notwithftanding all the reftri&tions with which commerce was oppreffed under the French government, the fur trade was extended to the immenfe diftance which has been already ftated; and furmounted many moft difcouraging difficulties, which will be hereafter noticed; while, at the fame time, no exertions were made from Hudfon's Bay to obtain even a fhare of the trade of a country which, according to the charter of that company, belonged to it, and, from its proximity, is fo much more acceffible to the mercantile adventurer.

Of thefe trading commanders, I underftood, that two attempted to penetrate to the Pacific Ocean, but the utmoft extent of their journey I could never learn; which may be attributed, indeed, to a failure of the undertaking.

For

For some time after the conquest of Canada, this trade was suspended, which must have been very advantageous to the Hudson's Bay Company, as all the inhabitants to the Westward of Lake Superior, were obliged to go to them for such articles as their habitual use had rendered necessary. Some of the Canadians who had lived long with them, and were become attached to a savage life, accompanied them thither annually, till mercantile adventurers again appeared from their own country, after an interval of several years, owing, as I suppose, to an ignorance of the country in the conquerors, and their want of commercial confidence in the conquered. There were, indeed, other discouragements, such as the immense length of the journey necessary to reach the limits beyond which this commerce must begin; the risk of property; the expences attending such a long transport; and an ignorance of the language of those who, from their experience, must be necessarily employed as the intermediate agents between them and the natives. But, notwithstanding these difficulties, the trade, by degrees, began to spread over the different parts to which it had been carried by the French, though at a great risk of the lives, as well as the property, of their new possessors, for the natives had been taught by their former allies to entertain hostile dispositions towards the English, from their having been in alliance with their natural enemies the Iroquois; and there were not wanting a sufficient number of discontented, disappointed people to keep alive such a notion; so that for a long time they were considered and treated as objects of hostility. To prove this disposition of the Indians, we have only to refer to the conduct of Pontiac, at Detroit, and the surprise and taking of Michilimakinac, about this period.

Hence

Hence it arofe, that it was fo late as the year 1766, before which, the trade I mean to confider, commenced from Michilimakinac. The firft who attempted it were fatisfied to go the length of the River Cameniftiquia, about thirty miles to the Eaftward of the Grande Portage, where the French had a principal eftablifhment, and was the line of their communication with the interior country. It was once deftroyed by fire. Here they went and returned fuccefsful in the following fpring to Michilimakinac. Their fuccefs induced them to renew their journey, and incited others to follow their example. Some of them remained at Cameniftiquia, while others proceeded to and beyond the Grande Portage, which, fince that time has become the principal entrepôt of that trade, and is fituated in a bay, in latitude 48. North, and longitude 90. Weft. After paffing the ufual feafon there, they went back to Michilimakinac as before, and encouraged by the trade, returned in increafed numbers. One of thefe, Thomas Curry, with a fpirit of enterprize fuperior to that of his contemporaries, determined to penetrate to the furtheft limits of the French difcoveries in that country; or at leaft till the froft fhould ftop him. For this purpofe he procured guides and interpreters, who were acquainted with the country, and with four canoes arrived at Fort Bourbon, which was one of their pofts, at the Weft end of the Cedar Lake, on the waters of the Safkatchiwine. His rifk and toil were well recompenfed, for he came back the following fpring with his canoes filled with fine furs, with which he proceeded to Canada, and was fatisfied never again to return to the Indian country.

From this period people began to fpread over every part of the country, particularly where the French had eftablifhed fettlements.

Mr. James

Mr. James Finlay was the firſt who followed Mr. Curry's example, and with the ſame number of canoes, arrived, in the courſe of the next ſeaſon, at Nipawee, the laſt of the French ſettlements on the bank of the Saſkatchiwine River, in latitude nearly 43¼ North, and longitude 103 Weſt: he found the good fortune, as he followed, in every reſpect, the example, of his predeceſſor.

As may be ſuppoſed, there were now people enough ready to replace them, and the trade was purſued with ſuch avidity, and irregularity, that in a few years it became the reverſe of what it ought to have been. An animated competition prevailed, and the contending parties carried the trade beyond the French limits, though with no benefit to themſelves or neighbours, the Hudſon's-Bay Company; who in the year 1774, and not till then, thought proper to move from home to the Eaſt bank of Sturgeon Lake, in latitude 53. 56. North, and longitude 102. 15. Weſt, and became more jealous of their fellow ſubjects; and, perhaps, with more cauſe, than they had been of thoſe of France. From this period to the preſent time, they have been following the Canadians to their different eſtabliſhments, while, on the contrary, there is not a ſolitary inſtance that the Canadians have followed them; and there are many trading poſts which they have not yet attained. This, however, will no longer be a myſtery when the nature and policy of the Hudſon's-Bay Company is compared with that which has been purſued by their rivals in this trade.—But to return to my ſubject.

This competition, which has been already mentioned, gave a fatal blow to the trade from Canada, and, with other incidental cauſes, in my

opinion,

opinion, contributed to its ruin. This trade was carried on in a very distant country, out of the reach of legal reftraint, and where there was a free fcope given to any ways or means in attaining advantage. The confequence was not only the lofs of commercial benefit to the perfons engaged in it, but of the good opinion of the natives, and the refpect of their men, who were inclined to follow their example ; fo that with drinking, caroufing, and quarrelling with the Indians along their route, and among themfelves, they feldom reached their winter quarters; and if they did, it was generally by dragging their property upon fledges, as the navigation was clofed up by the froft. When at length they were arrived, the object of each was to injure his rival traders in the opinion of the natives as much as was in their power, by mifreprefentation and prefents, for which the agents employed were peculiarly calculated. They confidered the command of their employer as binding on them, and however wrong or irregular the tranfaction, the refponfibility refted with the principal who directed them. This is Indian law. Thus did they wafte their credit and their property with the natives, till the firft was paft redemption, and the laft was nearly exhaufted ; fo that towards the fpring in each year, the rival parties found it abfolutely neceffary to join, and make one common ftock of what remained, for the purpofe of trading with the natives, who could entertain no refpect for perfons who had conducted themfelves with fo much irregularity and deceit. The winter, therefore was one continued fcene of difagreements and quarrels. If any one had the precaution or good fenfe to keep clear of thefe proceedings, he derived a proportionable advantage from his good conduct, and frequently proved a peace-maker between the parties. To fuch an height had they carried this licentious conduct, that they

were

were in a continual ftate of alarm, and were even frequently ftopped to pay tribute on their route into the country; though they had adopted the plan of travelling together in parties of thirty or forty canoes, and keeping their men armed; which fometimes, indeed, proved neceffary for their defence.

Thus was the trade carried on for feveral years, and confequently becoming worfe and worfe, fo that the partners, who met them at the Grande Portage, naturally complained of their ill fuccefs. But fpecious reafons were always ready to prove that it arofe from circumftances which they could not at that time control; and encouragements were held forth to hope that a change would foon take place, which would make ample amends for paft difappointments.

It was about this time, that Mr. Jofeph Frobifher, one of the gentlemen engaged in the trade, determined to penetrate into the country yet unexplored, to the North and Weftward, and, in the fpring of the year 1775, met the Indians from that quarter on their way to Fort Churchill, at Portage de Traite, fo named from that circumftance on the banks of the Miffinipi, or Churchill River, latitude 55. 25. North, longitude 103¼. Weft. It was, indeed, with fome difficulty that he could induce them to trade with him, but he at length procured as many furs as his canoes could carry. In this perilous expedition he fuftained every kind of hardfhip incident to a journey through a wild and favage country, where his fubfiftence depended on what the woods and the waters produced. Thefe difficulties, neverthelefs, did not difcourage him from returning in the following year, when he was equally fuccefsful.

He

He then fent his brother to explore the country ftill further Weft, who penetrated as far as the lake of Ifle a la Croix, in latitude 55. 26. North, and longitude 108 Weft.

He, however, never after wintered among the Indians, though he retained a large intereft in the trade, and a principal fhare in the direction of it till the year 1798, when he retired to enjoy the fruits of his labours; and, by his hofpitality, became known to every refpeƈtable ftranger who vifited Canada.

The fuccefs of this gentleman induced others to follow his example, and in the fpring of the year 1778, fome of the traders on the Safkatchiwine River, finding they had a quantity of goods to fpare, agreed to put them into a joint ftock, and gave the charge and management of them to Mr. Peter Pond, who, in four canoes, was direƈted to enter the Englifh River, fo called by Mr. Frobifher, to follow his track, and proceed ftill further; if poffible, to Athabafca, a country hitherto unknown but from Indian report. In this enterprife he at length fucceeded, and pitched his tent on the banks of the Elk River, by him erroneoufly called the Athabafca River, about thirty miles from the Lake of the Hills, into which it empties itfelf.

Here he paffed the winter of 1778-9; faw a vaft concourfe of the Knifteneaux and Chepewyan tribes, who ufed to carry their furs annually to Churchill; the latter by the barren grounds, where they fuffered innumerable hardfhips, and were fometimes even ftarved to death. The former followed the courfe of the lakes and rivers, through a country

that

that abounded in animals, and where there was plenty of fish : but though they did not fuffer from want of food, the intolerable fatigue of fuch a journey could not be eafily repaid to an Indian : they were, there-fore, highly gratified by feeing people come to their country to relieve them from fuch long, toilfome, and dangerous journies; and were im-mediately reconciled to give an advanced price for the articles neceffary to their comfort and convenience. Mr. Pond's reception and fuccefs was accordingly beyond his expectation; and he procured twice as many furs as his canoes would carry. They alfo fupplied him with as much provifion as he required during his refidence among them, and fufficient for his homeward voyage. Such of the furs as he could not embark, he fecured in one of his winter huts, and they were found the following feafon, in the fame ftate in which he left them.

Thefe, however, were but partial advantages, and could not prevent the people of Canada from feeing the improper conduct of fome of their affociates, which rendered it dangerous to remain any longer among the natives. Moft of them who paffed the winter at the Safkatchiwine, got to the Eagle hills, where, in the fpring of the year 1780, a few days pre-vious to their intended departure, a large band of Indians being engaged in drinking about their houfes, one of the traders, to eafe himfelf of the troublefome importunities of a native, gave him a dofe of laudanum in a glafs of grog, which effectually prevented him from giving further trouble to any one, by fetting him afleep for ever. This accident pro-duced a fray, in which one of the traders, and feveral of the men, were killed, while the reft had no other means to fave themfelves but by a precipitate flight, abandoning a confiderable quantity of goods, and

near

near half the furs which they had collected during the winter and the spring.

About the same time, two of the eftablishments on the Assiniboin river, were attacked with less juftice, when several white men, and a greater number of Indians were killed. In short, it appeared, that the natives had formed a refolution to extirpate the traders; and, without entering into any further reasonings on the subject, it appears to be incontrovertible, that the irregularity purfued in carrying on the trade has brought it into its prefent forlorn fituation; and nothing but the greateft calamity that could have befallen the natives, faved the traders from deftruction: this was the fmall pox, which spread its deftructive and defolating power, as the fire confumes the dry grafs of the field. The fatal infection fpread around with a baneful rapidity which no flight could efcape, and with a fatal effect that nothing could refift. It deftroyed with its peftilential breath whole families and tribes; and the horrid fcene prefented to those who had the melancholy and afflicting opportunity of beholding it, a combination of the dead, the dying, and fuch as to avoid the horrid fate of their friends around them, prepared to difappoint the plague of its prey, by terminating their own exiftence.

The habits and lives of these devoted people, which provided not to-day for the wants of to-morrow, muft have heightened the pains of fuch an affliction, by leaving them not only without remedy, but even without alleviation. Nought was left them but to fubmit in agony and defpair.

To

To aggravate the picture, if aggravation were poffible, may be added, the putrid carcafes which the wolves, with a furious voracity, dragged forth from the huts, or which were mangled within them by the dogs, whofe hunger was fatisfied with the disfigured remains of their mafters. Nor was it uncommon for the father of a family, whom the infection had not reached, to call them around him, to reprefent the cruel fufferings and horrid fate of their relations, from the influence of fome evil fpirit who was preparing to extirpate their race ; and to incite them to baffle death, with all its horrors, by their own poniards. At the fame time, if their hearts failed them in this neceffary act, he was himfelf ready to perform the deed of mercy with his own hand, as the laft act of his affection, and inftantly to follow them to the common place of reft and refuge from human evil.

It was never fatisfactorily afcertained by what means this malignant diforder was introduced, but it was generally fuppofed to be from the Miffiffoaic, by a war party.

The confequence of this melancholy event to the traders muft be felf-evident; the means of difpofing of their goods were cut off; and no furs were obtained, but fuch as had been gathered from the habitations of the deceafed Indians, which could not be very confiderable : nor did they look from the loffes of the prefent year, with any encouraging expectations to thofe which were to come. The only fortunate people confifted of a party who had again penetrated to the Northward and Weftward in 1780, at fome diftance up the Miffinipi, or Englifh River,

to

to Lake la Rouge.   Two unfortunate circumſtances, however, happened to them; which are as follow.

Mr. Wadin, a Swiſs gentleman, of ſtrict probity and known ſobriety, had gone there in the year 1779, and remained during the ſummer 1780. His partners and others, engaged in an oppoſite intereſt, when at the Grande Portage, agreed to ſend a quantity of goods on their joint account, which was accepted, and Mr. Pond was propoſed by them to be their repreſentative to act in conjunction with Mr. Wadin.   Two men, of more oppoſite characters, could not, perhaps, have been found.   In ſhort from various cauſes, their ſituations became very uncomfortable to each other, and mutual ill-will was the natural conſequence: without entering, therefore, into a minute hiſtory of theſe tranſactions, it will be ſufficient to obſerve, that, about the end of the year 1780, or the beginning of the year 1781, Mr. Wadin had received Mr. Pond and one of his own clerks to dinner; and, in the courſe of the night, the former was ſhot through the lower part of the thigh, when it was ſaid that he expired from the loſs of blood, and was buried next morning at eight o'clock.   Mr. Pond, and the clerk, were tried for this murder at Montreal, and acquitted: neverthelefs, their innocence was not ſo apparent as to extinguiſh the original ſuſpicion.

The other circumſtance was this.   In the ſpring of the year, Mr. Pond ſent the abovementioned clerk to meet the Indians from the Northward, who uſed to go annually to Hudſon's Bay; when he eaſily perſuaded them to trade with him, and return back, that they might not

take

take the contagion which had depopulated the country to the Eastward of them : but most unfortunately they caught it here, and carried it with them, to the destruction of themselves and the neighbouring tribes.

The country being thus depopulated, the traders and their friends from Canada, who, from various causes already mentioned, were very much reduced in number, became confined to two parties, who began seriously to think of making permanent establishments on the Missinipi river, and at Athabasca ; for which purpose, in 1781-2, they selected their best canoe-men, being ignorant that the small pox penetrated that way. The most expeditious party got only in time to the Portage la Loche, or Mithy-Ouinigam Portage, which divides the waters of the Missinipi from those that fall into the Elk river, to dispatch one canoe strong handed, and light-loaded, to that country ; but, on their arrival there, they found, in every direction, the ravages of the small pox ; so that, from the great diminution of the natives, they returned in the spring with no more than seven packages of beaver. The strong woods and mountainous countries afforded a refuge to those who fled from the contagion of the plains ; but they were so alarmed at the surrounding destruction, that they avoided the traders, and were dispirited from hunting except for their subsistence. The traders, however, who returned into the country in the year 1782-3, found the inhabitants in some sort of tranquillity, and more numerous than they had reason to expect, so that their success was proportionably better.

During the winter of 1783-4, the merchants of Canada, engaged in this trade, formed a junction of interests, under the name of the North-
Weft

Weſt Company, and divided it into ſixteen ſhares, without depoſiting any capital; each party furniſhing a proportion or quota of ſuch articles as were neceſſary to carry on the trade : the reſpective parties agreeing to ſatisfy the friends they had in the country, who were not provided for, according to this agreement, out of the proportions which they held. The management of the whole was accordingly entruſted to Meſſrs. Benjamin and Joſeph Frobiſher, and Mr. Simon M'Taviſh, two diſtinct houſes, who had the greateſt intereſt and influence in the country, and for which they were to receive a ſtipulated commiſſion in all tranſactions.

In the ſpring, two of thoſe gentlemen went to the Grande Portage with their credentials, which were confirmed and ratified by all the parties having an option, except Mr. Peter Pond, who was not ſatisfied with the ſhare allotted him. Accordingly he, and another gentleman, Mr. Peter Pangman, who had a right to be a partner, but for whom no proviſion had been made, came to Canada, with a determination to return to the country, if they could find any perſons to join them, and give their ſcheme a proper ſupport.

The traders in the country, and merchants at Montreal, thus entered into a co-partnerſhip, which, by theſe means, was conſolidated and directed by able men, who, from the powers with which they were entruſted, could carry on the trade to the utmoſt extent it would bear. The traders in the country, therefore, having every reaſon to expect that their paſt and future labours would be recompenſed, forgot all their former animoſities, and engaged with the utmoſt ſpirit and activity, to forward the general intereſt; ſo that, in the following year,

they

they met their agents at the Grande Portage, with their canoes laden with rich furs from the different parts of that immenfe tract of country. But this fatisfaction was not to be enjoyed without fome interruption; and they were mortified to find that Mr. Pangman had prevailed on Meffrs. Gregory and Macleod to join him, and give him their fupport in the bufinefs, though deferted by Mr. Pond, who accepted the terms offered by his former affociates.

In the counting houfe of Mr. Gregory I had been five years; and at this period had left him, with a fmall adventure of goods, with which he had entrufted me, to feek my fortune at Detroit. He, without any folicitation on my part, had procured an infertion in the agreement, that I fhould be admitted a partner in this bufinefs, on condition that I would proceed to the Indian country in the following fpring, 1785. His partner came to Detroit to make me fuch a propofition. I readily affented to it, and immediately proceeded to the Grande Portage, where I joined my affociates.

We now found that independent of the natural difficulties of the undertaking, we fhould have to encounter every other which they, who were already in poffeffion of the trade of the country, could throw in our way, and which their circumftances enabled them to do. Nor did they doubt, from their own fuperior experience, as well as that of their clerks and men, with their local knowledge of the country and its inhabitants, that they fhould foon compel us to leave the country to them. The event, however, did not juftify their expectations; for, after the fevereft ftruggle ever known in that part of the world,

world, and fuffering every oppreffion which a jealous and rival fpirit could inftigate; after the murder of one of our partners, the laming of another, and the narrow efcape of one of our clerks, who received a bullet through his powder horn, in the execution of his duty, they were compelled to allow us a fhare of the trade. As we had already incurred a lofs, this union was, in every refpect, a defirable event to us, and was concluded in the month of July 1787.

This commercial eftablifhment was now founded on a more folid bafis than any hitherto known in the country; and it not only continued in full force, vigour, and profperity, in fpite of all interference from Canada, but maintained at leaft an equal fhare of advantage with the Hudfon's-Bay Company, notwithftanding the fuperiority of their local fituation. The following account of this felf-erected concern will manifeft the caufe of its fuccefs.

It affumed the title of the North-Weft Company, and was no more than an affociation of commercial men, agreeing among themfelves to carry on the fur trade, unconnected with any other bufinefs, though many of the parties engaged had extenfive concerns altogether foreign to it. It may be faid to have been fupported entirely upon credit; for, whether the capital belonged to the proprietor, or was borrowed, it equally bore intereft, for which the affociation was annually accountable. It confifted of twenty fhares, unequally divided among the perfons concerned. Of thefe, a certain proportion was held by the people who managed the bufinefs in Canada, and were ftyled agents for the Company. Their duty was to import the neceffary goods from

England

England, ſtore them at their own expence at Montreal, get them made up into the articles ſuited to the trade, pack and forward them, and ſupply the caſh that might be wanting for the outfits; for which they received, independent of the profit on their ſhares, a commiſſion on the amount of the accounts, which they were obliged to make out annually, and keep the adventure of each year diſtinct. Two of them went annually to the Grande Portage, to manage and tranſact the buſineſs there, and on the communication at Detroit, Michilimakinac, St. Mary's, and Montreal, where they received ſtores, packed up, and ſhipped the company's furs for England, on which they had alſo a ſmall commiſſion. The remaining ſhares were held by the proprietors, who were obliged to winter and manage the buſineſs of the concern with the Indians, and their reſpective clerks, &c. They were not ſuppoſed to be under any obligation to furniſh capital, or even credit. If they obtained any capital by the trade, it was to remain in the hands of the agents; for which they were allowed intereſt. Some of them, from their long ſervices and influence, held double ſhares, and were allowed to retire from the buſineſs at any period of the exiſting concern, with one of thoſe ſhares, naming any young man in the company's ſervice to ſucceed him in the other. Seniority and merit were, however, conſidered as affording a claim to the ſucceſſion, which, neverthelefs, could not be diſpoſed of without the concurrence of the majority of the concern; who, at the ſame time relieved the ſeceding perſon from any reſponſibility reſpecting the ſhare that he transferred, and accounted for it according to the annual value or rate of the property; ſo that the ſeller could have no advantage but that of getting the ſhare of ſtock which he retained realiſed, and receiving for the transferred ſhare what was fairly determined to be the worth of it. The

former

former was alfo difcharged from all duty, and became a dormant partner. Thus, all the young men who were not provided for at the beginning of the contract, fucceeded in fucceffion to the character and advantages of partners. They entered into the Company's fervice for five or
feven years, under fuch expectations, and their reafonable profpects were
feldom difappointed : there were, indeed, inftances when they fucceeded
to fhares, before their apprenticefhip was expired, and it frequently happened that they were provided for while they were in a ftate of articled
clerkfhip. Shares were transferrable only to the concern at large, as no
perfon could be admitted as a partner who had not ferved his time to
the trade. The dormant partner indeed might difpofe of his intereft to
any one he chofe, but if the tranfaction were not acknowledged by his
affociates, the purchafer could only be confidered as his agent or attor-
ney. Every fhare had a vote, and two thirds formed a majority. This
regular and equitable mode of providing for the clerks of the company,
excited a fpirit of emulation in the difcharge of their various duties, and
in fact, made every agent a principal, who perceived his own profperity
to be immediately connected with that of his employers. Indeed, without fuch a fpirit, fuch a trade could not have become fo extended and
advantageous, as it has been and now is.

In 1788, the grofs amount of the adventure for the year did not exceed forty thoufand pounds,* but by the exertion, enterprife, and in-
duftry of the proprietors, it was brought in eleven years to triple that

---

* This might be properly called the ftock of the company, as it included, with the expenditure of
the year, the amount of the property unexpended, which had been appropriated for the adventure of
that year, and was carried on to the account of the following adventure.

amount

amount and upwards; yielding proportionate profits, and furpaffing, in fhort, any thing known in America.

Such, therefore, being the profperous ftate of the company, it, very naturally, tempted others to interfere with the concern in a manner by no means beneficial to the company, and commonly ruinous to the undertakers.

In 1798 the concern underwent a new form, the fhares were increafed to forty-fix, new partners being admitted, and others retiring. This period was the termination of the company, which was not renewed by all the parties concerned in it, the majority continuing to aft upon the old ftock, and under the old firm; the others beginning a new one; and it now remains to be decided, whether two parties, under the fame regulations and by the fame exertions, though unequal in number, can continue to carry on the bufinefs to a fuccefsful iffue. The contrary opinion has been held, which, if verified, will make it the intereft of the parties again to coalefce; for neither is deficient in capital to fupport their obftinacy in a lofing trade, as it is not to be fuppofed that either will yield on any other terms than perpetual participation.

It will not be fuperfluous in this place, to explain the general mode of carrying on the fur trade.

The agents are obliged to order the neceffary goods from England in the month of October, eighteen months before they can leave Montreal; that is, they are not fhipped from London until the fpring following,

lowing, when they arrive in Canada in the fummer. In the courfe of the following winter they are made up into fuch articles as are required for the favages; they are then packed into parcels of ninety pounds weight each, but cannot be fent from Montreal until the May following; fo that they do not get to market until the enfuing winter, when they are exchanged for furs, which come to Montreal the next fall, and from thence are fhipped, chiefly to London, where they are not fold or paid for before the fucceeding fpring, or even as late as June; which is forty-two months after the goods were ordered in Canada; thirty-fix after they had been fhipped from England, and twenty-four after they had been forwarded from Montreal; fo that the merchant, allowing that he has twelve months credit, does not receive a return to pay for thofe goods, and the neceffary expences attending them, which is about equal to the value of the goods themfelves, till two years after they are confidered as cafh, which makes this a very heavy bufinefs. There is even a fmall proportion of it that requires twelve months longer to bring round the payment, owing to the immenfe diftance it is carried, and from the fhortnefs of the feafons, which prevents the furs, even after they are collected, from coming out of the country for that period.

* This will be better illuftrated by the following ftatement :

We will fuppofe the goods for 1798 ;

The orders for the goods are fent to this country	25th Oct. 1796.
They are fhipped from London	March 1797.
They arrive in Montreal	June 1797.
They are made up in the courfe of that fummer and winter.	
They are fent from Montreal	May 1798.
They arrive in the Indian country, and are exchanged for furs the following winter	1798-9.
Which furs come to Montreal	Sept. 1799.
And are fhipped for London, where they are fold in March and April, and paid for in May or June	1800.

The

The articles neceffary for this trade, are coarfe woollen cloths of different kinds; milled blankets of different fizes; arms and ammunition; twift and carrot tobacco; Manchefter goods; linens, and coarfe fheetings; thread, lines and twine; common hardware; cutlery and iron-mongery of feveral defcriptions; kettles of brafs and copper, and fheet-iron; filk and cotton handkerchiefs; hats, fhoes and hofe; calicoes and printed cottons, &c. &c. &c. Spirituous liquors and provifions are purchafed in Canada. Thefe, and the expence of tranfport to and from the Indian country, including wages to clerks, interpreters, guides, and canoe-men, with the expence of making up the goods for the market, form about half the annual amount againft the adventure.

This expenditure in Canada ultimately tends to the encouragement of Britifh manufactory, for thofe who are employed in the different branches of this bufinefs, are enabled by their gains to purchafe fuch Britifh articles as they muft otherwife forego.

The produce of the year of which I am now fpeaking, confifted of the following furs and peltries :

106,000 Beaver fkins,	6000 Lynx fkins,
2160 Bear fkins,	600 Wolverine fkins,
1500 Fox fkins,	1650 Fifher fkins,
4000 Kitt Fox fkins,	100 Rackoon fkins,
4600 Otter fkins,	3800 Wolf fkins,
17,000 Mufquafh fkins,	700 Elk fkins,
32,000 Marten fkins,	750 Deer fkins,
1800 Mink fkins,	1200 Deer fkins, dreffed,
500 Buffalo robes, and a quantity of caftorum.	

Of

Of thefe were diverted from the Britifh market, being fent through the United States to China, 13,364 fkins, fine beaver, weighing 19283 pounds; 1250 fine otters, and 1724 kitt foxes. They would have found their way to the China market at any rate, but this deviation from the Britifh channel arofe from the following circumftance :

An adventure of this kind was undertaken by a refpectable houfe in London, half concerned with the North-Weft Company in the year 1792. The furs were of the beft kind, and fuitable to the market; and the adventurers continued this connexion for five fucceffive years, to the annual amount of forty thoufand pounds. At the winding up of the concern of 1792, 1793, 1794, 1795, in the year 1797, (the adventure of 1796 not being included, as the furs were not fent to China, but difpofed of in London), the North-Weft Company experienced a lofs of upwards of £40,000 (their half,) which was principally owing to the difficulty of getting home the produce procured in return for the furs from China, in the Eaft India Company's fhips, together with the duty payable, and the various reftrictions of that company. Whereas, from America there are no impediments; they get immediately to market, and the produce of them is brought back, and perhaps fold in the courfe of twelve months. From fuch advantages the furs of Canada will no doubt find their way to China by America, which would not be the cafe if Britifh fubjects had the fame privileges that are allowed to foreigners, as London would then be found the beft and fafeft market.

But to return to our principal fubject.—We fhall now proceed to confider the number of men employed in the concern : viz. fifty clerks,

feventy-

feventy-one interpreters and clerks, one thoufand one hundred and twenty canoe men, and thirty-five guides. Of thefe, five clerks, eighteen guides, and three hundred and fifty canoe men, were employed for the fummer feafon in going from Montreal to the Grande Portage, in canoes, part of whom proceeded from thence to Rainy Lake, as will be hereafter explained, and are called Pork-eaters, or Goers and Comers. Thefe were hired in Canada or Montreal, and were abfent from the 1ft of May till the latter end of September. For this trip the guides had from eight hundred to a thoufand livres, and a fuitable equipment; the foreman and fteerfman from four to fix hundred livres; the middlemen from two hundred and fifty to three hundred and fifty livres, with an equipment of one blanket, one fhirt, and one pair of trowfers; and were maintained during that period at the expence of their employers. Independent of their wages, they were allowed to traffic, and many of them earned to the amount of their wages. About one third of thefe went to winter, and had more than double the above wages and equipment. All the others were hired by the year, and fome times for three years; and of the clerks many were apprentices, who were generally engaged for five or feven years, for which they had only one hundred pounds, provifion and clothing. Such of them who could not be provided for as partners, at the expiration of this time, were allowed from one hundred pounds to three hundred pounds per annum, with all neceffaries, till provifion was made for them. Thofe who acted in the two-fold capacity of clerk and interpreter, or were fo denominated, had no other expectation than the payment of wages to the amount of from one thoufand to four thoufand livres per annum, with clothing and provifions. The guides, who are a very ufeful fet of men, acted alfo in the additional capacity of interpreters,

and

and had a stated quantity of goods, considered as sufficient for their wants, their wages being from one to three thousand livres. The canoe men are of two descriptions, foremen and steersmen, and middlemen. The two first were allowed annually one thousand two hundred, and the latter four hundred, livres each. The first class had what is called an equipment, consisting of two blankets, two shirts, two pair of trowsers, two handkerchiefs, fourteen pounds of carrot tobacco, and some trifling articles. The latter had ten pounds of tobacco, and all the other articles: those are called North Men, or Winterers; and to the last class of people were attached upwards of seven hundred Indian women and children, victualled at the expence of the company.

This first class of people are hired in Montreal five months before they set out, and receive their equipments, and one third of their wages in advance; and an adequate idea of the labour they undergo may be formed from the following account of the country through which they pass, and their manner of proceeding.

The necessary number of canoes being purchased, at about three hundred livres each, the goods formed into packages, and the lakes and rivers free of ice, which they usually are in the beginning of May, they are then dispatched from La Chine, eight miles above Montreal, with eight or ten men in each canoe, and their baggage; and sixty-five packages of goods, six hundred weight of biscuit, two hundred weight of pork, three bushels of pease, for the men's provision; two oil cloths to cover the goods, a sail, &c. an axe, a towing-line, a kettle, and a sponge to bail out the water, with a quantity of gum, bark, and watape, to

repair

repair the veffel.   An European on feeing one of thefe flender veffels thus laden, heaped up, and funk with her gunwale within fix inches of the water, would think his fate inevitable in fuch a boat, when he reflected on the nature of her voyage; but the Canadians are fo expert that few accidents happen.

Leaving La Chine, they proceed to St. Ann's, within two miles of the Weftern extremity of the ifland of Montreal, the lake of the two mountains being in fight, which may be termed the commencement of the Utawas River.   At the rapid of St. Ann they are obliged to take out part, if not the whole of their lading.   It is from this fpot that the Canadians confider they take their departure, as it poffeffes the laft church on the ifland, which is dedicated to the tutelar faint of voyagers.

The lake of the two mountains is about twenty miles long, but not more than three wide, and furrounded by cultivated fields, except the Seignory belonging to the clergy, though nominally in poffeffion of the two tribes of Iroquois and Algonquins, whofe village is fituated on a delightful point of land under the hills, which, by the title of mountains, give a name to the lake.   Near the extremity of the point their church is built, which divides the village in two parts, forming a regular angle along the water fide.   On the Eaft is the ftation of the Algonquins, and on the Weft, one of the Iroquois, confifting in all of about five hundred warriors. Each party has its miffionary, and divine worfhip is performed accord-ing to the rites of the Roman Catholic religion, in their refpective lan-guages in the fame church: and fo affiduous have their paftors been, that thefe people have been inftructed in reading and writing in their

own

own language, and are better inftructed than the Canadian inhabitants of the country of the lower ranks: but notwithftanding thefe advantages, and though the eftablifhment is nearly coeval with the colonization of the country, they do not advance towards a ftate of civilization, but retain their ancient habits, language, and cuftoms, and are becoming every day more depraved, indigent, and infignificant. The country around them, though very capable of cultivation, prefents only a few miferable patches of ground, fown by the women with maize and vegetables. During the winter feafon, they leave their habitations, and pious paftors, to follow the chafe, according to the cuftom of their forefathers. Such is, indeed, the ftate of all the villages near the cultivated parts of Canada. But we fhall now leave them to proceed on our voyage.

At the end of the lake the water contracts into the Utawas River, which, after a courfe of fifteen miles, is interrupted by a fucceffion of rapids and cafcades for upwards of ten miles, at the foot of which the Canadian Seignories terminate; and all above them were wafte land, till the conclufion of the American war, when they were furveyed by order of government, and granted to the officers and men of the eighty-fourth regiment, when reduced; but principally to the former, and confequently little inhabited, though very capable of cultivation.

The voyagers are frequently obliged to unload their canoes, and carry the goods upon their backs, or rather fufpended in flings from their heads. Each man's ordinary load is two packages, though fome carry three. Here the canoe is towed by a ftrong line. There are fome places where the ground will not admit of their carrying the whole;

they

they then make two trips, that is, leave half their lading, and go and land it at the diftance required; and then return for that which was left. In this diftance are three carrying-places, the length of which depends in a great meafure upon the ftate of the water, whether higher or lower; from the laft of thefe the river is about a mile and an half wide, and has a regular current for about fixty miles, when it ends at the firft Portage de Chaudiere, where the body of water falls twenty-five feet, over cragged, excavated rocks, in a moft wild, romantic manner. At a fmall diftance below, is the river Rideau on the left, falling over a perpendicular rock, near forty feet high, in one fheet, affuming the appearance of a curtain; and from which circumftance it derives its name. To this extent the lands have been furveyed, as before obferved, and are very fit for culture. Many loyalifts are fettled upon the river Rideau, and have, I am told, thriving plantations. Some American families preferring the Britifh territory, have alfo eftablifhed themfelves along a river on the oppofite fide, where the foil is excellent. Nor do I think the period is far diftant, when the lands will become fettled from this vicinity to Montreal.

Over this portage, which is fix hundred and forty-three paces long, the canoe and all the lading is carried. The rock is fo fteep and difficult of accefs, that it requires twelve men to take the canoe out of the water: it is then carried by fix men, two at each end on the fame fide, and two under the oppofite gunwale in the middle. From hence to the next is but a fhort diftance, in which they make two trips over the fecond Portage de Chaudiere, which is feven hundred paces, to carry the loading alone. From hence to the next and laft Chaudiere, or Portage des Chenes, is about

fix

fix miles, with a very ftrong current, where the goods are carried feven hundred and forty paces; the canoe being towed up by the line, when the water is not very high. We now enter Lac des Chaudieres, which is computed to be thirty miles in length. Though it is called a lake, there is a ftrong draught downwards, and its breadth is from two to four miles. At the end of this is the Portage des Chats, over which the canoe and lading are carried two hundred and feventy-four paces; and very difficult it is for the former. The river is here barred by a ridge of black rocks, rifing in pinnacles and covered with wood, which, from the fmall quantity of foil that nourifhes it, is low and ftinted. The river finds its way over and through thefe rocks, in numerous channels, falling fifteen feet and upwards. From hence two trips are made through a ferpentine channel, formed by the rocks, for feveral miles, when the current flackens, and is accordingly called the Lake des Chats. At the channels of the grand Calumet, which are computed to be at the diftance of eighteen miles, the current recovers its ftrength, and proceeds to the Portage Dufort, which is two hundred and forty-five paces long; over which the canoe and baggage are tranfported. From hence the current becomes more rapid, and requires two trips to the Décharge des Sables*, where the goods are carried one hundred and thirty-five paces, and the canoe towed. Then follows the Mountain Portage, where the canoe and lading are alfo carried three hundred and eighty-five paces; then to the Décharge of the Derigé where the goods are carried two hundred and fifty paces; and thence to the grand Calumet. This is the longeft

---

* The place where the goods alone are carried, is called a *Décharge*, and that where goods and canoes are both tranfported, overland, is denominated a *Portage*.

carrying-

carrying-place in this river, and is about two thousand and thirty-five paces. It is a high hill or mountain. From the upper part of this Portage the current is steady, and is only a branch of the Utawas River, which joins the main channel, that keeps a more Southern course, at the distance of twelve computed leagues. Six leagues further it forms Lake Coulonge, which is about four leagues in length : from thence it proceeds through the channels of the Allumettes to the Portage, where part of the lading is taken out, and carried three hundred and forty-two paces. Then succeeds the Portage des Allumettes, which is but twenty-five paces, over a rock difficult of access, and but a very short distance from Lake Coulonge. From Portage de Chenes to this spot, is a fine deer-hunting country, and the land in many parts very fit for cultivation. From hence the river spreads wide, and is full of islands, with some current for seven leagues, to the beginning of *Riviere Creuse*, or Deep River, which runs in the form of a canal, about a mile and an half wide, for about thirty-six miles ; bounded upon the North by very high rocks, with low land on the South, and sandy ; it is intercepted again by falls and cataracts, so that the Portages of the two Joachins almost join. The first is nine hundred and twenty-six paces, the next seven hundred and twenty, and both very bad roads. From hence is a steady current of nine miles to the River du Moine, where there has generally been a trading house ; the stream then becomes strong for four leagues, when a rapid succeeds, which requires two trips. A little way onward is the Décharge, and close to it, the Portage of the Roche Capitaine, seven hundred and ninety-seven paces in length. From hence two trips are made through a narrow channel of the Roche Capitaine, made by an island four miles in length. A strong current now succeeds, for about six leagues to the

Portage

Portage of the two rivers, which is about eight hundred and twenty paces; from thence it is three leagues to the Décharge of the Trou, which is three hundred paces. Near adjoining is the rapid of Levellier; from whence, including the rapids of Matawoen, where there is no carrying-place, it is about thirty-fix miles to the forks of the fame name; in latitude 46¼. North, and longitude 78¼. Weft, and is at the computed diftance of four hundred miles from Montreal. At this place the Petite Riviere falls into the Utawas. The latter comes in a North-Wefterly direction, forming feveral lakes in its courfe. The principal of them is Lake Temefcamang, where there has always been a trading poft, which may be faid to continue, by a fucceffion of rivers and lakes, upwards of fifty leagues from the Forks, paffing near the waters of the Lake Abbitiby, in latitude 48½. which is received by the Moofe River, that empties itfelf into James Bay.

The Petite Riviere takes a South-Weft direction, is full of rapids and cataracts to its fource, and is not more than fifteen leagues in length, in the courfe of which are the following interruptions—The Portage of Plein Champ, three hundred and nineteen paces; the Décharge of the Rofe, one hundred and forty-five paces; the Décharge of Campion, one hundred and eighty-four paces; the Portage of the Groffe Roche, one hundred and fifty paces; the Portage of Pareffeux, four hundred and two paces; the Portage of Priarie, two hundred and eighty-feven paces; the Portage of La Cave, one hundred paces; Portage of Talon, two hundred and feventy-five paces; which, for its length, is the worft on the communication; Portage Pin de Mufique, four hundred and fifty-fix paces, where many men have been crufhed to death by the

canoes,

canoes, and others have received irrecoverable injuries.   The laſt in this
river is the Turtle Portage, eighty-three paces, on entering the lake of
that name, where, indeed, the river may be ſaid to take its ſource.   From
the firſt vaſe to the great river, the country has the appearance of having
been over-run by fire, and conſiſts in general of huge rocky hills.   The
whole diſtance which is the height of land, between the waters of the
St. Laurence and the Utawas, is one thouſand five hundred and thirteen
paces to a ſmall canal in a plain, that is juſt ſufficient to carry the
loaded canoe about one mile to the next vaſe, which is ſeven hundred
and twenty-five paces.   It would be twice this diſtance, but the narrow
creek is dammed in the beaver faſhion, to float the canoes to this barrier,
through which they paſs, when the river is juſt ſufficient to bear them
through a ſwamp of two miles to the laſt vaſe, of one thouſand
and twenty-four paces in length.   Though the river is increaſed in this
part, ſome care is neceſſary to avoid rocks and ſtumps of trees.   In about
ſix miles is the lake Nepiſingui, which is computed to be twelve leagues
long, though the route of the canoes is ſomething more: it is about fifteen miles wide in the wideſt part, and bounded with rocks.   Its inhabitants conſiſt of the remainder of a numerous converted tribe, called
Nepiſinguis of the Algonquin nation.   Out of it flows the Riviere des
François, over rocks of a conſiderable height.   In a bay to the Eaſt of
this, the road leads over the Portage of the Chaudiere des François, five
hundred and forty-four paces, to ſtill water.   It muſt have acquired the
name of Kettle, from a great number of holes in the ſolid rock of a
cylindrical form, and not unlike that culinary utenſil.   They are obſerv-
able in many parts along ſtrong bodies of water, and where, at certain
ſeaſons, and diſtinct periods, it is well known the water inundates; at
the

the bottom of them are generally found a number of fmall ftones and pebbles. This circumftance juftifies the conclufion, that at fome former period thefe rocks formed the bed of a branch of the difcharge of this lake, although fome of them are upwards of ten feet above the prefent level of the water at its greateft height. They are, indeed, to be feen in every lake and river throughout this wide extended country. The French river is very irregular, both as to its breadth and form, and is fo interfperfed with iflands, that in the whole courfe of it the banks are fel-dom vifible. Of its various channels, that which is generally followed by the canoes is obftructed by the following Portages, viz. des Pins, fifty-two paces; Feaufille, thirty-fix paces; Parifienne, one hundred paces; Recolet, forty-five paces; and the Petite Feaufille, twenty-five paces. In feveral parts there are guts or channels, where the water flows with great velocity, which are not more than twice the breadth of a canoe. The diftance to Lake Huron is eftimated at twenty-five leagues, which this river enters in the latitude 45. 53. North, that is, at the point of land three or four miles within the lake. There is hardly a foot of foil to be feen from one end of the French river to the other, its banks confifting of hills of entire rock. The coaft of the lake is the fame, but lower, backed at fome diftance by high lands. The courfe runs through numerous iflands to the North of Weft to the river Teffalon, computed to be about fifty leagues from the French river, and which I found to be in latitude 46. 12. 21. North; and from thence croffing, from ifland to ifland, the arm of the lake that receives the water of Lake Superior (which continues the fame courfe), the route changes to the South of Weft ten leagues to the Detour, paffing the end of the ifland of St. Jofeph, within fix miles of the former place. On that ifland there

has

has been a military eſtabliſhment ſince the upper poſts were given up to the Americans in the year 1794; and is the Weſternmoſt military poſition which we have in this country. It is a place of no trade, and the greater part, if not the whole of the Indians, come here for no other purpoſe but to receive the preſents which our government annually allows them. They are from the American territory (except about thirty families, who are the inhabitants of the lake from the French river, and of the Algonquin nation) and trade in their peltries, as they uſed formerly to do at Michilimakinac, but principally with Britiſh ſubjeɛts. The Americans pay them very little attention, and tell them that they keep poſſeſſion of their country by right of conqueſt: that, as their brothers, they will be friends with them while they deſerve it; and that their traders will bring them every kind of goods they require, which they may procure by their induſtry.

Our commanders treat them in a very different manner, and, under the charaɛter of the repreſentatives of their father; (which parental title the natives give to his preſent Majeſty, the common father of all his people) preſent them with ſuch things as the aɛtual ſtate of their ſtores will allow.

How far this conduɛt, if continued, **may**, at a future exigency, keep theſe people in our intereſt, if they are even worthy of it, is not an objeɛt of my preſent conſideration: at the ſame time, I cannot avoid expreſ-ſing my perfeɛt conviɛtion, that it would not be of the leaſt advantage to our preſent or future commerce in that country, or to the people themſelves; as it only tends to keep many of them in a ſtate of idleneſs

about

about our military eftablifhments. The ammunition which they receive is employed to kill game, in order to procure rum in return, though their families may be in a ftarving condition : hence it is, that, in confequence of flothful and diffolute lives, their numbers are in a very perceptible ftate of diminution.

From the Detour to the ifland of Michilimakinac, at the confluence of the Lakes Huron and Michigan, in latitude 45. 54. North is about forty-miles. To keep the direct courfe to Lake Superior, the north fhore from the river Teffalon fhould be followed ; croffing to the North-Weft end of St. Jofeph, and paffing between it and the adjacent iflands, which makes a diftance of fifty miles to the fall of St. Mary, at the foot of which, upon the South fhore, there is a village, formerly a place of great refort for the inhabitants of Lake Superior, and confequently of confiderable trade : it is now, however, dwindled to nothing, and reduced to about thirty families, of the Algonquin nation, who are one half of the year ftarving, and the other half intoxicated, and ten or twelve Canadians, who have been in the Indian country from an early period of life, and intermarried with the natives who have brought them families. Their inducement to fettle there, was the great quantity of white fifh that are to be taken in and about the falls, with very little trouble, particularly in the autumn, when that fifh leaves the lakes, and comes to the running and fhallow waters to fpawn. Thefe, when falt can be procured, are pickled juft as the froft fets in, and prove very good food with potatoes, which they have of late cultivated with fuccefs. The natives live chiefly on this fifh, which they hang up by the tails, and preferve throughout the winter, or at leaft as long as they laft ; for whatever

quantity

quantity they may have taken, it is never known that their œconomy is fuch as to make them laft through the winter, which renders their fituation very diftreffing ; for if they had activity fufficient to purfue the labours of the chafe, the woods are become fo barren of game as to afford them no great profpect of relief. In the fpring of the year they, and the other inhabitants, make a quantity of fugar from the maple tree, which they exchange with the traders for neceffary articles, or carry it to Michilimakinac, where they expect a better price. One of thefe traders was agent for the North-Weft Company, receiving, ftoring, and forwarding fuch articles as come by the way of the lakes upon their veffels : for it is to be obferved, that a quantity of their goods are fent by that route from Montreal in boats to Kingfton, at the entrance of Lake Ontario, and from thence in veffels to Niagara, then over land ten miles to a water communication, by boats, to Lake Erie, where they are again received into veffels, and carried over that lake up the river Detroit, through the lake and river Sinclair to Lake Huron, and from thence to the Falls of St. Mary's, when they are again landed and carried for a mile above the falls, and fhipped over Lake Superior to the Grande Portage. This is found to be a lefs expenfive method than by canoes, but attended with more rifk, and requiring more time, than one fhort feafon of this country will admit ; for the goods are always fent from Montreal the preceding fall ; and befides, the company get the whole of their provifions from Detroit, as flour and Indian corn ; as alfo confiderable fupplies from Michilimakinac of maple fugar, tallow, gum, &c. &c.

For the purpofe of conveying all thefe things, they have two veffels
upon

upon the Lakes Erie and Huron, and one on Lake Superior, of from fifty to feventy tons burthen. This being, therefore, the depot for tranfports, the Montreal canoes, on their arrival, were forwarded over Lake Superior, with only five men in each; the others were fent to Michilimakinac for additional canoes, which were required to profecute the trade, and then take a lading there, or at St. Mary's, and follow the others. At length they all arrive at the Grande Portage, which is one hundred and fixty leagues from St. Mary's, and fituated on a pleafant bay on the North fide of the lake, in latitude 48. North and longitude 90. Weft from Greenwich, where the compafs has not above five degrees Eaft variation.

At the entrance of the bay is an ifland which fcreens the harbour from every wind except the South. The fhallownefs of the water, however, renders it neceffary for the veffel to anchor near a mile from the fhore, where there is not more than fourteen feet water. This lake juftifies the name that has been given to it: the Falls of St. Mary, which is its Northern extremity, being in latitude 46. 31. North, and in longitude 84 Weft, where there is no variation of the compafs whatever, while its Southern extremity, at the River St. Louis, is in latitude 46. 45. North, and longitude 92. 10. Weft: its greateft breadth is one hundred and twenty miles, and its circumference, including its various bays, is not lefs than one thoufand two hundred miles. Along its North fhore is the fafeft navigation, as it is a continued mountainous embankment of rock, from three hundred to one thoufand five hundred feet in height. There are numerous coves and fandy bays to land, which are frequently fheltered by iflands from the fwell of the lake. This is particularly the cafe at the diftance of one hundred miles to the Eaftward of the Grande Portage, and is called the Pays Plat.

This

This feems to have been caufed by fome convulfion of nature, for many of the iflands difplay a compofition of lava, intermixed with round ftones of the fize of a pigeon's egg. The furrounding rock is generally hard, and of a dark blue-grey, though it frequently has the appearance of iron and copper. The South fide of the lake, from Point Shagoimigo Eaft, is almoft a continual ftraight line of fandy beach, interfperfed with rocky precipices of lime-ftones, fometimes rifing to an hundred feet in height, without a bay. The embankments from that point Weftward are, in general, of ftrong clay, mixed with ftones, which renders the navigation irkfome and dangerous. On the fame fide, at the River Tonnagan, is found a quantity of virgin copper. The Americans, foon after they got poffeffion of that country, fent an engineer thither; and I fhould not be furprifed to hear of their employing people to work the mine. Indeed, it might be well worthy the attention of the Britifh fubjects to work the mines on the North coaft, though they are not fuppofed to be fo rich as thofe on the South.

Lake Superior is the largeft and moft magnificent body of frefh water in the world: it is clear and pellucid, of great depth, and abounding in a great variety of fifh, which are the moft excellent of their kind. There are trouts of three kinds, weighing from five to fifty pounds, fturgeon, pickerel, pike, red and white carp, black bafs, herrings, &c. &c. and the laft and beft of all, the Ticamang, or white fifh, which weighs from four to fixteen pounds, and is of a fuperior quality in thefe waters.

This lake may be denominated the grand refervoir of the River St. Laurence, as no confiderable rivers difcharge themfelves into it.

The

The principal ones are, the St. Louis, the Nipigon, the Pic, and the Michipicoten. Indeed, the extent of country from which any of them flow, or take their courfe, in any direction, cannot admit of it, in confequence of the ridge of land that feparates them from the rivers that empty themfelves into Hudfon's-Bay, the gulph of Mexico, and the waters that fall in Lake Michegan, which afterwards become a part of the St. Laurence.

This vaft collection of water is often covered with fog, particularly when the wind is from the Eaft, which, driving againft the high barren rocks on the North and Weft fhore, diffolves in torrents of rain. It is very generally faid, that the ftorms on this lake are denoted by a fwell on the preceding day; but this circumftance did not appear from my obfervation to be a regular phenomenon, as the fwells more frequently fubfided without any fubfequent wind.

Along the furrounding rocks of this immenfe lake, evident marks appear of the decreafe of its water, by the lines obfervable along them. The fpace, however, between the higheft and the loweft, is not fo great as in the fmaller lakes, as it does not amount to more than fix feet, the former being very faint.

The inhabitants that are found along the coaft of this water, are all of the Algonquin nation, the whole of which do not exceed 150 families.*

* In the year 1668, when the firft miffionaries vifited the South of this lake, they found the country full of inhabitants. They relate, that, about this time a band of the Nepifingues, who were converted, emigrated to the Nipigon country, which is to the North of Lake Superior. Few of their defcendants are now remaining, and not a trace of the religion communicated to them is to be difcovered.

Thefe

Thefe people live chiefly on fifh; indeed, from what has been faid of the country, it cannot be expected to abound in animals, as it is totally deftitute of that fhelter, which is fo neceffary to them. The rocks appear to have been over-run by fire, and the ftinted timber, which once grew there, is frequently feen lying along the furface of them: but it is not eafy to be reconciled, that any thing fhould grow where there is fo little appearance of foil. Between the fallen trees there are briars, with hurtleberry and goofeberry bufhes, rafp-berries, &c. which invite the bears in greater or leffer numbers, as they are a favourite food of that animal: beyond thefe rocky banks are found a few moofe and fallow deer. The waters alone are abun-dantly inhabited.

A very curious phenomenon was obferved fome years ago at the Grande Portage, for which no obvious caufe could be affigned. The water withdrew with great precipitation, leaving the ground dry that had never before been vifible, the fall being equal to four perpendicular feet, and rufhing back with great velocity above the common mark. It con-tinued thus falling and rifing for feveral hours, gradually decreafing till it ftopped at its ufual height. There is frequently an irregular influx and deflux, which does not exceed ten inches, and is attributed to the wind.

The bottom of the bay, which forms an amphitheatre, is clear and inclofed; and on the left corner of it, beneath an hill, three or four hundred feet in height, and crowned by others of a ftill greater altitude,

is

is the fort, picketed in with cedar pallifadoes, and inclofing houfes built with wood and covered with fhingles. They are calculated for every convenience of trade, as well as to accommodate the proprietors and clerks during their fhort refidence there. The North men live under tents : but the more frugal pork-eater lodges beneath his canoe. The foil immediately bordering on the lake has not proved very propitious, as nothing but potatoes have been found to anfwer the trouble of cultivation. This circumftance is probably owing to the cold damp fogs of the lake, and the moifture of the ground from the fprings that iffue from beneath the hills. There are meadows in the vicinity that yield abundance of hay for the cattle; but, as to agriculture, it has not hitherto been an object of ferious confideration.

I fhall now leave thefe geographical notices, to give fome further account of the people from Montreal.—When they are arrived at the Grande Portage, which is near nine miles over, each of them has to carry eight packages of fuch goods and provifions as are neceffary for the interior country. This is a labour which cattle cannot conveniently perform in fummer, as both horfes and oxen were tried by the company without fuccefs. They are only ufeful for light, bulky articles; or for tranfporting upon fledges, during the winter, whatever goods may remain there, efpecially provifion, of which it is ufual to have a year's ftock on hand.

Having finifhed this toilfome part of their duty, if more goods are neceffary to be tranfported, they are allowed a Spanifh dollar for each
package :

package: and so inured are they to this kind of labour, that I have known some of them set off with two packages of ninety pounds each, and return with two others of the same weight, in the course of six hours, being a distance of eighteen miles over hills and mountains. This necessary part of the business being over, if the season be early they have some respite, but this depends upon the time the North men begin to arrive from their winter quarters, which they commonly do early in July. At this period, it is necessary to select from the pork-eaters, a number of men, among whom are the recruits, or winterers, sufficient to man the North canoes necessary to carry, to the river of the rainy lake, the goods and provision requisite for the Athabasca country; as the people of that country, (owing to the shortness of the season and length of the road, can come no further), are equipped there, and exchange ladings with the people of whom we are speaking, and both return from whence they came. This voyage is performed in the course of a month, and they are allowed proportionable wages for their services.

The north men being arrived at the Grande Portage, are regaled with bread, pork, butter, liquor, and tobacco, and such as have not entered into agreements during the winter, which is customary, are contracted with, to return and perform the voyage for one, two, or three years: their accounts are also settled, and such as choose to send any of their earnings to Canada, receive drafts to transmit to their relations or friends: and as soon as they can be got ready, which requires no more than a fortnight, they are again dispatched to their respective departments.

ments. It is, indeed, very creditable to them as fervants, that though they are fometimes affembled to the number of twelve hundred men, indulging themfelves in the free ufe of liquor, and quarrelling with each other, they always fhew the greateft refpect to their employers, who are comparatively but few in number, and beyond the aid of any legal power to enforce due obedience. In fhort, a degree of fubordination can only be maintained by the good opinion thefe men entertain of their employers, which has been uniformly the cafe, fince the trade has been formed and conducted on a regular fyftem.

The people being difpatched to their refpective winter quarters, the agents from Montreal, affifted by their clerks, prepare to return there, by getting the furs acrofs the portage, and re-making them into packages of one hundred pounds weight each, to fend them to Montreal; where they commonly arrive about the month of September.

The mode of living at the Grande Portage, is as follows: The proprietors, clerks, guides, and interpreters, mefs together, to the number of fometimes an hundred, at feveral tables, in one large hall, the provifion confifting of bread, falt pork, beef, hams, fifh, and venifon, butter, peas, Indian corn, potatoes, tea, fpirits, wine, &c. and plenty of milk, for which purpofe feveral milch cows are conftantly kept. The mechanics have rations of fuch provifion, but the canoe-men, both from the North and Montreal, have no other allowance here, or in the voyage, than Indian corn and melted fat. The corn for this purpofe is prepared

pared before it leaves Detroit, by boiling it in a ftrong alkali, which takes off the outer hufk; it is then well wafhed, and carefully dried upon ftages, when it is fit for ufe. One quart of this is boiled for two hours, over a moderate fire, in a gallon of water; to which, when it has boiled a fmall time, are added two ounces of melted fuet; this caufes the corn to fplit, and in the time mentioned makes a pretty thick pudding. If to this is added a little falt, (but not before it is boiled, as it would interrupt the operation), it makes an wholefome, palatable food, and eafy of digeftion. This quantity is fully fufficient for a man's fubfiftence during twenty-four hours; though it is not fufficiently heartening to fuftain the ftrength neceffary for a ftate of active labour. The Americans call this difh hominee*.

The trade from the Grande Portage, is, in fome particulars, carried on in a different manner with that from Montreal. The canoes ufed in the latter tranfport are now too large for the former, and fome of about half the fize are procured from the natives, and are navigated by four, five, or fix men, according to the diftance which they have to go. They carry a lading of about thirty-five packages, on an average; of thefe twenty-three are for the purpofe of trade, and the reft are employed for provifions, ftores, and baggage. In each of thefe canoes are a foreman and fteerfman; the one to be always on the look out, and direct the paffage of the veffel, and the other to attend the helm. They alfo carry her, whenever that office is neceffary. The foreman has the command,

---

* Corn is the cheapeft provifion that can be procured, though from the expence of tranfport, the bufhel cofts about twenty fhillings fterling, at the Grande Portage. A man's daily allowance does not exceed ten-pence.

and the middle-men obey both; the latter earn only two-thirds of the wages which are paid the two former.   Independent of thefe a conductor or pilot is appointed to every four or fix of thefe canoes, whom they are all obliged to obey; and is, or at leaft is intended to be, a perfon of fuperior experience, for which he is proportionably paid.

In thefe canoes, thus loaded, they embark at the North fide of the portage, on the river Au Tourt, which is very inconfiderable; and after about two miles of a Wefterly courfe, is obftructed by the Par-tridge Portage, fix hundred paces long.   In the fpring this makes a con-fiderable fall, when the water is high, over a perpendicular rock of one hundred and twenty feet.   From thence the river continues to be fhal-low, and requires great care to prevent the bottom of the canoe from being injured by fharp rocks, for a diftance of three miles and an half to the Priarie, or Meadow, when half the lading is taken out, and carried by part of the crew, while two of them are conducting the canoe among the rocks, with the remainder, to the Carreboeuf Portage, three miles and an half more, when they unload and come back two miles, and embark what was left for the other hands to carry, which they alfo land with the former; all of which is carried fix hundred and eighty paces, and the canoe led up againft the rapid.   From hence the water is better calculated to carry canoes, and leads by a winding courfe to the North of Weft three miles to the Outard Portage, over which the canoe, and every thing in her, is carried for two thoufand four hundred paces. At the further end is a very high hill to defcend, over which hangs a rock upwards of feven hundred feet high.   Then fucceeds the Outard Lake, about fix miles long, lying in a North-Weft courfe, and about two

miles

miles wide in the broadeſt part. After paſſing a very ſmall rivulet, they come to the Elk Portage, over which the canoe and lading are again carried one thouſand one hundred and twenty paces; when they enter the lake of the ſame name, which is an handſome piece of water, running North-Weſt about four miles, and not more than one mile and an half wide*. They then land at the Portage de Ceriſe, over which, and in the face of a conſiderable hill, the canoe and cargo are again tranſported for one thouſand and fifty paces. This is only ſeparated from the ſecond Portage de Ceriſe, by a mud-pond (where there is plenty of water lilies), of a quarter of a mile in length; and this is again ſeparated by a ſimilar pond, from the laſt Portage de Ceriſe, which is four hundred and ten paces. Here the ſame operation is to be performed for three hundred and eighty paces. They next enter on the Mountain Lake, running North-Weſt by Weſt ſix miles long, and about two miles in its greateſt breadth. In the centre of this lake, and to the right is the Old Road, by which I never paſſed; but an adequate notion may be formed of it from the road I am going to deſcribe, and which is univerſally preferred. This is firſt, the ſmall new portage over which every thing is carried for ſix hundred and twenty-ſix paces, over hills and gullies; the whole is then embarked on a narrow line of water, that meanders South-Weſt about two miles and an half. It is neceſſary to unload here, for the length of the canoe, and then proceed Weſt half a mile, to the new Grande Portage, which is three thouſand one hundred paces in length, and over very rough ground, which requires the utmoſt exertions of the men, and frequently lames them: from hence they approach the Roſe Lake, the portage of

---

* Here is a moſt excellent fiſhery for white fiſh, which are exquiſite.

that

that name being oppofite to the junction of the road from the Mountain Lake. They then embark on the Rofe Lake, about one mile from the Eaft end of it, and fteer Weft by South, in an oblique courfe, acrofs it two miles; then Weft-North-Weft paffing the Petite Perche to the Marten Portage three miles. In this part of the lake the bottom is mud and flime, with about three or four feet of water over it; and here I frequently ftruck a canoe pole of twelve feet long, without meeting any other obftruction than if the whole were water: it has, however, a peculiar fuction or attractive power, fo that it is difficult to paddle a canoe over it. There is a fmall fpace along the South fhore, where the water is deep, and this effect is not felt. In proportion to the diftance from this part, the fuction becomes more powerful: I have, indeed been told that loaded canoes have been in danger of being fwallowed up, and have only owed their prefervation to other canoes, which were lighter. I have, myfelf, found it very difficult to get away from this attractive power, with fix men, and great exertion, though they did not appear to be in any danger of finking.

Over againft this is a very high, rocky ridge, on the South fide, called Marten Portage, which is but twenty paces long, and feparated from the Perche Portage, which is four hundred and eighty paces, by a mud-pond, covered with white lillies. From hence the courfe is on the lake of the fame name, Weft-South-Weft three miles to the height of land, where the waters of the Dove or Pigeon River terminate, and which is one of the fources of the great St. Laurence in this direction. Having carried the canoe and lading over it, fix hundred and feventy-nine paces, they

embark

embark on the lake of Hauteur de Terre*, which is in the fhape of an horfe-fhoe. It is entered near the curve, and left at the extremity of the Weftern limb, through a very fhallow channel, where the canoe paffes half loaded for thirty paces with the current, which leads through the fucceeding lakes and rivers, and difembogues itfelf, by the river Nelfon, into Hudfon's-Bay. The firft of thefe is Lac de pierres à fufil, running Weft-South-Weft feven miles long, and two wide, and, making an angle at North-Weft one mile more, becomes a river for half a mile, tumbling over a rock, and forming a fall and portage, called the Efcalier, of fifty-five paces; but from hence it is neither lake or river, but poffeffes the character of both, and ends between large rocks, which caufe a current or rapid, falling into a lake-pond for about two miles and an half, Weft-North-Weft, to the portage of the Cheval du Bois. Here the canoe and contents are carried three hundred and eighty paces, between rocks; and within a quarter of a mile is the Portage des Gros Pins, which is fix hundred and forty paces over an high ridge. The oppofite fide of it is wafhed by a fmall lake three miles round; and the courfe is through the Eaft end or fide of it, three quarters of a mile North-Eaft, where there is a rapid. An irregular, meandering channel, between rocky banks, then fucceeds, for feven miles and an half, to the Maraboeuf Lake, which extends North four miles; and is three quarters of a mile wide, terminating by a rapid and décharge, of one hundred and eighty paces, the rock of Saginaga being in fight, which caufes a fall of about feven feet, and a portage of fifty-five paces.

* The route which we have been travelling hitherto, leads along the high rocky land or bank of Lake Superior on the left. The face of the country offers a wild fcene of huge hills and rocks, feparated by ftony vallies, lakes, and ponds. Wherever there is the leaft foil, it is well covered with trees.

Lake

Lake Saginaga takes its names from its numerous Iflands. Its greateft length from Eaft to Weft is about fourteen miles, with very irregular inlets, is no where more than three miles wide, and terminates at the fmall portage of La Roche, of forty-three paces. From thence is a rocky, ftony paffage of one mile, to Priarie Portage, which is very improperly named, as there is no ground about it that anfwers to that defcription, except a fmall fpot at the embarking place at the Weft end: to the Eaft is an entire bog; and it is with great difficulty that the lading can be landed upon ftages, formed by driving piles into the mud, and fpreading branches of trees over them. The portage rifes on a ftony ridge, over which the canoe and cargo muft be carried for fix hundred and eleven paces. This is fucceeded by an embarkation on a fmall bay, where the bottom is the fame as has been defcribed in the Weft end of Rofe Lake, and it is with great difficulty that a laden canoe is worked over it, but it does not comprehend more than a diftance of two hundred yards. From hence the progrefs continues through irregular channels, bounded by rocks, in a Wefterly courfe for about five miles, to the little Portage des Couteaux, of one hundred and fixty-five paces, and the Lac des Couteaux, running about South-Weft by Weft twelve miles, and from a quarter to two miles wide. A deep bay runs Eaft three miles from the Weft end, where it is difcharged by a rapid river, and after running two miles Weft, it again becomes ftill water. In this river are two carrying-places, the one fifteen, and the other one hundred and ninety paces. From this to the Portage des Carpes is one mile North-Weft, leaving a narrow lake on the Eaft that runs parallel with the Lake des Couteaux, half its length, where there is a carrying-place, which is ufed when the water in the river laft mentioned is too low. The

Portage

Portage des Carpes is three hundred and ninety paces, from whence the water fpreads irregularly between rocks, five miles North-Weft and South-Eaft to the portage of Lac Bois Blanc, which is one hundred and eighty paces. Then follows the lake of that name, but I think improperly fo called, as the natives name it the Lake Pafcau Minac Sagaigan, or Dry Berries.

Before the fmall pox ravaged this country, and completed, what the Nodowafis, in their warfare, had gone far to accomplifh, the deftruction of its inhabitants, the population was very numerous: this was alfo a favourite part, where they made their canoes, &c. the lake abounding in fifh, the country round it being plentifully fupplied with various kinds of game, and the rocky ridges, that form the boundaries of the water, covered with a variety of berries.

When the French were in poffeffion of this country, they had feveral trading eftablifhments on the iflands and banks of this lake. Since that period, the few people remaining, who were of the Algonquin nation, could hardly find fubfiftence; game having become fo fcarce, that they depended principally for food upon fifh, and wild rice which grows fpontaneoufly in thefe parts.

This lake is irregular in its form, and its utmoft extent from Eaft to Weft is fifteen miles; a point of land, called Point au Pin, jutting into it, divides it in two parts: it then makes a fecond angle at the Weft end, to the leffer Portage de Bois Blanc, two hundred paces in length. This channel is not wide, and is intercepted by feveral rapids in the courfe of a

mile:

mile: it runs Weſt-North-Weſt to the Portage des Pins, over which the canoe and lading is again carried four hundred paces. From hence the channel is alſo intercepted by very dangerous rapids for two miles Weſterly, to the point of Portage du Bois, which is two hundred and eighty paces. Then ſucceeds the portage of Lake Croche one mile more, where the carrying-place is eighty paces, and is followed by an embarkation on that lake, which takes its name from its figure. It extends eighteen miles, in a meandering form, and in a weſterly direction; it is in general very narrow, and at about two-thirds of its length becomes very contracted, with a ſtrong current.

Within three miles of the laſt Portage is a remarkable rock, with a ſmooth face, but ſplit and cracked in different parts, which hang over the water. Into one of its horizontal chaſms a great number of arrows have been ſhot, which is ſaid to have been done by a war party of the Nadowaſis or Sieux, who had done much miſchief in this country, and left theſe weapons as a warning to the Chebois or natives, that, notwithſtanding its lakes, rivers, and rocks, it was not inacceſſible to their enemies.

Lake Croche is terminated by the Portage de Rideau, four hundred paces long, and derives its name from the appearance of the water, falling over a rock of upwards of thirty feet. Several rapids ſucceed, with intervals of ſtill water, for about three miles to the Flacon portage, which is very difficult, is four hundred paces long, and leads to the Lake of La Croix, ſo named from its ſhape. It runs about North-Weſt eighteen miles to the Beaver Dam, and then ſinks into a deep bay nearly Eaſt. The courſe to

the

the Portage is Weſt by North for ſixteen miles more from the Beaver Dam, and into the Eaſt bay is a road which was frequented by the French, and followed through lakes and rivers until they came to Lake Superior by the river Caminiſtiquia, thirty miles Eaſt of the Grand Portage.

Portage la Croix is ſix hundred paces long: to the next portage is a quarter of a mile, and its length is forty paces; the river winding four miles to Vermillion Lake, which runs ſix or ſeven miles North-North-Weſt, and by a narrow ſtrait communicates with Lake Namaycan, which takes its name from a particular place at the foot of a fall, where the natives ſpear ſturgeon: Its courſe is about North-North-Weſt and South-South-Eaſt, with a bay running Eaſt, that gives it the form of a triangle: its length is about ſixteen miles to the Nouvelle Portage. The diſcharge of the lake is from a bay on the left, and the portage one hundred and eighty paces, to which ſucceeds a very ſmall river, from whence there is but a ſhort diſtance to the next Nouvelle Portage, three hundred and twenty paces long. It is then neceſſary to embark on a ſwamp, or over-flowed country, where wild rice grows in great abundance. There is a channel or ſmall river in the centre of this ſwamp, which is kept with difficulty, and runs South and North one mile and a half, with deepening water. The courſe continues North-North-Weſt one mile to the Chaudiere Portage, which is cauſed by the diſcharge of the waters running on the left of the road from Lake Naymaycan, which uſed to be the common route, but that which I have deſcribed is the ſafeſt as well as ſhorteſt. From hence there is ſome current though the water is wide ſpread, and its courſe about North by Weſt three miles and an half to

the

the Lac de la Pluie, which lies nearly Eaſt and Weſt; from thence about fifteen miles is a narrow ſtrait that divides the land into two un-equal parts, from whence to its diſcharge is a diſtance of twenty-four miles. There is a deep bay running North-Weſt on the right, that is not included, and is remarkable for furniſhing the natives with a kind of ſoft, red ſtone, of which they make their pipes; it alſo affords an excel-lent fiſhery both in the ſummer and winter; and from it is an eaſy, ſafe, and ſhort road to the Lake du Bois, (which I ſhall mention preſently) for the Indians to paſs in their ſmall canoes, through a ſmall lake and on a ſmall river, whoſe banks furniſh abundance of wild rice. The dif-charge of this lake is called Lake de la Pluie River, at whoſe entrance there is a rapid, below which is a fine bay, where there had been an ex-tenſive picketted fort and building when poſſeſſed by the French: the ſite of it is at preſent a beautiful meadow, ſurrounded with groves of oaks. From hence there is a ſtrong current for two miles, where the water falls over a rock twenty feet, and, from the conſequent turbulence of the water, the carrying-place, which is three hundred and twenty paces long, derives the name of Chaudiere. Two miles onward is the preſent trading eſtabliſhment, ſituated on an high bank on the North ſide of the river, in 48. 37. North latitude.

Here the people from Montreal come to meet thoſe who arrive from the Athabaſca country, as has been already deſcribed, and exchange lading with them. This is alſo the reſidence of the firſt chief, or Sachem, of all the Algonquin tribes, inhabiting the different parts of this country. He is by diſtinction called Nectam, which implies perſonal pre-eminence. Here alſo the elders meet in council to treat of peace or war.

This

This is one of the fineſt rivers in the North-Weſt, and runs a courſe Weſt and Eaſt one hundred and twenty computed miles; but in taking its courſe and diſtance minutely I make it only eighty. Its banks are covered with a rich ſoil, particularly to the North, which, in many parts, are clothed with fine open groves of oak, with the maple, the pine, and the cedar. The Southern bank is not ſo elevated, and diſplays the maple, the white birch, and the cedar, with the ſpruce, the alder, and various underwood. Its waters abound in fiſh, particularly the ſturgeon, which the natives both ſpear and take with drag-nets. But notwithſtanding the promiſe of this ſoil, the Indians do not attend to its cultivation, though they are not ignorant of the common proceſs, and are fond of the Indian corn, when they can get it from us.

Though the ſoil at the fort is a ſtiff clay, there is a garden, which, unaſſiſted as it is by manure, or any particular attention, is tolerably productive.

We now proceed to mention the Lake du Bois, into which this river diſcharges itſelf in latitude 49. North, and was formerly famous for the richneſs of its banks and waters, which abounded with whatever was neceſſary to a ſavage life. The French had ſeveral ſettlements in and about it; but it might be almoſt concluded, that ſome fatal circumſtance had deſtroyed the game, as war and the ſmall pox had diminiſhed the inhabitants, it having been very unproductive in animals ſince the Britiſh ſubjects have been engaged in travelling through it; though it now appears to be recovering its priſtine ſtate. The few Indians who inhabit

it

it might live very comfortably, if they were not so immoderately fond of spirituous liquors.

This lake is also rendered remarkable, in consequence of the Americans having named it as the spot, from which a line of boundary, between them and British America, was to run West, until it struck the Mississippi; which, however, can never happen, as the North-West part of the Lake du Bois is in latitude 49. 37. North, and longitude 94. 31 West, and the Northernmost branch of the source of the Mississippi is in latitude 47. 38. North, and longitude 95. 6. West, ascertained by Mr. Thomson, astronomer to the North-West Company, who was sent expressly for that purpose in the spring of 1798. He, in the same year, determined the Northern bend of the Missisoury to be in latitude 47. 32. North, and longitude 101. 25. West; and, according to the Indian accounts, it runs to the south of West, so that if the Missisoury were even to be considered as the Mississippi, no Western line could strike it.

It does not appear to me to be clearly determined what course the Line is to take, or from what part of Lake Superior it strikes through the country to the Lake du Bois: were it to follow the principal waters to their source, it ought to keep through Lake Superior to the River St. Louis, and follow that river to its source; close to which is the source of the waters falling into the river of Lake la Pluie, which is a common route of the Indians to the Lake du Bois: the St. Louis passes within a short distance of a branch of the Mississippi, where it becomes navigable for canoes. This will appear more evident from consulting

the

the map; and if the navigation of the Miffiffippi is confidered as of any confequence, by this country, from that part of the globe, fuch is the neareft way to get at it.

But to return to our narrative. The Lake du Bois is, as far as I could learn, nearly round, and the canoe courfe through the centre of it among a clufter of iflands, fome of which are fo extenfive that they may be taken for the main land. The reduced courfe would be nearly South and North. But following the navigating courfe, I make the diftance feventy-five miles, though in a direct line it would fall very fhort of that length. At about two-thirds of it there is a fmall carrying-place, when the water is low. The carrying-place out of the lake is on an ifland, and named Portage du Rat, in latitude 49. 37. North and longitude 94¼. Weft, it is about fifty paces long. The lake difcharges itfelf at both ends of this ifland, and forms the River Winipic, which is a large body of water, interfperfed with numerous iflands, caufing various channels and interruptions of portages and rapids. In fome parts it has the appearance of lakes, with fteady currents; I eftimate its winding courfe to the Dalles eight miles; to the Grand Dé-charge twenty-five miles and an half, which is a long carrying-place for the goods; from thence to the little Décharge one mile and an half; to the Terre Jaûne Portage two miles and an half; then to its galet feventy yards; two miles and three quarters to the Terre Blanche, near which is a fall of from four to five feet; three miles and an half to Por-tage de L'Ifle, where there is a trading-poft, and, about eleven miles, on the North fhore, a trading eftablifhment, which is the road, in boats,

to

to Albany River, and from thence to Hudfon's Bay. There is alfo a
communication with Lake Superior, through what is called the Nipigan
country, that enters the Lake Winipic about thirty-five leagues Eaft of the
Grande Portage. In fhort, the country is fo broken by lakes and rivers,
that people may find their way in canoes in any direction they pleafe.
It is now four miles to Portage de L'ifle, which is but fhort, though
feveral canoes have been loft in attempting to run the rapid. From
thence it is twenty-fix miles to Jacob's Falls, which are about fifteen feet
high; and fix miles and an half to the woody point; forty yards from which
is another Portage. They both form an high fall, but not perpendicular.
From thence to another galet, or rocky Portage, is about two miles,
which is one continual rapid and cafcade; and about two miles further
is the Chute à l'Efclave, which is upwards of thirty feet. The Portage
is long, through a point covered with wood: it is fix miles and an half
more to the barrier, and ten miles to the Grand Rapid. From thence,
on the North fide, is a fafe road, when the waters are high, through fmall
rivers and lakes, to the Lake du Bonnet, called the Pinnawas, from the
man who difcovered it: to the White River, fo called from its being, for
a confiderable length, a fucceffion of falls and cataracts, is twelve miles.
Here are feven portages, in fo fhort a fpace, that the whole of them are
difcernible at the fame moment. From this to Lake du Bonnet is fifteen
miles more, and four miles acrofs it to the rapid. Here the Pinnawas
road joins, and from thence it is two miles to the Galet du Lac du Bonnet;
from this to the Galet du Bonnet one mile and an half; thence to the Portage of the fame name is three miles. This Portage is near half a league
in length, and derives its name from a cuftom the Indians have of crown-
ing ftones, laid in a circle, on the higheft rock in the portage, with
                                                                    wreaths,

wreaths of herbage and branches. There have been examples of men taking seven packages of ninety pounds each, at one end of the portage, and putting them down at the other without stopping.

To this, another small portage immediately succeeds, over a rock producing a fall. From thence to the fall of Terre Blanche is two miles and an half; to the first portage Des Eaux qui Remuent is three miles; to the next, of the same name, is but a few yards distant; to the third and last, which is a Décharge, is three miles and an half; and from this to the last Portage of the river one mile and an half; and to the establishment, or provision house, is two miles and an half. Here also the French had their principal inland depôt, and got their canoes made.

It is here, that the present traders, going to great distances, and where provision is difficult to procure, receive a supply to carry them to the Rainy Lake, or Lake Superior. From the establishment to the entrance of Lake Winipic is four miles and an half, latitude 50. 37. North.

The country, soil, produce, and climate, from Lake Superior to this place bear a general resemblance, with a predominance of rock and water: the former is of the granite kind. Where there is any soil it is well covered with wood, such as oak, elm, ash of different kinds, maple of two kinds, pines of various descriptions, among which are what I call the cypress, with the hickory, iron-wood, liard, poplar, cedar, black and white birch, &c. &c. Vast quantities of wild rice are seen throughout the country, which the natives

collect

collect in the month of Auguſt for their winter ſtores.* To the North of fifty degrees, it is hardly known, or at leaſt does not come to maturity.

Lake Winipic is the great reſervoir of ſeveral large rivers, and diſcharges itſelf by the River Nelſon into Hudſon's Bay. The firſt in rotation, next to that I have juſt deſcribed, is the Aſſiniboin, or Red River, which, at the diſtance of forty miles coaſtwiſe, diſembogues on the South-Weſt ſide of the lake Winipic. It alternately receives thoſe two denominations from its dividing, at the diſtance of about thirty miles from the lake, into two large branches. The Eaſtern branch, called the Red River, runs in a Southern direction to near the head waters of the Miſſiſſippi. On this are two trading eſtabliſhments. The country on either ſide is but partially ſupplied with wood, and conſiſts of plains covered with herds of the buffalo and the elk, eſpecially on the Weſtern ſide. On the Eaſtern ſide are lakes and rivers, and the whole country is well wooded, level, abounding in beaver, bears, mooſe-deer, fallow-deer, &c. &c. The natives, who are of the Algonquin tribe, are not very numerous, and are conſidered as the natives of Lake Superior. This country being near the Miſſiſſippi, is alſo inhabited by the Nadowaſis, who are the natural enemies of the former; the head of the water being the war-line, they are in a continual ſtate of hoſtility; and though the Algonquins are equally brave, the others generally out-number them; it is very probable, therefore, that if the latter continue to venture out of the woods, which form their only protection, they will ſoon

---

* The fruits are, ſtrawberries, hurtleberries, plumbs, and cherries, hazlenuts, gooſeberries, currants, raſpberries, poires, &c.

be

be extirpated. There is not, perhaps, a finer country in the world for the refidence of uncivilifed man, than that which occupies the fpace between this river and Lake Superior. It abounds in every thing neceffary to the wants and comforts of fuch a people. Fifh, venifon, and fowl, with wild rice, are in great plenty; while, at the fame time, their fubfiftence requires that bodily exercife fo neceffary to health and vigour.

This great extent of country was formerly very populous, but from the information I received, the aggregate of its inhabitants does not exceed three hundred warriors; and, among the few whom I faw, it appeared to me that the widows were more numerous than the men. The rackoon is a native of this country, but is feldom found to the Northward of it.

The other branch is called after the tribe of the Nadawafis, who here go by the name of Affiniboins, and are the principal inhabitants of it. It runs from off the North-North-Weft, and, in the latitude of $51\frac{1}{4}$. Weft, and longitude $103\frac{1}{3}$. rifing in the fame mountains as the river Dauphin, of which I fhall fpeak in due order. They muft have feparated from their nation at a time beyond our knowledge, and live in peace with the Algonquins and Knifteneaux.

The country between this and the Red River, is almoft a continual plain to the Miffifoury. The foil is fand and gravel, with a flight intermixture of earth, and produces a fhort grafs. Trees are very rare; nor are there on the banks of the river fufficient, except in particular fpots, to build houfes and fupply fire-wood for the trading

eftablifhments

eftablifhments, of which there are four principal ones. Both thefe rivers are navigable for canoes to their fource, without a fall; though in fome parts there are rapids, caufed by occafional beds of lime-ftone, and gravel; but in general they a fandy bottom.

The Affiniboins, and fome of the Fall, or Big-bellied Indians, are the principal inhabitants of this country, and border on the river, occupying the centre part of it; that next Lake Winipic, and about its fource, being the ftation of the Algonquins and Knifteneaux, who have chofen it in preference to their own country. They do not exceed five hundred families. They are not beaver hunters, which accounts for their allowing the divifion juft mentioned, as the lower and upper parts of this river have thofe animals, which are not found in the intermediate diftrict. They confine themfelves to hunting the buffalo, and trapping wolves, which cover the country. What they do not want of the former for raiment and food, they fometimes make into pemmican, or pounded meat, while they melt the fat, and prepare the fkins in their hair, for winter. The wolves they never eat, but produce a tallow from their fat, and prepare their fkins; all which they bring to exchange for arms and ammunition, rum, tobacco, knives, and various baubles, with thofe who go to traffic in their country.

The Algonquins, and the Knifteneaux, on the contrary, attend to the fur-hunting, fo that they acquire the additional articles of cloth, blankets, &c. but their paffion for rum often puts it out of their power to fupply themfelves with real neceffaries.

The

The next river of magnitude is the river Dauphin, which empties itfelf at the head of St. Martin's Bay, on the Weft fide of the Lake Winipic, latitude nearly 52. 15. North, taking its fource in the fame mountains as the laft-mentioned river, as well as the Swan and Red-Deer River, the latter paffing through the lake of the fame name, as well as the former, and both continuing their courfe through the Manitoba Lake, which, from thence, runs parallel with Lake Winipic, to within nine miles of the Red River, and by what is called the river Dauphin, difembogues its waters, as already defcribed, into that lake. Thefe rivers are very rapid, and interrupted by falls, &c. the bed being generally rocky. All this country, to the South branch of the Safkatchiwine, abounds in beaver, moofe-deer, fallow-deer, elks, bears, buffalos, &c. The foil is good, and wherever any attempts have been made to raife the efculent plants, &c. it has been found productive.

On thefe waters are three principal forts for trade. Fort Dauphin, which was eftablifhed by the French before the conqueft. Red-Deer-River, and Swan-River Forts, with occafional detached pofts from thefe. The inhabitants are the Knifteneaux, from the North of Lake Winipic; and Algonquins from the country between the Red River and Lake Superior; and fome from the Rainy Lake: but as they are not fixed inhabitants, their number cannot be determined: they do not, however, at any time exceed two hundred warriors. In general they are good hunters. There is no other confiderable river except the Safkatchiwine, which I fhall mention prefently, that empties itfelf into the Lake Winipic.

Thofe

Thofe on the North fide are inconfiderable, owing to the comparative vicinity of the high land that feparates the waters coming this way, from thofe difcharging into Hudfon's bay, The courfe of the lake is about Weft-North-Weft, and South-South-Eaft, and the Eaft end of it is in 50. 37. North. It contracts at about a quarter of its length to a ftrait, in latitude 51. 45. and is no more than two miles broad, where the South fhore is gained through iflands, and croffing various bays to the difcharge of the Safkatchiwine, in latitude 53. 15. This lake, in common with thofe of this country, is bounded on the North with banks of black and grey rock, and on the South by a low, level country, occafionally interrupted with a ridge or bank of lime-ftones, lying in ftratas, and rifing to the perpendicular height of from twenty to forty feet; thefe are covered with a fmall quantity of earth, forming a level furface, which bears timber, but of a moderate growth, and declines to a fwamp. Where the banks are low, it is evident in many places that the waters are withdrawn, and never rife to thofe heights which were formerly wafhed by them.

The inhabitants who are found along this lake, are of the Knifteneaux and Algonquin tribes, and but few in number, though game is not fcarce, and there is fifh in great abundance. The black bafs is found there, and no further Weft; and beyond it no maple trees are feen, either hard or foft.

On entering the Safkatchiwine, in the courfe of a few miles, the great rapid interrupts the paffage. It is about three miles long. Through the greateft part of it the canoe is towed, half or full laden, according to

the

the ſtate of the waters: the canoe and its contents are then carried one thouſand one hundred paces. The channel here is near a mile wide, the waters tumbling over ridges of rocks that traverſe the river. The ſouth bank is very high, riſing upwards of fifty feet, of the ſame rock as ſeen on the South ſide of the Lake Winipic, and the North is not more than a third of that height. There is an excellent ſturgeon-fiſhery at the foot of this caſcade, and vaſt numbers of pelicans, cormo-rants, &c. frequent it, where they watch to ſeize the fiſh that may be killed or diſabled by the force of the waters.

About two miles from this Portage the navigation is again inter-rupted by the Portage of the Roché Rouge, which is an hundred yards long; and a mile and an half from thence the river is barred by a range of iſlands, forming rapids between them; and through theſe it is the ſame diſtance to the rapid of Lake Travers, which is four miles right acroſs, and eight miles in length. Then ſucceeds the Grande Décharge, and ſeveral rapids, for four miles to the Cedar Lake, which is entered through a ſmall channel on the left, formed by an iſland, as going round it would occaſion loſs of time. In this diſ-tance banks of rocks (ſuch as have already been deſcribed), appear at intervals on either ſide; the reſt of the country is low. This is the caſe along the South bank of the lake and the iſlands, while the North ſide, which is very uncommon, is level throughout. This lake runs firſt Weſt four miles, then as much more Weſt-South-Weſt, acroſs a deep bay on the right, then ſix miles to the Point de Lievre, and acroſs another bay again on the right; then North-Weſt eight miles, acroſs a ſtill deeper bay on the right; and ſeven miles parallel with the North coaſt, North-North-Weſt

through

through iflands, five miles more to Fort Bourbon*, fituated on a fmall ifland, dividing this from Mud-Lake.

The Cedar Lake is from four to twelve miles wide, exclufive of the bays. Its banks are covered with wood, and abound in game, and its waters produce plenty of fifh, particularly the fturgeon. The Mud-Lake, and the neighbourhood of the Fort Bourbon, abound with geefe, ducks, fwans, &c. and was formerly remarkable for a vaft number of martens, of which it cannot now boaft but a very fmall proportion.

The Mud-Lake muft have formerly been a part of the Cedar Lake, but the immenfe quantity of earth and fand, brought down by the Safkatchi-wine, has filled up this part of it for a circumference whofe diameter is at leaft fifteen or twenty miles: part of which fpace is ftill covered with a few feet of water, but the greateft proportion is fhaded with large trees, fuch as the liard, the fwamp-afh, and the willow. This land confifts of many iflands, which confequently form various channels, feveral of which are occafionally dry, and bearing young wood. It is, indeed, more than pro-bable that this river will, in the courfe of time, convert the whole of the Cedar Lake into a foreft. To the North-Weft the cedar is not to be found.

From this lake the Safkatchiwine may be confidered as navigable to near its fources in the rocky mountains, for canoes, and without a carrying-place, making a great bend to Cumberland Houfe, on Sturgeon Lake. From the confluence of its North and South branches its courfe

This was alfo a principal poft of the French, who gave it its name.

is

is Wefterly; fpreading itfelf, it receives feveral tributary ftreams, and encompaffes a large track of country, which is level, particularly along the South branch, but is little known. Beaver, and other animals, whofe furs are valuable, are amongft the inhabitants of the North-Weft branch, and the plains are covered with buffalos, wolves, and fmall foxes; particularly about the South branch, which, however, has of late claimed fome attention, as it is now underftood, that where the plains terminate towards the rocky mountain, there is a fpace of hilly country clothed with wood, and inhabited alfo by animals of the fur kind. This has been actually determined to be the cafe towards the head of the North branch, where the trade has been carried to about the latitude 54 North, and longitude 114½. Weft. The bed and banks of the latter, in fome few places, difcover a ftratum of free-ftone; but, in general, they are compofed of earth and fand. The plains are fand and gravel, covered with fine grafs, and mixed with a fmall quanty of vegetable earth. This is particularly obfervable along the North branch, the Weft fide of which is covered with wood.

There are on this river five principal factories for the convenience of trade with the natives. Nepawi Houfe, South-branch Houfe, Fort-George Houfe, Fort-Auguftus Houfe, and Upper Eftablifhment. There have been many others, which, from various caufes, have been changed for thefe, while there are occafionally others depending on each of them.

The inhabitants, from the information I could obtain, are as fol-low:

At

At Nepawi, and South-Branch Houfe, about thirty tents of Knifte-neaux, or ninety warriors; and fixty tents of Stone-Indians, or Affiniboins, who are their neighbours, and are equal to two hundred men: their hunting ground extends upwards to about the Eagle Hills. Next to them are thofe who trade at Forts George and Auguftus, and are about eighty tents or upwards of Knifteneaux: on either fide of the river, their number may be two hundred. In the fame country are one hundred and forty tents of Stone-Indians; not quite half of them inhabit the Weft woody country; the others never leave the plains, and their numbers cannot be lefs than four hundred and fifty men. At the Southern Head-waters of the North branch dwells a tribe called Sarfees, confifting of about thirty-five tents, or one hundred and twenty men. Oppofite to thofe Eaftward, on the head-waters of the South Branch, are the Pica-neaux, to the number of from twelve to fifteen hundred men. Next to them, on the fame water, are the Blood-Indians, of the fame nation as the laft, to the number of about fifty tents, or two hundred and fifty men. From them downwards extend the Black-Feet Indians, of the fame nation as the two laft tribes: their number may be eight hundred men. Next to them, and who extend to the confluence of the South and North branch, are the Fall, or Big-bellied Indians, who may amount to about fix hundred warriors.

Of all thefe different tribes, thofe who inhabit the broken country on the North-Weft fide, and the fource of the North branch, are beaver-hunters; the others deal in provifions, wolf, buffalo, and fox fkins; and many people on the South branch do not trouble themfelves to come near

the

the trading eftablifhments.   Thofe who do, choofe fuch eftablifhments as
are next to their country.   The Stone-Indians here, are the fame people
as the Stone-Indians, or Affiniboins, who inhabit the river of that name already defcribed, and both are detached tribes from the Nadawafis, who inhabit the Weftern fide of the Miffiffippi, and lower part of the Miffifoury.
The Fall, or Big-bellied Indians, are from the South-Eaftward alfo, and
of a people who inhabit the plains from the North bend of the laft mentioned river, latitude 47. 32. North, longitude 101. 25. Weft, to the
South bend of the Affiniboin River, to the number of feven hundred
men.   Some of them occafionally come to the latter river to exchange
dreffed buffalo robes, and bad wolf-fkins for articles of no great
value.

The Picaneaux, Black-Feet, and Blood-Indians, are a diftinct people,
fpeak a language of their own, and, I have reafon to think, are travelling North-Weftward, as well as the others juft mentioned: nor have
I heard of any Indians with whofe language, that which they fpeak has
any affinity.   They are the people who deal in horfes and take them
upon the war-parties towards Mexico; from which, it is evident, that
the country to the South-Eaft of them, confifts of plains, as thofe
animals could not well be conducted through an hilly and woody country, interfected by waters.

The Sarfees, who are but few in number, appear from their language, to come on the contrary from the North-Weftward, and are
of the fame people as the Rocky-Mountain Indians defcribed in my

fecond

second journal, who are a tribe of the Chepewyans; and, as for the Knifteneaux, there is no queftion of their having been, and continuing to be, invaders of this country, from the Eaftward.   Formerly, they ftruck terror into all the other tribes whom they met; but now they have loft the refpect that was paid them; as thofe whom they formerly confidered as barbarians, are now their allies, and confequently become better acquainted with them, and have acquired the ufe of fire-arms.   The former are ftill proud without power, and affect to confider the others as their inferiors: thofe confequently are extremely jealous of them, and, depending upon their own fuperiority in numbers, will not fubmit tamely to their infults; fo that the confequences often prove fatal, and the Knifteneaux are thereby decreafing both in power and number: fpirituous liquors alfo tend to their diminution, as they are inftigated thereby to engage in quarrels which frequently have the moft difaftrous termination among themfelves.

The Stone-Indians muft not be confidered in the fame point of view refpecting the Knifteneaux, for they have been generally obliged, from various caufes, to court their alliance.   They, however, are not without their difagreements, and it is fometimes very difficult to compofe their differences.   Thefe quarrels occafionally take place with the traders, and fometimes have a tragical conclufion.   They generally originate in confequence of ftealing women and horfes: they have great numbers] of the latter throughout their plains, which are brought, as has been obferved, from the Spanifh fettlements in Mexico; and many of them have been feen even in the back parts of this country, branded with the initials of their original owners names.

Thofe

Thofe horfes are diftinctly employed as beafts of burden, and to chafe the buffalo. The former are not confidered as being of much value, as they may be purchafed for a gun, which cofts no more than twenty-one pounds in Great-Britain. Many of the hunters cannot be purchafed with ten, the comparative value, which exceeds the property of any native.

Of thefe ufeful animals no care whatever is taken, as when they are no longer employed, they are turned loofe winter and fummer to provide for themfelves. Here, it is to be obferved, that the country, in general, on the Weft and North fide of this great river, is broken by the lakes and rivers with fmall intervening plains, where the foil is good, and the grafs grows to fome length. To thefe the male buffalos refort for the winter, and if it be very fevere, the females alfo are obliged to leave the plains.

But to return to the route by which the progrefs Weft and North is made through this continent.

We leave the Safkatchiwine * by entering the river which forms the difcharge of the Sturgeon Lake, on whofe Eaft bank is fituated Cumberland houfe, in latitude 53. 56. North, longitude 102. 15. The diftance between the entrance of the lake and Cumberland houfe is eftimated at twenty miles. It is very evident that the mud which is carried down by

---

* It may be proper to obferve, that the French had two fettlements upon the Safkatchiwine, long before, and at the conqueft of Canada ; the firft at the Pafquia, near Carrot River, and the other at Nipawi, where they had agricultural inftruments and wheel carriages, marks of both being found about thofe eftablifhments, where the foil is excellent.

the

the Saſkatchiwine River, has formed the land that lies between it and the lake, for the diſtance of upwards of twenty miles in the line of the river, which is inundated during one half of the ſummer, though covered with wood.   This lake forms an irregular horſe-ſhoe, one ſide of which runs to the North-Weſt, and bears the name of Pine-Iſland Lake, and the other known by the name already mentioned, runs to the Eaſt of North, and is the largeſt : its length is about twenty-ſeven miles, and its greateſt breadth about ſix miles.   The North ſide of the latter is the ſame kind of rock as that deſcribed in Lake Winipic, on the Weſt ſhore.   In lati-tude 54. 16. North, the Sturgeon-Weir River diſcharges itſelf into this lake, and its bed appears to be of the ſame kind of rock, and is almoſt a continual rapid.   Its direct courſe is about Weſt by North, and with its windings, is about thirty miles.   It takes its waters into the Beaver Lake, the South-Weſt ſide of which conſiſts of the ſame rock lying in thin ſtratas : the route then proceeds from iſland to iſland for about twelve miles, and along the North ſhore, for four miles more, the whole being a North-Weſt courſe to the entrance of a river, in latitude 54. 32. North. The lake, for this diſtance, is about four or five miles wide, and abounds with fiſh common to the country.   The part of it upon the right of that which has been deſcribed, appears more conſiderable.   The iſlands are rocky, and the lake itſelf ſurrounded by rocks.   The communication from hence to the Bouleau Lake, alternately narrows into rivers and ſpreads into ſmall lakes.   The interruptions are, the Pente Portage, which is ſucceeded by the Grand Rapid, where there is a Décharge, the Carp Portage, the Bouleau Portage in latitude 54. 50. North, in-cluding a diſtance, together with the windings, of thirty-four miles, in a Weſterly direction.   The Lake de Bouleau then follows.   This

lake

lake might with greater propriety, be denominated a canal, as it is not more than a mile in breadth. Its courfe is rather to the Eaft of North for twelve miles to Portage de L'Ifle. From thence there is ftill water to Portage d'Epinettes, except an adjoining rapid. The diftance is not more than four miles Wefterly. After croffing this Portage, it is not more than two miles to Lake Miron, which is in latitude 55. 7. North. Its length is about twelve miles, and its breadth irregular, from two to ten miles. It is only feparated from Lake du Chitique, or Pelican Lake, by a fhort, narrow, and fmall ftrait. That lake is not more than feven miles long, and its courfe about North-Weft. The Lake des Bois then fucceeds, the paffage to which is through fmall lakes, feparated by falls and rapids. The firft is a Décharge: then follow the three galets, in immediate fuc-ceffion. From hence Lake des Bois runs about twenty-one miles. Its courfe is South-South-Eaft, and North-North-Weft, and is full of iflands. The paffage continues through an intricate, narrow, winding, and fhallow channel for eight miles. The interruptions in this diftance are frequent, but depend much on the ftate of the waters. Having paffed them, it is neceffary to crofs the Portage de Traite, or, as it is called by the Indians, Athiquifipichigan Ouinigam, or the Portage of the Stretched Frog-Skin, to the Miffinipi. The waters already defcribed difcharge themfelves into Lake Winipic, and augment thofe of the river Nelfon. Thefe which we are now entering are called the Miffinipi, or great Churchill River.

All the country to the South and Eaft of this, within the line of the progrefs that has been defcribed, is interfperfed by lakes, hills, and rivers, and is full of animals, of the fur-kind, as well as the moofe-deer.

Its

Its inhabitants are the Knifteneaux Indians, who are called by the fervants of the Hudfon's-Bay Company, at York, their home-guards.

The traders from Canada fucceeded for feveral years in getting the largeft proportion of their furs, till the year 1793, when the fervants of that company thought proper to fend people amongft them, (and why they did not do it before is beft known to themfelves), for the purpofe of trade, and fecuring their credits, which the Indians were apt to forget. From the fhort diftance they had to come, and the quantity of goods they fupplied, the trade has, in a great meafure, reverted to them, as the merchants from Canada could not meet them upon equal terms. What added to the lofs of the latter, was the murder of one of their traders, by the Indians, about this period. Of thefe people not above eighty men have been known to the traders from Canada, but they confift of a much greater number.

The Portage de Traite, as has been already hinted, received its name from Mr. Jofeph Frobifher, who penetrated into this part of the country from Canada, as early as the years 1774 and 1775, where he met with the Indians in the fpring, on their way to Churchill, according to annual cuftom, with their canoes full of valuable furs. They traded with him for as many of them as his canoes could carry, and in confequence of this tranfaction, the Portage received and has fince retained its prefent appellation. He alfo denominated thefe waters the Englifh River. The Miffinipi, is the name which it received from the Knifteneaux, when they firft came to this country, and either deftroyed or drove back the natives, whom they held in great contempt, on many accounts, but particularly for their ignorance in hunting

the

the beaver, as well as in preparing, ſtretching, and drying the ſkins of thoſe animals. And as a ſign of their deriſion, they ſtretched the ſkin of a frog, and hung it up at the Portage. This was, at that time, the utmoſt extent of their conqueſt or warfaring-progreſs Weſt, and is in latitude 55. 25. North, and longitude 103¾. Weſt. The river here, which bears the appearance of a lake, takes its name from the Portage, and is full of iſlands. It runs from Eaſt to Weſt about ſixteen miles, and is from four to five miles broad. Then ſucceed falls and caſcades which form what is called the grand rapid. From thence there is a ſucceſſion of ſmall lakes and rivers, interrupted by rapids and falls, viz. the Portage de Bareel, the Portage de L'Iſle, and that of the Rapid River. The courſe is twenty miles from Eaſt-South-Eaſt to North-North-Weſt. The Rapid-River Lake then runs Weſt five miles, and is of an oval form. The rapid river is the diſcharge of Lake la Ronge, where there has been an eſtabliſhment for trade from the year 1782. Since the ſmall pox ravaged theſe parts, there have been but few inhabi-tants; theſe are of the Kniſteneaux tribe, and do not exceed thirty men. The direct navigation continues to be through rivers and canals, interrupted by rapids; and the diſtance to the firſt Décharge is four miles, in a Weſterly direction. Then follows Lake de la Montagne, which runs South-South-Weſt three miles and an half, then North ſix miles, through narrow channels, formed by iſlands, and continues North-North-Weſt five miles, to the portage of the ſame name, which is no ſooner croſſed, than another appears in ſight, leading to the Otter Lake, from whence it is nine miles Weſterly to the Otter Portage, in latitude 55. 39. Between this and the Portage du Diable, are ſeveral rapids, and the diſtance three miles and an half. Then ſuc-ceeds the lake of the ſame name, running from South-Eaſt to North-Weſt,

Weſt, five miles, and Weſt four miles and an half. There is then a ſucceſſion of ſmall lakes, rapids, and falls, producing the Portage des Ecors,
Portage du Galet, and Portage des Morts, the whole comprehending a
diſtance of ſix miles, to the lake of the latter name. On the left ſide
is a point covered with human bones, the relics of the ſmall pox; which
circumſtance gave the Portage and the lake this melancholy denomination. Its courſe is South-Weſt fifteen miles, while its breadth does not
exceed three miles. From thence a rapid river leads to Portage de
Hallier, which is followed by Lake de L'Iſle d'Ours: it is, however, improperly called a lake, as it contains frequent impediments amongſt its
iſlands, from rapids. There is a very dangerous one about the centre of
it, which is named the Rapid qui ne parle point, or that never ſpeaks,
from its ſilent whirlpool-motion. In ſome of the whirlpools the
ſuċtion is ſo powerful, that they are carefully avoided. At ſome diftance from the ſilent rapid, is a narrow ſtrait, where the Indians
have painted red figures on the face of a rock, and where it was their
cuſtom formerly to make an offering of ſome of the articles which they
had with them, in their way to and from Churchill. The courſe in this
lake, which is very meandering, may be eſtimated at thirty-eight miles,
and is terminated by the Portage du Canot Tourner, from the danger to
which thoſe are ſubjeċt who venture to run this rapid. From thence a
river of one mile and an half North-Weſt courſe leads to the Portage de
Bouleau, and in about half a mile to Portage des Epingles, ſo called from
the ſharpneſs of its ſtones. Then follows the Lake des Souris, the direction acroſs which is amongſt iſlands, North-Weſt by Weſt ſix miles. In
this traverſe is an iſland, which is remarkable for a very large ſtone, in
the form of a bear, on which the natives have painted the head and

ſnout

fnout of that animal; and here they alfo were formerly accuftomed to offer facrifices. This lake is feparated only by a narrow ftrait from the Lake du Serpent, which runs North-North-Weft feven miles, to a narrow channel, that connects it with another lake, bearing the fame name, and running the fame courfe for eleven miles, when the rapid of the fame denomination is entered on the Weft fide of the lake. It is to be remarked here, that for about three or four miles on the North-Weft fide of this lake, there is an high bank of clay and fand, clothed with cyprefs trees, a circumftance which is not obfervable on any lakes hitherto mentioned, as they are bounded, particularly on the North, by black and grey rocks. It may alfo be confidered as a moft extraordinary circumftance, that the Chepewyans, go North-Weft from hence to the barren grounds, which are their own country, without the affiftance of canoes; as it is well known that in every other part which has been defcribed, from Cumberland Houfe, the country is broken on either fide of the direction to a great extent: fo that a traveller could not go at right angles with any of the waters already mentioned, without meeting with others in every eight or ten miles. This will alfo be found to be very much the cafe in proceeding to Portage la Loche.

The laft mentioned rapid is upwards of three miles long, North-Weft by Weft; there is, however, no carrying, as the line and poles are fufficient to drag and fet the canoe againft the current. Lake Croche is then croffed in a Wefterly direction of fix miles, though its whole length may be twice that diftance; after which it contracts to a river that runs Wefterly for ten miles, when it forms a bend, which is left to the

South

South, and entering a portion of its waters called the **Grafs River**, whofe meandering courfe is about fix miles, but in a direct line not more than half that length, where it receives its waters from the great river, which then runs Wefterly eleven miles before it forms the Knee Lake, whofe direction is to the North of Weft.   It is full of iflands for eighteen miles, and its greateft apparent breadth is not more than five miles.   The portage of the fame name is feveral hundred yards long, and over large ftones.   Its latitude is 55. 50. and longitude 106. 30.   Two miles further North is the commencement of the Croche Rapid, which is a fucceffion of cafcades for about three miles, making a bend due South to the Lake du Primeau, whofe courfe is various, and through iflands, to the diftance of about fifteen miles.   The banks of this lake are low, ftony, and marfhy, whofe grafs and rufhes, afford fhelter and food to great numbers of wild fowl.   At its Weftern extremity is Portage la Puife, from whence the river takes a meandering courfe, widening and contracting at intervals, and is much interrupted by rapids.   After a Wefterly courfe of twenty miles, it reaches Portage Pellet.   From hence, in the courfe of feven miles, are three rapids, to which fucceeds the Shagoina Lake, which may be eighteen miles in circumference. Then Shagoina ftrait and rapid lead into the Lake of Ifle a la Croifé, in which the courfe is South twenty miles, and South-South-Weft fourteen miles, to the Point au Sable; oppofite to which is the difcharge of the Beaver-River, bearing South fix miles: the lake in the diftance run, does not exceed twelve miles in its greateft breadth.   It now turns Weft-South-Weft, the ifle a la Croifé being on the South, and the main land on the North; and it clears the one and the other in the diftance of three miles, the water prefenting an open horizon to right and left: that on the left formed by a deep narrow bay, about ten leagues

in

in depth; and that to the right by what is called la Riviere Creufe, or Deep River, being a canal of ftill water, which is here four miles wide. On following the laft courfe, Ifle a la Croffe Fort appears on a low ifthmus, at the diftance of five miles, and is in latitude 55. 25. North, and longitude 107. 48. Weft.

This lake and fort take their names from the ifland juft mentioned, which, as has been already obferved, received it denomination from the game of the crofs, which forms a principal amufement among the natives.

The fituation of this lake, the abundance of the fineft fifh in the world to be found in its waters, the richnefs of its furrounding banks and forefts, in moofe and fallow deer, with the vaft numbers of the fmaller tribes of animals, whofe fkins are precious, and the numerous flocks of wild fowl that frequent it in the fpring and fall, make it a moft defirable fpot for the conftant refidence of fome, and the occafional rendez-vous of others of the inhabitants of the country, particularly of the Knifteneaux.

Who the original people were that were driven from it, when con-quered by the Knifteneaux is not now known, as not a fingle veftige re-mains of them. The latter, and the Chepewyans, are the only people that have been known here; and it is evident that the laft-mentioned confider themfelves as ftrangers, and feldom remain longer than three or four years, without vifiting their relations and friends in the barren grounds, which they term their native country. They were for fometime treated by

the

the Knifteneaux as enemies; who now allow them to hunt to the North of the track which has been defcribed, from Fort du Traite upwards, but when they occafionally meet them, they infift on contributions, and frequently punifh refiftance with their arms. This is fometimes done at the forts, or places of trade, but then it appears to be a voluntary gift. A treat of rum is expected on the occafion, which the Chepewyans on no other account ever purchafe; and thofe only who have had frequent intercourfe with the Knifteneaux have any inclination to drink it.

When the Europeans firft penetrated into this country, in 1777, the people of both tribes were numerous, but the fmall pox was fatal to them all, fo that there does not exift of the one, at prefent, more than forty refident families; and the other has been from about thirty to two hundred families. Thefe numbers are applicable to the conftant and lefs ambitious inhabitants, who are fatisfied with the quiet poffeffion of a country affording, without rifk or much trouble, every thing neceffary to their comfort; for fince traders have fpread themfelves over it, it is no more the rendezvous of the errant Knifteneaux, part of whom ufed annually to return thither from the country of the Beaver River, which they had explored to its fource in their war and hunting excurfions and as far as the Safkatchiwine, where they fometimes met people of their own nation, who had profecuted fimilar conquefts up that river. In that country they found abundance of fifh and animals, fuch as have been already defcribed, with the addition of the buffalos, who range in the partial patches of meadow fcattered along the rivers and lakes. From thence they returned in the fpring to the friends whom they had left; and, at the fame

time

time met with others who had penetrated, with the same defigns, into the Athabafca country, which will be defcribed hereafter.

The fpring was the period of this joyful meeting, when their time was occupied in feafting, dancing, and other paftimes, which were occafionally fufpended for facrifice, and religious folemnity : while the narratives of their travels, and the hiftory of their wars, amufed and animated the feftival. The time of rejoicing was but fhort, and was foon interrupted by the neceffary preparations for their annual journey to Churchill, to exchange their furs for fuch European articles as were now become neceffary to them. The fhortnefs of the feafons, and the great length of their way requiring the utmoft difpatch, the moft active men of the tribe, with their youngeft women, and a few of their children undertook the voyage, under the direction of fome of their chiefs, following the waters already defcribed, to their difcharge at Churchill Factory, which are called, as has already been obferved, the Miffinipi, or Great Waters. There they remained no longer than was fufficient to barter their commodities, with a fupernumerary, and a day or two to gratify themfelves with the indulgence of fpirituous liquors. At the fame time the inconfiderable quantity they could purchafe to carry away with them, for a regale with their friends, was held facred, and referved to heighten the enjoyment of their return home, when the amufements, feftivity, and religious folemnities of the fpring were repeated. The ufual time appropriated to thefe convivialities being completed, they feparated, to purfue their different objects; and if they were determined to go to war, they made the neceffary arrangements for their future operations.

But

But we muſt now renew the progreſs of the route. It is not more than two miles from Iſle a la Croſſe Fort, to a point of land which forms a cheek of that part of the lake called the Riviere Creuſe, which preſerves the breadth already mentioned for upwards of twenty miles; then contraȼts to about two, for the diſtance of ten miles more, when it opens to Lake Clear, which is very wide, and commands an open horizon, keeping the Weſt ſhore for ſix miles. The whole of the diſtance mentioned is about North-Weſt, when, by a narrow, crooked channel, turning to the South of Weſt, the entry is made into Lake du Boeuf, which is contraȼted near the middle, by a projeȼting ſandy point; independent of which it may be deſcribed as from ſix to twelve miles in breadth, thirty-ſix miles long, and in a North-Weſt direȼtion. At the North-Weſt end, in latitude 56. 8. it receives the waters of the river la Loche, which, in the fall of the year, is very ſhallow, and navigated with difficulty even by half-laden canoes. Its water is not ſufficient to form ſtrong rapids, though from its rocky bottom the canoes are frequently in conſiderable danger. Including its meanders, the courſe of this river may be computed at twenty-four miles, and receives its firſt waters from the lake of the ſame name, which is about twenty miles long, and ſix wide; into which a ſmall river flows, ſufficient to bear loaded canoes, for about a mile and an half, where the navigation ceaſes; and the canoes, with their lading, are carried over the Portage la Loche for thirteen miles.

This portage is the ridge that divides the waters which diſcharge themſelves into Hudſon's Bay, from thoſe that flow into the Northern ocean, and is in the latitude 56. 20. and longitude 109. 15. Weſt. It runs South

Weſt

Weſt until it loſes its local height between the Saſkatchiwine and Elk Rivers; cloſe on the bank of the former, in latitude 53. 36. North, and longitude 113. 45. Weſt, it may be traced in an Eaſterly direction toward latitude 58. 12. North, and longitude 103½. Weſt, when it appears to take its courſe due North, and may probably reach the Frozen Seas.

From Lake le Souris, the banks of the rivers and lakes diſplay a ſmaller portion of ſolid rock. The land is low and ſtony, intermixed with a light, ſandy ſoil, and clothed with wood. That of the Beaver River is of a more productive quality: but no part of it has ever been cultivated by the natives or Europeans, except a ſmall garden at the Iſle a la Croſſe, which well repaid the labour beſtowed upon it.

The Portage la Loche is of a level ſurface, in ſome parts abounding with ſtones, but in general it is an entire ſand, and covered with the cypreſs, the pine, the ſpruce fir, and other trees natural to its ſoil. Within three miles of the North-Weſt termination, there is a ſmall round lake, whoſe diameter does not exceed a mile, and which affords a trifling reſpite to the labour of carrying. Within a mile of the termination of the Portage is a very ſteep precipice, whoſe aſcent and deſcent appears to be equally impracticable in any way, as it conſiſts of a ſucceſſion of eight hills, ſome of which are almoſt perpendicular; neverthelefs, the Canadians contrive to ſurmount all theſe difficulties, even with their canoes and lading.

This precipice, which riſes upwards of a thouſand feet above the plain beneath it, commands a moſt extenſive, romantic, and raviſhing proſpect.

From

From thence the eye looks down on the courfe of the little river, by fome called the Swan river, and by others, the Clear-Water and Pelican river, beautifully meandering for upwards of thirty miles. The valley, which is at once refrefhed and adorned by it, is about three miles in breadth, and is confined by two lofty ridges of equal height, difplaying a moft delightful intermixture of wood and lawn, and ftretching on till the blue mift obfcures the profpect. Some parts of the inclining heights are covered with ftately forefts, relieved by promontories of the fineft verdure, where the elk and buffalo find pafture. Thefe are contrafted by fpots where fire has deftroyed the woods, and left a dreary void behind it. Nor, when I beheld this wonderful difplay of uncultivated nature, was the moving fcenery of human occupation wanting to complete the picture. From this elevated fituation, I beheld my people, diminifhed, as it were, to half their fize, employed in pitching their tents in a charming meadow, and among the canoes, which, being turned upon their fides, prefented their reddened bottoms in contraft with the furrounding verdure. At the fame time, the procefs of gumming them produced numerous fmall fpires of fmoke, which, as they rofe, enlivened the fcene, and at length blended with the larger columns that afcended from the fires where the fuppers were preparing. It was in the month of September when I enjoyed a fcene, of which I do not prefume to give an adequate defcription; and as it was the rutting feafon of the elk, the whiftling of that animal was heard in all the variety which the echoes could afford it.

This river, which waters and reflects fuch enchanting fcenery, runs, including its windings, upwards of eighty miles, when it difcharges itfelf in the Elk River, according to the denomination of the natives, but

commonly

commonly called by the white people, the Athabafca River, in latitude 56. 42. North.

At a fmall diftance from Portage la Loche, feveral carrying-places interrupt the navigation of the river; about the middle of which are fome mineral fprings, whofe margins are covered with fulphureous incruftations. At the junction or fork, the Elk River is about three quarters of a mile in breadth, and runs in a fteady current, fometimes contracting, but never increafing its channel, till, after receiving feveral fmall ftreams, it difcharges itfelf into the Lake of the Hills, in latitude 58. 36. North. At about twenty-four miles from the Fork, are fome bitumenous fountains, into which a pole of twenty feet long may be inferted without the leaft refiftance. The bitumen is in a fluid ftate, and when mixed with gum, or the refinous fubftance collected from the fpruce fir, ferves to gum the canoes. In its heated ftate it emits a fmell like that of fea-coal. The banks of the river, which are there very elevated, difcover veins of the fame bitumenous quality. At a fmall diftance from the Fork, houfes have been erected for the convenience of trading with a party of the Knifteneaux, who vifit the adjacent country for the purpofe of hunting.

At the diftance of about forty miles from the lake, is the Old Eftablifhment, which has been already mentioned, as formed by Mr. Pond in the year 1778-9, and which was the only one in this part of the world, till the year 1785. In the year 1788, it was transferred to the Lake of the Hills, and formed on a point on its Southern fide, at about eight miles from the difcharge of the river. It was named Fort Chepewyan, and is in latitude 58. 38. North, longitude 110. 26. Weft, and much

better

better fituated for trade and fifhing, as the people here have recourfe to water for their fupport.

This being the place which I made my head-quarters for eight years, and from whence I took my departure, on both my expeditions, I fhall give fome account of it, with the manner of carrying on the trade there, and other circumftances connected with it.

The laden canoes which leave Lake la Pluie about the firft of Auguft, do not arrive here till the latter end of September, or the beginning of October, when a neceffary proportion of them is difpatched up the Peace River to trade with the Beaver and Rocky-Mountain Indians. Others are fent to the Slave River and Lake, or beyond them, and traffic with the inhabitants of that country. A fmall part of them, if not left at the Fork of the Elk River, return thither for the Knifteneaux, while the reft of the people and merchandife remain here to carry on trade with the Chepewyans.

Here have I arrived with ninety or an hundred men without any provifion for their fuftenance; for whatever quantity might have been obtained from the natives during the fummer, it could not be more than fufficient for the people difpatched to their different pofts; and even if there were a cafual fuperfluity, it was abfolutely neceffary to preferve it untouched, for the demands of the fpring. The whole dependance, therefore, of thofe who remained, was on the lake, and fifhing implements for the means of our fupport. The nets are fixty fathom in length, when fet, and contain fifteen mefhes of five inches in depth. The manner of ufing them is as follows: A fmall ftone and wooden

buoy

buoy are faftened to the fide-line oppofite to each other, at about the diftance of two fathoms : when the net is carefully thrown into the water,
the ftone finks it to the bottom, while the buoy keeps it at its full extent, and it is fecured in its fituation by a ftone at either end. The
nets are vifited every day, and taken out every other day to be cleaned
and dried. This is a very ready operation when the waters are not
frozen, but when the froft has fet in, and the ice has acquired its greateft
thicknefs, which is fometimes as much as five feet, holes are cut in it at
the diftance of thirty feet from each other, to the full length of the net ;
one of them is larger than the reft, being generally about four feet fquare,
and is called the bafon : by means of them, and poles of a proportionable length, the nets are placed in and drawn out of the water.
The fetting of hooks and lines is fo fimple an employment as to render
a defcription unneceffary. The white fifh are the principal object of
purfuit : they fpawn in the fall of the year, and, at about the fetting
in of the hard froft, crowd in fhoals to the fhallow water, when as
many as poffible are taken, in order that a portion of them may be laid by
in the froft to provide againft the fcarcity of winter ; as, during that feafon,
the fifh of every defcription decreafe in the lakes, if they do not altogether
difappear. Some have fuppofed that during this period they are ftationary, or affume an inactive ftate. If there fhould be any intervals of
warm weather during the fall, it is neceffary to fufpend the fifh by the
tail, though they are not fo good as thofe which are altogether preferved
by the froft. In this ftate they remain to the beginning of April, when
they have been found as fweet as when they were caught.*

---

* This fifhery requires the moft unremitting attention, as the voyaging Canadians are equally in-
dolent, extravagant, and improvident, when left to themfelves, and rival the favages in a neglect of
the morrow.

Thus

Thus do thefe voyagers live, year after year, entirely upon fifh, without even the quickening flavour of falt, or the variety of any farinaceous
root or vegetable.   Salt, however, if their habits had not rendered it
unneceffary, might be obtained in this country to the Weftward of the
Peace River, where it lofes its name in that of the Slave River, from the
numerous falt-ponds and fprings to be found there, which will fupply in
any quantity, in a ftate of concretion, and perfectly white and clean.
When the Indians pafs that way they bring a fmall quantity to the fort,
with other articles of traffic.

During a fhort period of the fpring and fall, great numbers of wild
fowl frequent this country, which prove a very gratifying food after fuch
a long privation of flefh-meat.   It is remarkable, however, that the Canadians who frequent the Peace, Safkatchiwine, and Affiniboin rivers,
and live altogether on venifon, have a lefs healthy appearance than thofe
whofe fuftenance is obtained from the waters.   At the fame time the
fcurvy is wholly unknown among them.

In the fall of the year the natives meet the traders at the forts, where
they barter the furs or provifions which they may have procured : they
then obtain credit, and proceed to hunt the beavers, and do not return
till the beginning of the year; when they are again fitted out in the
fame manner and come back the latter end of March, or the beginning
of April.   They are now unwilling to repair to the beaver hunt until the
waters are clear of ice, that they may kill them with fire-arms, which
the Chepewyans are averfe to employ.   The major part of the latter
return to the barren grounds, and live during the fummer with their

relations

relations and friends in the enjoyment of that plenty which is derived from numerous herds of deer. But thofe of that tribe who are moft partial to thefe defarts, cannot remain there in winter, and they are obliged, with the deer, to take fhelter in the woods during that rigorous feafon, when they contrive to kill a few beavers, and fend them by young men, to exchange for iron utenfils and ammunition.

Till the year 1782, the people of Athabafca fent or carried their furs regularly to Fort Churchill, Hudfon's Bay; and fome of them have, fince that time, repaired thither, notwithftanding they could have provided themfelves with all the neceffaries which they required. The difference of the price fet on goods here and at that factory, made it an object with the Chepewyans, to undertake a journey of five or fix months, in the courfe of which they were reduced to the moft painful extremities, and often loft their lives from hunger and fatigue. At prefent, however, this traffic is in a great meafure difcontinued, as they were obliged to expend in the courfe of their journey, that very ammunition which was its moft alluring object.

Some Account of the Knisteneaux Indians.

THESE people are fpread over a vaft extent of country. Their language is the fame as that of the people who inhabit the coaft of

Britifh

Britifh America on the Atlantic, with the exception of the Efqui-maux*, and continues along the Coaft of Labrador, and the gulph and banks of St. Laurence to Montreal. The line then follows the Utawas river to its fource; and continues from thence nearly Weft along the high lands which divide the waters that fall into Lake Superior and Hudfon's Bay. It then proceeds till it ftrikes the middle part of the river Winipic, following that water through the Lake Winipic, to the difcharge of the Safkatchiwine into it; from thence it accompanies the latter to Fort George, when the line, ftriking by the head of the Beaver River to the Elk River, runs along its banks to its dif-charge in the Lake of the Hills; from which it may be carried back Eaft, to the Ifle á la Croffe, and fo on to Churchill by the Miffinipi. The whole of the tract between this line and Hudfon's Bay and Straits, (except that of the Efquimaux in the latter), may be faid to be exclufively the country of the Knifteneaux. Some of them, indeed, have penetrated further Weft and South to the Red River, to the South of Lake Winipic, and the South branch of the Safkatchiwine.

They are of a moderate ftature, well proportioned, and of great activity. Examples of deformity are feldom to be feen among them. Their complexion is of a copper colour, and their hair black, which is common to all the natives of North America. It is cut in vari-ous forms, according to the fancy of the feveral tribes, and by fome is

---

* The fimilarity between their language, and that of the Algonquins, is an unequivocal proof that they are the fame people. Specimens of their refpective tongues will be hereafter given.

left

left in the long, lank, flow of nature. They very generally extract their beards, and both fexes manifeft a difpofition to pluck the hair from every part of the body and limbs. Their eyes are black, keen, and penetrating; their countenance open and agreeable, and it is a principal object of their vanity to give every poffible decoration to their perfons. A material article in their toilettes is vermilion, which they contraft with their native blue, white, and brown earths, to which charcoal is frequently added.

Their drefs is at once fimple and commodious. It confifts of tight leggins, reaching near the hip: a ftrip of cloth or leather, called affian, about a foot wide, and five feet long, whofe ends are drawn inwards and hang behind and before, over a belt tied round the waift for that purpofe: a clofe veft or fhirt reaching down to the former garment, and cinctured with a broad ftrip of parchment faftened with thongs behind; and a cap for the head, confifting of a piece of fur, or fmall fkin, with the brufh of the animal as a fufpended ornament: a kind of robe is thrown occafionally over the whole of the drefs, and ferves both night and day. Thefe articles, with the addition of fhoes and mittens, conftitute the variety of their apparel. The materials vary according to the feafon, and confift of dreffed moofe-fkin, beaver prepared with the fur, or European woollens. The leather is neatly painted, and fancifully worked in fome parts with porcupine quills, and moofe-deer hair: the fhirts and leggins are alfo adorned with fringe and taffels; nor are the fhoes and mittens without fomewhat of appropriate decoration, and worked with a confiderable degree of fkill and tafte. Thefe habiliments are put on, however,

ever, as fancy or convenience fuggefts; and they will fometimes proceed to the chafe in the fevereft froft, covered only with the flighteft of them. Their head-dreffes are compofed of the feathers of the fwan, the eagle, and other birds. The teeth, horns, and claws of different animals, are alfo the occafional ornaments of the head and neck. Their hair, however arranged, is always befmeared with greafe. The making of every article of drefs is a female occupation; and the women, though by no means inattentive to the decoration of their own per-fons, appear to have a ftill greater degree of pride in attending to the appearance of the men, whofe faces are painted with more care than thofe of the women.

The female drefs is formed of the fame materials as thofe of the other fex, but of a different make and arrangement. Their fhoes are commonly plain, and their leggins gartered beneath the knee. The coat, or body covering, falls down to the middle of the leg, and is faftened over the fhoulders with cords, a flap or cape turning down about eight inches, both before and behind, and agreeably ornamented with quill-work and fringe; the bottom is alfo fringed, and fancifully painted as high as the knee. As it is very loofe, it is enclofed round the waift with a ftiff belt, decorated with taffels, and faftened behind. The arms are covered to the wrift, with detached fleeves, which are fewed as far as the bend of the arm; from thence they are drawn up to the neck, and the cor-ners of them fall down behind, as low as the waift. The cap, when they wear one, confifts of a certain quantity of leather or cloth, fewed at one end, by which means it is kept on the head, and, hanging down

the

the back, is faftened to the belt, as well as under the chin. The upper garment is a robe like that worn by the men. Their hair is divided on the crown, and tied behind, or fometimes faftened in large knots over the ears. They are fond of European articles, and prefer them to their own native commodities. Their ornaments confift in common with all favages, in bracelets, rings, and fimilar baubles. Some of the women tatoo three perpendicular lines, which are fometimes double: one from the centre of the chin to that of the under lip, and one parallel on either fide to the corner of the mouth.

Of all the nations which I have feen on this continent, the Knifteneaux women are the moft comely. Their figure is generally well proportioned, and the regularity of their features would be acknowledged by the more civilized people of Europe. Their complexion has lefs of that dark tinge which is common to thofe favages who have lefs cleanly habits.

Thefe people are, in general, fubject to few diforders. The lues venerea, however, is a common complaint, but cured by the application of fimples, with whofe virtues they appear to be well acquainted. They are alfo fubject to fluxes, and pains in the breaft, which fome have attributed to the very cold and keen air which they inhale; but I fhould imagine that thefe complaints muft frequently proceed from their immoderate indulgence in fat meat at their feafts, particularly when they have been preceded by long fafting.

They are naturally mild and affable, as well as juft in their deal-

ings,

ings, not only among themfelves, but with ftrangers*. They are alfo generous and hofpitable, and good-natured in the extreme, except when their nature is perverted by the inflammatory influence of fpirituous liquors. To their children they are indulgent to a fault. The father, though he affumes no command over them, is ever anxious to in-ftruct them in all the preparatory qualifications for war and hunt-ing; while the mother is equally attentive to her daughters in teaching them every thing that is confidered as neceffary to their character and fituation. It does not appear that the hufband makes any diftinction between the children of his wife, though they may be the offspring of different fathers. Illegitimacy is only attached to thofe who are born before their mothers have cohabited with any man by the title of hufband.

It does not appear, that chaftity is confidered by them as a virtue; or that fidelity is believed to be effential to the happinefs of wedded life. Though it fometimes happens that the infidelity of a wife is punifhed by the hufband with the lofs of her hair, nofe, and perhaps life; fuch feverity proceeds from its having been practifed without his permiffion: for a temporary interchange of wives is not uncommon; and the offer of their perfons is confidered as a neceffary part of the hofpitality due to ftrangers.

When a man lofes his wife, it is confidered as a duty to marry her

---

* They have been called thieves, but when that vice can with juftice be attributed to them, it may be traced to their connection with the civilized people who come into their country to traffic.

fifter,

fifter, if fhe has one; or he may, if he pleafes, have them both at the fame time.

It will appear from the fatal confequences I have repeatedly imputed to the ufe of fpirituous liquors, that I more particularly confider thefe people as having been, morally fpeaking, great fufferers from their communication with the fubjects of civilized nations. At the fame time they were not, in a ftate of nature, without their vices, and fome of them of a kind which is the moft abhorrent to cultivated and reflecting man. I fhall only obferve that inceft and beftiality are among them.

When a young man marries, he immediately goes to live with the father and mother of his wife, who treat him, neverthelefs, as a perfect ftranger, till after the birth of his firft child: he then attaches himfelf more to them than his own parents; and his wife no longer gives him any other denomination than that of the father of her child.

The profeffion of the men is war and hunting, and the more active fcene of their duty is the field of battle, and the chafe in the woods. They alfo fpear fifh, but the management of the nets is left to the women. The females of this nation are in the fame fubordinate ftate with thofe of all other favage tribes; but the feverity of their labour is much diminifhed by their fituation on the banks of lakes and rivers, where they employ canoes. In the winter, when the waters are frozen, they make their journies, which are never of any great length, with fledges drawn by dogs. They

They are, at the fame time fubject to every kind of domeftic drudgery: they drefs the leather, make the clothes and fhoes, weave the nets, collect wood, erect the tents, fetch water, and perform every culinary fervice; fo that when the duties of maternal care are added, it will appear that the life of thefe women is an uninterrupted fucceffion of toil and pain. This, indeed, is the fenfe they entertain of their own fituation; and, under the influence of that fentiment, they are fometimes known to deftroy their female children, to fave them from the miferies which they themfelves have fuffered. They alfo have a ready way, by the ufe of certain fimples, of procuring abortions, which they fometimes practife, from their hatred of the father, or to fave themfelves the trouble which children occafion: and, as I have been credibly informed, this unnatural act is repeated without any injury to the health of the women who perpetrate it.

The funeral rites begin, like all other folemn ceremonials, with fmoking, and are concluded by a feaft. The body is dreffed in the beft habiliments poffeffed by the deceafed, or his relations, and is then depofited in a grave, lined with branches: fome domeftic utenfils are placed on it, and a kind of canopy erected over it. During this ceremony, great lamentations are made, and if the departed perfon is very much regretted the near relations cut off their hair, pierce the flefhy part of their thighs and arms with arrows, knives, &c. and blacken their faces with charcoal. If they have diftinguifhed themfelves in war, they are fometimes laid on a kind of fcaffolding; and I have been informed that women, as in the Eaft, have been known to facrifice themfelves to the manes of their hufbands. The whole of the property belonging to the departed perfon

is

is deftroyed, and the relations take in exchange for the wearing apparel, any rags that will cover their nakednefs. The feaft beftowed on the occafion, which is, or at leaft ufed to be, repeated annually, is accompanied with eulogiums on the deceafed, and without any acts of ferocity. On the tomb are carved or painted the fymbols of his tribe, which are taken from the different animals of the country.

Many and various are the motives which induce a favage to engage in war. To prove his courage, or to revenge the death of his relations, or fome of his tribe, by the maffacre of an enemy. If the tribe feel themfelves called upon to go to war, the elders convene the people, in order to know the general opinion. If it be for war, the chief publifhes his intention to fmoke in the facred ftem at a certain period, to which folemnity, meditation and fafting are required as preparatory ceremonials. When the people are thus affembled, and the meeting fanctified by the cuftom of fmoking, the chief enlarges on the caufes which have called them together, and the neceffity of the meafures propofed on the occafion. He then invites thofe who are willing to follow him, to fmoke out of the facred ftem, which is confidered as the token of enrolment; and if it fhould be the general opinion, that affiftance is neceffary, others are invited, with great formality, to join them. Every individual who attends thefe meetings brings fomething with him as a token of his warlike intention, or as an object of facrifice, which, when the affembly diffolves, is fufpended from poles near the place of council.

They have frequent feafts, and particular circumftances never fail to
produce

produce them; fuch as a tedious illnefs, long fafting, &c. On thefe occafions it is ufual for the perfon who means to give the entertainment, to announce his defign, on a certain day, of opening the medicine bag and fmoking out of his facred ftem. This declaration is confidered as a facred vow that cannot be broken. There are alfo ftated periods, fuch as the fpring and autumn, when they engage in very long and folemn ceremonies. On thefe occafions dogs are offered as facrifices, and thofe which are very fat, and milk-white, are preferred. They alfo make large offerings of their property, whatever it may be. The fcene of thefe ceremonies is in an open inclofure on the bank of a river or lake, and in the moft confpicuous fituation, in order that fuch as are paffing along or travelling, may be induced to make their offerings. There is alfo a particular cuftom among them, that, on thefe occafions, if any of the tribe, or even a ftranger, fhould be paffing by, and be in real want of any thing that is difplayed as an offering, he has a right to take it, fo that he replaces it with fome article he can fpare, though it be of far inferior value: but to take or touch any thing wantonly is confidered as a facrilegious act, and highly infulting to the great Mafter of Life, to ufe their own expreffion, who is the facred object of their devotion.

The fcene of private facrifice is the lodge of the perfon who performs it, which is prepared for that purpofe by removing every thing out of it, and fpreading green branches in every part. The fire and afhes are alfo taken away. A new hearth is made of frefh earth, and another fire is lighted. The owner of the dwelling remains alone in it; and he begins the ceremony by fpreading a piece of new cloth, or a well-dreffed moofe-fkin neatly painted, on which he opens his medicine-bag and

expofes

expofes its contents, confifting of various articles. The principal of them is a kind of houfehold god, which is a fmall carved image about eight inches long. Its firft covering is of down, over which a piece of beech bark is clofely tied, and the whole is enveloped in feveral folds of red and blue cloth. This little figure is an objeft of the moft pious re-gard. The next article is his war-cap, which is decorated with the fea-thers and plumes of fcarce birds, beavers, and eagle's claws, &c. There is alfo fufpended from it a quill or feather for every enemy whom the owner of it has flain in battle. The remaining contents of the bag are, a piece of Brazil tobacco, feveral roots and fimples, which are in great eftimation for their medicinal qualities, and a pipe. Thefe articles being all expofed, and the ftem refting upon two forks, as it muft not touch the ground, the mafter of the lodge fends for the perfon he moft efteems, who fits down oppofite to him; the pipe is then filled and fixed to the ftem. A pair of wooden pincers is provided to put the fire in the pipe, and a double-pointed pin, to empty it of the remnant of tobacco which is not confumed. This arrangement being made, the men affemble, and fome-times the women are allowed to be humble fpeftators, while the moft re-ligious awe and folemnity pervades the whole. The Michiniwais, or Affiftant, takes up the pipe, lights it, and prefents it to the officiating perfon, who receives it ftanding and holds it between both his hands. He then turns himfelf to the Eaft, and draws a few whiffs, which he blows to that point. The fame ceremony he obferves to the other three quarters, with his eyes direfted upwards during the whole of it. He holds the ftem about the middle between the three firft fingers of both hands, and raifing them upon a line with his forehead, he fwings it three times round from the Eaft, with the fun, when, after pointing and balancing it

in

in various directions, he repofes it on the forks : he then makes a fpeech to explain the defign of their being called together, which concludes with an acknowledgment of paft mercies, and a prayer for the continuance of them, from the Mafter of Life. He then fits down, and the whole company declare their approbation and thanks by uttering the word *ho !* with an emphatic prolongation of the laft letter. The Michiniwais then takes up the pipe and holds it to the mouth of the officiating perfon, who, after fmoking three whiffs out of it, utters a fhort prayer, and then goes round with it, taking his courfe from Eaft to Weft, to every perfon prefent, who individually fays fomething to him on the occafion : and thus the pipe is generally fmoked out; when, after turning it three or four times round his head, he drops it downwards, and replaces it in its original fituation. He then returns the company thanks for their attendance, and wifhes them, as well as the whole tribe, health and long life.

Thefe fmoking rites precede every matter of great importance, with more or lefs ceremony, but always with equal folemnity. The utility of them will appear from the following relation.

If a chief is anxious to know the difpofition of his people towards him, or if he wifhes to fettle any difference between them, he announces his intention of opening his medicine-bag and fmoking in his facred ftem ; and no man who entertains a grudge againft any of the party thus affembled can fmoke with the facred ftem; as that ceremony diffipates all differences, and is never violated.

No

No one can avoid attending on thefe occafions; but a perfon may attend and be excufed from affifting at the ceremonies, by acknowledging that he has not undergone the neceffary purification. The having cohabited with his wife, or any other woman, within twenty-four hours preceding the ceremony, renders him unclean, and, confequently, difqualifies him from performing any part of it. If a contract is entered into and folemnifed by the ceremony of fmoking, it never fails of being faithfully fulfilled. If a perfon, previous to his going a journey, leaves the facred ftem as a pledge of his return, no confideration whatever will prevent him from executing his engagement.*

The chief, when he propofes to make a feaft, fends quills, or fmall pieces of wood, as tokens of invitation to fuch as he wifhes to partake of it. At the appointed time the guefts arrive, each bringing a difh or platter, and a knife, and take their feats on each fide of the chief, who receives them fitting, according to their refpective ages. The pipe is then lighted, and he makes an equal divifion of every thing that is provided. While the company are enjoying their meal, the chief fings, and accompanies his fong with the tambourin, or fhifhiquoi, or rattle. The gueft who has firft eaten his portion is confidered as the moft diftinguifhed perfon. If there fhould be any who cannot finifh the whole of their mefs, they endeavour to prevail on fome of their friends to eat it for them, who are rewarded for their affiftance with ammunition and tobacco. It is proper alfo to remark, that at

* It is however to be lamented, that of late there is a relaxation of the duties originally attached to thefe feftivals.

thefe

thefe feafts a fmall quantity of meat or drink is facrificed, before they begin to eat, by throwing it into the fire, or on the earth.

Thefe feafts differ according to circumftances; fometimes each man's allowance is no more than he can difpatch in a couple of hours. At other times the quantity is fufficient to fupply each of them with food for a week, though it muft be devoured in a day. On thefe occafions it is very difficult to procure fubftitutes, and the whole muft be eaten whatever time it may require. At fome of thefe entertainments there is a more rational arrangement, when the guefts are allowed to carry home with them the fuperfluous part of their portions. Great care is always taken that the bones may be burned, as it would be confidered a profanation were the dogs permitted to touch them.

The public feafts are conducted in the fame manner, but with fome additional ceremony. Several chiefs officiate at them, and procure the neceffary provifions, as well as prepare a proper place of reception for the numerous company. Here the guefts difcourfe upon public topics, repeat the heroic deeds of their forefathers, and excite the rifing generation to follow their example. The entertainments on thefe occafions confift of dried meats, as it would not be practicable to drefs a fufficient quantity of frefh meat for fuch a large affembly; though the women and children are excluded.

Similar feafts ufed to be made at funerals, and annually, in honour of the dead; but they have been, for fome time, growing into difufe, and I never had an opportunity of being prefent at any of them.

The

The women, who are forbidden to enter the places facred to thefe feftivals, dance and fing around them, and fometimes beat time to the mufic within them; which forms an agreeable contraſt.

With refpeƈt to their divifions of time, they compute the length of their journies by the number of nights paffed in performing them; and they divide the year by the fucceffion of moons. In this calculation, however, they are not altogether correƈt, as they cannot account for the odd days.

The names which they give to the moons are defcriptive of the feveral feafons.

May	Atheiky o Pifhim	Frog-Moon.
June	Oppinu o Pifhim	The Moon in which birds begin to lay their eggs.
July	Aupafcen o Pifhim	The Moon when birds caſt their feathers.
Auguſt	Aupahou o Pifhim	The Moon when the young birds begin to fly.
September	Wafkifcon o Pifhim	The Moon when the moofe-deer caſt their horns.
Oƈtober	Wifac o Pifhim	The Rutting-Moon.
November	Thithigon Pewai o Pifhim	Hoar-Froſt-Moon.
	Kufkatinayoui o Pifhim	Ice-Moon.
December	Pawatchicananafis o Pifhim	Whirlwind-Moon.
January	Kufhapawaſticanum o Pifhim	Extreme cold Moon.

February

February -	Kichi Piſhim	-	-	-	Big Moon; ſome ſay, Old Moon.
March -	Mickyſue Piſhim		-	-	Eagle Moon.
April -	Niſcaw o Piſhim		-	-	Gooſe-Moon.

Theſe people know the medicinal virtues of many herbs and ſimples, and apply the roots of plants and the bark of trees with ſucceſs. But the conjurers, who monopolize the medical ſcience, find it neceſſary to blend myſtery with their art, and do not communicate their knowledge. Their materia medica they adminiſter in the form of purges and clyſters; but the remedies and ſurgical operations are ſuppoſed to derive much of their effect from magic and incantation. When a bliſter riſes in the foot from the froſt, the chaffing of the ſhoe, &c. they immediately open it, and apply the heated blade of a knife to the part, which, painful as it may be, is found to be efficacious. A ſharp flint ſerves them as a lancet for letting blood, as well as for ſcarification in bruiſes and ſwellings. For ſprains, the dung of an animal juſt killed is confidered as the beſt remedy. They are very fond of European medicines, though they are ignorant of their application : and thoſe articles form a confiderable part of the European traffic with them.

Among their various ſuperſtitions, they believe that the vapour which is ſeen to hover over moiſt and ſwampy places, is the ſpirit of ſome perſon lately dead. They alſo fancy another ſpirit which appears, in the ſhape of a man, upon the trees near the lodge of a perſon deceaſed, whoſe property has not been interred with them. He is repreſented as bearing a gun in his hand, and it is believed that he does not return to his reſt, till the property that has been withheld from the grave has been ſacrificed to it.

Examples

Examples of the Knifteneaux and Algonquin Tongues.

	Knifteneaux.	Algonquin.
Good Spirit	Ki jai Manitou	Ki jai Maritou.
Evil Spirit	Matchi manitou	Matchi manitou.
Man	Ethini	Inini.
Woman	Efquois	Ich-quois.
Male	Nap hew	Aquoifi.
Female	Non-genfe	Non-genfe
Infant	A' wafh ifh	Abi nont-chen.
Head	Us ti quoin	O'chiti-goine.
Forehead	Es caa tick	O catick.
Hair	Wes ty-ky	Wineffis.
Eyes	Es kis och	Ofkingick.
Nofe	Ofkiwin	O'chengewane.
Noftrils	Oo tith ee go mow	Ni-de-ni-guom.
Mouth	O toune	O tonne.
My teeth	Wip pit tah	Nibit.
Tongue	Otaithani	O-tai-na-ni.
Beard	Michitoune	Omichitonn.
Brain	With i tip	Aba-e winikan.
Ears	O tow ee gie	O-ta wagane.
Neck	O qui ow	O'quoi gan.
Throat	O koot tas gy	Nigon dagane.
Arms	O nifk	O nic.
Fingers	Che chee	Ni nid gines.
Nails	Wos kos fia	Os-kenge.
Side	O's fpig gy	Opikegan.
My back	No pis quan	Ni-pi quoini.
My belly	Nattay	Ni my fat.
Thighs	O povam	Obouame
My knees	No che quoin nah	Ni gui tick.
Legs	Nofk	Ni gatte.
Heart	O thea	Othai.
My father	Noo ta wie	Noffai.
My mother	Nigah wei	Nigah.
My boy (fon)	Negoufis	Nigouiffés
My girl (daughter)	Netanis	Nidanifs.

My

	Kniſteneaux.	Algonquin.
My brother, elder	Ni ſteſs	Nis-a-yen.
My ſiſter, elder	Ne miſs	Nimiſain.
My grandfather	Ne moo ſhum	Ni-mi-chomiſs.
My grandmother	N' o kum	No-co-miſs.
My uncle	N' o'ka miſs	Ni ni michomen.
My nephew	Ne too ſim	Ne do jim.
My niece	Ne too ſim eſquois	Ni-do jim equois.
My mother in law	Niſigouſe	Ni ſigouſiſs.
My brother in law	Niſtah	Nitah.
My companion	Ne wechi wagan	Ni-wit-chi-wagan.
My huſband	Ni nap pem	Ni na bem.
Blood	Mith coo	Miſquoi.
Old Man	Shi nap	Aki win ſe.
I am angry	Ne kis ſi waſh en	Niſ katiſſiwine.
I fear	Ne goos tow	Niſeſt guſe.
Joy	Ne hea tha tom	Mamoud gikiſi.
Hearing	Pethom	Oda wagan.
Track	Mis conna	Pemi ka wois.
Chief, great ruler	Haukimah	Kitchi onodis.
Thief	Kiſmoutheſk	Ke moutiſké.
Excrement	Meyee	Moui.
Buffalo	Mouſtouche	Pichike.
Ferret	Sigous	Shingouſs.
Polecat	Shicak	Shi-kâk.
Elk	Mouſtouche	Michai woi.
Rein deer	Attick	Atick.
Fallow deer	Attick	Wa waſqueſh.
Beaver	Amiſk	Amic.
Woolverine	Qui qua katch	Quin quoagki.
Squirrel	Ennequachas	Otchi ta mou.
Minx	Sa quaſue	Shaugouch.
Otter	Nekick	Ni guick.
Wolf	Mayegan	Maygan.
Hare	Wapouce	Wapouce.
Marten	Wappiſtan	Wabichinſe.
Mooſe	Mouſwah	Monſe
Bear	Maſquâ	Macqua.
Fiſher	Wijaſk	Od-jiſck.

Lynx

	Knifteneaux.		Algonquin.
Lynx -	- Picheu -	-	Pechou.
Porcupine -	- Cau quah -	-	Kack.
Fox -	- Ma kifew -	-	Wagouche.
Mufk Rat	- Wajafk -	-	Wa-jack.
Moufe -	- Abicufhifs -	-	Wai wa be gou noge.
Cow Buffalo	- Nofhi Mouftouche	-	Nochena pichik.
Meat-flefh	- Wias -	-	Wi-afs.
Dog -	- Atim -	-	Ani-moufe.
Eagle -	- Makufue -	-	Me-guiffis.
Duck -	- Sy Sip -	-	Shi-fip.
Crow, Corbeau	- Ca Cawkeu -	-	Ka Kak.
Swan -	- Wapifeu -	-	Wa-pe-fy.
Turkey -	- Mes fei thew -	-	Miffiffay.
Pheafants -	- Okes kew -	-	Ajack.
Bird -	- Pethefew -	-	Pi-na-fy.
Outard -	- Nifcag -	-	Nic kack.
White Goofe	- Wey Wois -	-	Woi wois.
Grey Goofe	- Peftafifh -	-	Pos ta kifk.
Partridge -	- Pithew -	-	Pen ainfe.
Water Hen	- Chiquibifh -	-	Che qui bis.
Dove -	- Omi Mee. -	-	O mi-mis.
Eggs -	- Wa Wah -	-	Wa Weni.
Pike or Jack	- Kenonge -	-	Kenongé.
Carp -	- Na may bin -	-	Na me bine.
Sturgeon -	- Na May -	-	Na Maiu.
White Fifh	- Aticaming -	-	Aticaming.
Pikrel -	- Oc-chaw -	-	Oh-ga.
Fifh (in general)	- Kenongé -	-	Ki-cons.
Spawn -	- Waquon -	-	Wa quock.
Fins -	- Chi chi kan -	-	O nidj-igan.
Trout -	- Nay goufe -	-	Na Men Goufe.
Craw Fifh -	- A fhag gee -	-	A cha kens chacque.
Frog -	- Athick -	-	O ma ka ki.
Wafp -	- Ah moo -	-	A mon.
Turtle -	- Mikinack -	-	Mi-ki-nack.
Snake -	- Kinibick -	-	Ki nai bick.
Awl -	- Ofcajick -	-	Ma-gofe.

Needle

	Kniſteneaux.	Algonquin.
Needle	Saboinigan	Sha-bo nigan.
Fire Steel	Appet	Scoutecgan.
Fire wood	Mich-tah	Miſſane.
Cradle	Teckinigan	Tickina-gan.
Dagger	Ta comagau	Na-ba-ke-gou-man.
Arrow	Auguſk or Atouche	Mettic ka nouins.
Fiſh Hook	Quoſquipichican	Maneton Miquiſcane.
Ax	Shegaygan	Wagagvette.
Ear-bob	Chi-kiſebiſoun	Na be chi be ſoun.
Comb	Sicahoun	Pin ack wan.
Net	Athabe	Aſſap.
Tree	Miſtick	Miti-coum.
Wood	Miſtick	Mitic.
Paddle	Aboi	Aboui.
Canoe	Chiman	S-chiman.
Birch Rind	Waſquoi	Wig naſs.
Bark	Waſquoi	On-na-guege.
Touch Wood	Pouſagan	Sa-ga-tagan.
Leaf	Nepeſhah	Ni-biche.
Graſs	Maſquoſi	Maſquoſi.
Raſpberries	Miſqui-meinac	Miſqui meinac.
Strawberries	O'-tai-e minac	O'-tai-e minac.
Aſhes	Pecouch	Pengoui.
Fire	Scou tay	Scou tay.
Grapes	Shomenac	Shomenac.
Fog	Pakiſhihow	A Winni.
Mud	Aſus ki	A Shiſki.
Currant	Kiſijiwin	Ki ſi chi woin.
Road	Meſcanah	Mickanan.
Winter	Pipoun	Pipone.
Iſland	Miniſtick	Miniſs.
Lake	Sagayigan	Sagayigan.
Sun	Piſim	Kijis.
Moon	Tibiſca peſim (the night Sun	Dibic kijiſs.
Day	Kigigah	Kigi gatte.
Night	Tibiſca	Dibic kawte.
Snow	Counah	So qui po.

Rain

	Knifteneaux.	Algonquin.
Rain	Kimiwoin	Ki mi woini.
Drift	Pewan	Pi-woine.
Hail	Shes eagan	Me qua menfan.
Ice	Mefquaming	Me quam.
Froft	Aquatin	Gas-ga-tin.
Mift	Picafyow	An-quo-et.
Water	Nepec	Ni-pei.
World	Meffe afky (all the earth)	Miffi achki.
Mountain	Wachee	Watchive.
Sea	Kitchi kitchi ga ming	Kitchi-kitchi ga ming.
Morning	Kequifhepe	Ki-ki-jep.
Mid-day	Abetah quifheik	Na ock quoi.
Portage	Unygam	Ouni-gam.
Spring	Menoufcaming	Mino ka ming.
River	Sipee	Sipi.
Rapid	Bawaftick	Ba wetick.
Rivulet	Sepeefis	Sipi wes chin.
Sand	Thocaw	Ne gawe.
Earth	Afkee	Ach ki.
Star	Attack	Anang.
Thunder	Pithufeu	Ni mi ki.
Wind	Thoutin	No tine.
Calm	Athawoftin	A-no-a-tine.
Heat	Quifhipoi	Aboycé.
Evening	Ta kafhiké	O'n-a guche.
North	Kywoitin	Ke woitinak.
South	Sawena woon	Sha-wa-na-wang.
Eaft	Cofhawcaftak	Wa-ba-no-notine.
Weft	Paquifimow	Panguis-chi-mo.
To-morrow	Wabank	Wa-bang.
Bone	Ofkann	Oc-kann.
Broth	Michim waboi	Thaboub.
Feaft	Ma qua fee	Wi con qui wine.
Greafe or oil	Pimis	Pimi-tais.
Marrow fat	Ofcan pimis	Ofka-pimitais.
Sinew	Afstis	Attifs.
Lodge	Wig-waum	Wi-gui-wam.
Bed	Ne pa win	Ne pai wine.

Within

	Knifteneaux.	Algonquin.
Within	Pendog ké	Pendig.
Door	Squandam	Scouandam.
Difh	Othagan	O' na gann.
Fort	Wafgaigan	Wa-kuigan.
Sledge	Tabanafk	Otabanac.
Cincture	Poquoatehoun	Ketche pifou.
Cap	Aftotin	Pe matinang.
Socks	Afhican	A chi-gan.
Shirt	Papackeweyan	Pa pa ki weyan.
Coat	Papife-co-wagan	Papife-co-wagan.
Blanket	Wape weyang	Wape weyan.
Cloth	Maneto weguin	Maneto weguin.
Thread	Affabab	Affabab.
Garters	Chi ki-bifoon	Ni gafke-tafe befoun.
Mittens	Aftiffack	Medjicawine.
Shoes	Mafkifin	Makifin.
Smoking bag	Kufquepetagan	Kafquepetagan.
Portage fling	Apifan	Apican.
Strait on	Goi afk	Goi-ack.
Medicine	Mas ki kee	Macki-ki.
Red	Mes coh	Mes-cowa.
Blue	Kafqutch (fame as black)	O-jawes-cowa.
White	Wabifca	Wabifca.
Yellow	Saw waw	O-jawa.
Green	Chibatiquare	O'jawes-cowa.
Brown		O'jawes-cowa.
Grey, &c.		O'jawes-cowa.
Ugly	Mache na goufeu	Mous-counu-goufe.
Handfome	Catawaffifeu	Nam biffa.
Beautiful	Kiffi Sawenogan	Quoi Natch.
Deaf	Nima petom	Ka ki be chai.
Good-natured	Mithiwafhin	Onichifhin.
Pregnant	Paawie	And'jioko.
Fat	Outhineu	Oui-ni-noe.
Big	Mufhikitee	Mefsha.
Small or little	Abifafheu	Agu-chin.
Short	Chemafifh	Tackofi.

Skin

	Knifteneaux.	Algonquin.
Skin	Wian	Wian.
Long	Kinwain	Kiniwa.
Strong	Mafcawa	{ Mache-cawa. Mas cawife.
Coward	Sagatahaw	Cha-goutai-ye.
Weak	Nitha miffew	Cha-goufi.
Lean	Mahta waw	Ka wa ca-tofa.
Brave	Nima Guftaw	Son qui taigé.
Young man	Ofquineguifh	Ofkinigui.
Cold	Kiffin	Kiffinan.
Hot	Kichatai	Kicha tai.
Spring	Minoufcaming	Minokaming.
Summer	Nibin	Nibiqui.
Fall	Tagowagonk	Tagowag.
One	Peyac	Pecheik.
Two	Nifheu	Nige.
Three	Nifhtou	Nis-wois.
Four	Neway	Ne-au.
Five	Ni-annan	Na-nan.
Six	Negoutawoefic	Ni gouta waswois.
Seven	Nifh woific	Nigi-was-wois.
Eight	Jannanew	She was wois.
Nine	Shack	Shang was wois.
Ten	Mitatat	Mit-affwois.
Eleven	Peyac ofap	Mitaffwois, hachi, pe-cheik.
Twelve	Nifheu ofap	Mitaffwois, hachi, nige.
Thirteen	Nichtou ofap	Mitaffwois, hachi, nif-wois.
Fourteen	Neway ofap	Mitaffwois, hachi, ne-au.
Fifteen	Niannan ofap	Mitaffwois, hachi, nanan.
Sixteen	Nigoutawoefic ofap	Mitaffwois, hachi, ne-goutawafwois.
Seventeen	Nifh woefic ofap	Mitaffwois, hachi, nigi wafwois.
Eighteen	Jannanew ofap	Mitaffwois, hachi, fhi-wafwois.
Nineteen	Shack ofap	Mitaffwois, hachi, fhang as wois.

Twenty

	Knifteneaux.	Algonquin.
Twenty	Nifheu mitenah	Nigeta-nan.
Twenty-one	Nifhew mitenah peyac ofap	Nigeta nan, hachi, pe-chic.
Twenty-two, &c.	Nifheu mitenah nifhew ofap	
Thirty	Nifhtou mitenah	Nifwois mitanan.
Forty	Neway mitenah	Neau mitanan.
Fifty	Niannan mitenah	Nanan mitanan.
Sixty	Negoutawoific mitenah	Nigouta was wois mi-tanan.
Seventy	Nifhwoific mitenah	Nigi was wois mitanan.
Eighty	Jannaeu mitenah	She was wois mitanan.
Ninety	Shack mitenah	Shang was wois mitanan.
Hundred	Mitana mitinah	Ningoutwack.
Two Hundred	Nefhew mitena a mite-nah }	Nige wack.
One thoufand	Mitenah mitena mite-nah }	Kitchi-wack.
Firft	Nican	Nitam.
Laft	Squayatch	Shaquoiyanque.
More	Minah	Awa chi min.
Better	Athiwack mithawafhin	Awachimin o nichi fhen.
Beft	Athiwack mithawafhin	Kitchi o nichi fhin.
I, or me	Nitha	Nin.
You, or thou	Kitha	Kin.
They, or them	Withawaw	Win na wa.
We	Nithawaw	Nina wa.
My, or mine	Nitayan	Nida yam.
Your's	Kitayan	Kitayam.
Who		Auoni.
Whom	Awoiné	Kegoi nin.
What		Wa.
His, or her's	Otayan	Otayim mis.
All	Kakithau	Kakenan.
Some, or fome few	Pey peyac	Pe-pichic.
The fame	Tabefcoutch	Mi ta yoche.
All the world	Miffi acki wanque	Mifhiwai afky.
All the men	Kakithaw Ethi nyock	Miffi Inini wock.

More

	Knifteneaux.	Algonquin.
More	Mina	Mina wa.
Now and then		Nannigoutengue.
Sometimes	I as-cow-puco	
Seldom		Wica-ac-ko.
Arrive	Ta couchin	Ta-gouchin.
Beat	Otamaha	Packit-ais.
To burn	Miftafcafoo	Icha-quifo.
To fing	Nagamoun	Nagam.
To cut	Kifquifhan	Qui qui jan.
To hide	Catann	Cafo tawe.
To cover	Acquahoun	A co na oune.
To believe	Taboitam	Tai boitam.
To fleep	Nepan	Ni pann.
To difpute	Ke ko mi towock	Ki quaidiwine.
To dance	Nemaytow	Nimic.
To give	Mith	Mih.
To do	Ogitann	O-gitoune.
To eat	Wiffinee	Wiffiniwin.
To die	Nepew	Ni po wen.
To forget	Winnekifkifew	Woi ni mi kaw.
To fpeak	Athimetakcoufé	Aninntagouffé.
To cry (tears)	Mantow	Ma wi.
To laugh	Papew	Pa-pe.
To fet down	Nematappe	Na matape win.
To walk	Pimoutais	Pemouffai.
To fall	Packifin	Panguifhin.
To work	Ah tus kew	Anokeh.
To kill	Nipahaw	Nifhi-woes.
To fell	Attawoin	Ata wois.
To live	Pimatife	Pematis.
To fee	Wabam	Wab.
To come	Aftamoteh	Pitta-fi-moufs.
Enough	Egothigog	Mi mi nic.
Cry (tears)	Manteau	Ambai ma wita.
It hails	Shifiagan	Sai faigaun.
There is } There is fome }	Aya wa	Aya wan.

It

	Knifteneaux.	Algonquin.
It rains	Quimiwoin	Qui mi woin.
After to-morrow	Awis wabank	Awes wabang.
To-day	Anoutch	Non gum.
Thereaway	Netoi	Awoité.
Much	Michett	Ni bi wa.
Prefently	Pichifqua	Pitchinac.
Make, heart	Quithipeh	Wai we be.
This morning	Shebas	Shai bas.
This night	Tibifcag	De bi cong.
Above	Efpiming	O kitchiai.
Below	Tabaffifh	Ana mai.
Truly	Taboiy	Ne da wache.
Already	Safhay	Sha fhaye.
Yet, more	Minah	Mina wa.
Yefterday	Tacoufhick	Pitchinago.
Far	Wathow	Waffa.
Near	Quifhiwoac	Paifhou.
Never	Nima wecatch	Ka wi ka.
No	Nima	Ka wine.
Yes	Ah	In.
By-and-bye	Pa-nima	Pa-nima.
Always	Ka-ki-kee	Ka qui nick.
Make hafte	Quethepeh	Niguim.
Its long fince	Mewaifha	Mon wifha.

Some Account of the Chepewyan Indians.

THEY are a numerous people, who confider the country between the parallels of latitude 60. and 65. North, and longitude 100. to 110. Weft, as their lands or home. They fpeak a copious language, which is very difficult to be attained, and furnifhes dialects to the various emigrant tribes which inhabit the following immenfe track of country, whofe boundary

boundary I fhall defcribe*.   It begins at Churchill, and runs along the line of feparation between them and the Knifteneaux, up the Miffinipi to the Ifle à la Croffe, paffing on through the Buffalo Lake, River Lake, and Portage la Loche: from thence it proceeds by the Elk River to the Lake of the Hills, and goes directly Weft to the Peace River; and up that river to its fource and tributary waters; from whence it proceeds to the waters of the river Columbia; and follows that river to latitude 52. 24. North, and longitude 122. 54. Weft, where the Chepewyans have the Atnah or Chin Nation for their neighbours.   It then takes a line due Weft to the fea-coaft, within which, the country is poffeffed by a people who fpeak their language†, and are confequently defcended from them: there can be no doubt, therefore, of their progrefs being to the Eaftward.   A tribe of them is even known at the upper eftablifhments on the Safkatchiwine; and I do not pretend to afcertain how far they may follow the Rocky Mountains to the Eaft.

It is not poffible to form any juft eftimate of their numbers, but it is apparent, neverthelefs, that they are by no means proportionate to the vaft extent of their territories, which may, in fome degree, be attributed to the ravages of the fmall pox, which are, more or lefs, evident thoughout this part of the continent.

The notion which thefe people entertain of the creation, is of a very

---

* Thofe of them who come to trade with us, do not exceed eight hundred men, and have a fmattering of the Knifteneaux tongue, in which they carry on their dealings with us.

† The coaft is inhabited on the North-Weft by the Efkimaux, and on the Pacific Ocean by a people different from both.

fingular

fingular nature. They believe that, at the firft, the globe was one vaft and entire ocean, inhabited by no living creature, except a mighty bird, whofe eyes were fire, whofe glances were lightning, and the clapping of whofe wings were thunder. On his defcent to the ocean, and touching it, the earth inftantly arofe, and remained on the furface of the waters. This omnipotent bird then called forth all the variety of animals from the earth, except the Chepewyans, who were produced from a dog; and this circumftance occafions their averfion to the flefh of that animal, as well as the people who eat it. This extraordinary tradition proceeds to relate, that the great bird, having finifhed his work, made an arrow, which was to be preferved with great care, and to remain untouched; but that the Chepewyans were fo devoid of underftanding, as to carry it away; and the facrilege fo enraged the great bird, that he has never fince appeared.

They have alfo a tradition amongft them, that they originally came from another country, inhabited by very wicked people, and had traverfed a great lake, which was narrow, fhallow, and full of iflands, where they had fuffered great mifery, it being always winter, with ice and deep fnow. At the Copper-Mine River, where they made the firft land, the ground was covered with copper, over which a body of earth had fince been collected, to the depth of a man's height. They believe, alfo, that in ancient times their anceftors lived till their feet were worn out with walking, and their throats with eating. They defcribe a deluge, when the waters fpread over the whole earth, except the higheft mountains, on the tops of which they preferved themfelves.

They

They believe, that immediately after their death, they pafs into another world, where they arrive at a large river, on which they embark in a
ftone canoe, and that a gentle current bears them on to an extenfive lake,
in the centre of which is a moft beautiful ifland; and that, in the view of
this delightful abode, they receive that judgment for their conduct during life, which terminates their final ftate and unalterable allotment. If
their good actions are declared to predominate, they are landed upon
the ifland, where there is to be no end to their happinefs; which, however, according to their notions, confifts in an eternal enjoyment of
fenfual pleafure, and carnal gratification. But if their bad actions weigh
down the balance, the ftone canoe finks at once, and leaves them up to
their chins in the water, to behold and regret the reward enjoyed by
the good, and eternally ftruggling, but with unavailing endeavours, to
reach the blifsful ifland, from which they are excluded for ever.

They have fome faint notions of the tranfmigration of the foul; fo
that if a child be born with teeth, they inftantly imagine, from its premature appearance, that it bears a refemblance to fome perfon who
had lived to an advanced period, and that he has affumed a renovated
life, with thefe extraordinary tokens of maturity.

The Chepewyans are fober, timorous, and vagrant, with a felfifh difpofition which has fometimes created fufpicions of their integrity. Their
ftature has nothing remarkable in it; but though they are feldom corpulent, they are fometimes robuft. Their complexion is fwarthy; their features coarfe, and their hair lank, but not always of a dingy black; nor have
they univerfally the piercing eye, which generally animates the Indian
countenance.

countenance. The women have a more agreeable afpect than the men, but their gait is awkward, which proceeds from their being accuftomed, nine months in the year, to travel on fnow-fhoes and drag fledges of a weight from two to four hundred pounds. They are very fubmiffive to their hufbands, who have, however, their fits of jealoufy; and, for very trifling caufes, treat them with fuch cruelty as fometimes to occafion their death. They are frequently objects of traffic; and the father poffeffes the right of difpofing of his daughter*. The men in general extract their beards, though fome of them are feen to prefer a bufhy, black beard, to a fmooth chin. They cut their hair in various forms, or leave it in a long, natural flow, according as their caprice or fancy fuggefts. The women always wear it in great length, and fome of them are very attentive to its arrangement. If they at any time appear defpoiled of their treffes, it is to be efteemed a proof of the hufband's jealoufy, and is confidered as a feverer punifhment than manual correction. Both fexes have blue or black bars, or from one to four ftraight lines on their cheeks or forehead, to diftinguifh the tribe to which they belong. Thefe marks are either tatooed, or made by drawing a thread, dipped in the neceffary colour, beneath the fkin.

There are no people more attentive to the comforts of their drefs, or lefs anxious refpecting its exterior appearance. In the winter it is compofed of the fkins of deer, and their fawns, and dreffed as fine as any chamois leather, in the hair. In the fummer their apparel is the fame, except that it is prepared without the hair. Their fhoes and leggins

---

* They do not, however, fell them as flaves, but as companions to thofe who are fuppofed to live more comfortably than themfelves.

are

are fewn together, the latter reaching upwards to the middle, and being fupported by a belt, under which a fmall piece of leather is drawn to cover the private parts, the ends of which fall down both before and behind. In the fhoes they put the hair of the moofe or rein-deer with additional pieces of leather as focks. The fhirt or coat, when girted round the waift, reaches to the middle of the thigh, and the mittens are fewed to the fleeves, or are fufpended by ftrings from the fhoulders, A ruff or tippet furrounds the neck, and the fkin of the head of the deer forms a curious kind of cap. A robe, made of feveral deer or fawn fkins fewed together, covers the whole. This drefs is worn fingle or double, but always in the winter, with the hair within and without. Thus arrayed, a Chepewyan will lay himfelf down on the ice in the middle of a lake, and repofe in comfort; though he will fometimes find a difficulty in the morning to difencumber himfelf from the fnow drifted on him during the night. If in his paffage he fhould be in want of provifion, he cuts an hole in the ice, when he feldom fails of taking fome trout or pike, whofe eyes he inftantly fcoops out, and eats as a great delicacy; but if they fhould not be fufficient to fatisfy his appetite, he will, in this neceffity make his meal of the fifh in its raw ftate; but, thofe whom I faw, preferred to drefs their victuals when circumftances admitted the neceffary preparation. When they are in that part of their country which does not produce a fufficient quantity of wood for fuel, they are reduced to the fame exigency, though they generally dry their meat in the fun.*

The

---

* The provifion called Pemican, on which the Chepewyans, as well as the other favages of this country, chiefly fubfift in their journies, is prepared in the following manner. The lean parts of the flefh of the larger animals are cut in thin flices, and are placed on a wooden grate over a flow fire, or

expofed

The dreſs of the women differs from that of the men. Their leggins are tied below the knee; and their coat or ſhift is wide, hanging down to the ancle, and is tucked up at pleaſure by means of a belt, which is faſtened round the waiſt. Thoſe who have children have theſe garments made very full about the ſhoulders, as when they are travelling they carry their infants upon their backs, next their ſkin, in which ſituation they are perfectly comfortable and in a poſition convenient to be ſuckled. Nor do they diſcontinue to give their milk to them till they have another child. Child-birth is not the object of that tender care and ſerious attention among the ſavages as it is among civiliſed people. At this period no part of their uſual occupation is omitted, and this continual and regular exerciſe muſt contribute to the welfare of the mother, both in the progreſs of parturition and in the moment of delivery. The women have a ſingular cuſtom of cutting off a ſmall piece of the navel-ſtring of the new-born children, and hang it about their necks: they are alſo curious in the covering they make for it, which they decorate with porcupine's quills and beads.

Though the women are as much in the power of the men, as any other articles of their property, they are always conſulted, and poſſeſs a

expoſed to the ſun, and ſometimes to the froſt. Theſe operations dry it, and in that ſtate it is pounded between two ſtones: it will then keep with care for ſeveral years. If, however, it is kept in large quantities, it is diſpoſed to ferment in the ſpring of the year, when it muſt be expoſed to the air, or it will ſoon decay. The inſide fat, and that of the rump, which is much thicker in theſe wild than our domeſtic animals, is melted down and mixed, in a boiling ſtate, with the pounded meat, in equal proportions: it is then put in baſkets or bags for the convenience of carrying it. Thus it becomes a nutritious food, and is eaten, without any further preparation, or the addition of ſpice, ſalt, or any vegetable or farinaceous ſubſtance. A little time reconciles it to the palate. There is another ſort made with the addition of marrow and dried berries, which is of a ſuperior quality.

very

very confiderable influence in the traffic with Europeans, and other important concerns.

Plurality of wives is common among them, and the ceremony of marriage is of a very fimple nature. The girls are betrothed at a very early period to thofe whom the parents think the beft able to fupport them : nor is the inclination of the woman confidered. Whenever a feparation takes place, which fometimes happens, it depends entirely on the will and pleafure of the hufband. In common with the other Indians of this country, they have a cuftom refpecting the periodical ftate of a woman, which is rigoroufly obferved : at that time fhe muft feclude herfelf from fociety. They are not even allowed in that fituation to keep the fame path as the men, when travelling : and it is confidered a great breach of decency for a woman fo circumftanced to touch any utenfils of manly occupation. Such a circumftance is fuppofed to defile them, fo that their fubfequent ufe would be followed by certain mifchief or misfortune. There are particular fkins which the women never touch, as of the bear and wolf; and thofe animals the men are feldom known to kill.

They are not remarkable for their activity as hunters, which is owing to the eafe with which they fnare deer and fpear fifh : and thefe occupations are not beyond the ftrength of their old men, women, and boys : fo that they participate in thofe laborious occupations, which among their neighbours, are confined to the women. They make war on the Efquimaux, who cannot refift their fuperior numbers, and put them to death, as it is a principle with them never to make prifoners. At the fame

time

time they tamely fubmit to the Knifteneaux, who are not fo numerous as themfelves, when they treat them as enemies.

They do not affect that cold referve at meeting, either among themfelves or ftrangers, which is common with the Knifteneaux, but communicate mutually, and at once, all the information of which they are poffeffed. Nor are they roufed like them from an apparent torpor to a ftate of great activity. They are confequently more uniform in this refpect, though they are of a very perfevering difpofition when their intereft is concerned.

As thefe people are not addicted to fpirituous liquors, they have a regular and uninterrupted ufe of their underftanding, which is always directed to the advancement of their own intereft; and this difpofition, as may be readily imagined, fometimes occafions them to be charged with fraudulent habits. They will fubmit with patience to the fevereft treatment, when they are confcious that they deferve it, but will never forget or forgive any wanton or unneceffary rigour. A moderate conduct I never found to fail, nor do I hefitate to reprefent them, altogether, as the moft peaceable tribe of Indians known in North America.

There are conjurers and high-priefts, but I was not prefent at any of their ceremonies; though they certainly operate in an extraordinary manner on the imaginations of the people in the cure of diforders. Their principal maladies are, rheumatic pains, the flux and confumption. The venereal complaint is very common; but though its progrefs is
flow,

flow, it gradually undermines the conftitution, and brings on premature decay. They have recourfe to fuperftition for their cure, and charms are their only remedies, except the bark of the willow, which being burned and reduced to powder, is ftrewed upon green wounds and ulcers, and places contrived for promoting perfpiration. Of the ufe of fimples and plants they have no knowledge; nor can it be expected, as their country does not produce them.

Though they have enjoyed fo long an intercourfe with Europeans, their country is fo barren, as not to be capable of producing the ordinary neceffaries naturally introduced by fuch a communication; and they continue, in a great meafure, their own inconvenient and awkward modes of taking their game and preparing it when taken. Sometimes they drive the deer into the fmall lakes, where they fpear them, or force them into inclofures, where the bow and arrow are employed againft them. Thefe animals are alfo taken in fnares made of fkin. In the former inftance the game is divided among thofe who have been engaged in the purfuit of it. In the latter it is confidered as private property; neverthelefs, any unfuccefsful hunter paffing by, may take a deer fo caught, leaving the head, fkin, and faddle for the owner. Thus, though they have no regular government, as every man is lord in his own family, they are influenced, more or lefs, by certain principles which conduce to their general benefit.

In their quarrels with each other, they very rarely proceed to a greater degree of violence than is occafioned by blows, wreftling, and pulling of

the

the hair, while their abufive language confifts in applying the name of the moft offenfive animal to the object of their difpleafure, and adding the term ugly, and chiay, or ftill-born.*

Their arms and domeftic apparatus, in addition to the articles procured from Europeans, are fpears, bows, and arrows, fifhing-nets, and lines made of green deer-fkin thongs. They have alfo nets for taking the beaver as he endeavours to efcape from his lodge when it is broken open. It is fet in a particular manner for the purpofe, and a man is employed to watch the moment when he enters the fnare, or he would foon cut his way through it. He is then thrown upon the ice, where he remains as if he had no life in him.

The fnow-fhoes are of very fuperior workmanfhip. The inner part of their frame is ftraight, the outer one is curved, and it is pointed at both ends, with that in front turned up. They are alfo laced with great neatnefs with thongs made of deer-fkin. The fledges are formed of thin flips of board turned up alfo in front, and are highly polifhed with crooked knives, in order to flide along with facility. Clofe-grained wood is, on that account, the beft; but theirs are made of the red or fwamp fpruce-fir tree.

The country, which thefe people claim as their land, has a very fmall quantity of earth, and produces little or no wood or herbage.

* This name is alfo applicable to the fœtus of an animal, when killed, which is confidered as one of the greateft delicacies.

Its

Its chief vegetable fubftance is the mofs, on which the deer feed; and a kind of rock mofs, which, in times of fcarcity, preferves the lives of the natives.   When boiled in water, it diffolves into a clammy, glutinous, fubftance, that affords a very fufficient nourifhment.   But, notwithftanding the barren ftate of their country, with proper care and economy, thefe people might live in great comfort, for the lakes abound with fifh, and the hills are covered with deer.   Though, of all the Indian people of this continent they are confidered as the moft provident, they fuffer feverely at certain feafons, and particularly in the dead of winter, when they are under the neceffity of retiring to their fcanty, ftinted woods. To the Weftward of them the mufk-ox may be found, but they have no dependence on it as an article of fuftenance.   There are alfo large hares, a few white wolves, peculiar to their country, and feveral kinds of foxes, with white and grey partridges, &c.   The beaver and moofe-deer they do not find till they come within 60 degrees North latitude; and the buffalo is ftill further South.   That animal is known to frequent an higher latitude to the Weftward of their country.   Thefe people bring pieces of beautiful variegated marble, which are found on the fur-face of the earth.   It is eafily worked, bears a fine polifh, and hardens with time; it endures heat, and is manufactured into pipes or calumets, as they are very fond of fmoking tobacco; a luxury which the Euro-peans communicated to them.

Their amufements or recreations are but few.   Their mufic is fo inharmonious, and their dancing fo awkward, that they might be fup-pofed to be afhamed of both, as they very feldom practife either. They alfo fhoot at marks, and play at the games common among them;

but

but in fact they prefer sleeping to either; and the greater part of their time is passed in procuring food, and resting from the toil necessary to obtain it.

They are also of a querulous disposition, and are continually making complaints; which they express by a constant repetition of the word eduiy, " it is hard," in a whining and plaintive tone of voice.

They are superstitious in the extreme, and almost every action of their lives, however trivial, is more or less influenced by some whimsical notion. I never observed that they had any particular form of religious worship; but as they believe in a good and evil spirit, and a state of future rewards and punishments, they cannot be devoid of religious impressions. At the same time they manifest a decided unwillingness to make any communications on the subject.

The Chepewyans have been accused of abandoning their aged and infirm people to perish, and of not burying their dead; but these are melancholy necessities, which proceed from their wandering way of life. They are by no means universal, for it is within my knowledge, that a man, rendered helpless by the palsy, was carried about for many years, with the greatest tenderness and attention, till he died a natural death. That they should not bury their dead in their own country cannot be imputed to them as a custom arising from a savage insensibility, as they inhabit such high latitudes that the ground never thaws; but it is well known, that when they are in the woods, they cover their dead with trees. Besides, they manifest no common respect to the
memory

memory of their departed friends, by a long period of mourning, cutting off their hair, and never making ufe of the property of the deceafed. Nay, they frequently deftroy or facrifice their own, as a token of regret and forrow.

If there be any people who, from the barren ftate of their country, might be fuppofed to be cannibals by nature, thefe people, from the difficulty they, at times, experience in procuring food, might be liable to that imputation. But, in all my knowledge of them, I never was acquainted with one inftance of that difpofition; nor among all the natives which I met with in a route of five thoufand miles, did I fee or hear of an example of cannibalifm, but fuch as arofe from that irrefiftible neceffity, which has been known to impel even the moft civilifed people to eat each other.

Example of the Chepewyan Tongue.

Man - - -	Dinnie.
Woman - -	Chequois.
Young man - -	Quelaquis.
Young woman - -	Quelaquis chequoi.
My fon - -	Zi azay.
My daughter - -	Zi lengai.
My hufband - -	Zi dinnie.
My wife - -	Zi zayunai.
My brother - -	Zi raing.
My father - -	Zi tah.
My mother - -	Zi nah.
My grandfather - -	Zi unai.
Me or my - -	See.
I - - -	Ne.
You - - -	Nun.
They - - -	Be.
Head - - -	Edthie.
	Hand

Hand	Law.
Leg	Edthen.
Foot	Cuh.
Eyes	Nackhay.
Teeth	Goo.
Side	Kac-hey.
Belly	Bitt.
Tongue	Edthu.
Hair	Thiegah.
Back	Loffeh.
Blood	Dell.
The Knee	Cha-gutt.
Clothes or Blanket	Etlunay.
Coat	Eeh.
Leggin	Thell.
Shoes	Kinchee.
Robe or Blanket	Thuth.
Sleeves	Bah.
Mittens	Geefe.
Cap	Sah.
Swan	Kagouce.
Duck	Keth.
Goofe	Gah.
White partridge	Cafs bah.
Grey partridge	Deyee.
Buffalo	Giddy.
Moofe deer	Dinyai.
Rein-deer	Edthun.
Beaver	Zah.
Bear	Zafs.
Otter	Naby-ai.
Martin	Thah.
Wolvereen	Naguiyai.
Wolf	Yefs (Nouneay.)
Fox	Naguethey.
Hare	Cah.
Dog	Sliengh.
Beaver-fkin	Zah thith.
Otter-fkin	Naby-ai thith.
Moofe-fkin	Deny-ai thith.
Fat	Icah.
Greafe	Thlefs.

Meat

Meat	-	-	-	Bid.
Pike	-	-	-	Uldiah.
White-fish	-	-	Slouey.
Trout	-	-	-	Slouyzinai.
Pickerel	-	-	-	O'Gah.
Fishhook	-	-	Ge-eth.
Fishline	-	-	Clulez.
One	-	-	Slachy.
Two	-	-	-	Naghur.
Three	-	-	-	Tagh-y.
Four	-	-	-	Dengk-y.
Five	-	-	Safoulachee.
Six	-	-	-	Alki tar-hy-y.
Seven	-	-	-	
Eight	-	-	-	Alki deing-hy
Nine	-	-	-	Cakina hanoth-na.
Ten	-	-	-	Ca noth na.
Twenty	-	-	Na ghur cha noth na.
Fire	-	-	-	Counn.
Water	-	-	-	Toue.
Wood	-	-	-	Dethkin.
Ice	-	-	-	Thun.
Snow	-	-	-	Yath.
Rain	-	-	-	Thinnelfee.
Lake	-	-	-	Touey.
River	-	-	-	Teffe.
Mountain	-	-	Zeth.
Stone	-	-	-	Thaih.
Berries	-	-	-	Gui-eh.
Hot	-	-	-	Edowh.
Cold	-	-	-	Edzah.
Ifland	-	-	-	Nouey.
Gun	-	-	-	Telkithy.
Powder	-	-	Telkithy counna.
Knife	-	-	-	Befs.
Axe	-	-	-	Thynle.
Sun	-	-	} Sah.
Moon	-	-	
Red	-	-	-	Deli coufe.
Black	-	-	-	Dell zin.
Trade, or barter	-	-	Na-houn-ny.
Good	-	-	-	Leyzong.

Not

Not good - -	Leyzong houlley.
Stinking - -	Geddey.
Bad, ugly - -	Slieney.
Long since - -	Galladinna.
Now, to-day - -	Ganneh.
To-morrow - -	Gambeh.
By-and-bye, or presently -	Carahoulleh.
House, or lodge - -	Cooen.
Canoe - - -	Shaluzee.
Door - - -	The o ball.
Leather-lodge - -	N'abalay.
Chief - - -	Buchahudry.
Mine - - -	Zidzy.
His - - -	Bedzy.
Yours' - -	Nuntzy.
Large - - -	Unshaw.
Small, or little - -	Chautah.
I love you - -	Ba ehoinichdinh.
I hate you - -	Bucnoinichadinh hillay.
I am to be pitied -	Est-chounest-hinay.
My relation - -	Sy lod, innay.
Give me water - -	Too hanniltu.
Give me meat - -	Beds-hanniltu.
Give me fish - -	Sloeeh anneltu.
Give me meat to eat -	Bid Barheether,
Give me water to drink -	To Barhithen.
Is it far off - -	Netha uzany.
Is it near - -	Nilduay uzany.
It is not far - -	Nitha-hillai.
It is near - - -	Nilduay.
How many - -	Etlaneldey.
What call you him, or that	Etla houllia.
Come here - -	Yeu dessay.
Pain, or suffering -	I-yah.
It's hard - -	Eduyah.
You lie - -	Untzee.
What then - -	Edlaw-gueh.

JOURNAL

OF A

VOYAGE, &c.

CHAPTER I.

Embarked at Fort Chepewyan, on the Lake of the Hills, in company with M. Le Roux. Account of the party, provisions, &c. Direction of the course. Enter one of the branches of the Lake. Arrive in the Peace River. Appearance of the land. Navigation of the river. Arrive at the mouth of the Dog River. Successive description of several carrying places. A canoe lost in one of the Falls. Encamp on Point de Roche. Course continued. Set the nets, &c. Arrive at the Slave Lake. The weather extremely cold. Banks of the river described, with its trees, soil, &c. Account of the animal productions, and the fishery of the Lake. Obliged to wait till the moving of the ice. Three families of Indians arrive from Athabasca. Beavers, geese, and swans killed. The nets endangered by ice. Re-imbark and land on a small island. Course continued along the shores, and across the bays of the Lake. Various successes of the hunters. Steer for an island where there was plenty of cranberries and small onions. Kill several rein deer. Land on an island named Isle à la Cache. Clouds of musquitoes.

WE embarked at nine o'clock in the morning, at Fort Chepewyan, on the South side of the Lake of the Hills, in latitude 58. 40. North, and longitude 110. 30. West from Greenwich, and compass has sixteen

degrees

degrees variation Eaſt, in a canoe made of birch bark.   The crew conſiſted of four Canadians, two of whom were attended by their wives,
and a German; we were accompanied alſo by an Indian, who had
acquired the title of Engliſh Chief, and his two wives, in a ſmall canoe,
with two young Indians; his followers in another ſmall canoe.   Theſe
men were engaged to ſerve us in the twofold capacity of interpreters
and hunters.   This Indian was one of the followers of the chief who
conducted Mr. Hearne to the copper-mine river, and has ſince been a
principal leader of his countrymen who were in the habit of carrying
furs to Churchill Factory, Hudſon's Bay, and till of late very much
attached to the intereſt of that company.   Theſe circumſtances procured him the appellation of the Engliſh Chief.

We were alſo accompanied by a canoe that I had equipped for the
purpoſe of trade, and given the charge of it to M. Le Roux, one of the
Company's clerks.   In this I was obliged to ſhip part of our proviſion;
which, with the clothing neceſſary for us on the voyage, a proper
aſſortment of the articles of merchandize as preſents, to enſure us a
friendly reception among the Indians, and the ammunition and arms
requiſite for defence, as well as a ſupply for our hunters, were more
than our own canoe could carry, but by the time we ſhould part company, there was every reaſon to ſuppoſe that our expenditure would
make ſufficient room for the whole.

We proceeded twenty-one miles to the Weſt, and then took a courſe
of nine miles to North-North-Weſt, when we entered the river, or one
of the branches of the lake, of which there are ſeveral.   We then ſteered
North five miles, when our courſe changed for two miles to North-
North

North-Eaft, and here at feven in the evening we landed and pitched
our tents. One of the hunters killed a goofe, and a couple of ducks; at the fame time the canoe was taken out of the water, to be gummed, which neceffary bufinefs was effectually performed.

We embarked at four this morning, and proceeded North-North- Eaft half a mile, North one mile and a half, Weft two miles, North-Weft two miles, Weft-North-Weft one mile and a half, North-North-Weft half a mile, and Weft-North-Weft two miles, when this branch lofes itfelf in the Peace River. It is remarkable, that the currents of thefe various branches of the lake, when the Peace River is high, as in May and Auguft, run into the lake, which in the other months of the year returns its waters to them; whence to this place, the branch is not more than two hundred yards wide, nor lefs than an hundred and twenty. The banks are rather low, except in one place, where an huge rock rifes above them. The low land is covered with wood, fuch as white birch, pines of different kinds, with the poplar, three kinds of willow, and the liard.

The Peace River is upwards of a mile broad at this fpot, and its current is ftronger than that of the channel which communicates with the lake. It here, indeed, affumes the name of the *Slave* River.* The courfe of this day was as follows:—North-Weft two miles, North-North-Weft, through iflands, fix miles, North four miles and a half, North by Eaft two miles, Weft by North fix miles, North one

---

* The Slave Indians having been driven from their original country, by their enemies the Kniftenaux, along the borders of this part of the river, it received that title, though it by no means involves the idea of fervitude, but was given to thefe fugitives as a term of reproach, that denoted more than common favagenefs.

mile,

mile, North-Eaft by Eaft two miles, North one mile. We now defcended a rapid, and proceeded North-Weft feven miles and a half, North-Weft nine miles, North by Weft fix miles, North-Weft by Weft one mile and a half, North-Weft by North half a mile, North-North-Weft fix miles, North one mile, North-Weft by Weft four miles, North-North-Eaft one mile. Here we arrived at the mouth of the Dog River, where we landed, and unloaded our canoes, at half paft feven in the evening, on the Eaft fide, and clofe by the rapids. At this ftation the river is near two leagues in breadth.

Friday 5.   At three o'clock in the morning we embarked, but unloaded our canoes at the firft rapid. When we had reloaded, we entered a fmall channel, which is formed by the iflands, and, in about half an hour, we came to the carrying place. It is three hundred and eighty paces in length, and very commodious, except at the further end of it. We found fome difficulty in reloading at this fpot, from the large quantity of ice which had not yet thawed. From hence to the next carrying place, called the *Portage d'Embarras*, is about fix miles, and is occafioned by the drift wood filling up the fmall channel, which is one thoufand and twenty paces in length; from hence to the next is one mile and a half, while the diftance to that which fucceeds, does not exceed one hundred and fifty yards. It is about the fame length as the laft; and from hence to the carrying place called the Mountain, is about four miles further; when we entered the great river. The fmaller one, or the channel, affords by far the beft paffage, as it is without hazard of any kind, though I believe a fhorter courfe would be found on the outfide of the iflands, and without fo many carrying places. That called the Mountain is three hundred and thirty-five paces in length; from thence to the next, named the Peli-

can,

can, there is about a mile of dangerous rapids. The landing is very ſteep, and cloſe to the fall. The length of this carrying-place is eight hundred and twenty paces.

The whole of the party were now employed in taking the baggage and the canoe up the hill. One of the Indian canoes went down the fall, and was daſhed to pieces. The woman who had the management of it, by quitting it in time, preſerved her life, though ſhe loſt the little property it contained.

The courſe from the place we quitted in the morning is about North-Weſt, and comprehends a diſtance of fifteen miles. From hence to the next and laſt carrying place, is about nine miles; in which diſtance there are three rapids: courſe North-Weſt by Weſt. The carrying path is very bad, and five hundred and thirty-five paces in length. Our canoes being lightened, paſſed on the outſide of the oppoſite iſland, which rendered the carrying of the baggage very ſhort indeed, being not more than the length of a canoe. In the year 1786, five men were drowned, and two canoes and ſome packages loſt, in the rapids on the other ſide of the river, which occaſioned this place to be called the *Portage des Noyés.* They were proceeding to the Slave Lake, in the fall of that year, under the direction of Mr. Cuthbert Grant. We proceeded from hence ſix miles, and encamped on Point de Roche, at half paſt five in the afternoon. The men and Indians were very much fatigued; but the hunters had provided ſeven geeſe, a beaver, and four ducks.

We embarked at half paſt two in the morning, and ſteered North-Weſt by North twenty-one miles, North-Weſt by Weſt five miles, Weſt-North-

North-Weſt four miles, Weſt ſix miles, doubled a point North-North-Eaſt one mile, Eaſt five miles, North two miles, North-Weſt by North one mile and a half, Weſt-North-Weſt three miles, North-Faſt by Eaſt two miles, doubled a point one mile and a half, Weſt by North nine miles, North-Weſt by Weſt ſix miles, North-North-Weſt five miles; here we landed at ſix o'clock in the evening, unloaded, and encamped. Nets were alſo ſet in a ſmall adjacent river. We had an head wind during the greater part of the day, and the weather was become ſo cold that the Indians were obliged to make uſe of their mittens. In this day's progreſs we killed ſeven geeſe and ſix ducks.

Sunday 7.   At half paſt three we renewed our voyage, and proceeded Weſt-North-Weſt one mile, round an iſland one mile, North-Weſt two miles and a half, South by Weſt three miles, Weſt-South-Weſt one mile, South-Weſt by South half a mile, North-Weſt three miles, Weſt-North-Weſt three miles and a half, North ſeven miles and a half, North-Weſt by North four miles, North two miles and a half, North-Weſt by North two miles. The rain, which had prevailed for ſome time, now came on with ſuch violence, that we were obliged to land and unload, to prevent the goods and baggage from getting wet; the weather, however, ſoon cleared up, ſo that we reloaded the canoe, and got under way. We now continued our courſe North ten miles, Weſt one mile and a half, and North one mile and a half, when the rain came on again, and rendered it abſo-lutely neceſſary for us to get on ſhore for the night, at about half paſt three. We had a ſtrong North-North-Eaſt wind throughout the day, which greatly impeded us; M. Le Roux, however, with his party, paſſed on in ſearch of a landing place more agreeable to them. The Indians killed a couple of geeſe, and as many ducks. The rain continued through the remaining part of the day.

The

The night was very boifterous, and the rain did not ceafe till two in the afternoon of this day; but as the wind did not abate of its violence, we were prevented from proceeding till the morrow.

We embarked at half paft two in the morning, the weather being calm and foggy. Soon after our two young men joined us, whom we had not feen for two days; but during their abfence they had killed four beavers and ten geefe. After a courfe of one mile North-Weft by North, we obferved an opening on the right, which we took for a fork of the river, but it proved to be a lake. We returned and fteered South-Weft by Weft one mile and a half, Weft-South-Weft one mile and a half, Weft one mile, when we entered a very fmall branch of the river on the Eaft bank; at the mouth of which I was informed there had been a carrying place, owing to the quantity of drift wood, which then filled up the paffage, but has fince been carried away. The courfe of this river is meandering, and tends to the North, and in about ten miles falls into the Slave Lake, where we arrived at nine in the morning, when we found a great change in the weather, as it was become extremely cold. The lake was entirely covered with ice, and did not feem in any degree to have given way, but near the fhore. The gnats and mufkitoes which were very troublefome during our paffage along the river, did not venture to accompany us to this colder region.

The banks of the river both above and below the rapids, were on both fides covered with the various kinds of wood common to this country; particularly the Weftern fide; the land being lower and confifting of a rich black foil. This artificial ground is carried down by the
ftream,

ſtream, and reſts upon drift wood, ſo as to be eight or ten feet deep. The eaſtern banks are more elevated, and the ſoil a yellow clay mixed with gravel; ſo that the trees are neither ſo large or numerous as on the oppoſite ſhore. The ground was not thawed above fourteen inches in depth; notwithſtanding the leaf was at its full growth; while along the lake there was ſcarcely any appearance of verdure.

The Indians informed me, that, at a very ſmall diſtance from either bank of the river, are very extenſive plains, frequented by large herds of buffaloes; while the mooſe and rein-deer keep in the woods that border on it. The beavers, which are in great numbers, build their habitations in the ſmall lakes and rivers, as, in the larger ſtreams, the ice carries every thing along with it, during the ſpring. The mud banks in the river are covered with wild fowl; and we this morning killed two ſwans, ten geeſe, and one beaver, without ſuffering the delay of an hour; ſo that we might have ſoon filled the canoe with them, if that had been our objeċt.

From the ſmall river we ſteered Eaſt, along the inſide of a long ſand-bank, covered with drift wood and enlivened by a few willows, which ſtretches on as far as the houſes erećted by Meſſrs. Grant and Le Roux, in 1785. We often ran aground, as for five ſucceſſive miles the depth of the water no where exceeded three feet. There we found our people, who had arrived early in the morning, and whom we had not ſeen ſince the preceding Sunday. We now unloaded the canoe, and pitched our tents, as there was every appearance that we ſhould be obliged to remain here for ſome time. I then ordered the nets to be ſet, as it was abſo-

lutely

lutely neceffary that the ftores provided for our future voyage fhould remain untouched. The fifh we now caught were carp, poiffon inconnu, white fifh, and trout.

It rained during the greateft part of the preceding night, and the weather did not clear up till the afternoon of this day. This circumftance had very much weakened the ice, and I fent two of the Indians on an hunting party to a lake at the diftance of nine miles, which, they informed me, was frequented by animals of various kinds. Our fifhery this day was not fo abundant as it had been on the preceding afternoon.

The weather was fine and clear with a ftrong wefterly wind. The women were employed in gathering berries of different forts, of which there are a great plenty; and I accompanied one of my people to a fmall adjacent ifland, where we picked up fome dozens of fwan, geefe, and duck-eggs; we alfo killed a couple of ducks and a goofe.

In the evening the Indians returned, without having feen any of the larger animals. A fwan and a grey crane were the only fruits of their expedition. We caught no other fifh but a fmall quantity of pike, which is too common to be a favourite food with the people of the country. The ice moved a little to the eaftward.

The weather continued the fame as yefterday, and the mufquitoes began to vifit us in great numbers. The ice moved again in the fame direction, and I afcended an hill, but could not perceive that it was broken in the middle of the lake. The hunters killed a goofe and three ducks.

The

The weather was cloudy, and the wind changeable till about fun-fet, when it fettled in the north. It drove back the ice which was now very much broken along the fhore, and covered our nets. One of the hunters who had been at the Slave River the preceding evening, returned with three beavers and fourteen geefe. He was accompanied by three families of Indians, who left Athabafca the fame day as myfelf: they did not bring me any fowl; and they pleaded in excufe, that they had travelled with fo much expedition, as to prevent them from procuring fufficient provifions for themfelves. By a meridian line, I found the variation of the compafs to be about twenty degrees eaft.

Sunday 14.   The weather was clear and the wind remained in the fame quarter. The ice was much broken, and driven to the fide of the lake, fo that we were apprehenfive for the lofs of our nets, as they could not, at prefent, be extricated. At fun-fet there was an appearance of a violent guft of wind from the fouthward, as the fky became on a fudden, in that quarter, of a very dufky blue colour, and the lightning was very frequent. But inftead of wind there came on a very heavy rain, which promifed to diminifh the quantity of broken ice.

Monday 15.   In the morning, the bay ftill continued to be fo full of ice, that we could not get at our nets. About noon, the wind veered to the Weftward, and not only uncovered the nets, but cleared a paffage to the oppofite iflands. When we raifed the nets we found them very much fhattered, and but few fifh taken. We now ftruck our tents, and embarked at fun-fet, when we made the traverfe, which was about eight miles North-Eaft by North in about two hours. At half paft eleven P. M. we landed on a
                                                                                    fmall

fmall ifland and proceeded to gum the canoe. At this time the atmofphere was fufficiently clear to admit of reading or writing without the aid of artificial light. We had not feen a ftar fince the fecond day after we left Athabafca. About twelve o'clock, the moon made its appearance above the tops of the trees, the lower horn being in a ftate of eclipfe, which continued for about fix minutes, in a cloudlefs fky.

I took foundings three times in the courfe of the traverfe, when I found fix fathoms water, with a muddy bottom.

We were prevented from embarking this morning by a very ftrong wind from the North, and the vaft quantity of floating ice. Some trout were caught with the hook and line, but the net was not fo fuccefsful. I had an obfervation which gave 61. 28. North latitude.

The wind becoming moderate, we embarked about one, taking a North-Weft courfe, through iflands of ten miles, in which we took in a confiderable quantity of water. After making feveral traverfes, we landed at five P. M. and having pitched our tents, the hooks, lines, and nets, were immediately fet. During the courfe of the day there was occafional thunder.

We proceeded, and taking up our nets as we paffed, we found no more than feventeen fifh, and were ftopped within a mile by the ice. The Indians, however, brought us back to a point where our fifhery was very fuccefsful. They proceeded alfo on an hunting party, as well as to difcover a paffage among the iflands; but at three in the after-

noon

noon they returned without having fucceeded in either object. We were, however, in expectation, that, as the wind blew very ftrong, it would force a paffage. About fun-fet, the weather became overcaft, with thunder, lightning, and rain.

Thurfday 18.   The nets were taken up at four this morning with abundance of fifh, and we fteered North-Weft four miles, where the ice again prevented our progrefs. A South-Eaft wind drove it among the iflands, in fuch a manner as to impede our paffage, and we could perceive at fome diftance a-head, that it was but little broken. We now fet our nets in four fathom water. Two of our hunters had killed a rein-deer and its fawn. They had met with two Indian families, and in the evening, a man belonging to one of them, paid us a vifit : he informed me, that the ice had not ftirred on the fide of the ifland oppofite to us. Thefe people live entirely on fifh, and were waiting to crofs the lake as foon as it fhould be clear of ice.

Friday 19.   This morning our nets were unproductive, as they yielded us no more than fix fifh, which were of a very bad kind. In the forenoon, the Indians proceeded to the large ifland oppofite to us, in fearch of game. The weather was cloudy, and the wind changeable : at the fame time, we were peftered by mufquitoes, though, in a great meafure, furrounded with ice.

Saturday 20.   We took up our nets, but without any fifh. It rained very hard during the night and this morning : neverthelefs, M. Le Roux and his people went back to the point which we had quitted on the 18th, but

I did

I did not think it prudent to move. As I was watching for a paſſage through the ice, I promiſed to ſend for them when I could obtain it. It rained at intervals till about five o'clock; when we loaded our canoe, and ſteered for the large iſland, Weſt ſix miles. When we came to the point of it, we found a great quantity of ice; we, however, ſet our nets, and ſoon caught plenty of fiſh. In our way thither we met our hunters, but they had taken nothing. I took ſoundings at an hundred yards from the iſland, when we were in twenty-one fathom water. Here we found abundance of cranberries and ſmall ſpring onions. I now diſpatched two men for M. Le Roux, and his people.

A Southerly wind blew through the night, and drove the ice to the Northward. The two men whom I had ſent to M. Le Roux, returned at eight this morning; they parted with him at a ſmall diſtance from us, but the wind blew ſo hard, that he was obliged to put to ſhore. Having a glimpſe of the ſun, when it was twelve by my watch, I found the latitude 61. 34. North latitude. At two in the afternoon, M. Le Roux, and his people arrived. At five, the ice being almoſt all driven paſt to the Northward, we accordingly embarked, and ſteered Weſt fifteen miles, through much broken ice, and on the outſide of the iſlands, though it appeared to be very ſolid to the North-Eaſt. I ſounded three times in this diſtance, and found it ſeventy-five, forty-four, and ſixty fathom water. We pitched our tents on one of a cluſter of ſmall iſlands that were within three miles of the main land, which we could not reach in conſequence of the ice.

We ſaw ſome rein-deer on one of the iſlands, and our hunters went

in

in purfuit of them, when they killed five large and two fmall ones, which was eafily accomplifhed, as the animals had no fhelter to which they could run for protection. They had, without doubt, croffed the ice to this fpot, and the thaw coming on had detained them there, and made them an eafy prey to the purfuer. This ifland was accordingly named Ifle de Carrebœuf.

I fat up the whole of this night to obferve the fetting and rifing of the fun. That orb was beneath the horizon four hours twenty-two minutes, and rofe North 20 Eaft by compafs. It, however, froze fo hard, that during the fun's difappearance the water was covered with ice half a quarter of an inch thick.

Monday 22.

We embarked at half paft three in the morning, and rounding the out-fide of the iflands, fteered North-Weft thirteen miles along the ice, edging in for the main land, the wind Weft, then Weft two miles; but it blew fo hard as to oblige us to land on an ifland at half paft nine, from whence we could juft diftinguifh land to the South-Eaft, at the diftance of about twelve leagues; though we could not determine, whether it was a con-tinuation of the iflands, or the fhores of the lake.* I took an obferva-tion at noon, which gave me 61. 53. North, the variation of the compafs being, at the fame time, about two points. M. Le Roux's people having provided two bags of *pemican*† to be left in the ifland againft their re-turn; it was called *Ifle à la Cache*.

* Sometimes the land looms, fo that there may be a great deception as to the diftance: and I think this was the cafe at prefent.

† Fifh dried in the fun, and afterwards pounded for the convenience of carriage.

The

The wind being moderated, we proceeded again at half paſt two in the afternoon, and ſteering Weſt by North among the iſlands, made a courſe of eighteen miles. We encamped at eight o'clock on a ſmall iſland, and ſince eight in the morning had not paſſed any ice. Though the weather was far from being warm, we were tormented, and our reſt interrupted, by the hoſt of muſquitoes that accompanied us.

CHAP.

CHAPTER II.

Landed at some lodges of Red-Knife Indians : procure one of them to assist in navigating the bays. Conference with the Indians. Take leave of M. Le Roux, and continue the voyage. Different appearances of the land; its vegetable produce. Visit an island where the wood had been felled. Further description of the Coast. Plenty of rein and moose-deer, and white partridges. Enter a very deep bay. Interrupted by ice. Very blowing weather. Continue to coast the bay. Arrive at the mouth of a river. Great numbers of fish and wild-fowl. Description of the land on either side. Curious appearance of woods that had been burned. Came in sight of the Horn Mountain. Continue to kill geese and swans, &c. Violent storm.

1789.
June.

Tuesday 23.

TOWARDS morning, the Indians who had not been able to keep up with us the preceding day, now joined us, and brought two swans and a goose. At half past three we re-embarked, and steering West by North a mile and an half, with a Northerly wind, we came to the foot of a traverse across a deep bay, West five miles, which receives a considerable river at the bottom of it; the distance about twelve miles. The North-West side of the bay was covered with many small islands that were surrounded with ice; but the wind driving it a little off the land, we had a clear passage on the inside of them. We steered South-West nine miles under

sail,

sail, then North-West nearly, through the islands, forming a course of sixteen miles. We landed on the main land at half past two in the afternoon at three lodges of Red-Knife Indians, so called from their copper knives. They informed us, that there were many more lodges of their friends at no great distance; and one of the Indians set off to fetch them: they also said, that we should see no more of them at present; as the Slave and Beaver Indians, as well as others of the tribe, would not be here till the time that the swans cast their feathers. In the afternoon it rained a torrent.

M. Le Roux purchased of these Indians upwards of eight packs of good beaver and marten skins; and there were not above twelve of them qualified to kill beaver. The English chief got upwards of an hundred skins on the score of debts due to him, of which he had many outstanding in this country. Forty of them he gave on account of debts due by him since the winters of 1786 and 1787, at the Slave Lake; the rest he exchanged for rum and other necessary articles; and I added a small quantity of that liquor as an encouraging present to him and his young men. I had several consultations with these Copper Indian people, but could obtain no information that was material to our expedition; nor were they acquainted with any part of the river, which was the object of my research, but the mouth of it. In order to save as much time as possible in circumnavigating the bays, I engaged one of the Indians to conduct us; and I accordingly equipped him with various articles of clothing, &c. I also purchased a large new canoe, that he might embark with the two young Indians in my service.

This day, at noon, I took an observation, which gave me 62. 24. North latitude:

latitude; the variation of the compaſs being about twenty-ſix or twenty-ſeven degrees to the Eaſt.

In the afternoon I aſſembled the Indians, in order to inform them that I ſhould take my departure on the following day; but that people would remain on the ſpot till their countrymen, whom they had mentioned, ſhould arrive; and that, if they brought a ſufficient quantity of ſkins to make it anſwer, the Frenchmen would return for more goods, with a view to winter here, and build a fort,* which would be continued as long as they ſhould be found to deſerve it.   They aſſured me, that it would be a great encouragement to them to have a ſettlement of ours in their country; and that they ſhould exert themſelves to the utmoſt to kill beaver, as they would then be certain of getting an adequate value for them.   Hitherto, they ſaid, the Chepewyans always pillaged them; or, at moſt, gave little or nothing for the fruits of their labour, which had greatly diſcouraged them; and that, in conſequence of this treatment, they had no motive to purſue the beaver, but to obtain a ſufficient quantity of food and raiment.

I now wrote to Meſſrs. Macleod and Mackenzie, and addreſſed my papers to the former, at Athabaſca.

Thurſday 25.   We left this place at three this morning, our canoe being deeply laden, as we had embarked ſome packages that had come in the canoes of M. Le Roux. We were ſaluted on our departure with ſome vollies of ſmall arms, which we returned. and ſteered South by Weſt ſtraight

---

* Fort, is the name given to any eſtabliſhment in this country

acroſs

acrofs the bay, which is here no more than two miles and a half broad, but, from the accounts of the natives, it is fifteen leagues in depth, with a much greater breadth in feveral parts, and full of iflands. I founded in the courfe of the traverfe and found fix fathoms with a fandy bottom. Here, the land has a very different appearance from that on which we have been fince we entered the lake. Till we arrived here there was one continued view of high hills and iflands of folid rock, whofe furface was occafionally enlivened with mofs, fhrubs, and a few fcattered trees, of a very ftinted growth from an in-fufficiency of foil to nourifh them. But, notwithftanding their barren appearance, almoft every part of them produces berries of various kinds, fuch as cranberries, juniper-berries, rafpberries, partridge berries, goofeberries, and the pathagomenan, which is fomething like a rafp-berry ; it grows on a fmall ftalk about a foot and a half high, in wet, moffy fpots. Thefe fruits are in great abundance, though they are not to be found in the fame places, but in fituations and afpects fuited to their peculiar natures.

The land which borders the lake in this part is loofe and fandy, but is well covered with wood, compofed of trees of a larger growth : it gradually rifes from the fhore, and at fome diftance forms a ridge of high land running along the coaft, thick with wood and a rocky fummit rifing above it.

We fteered South-South-Eaft nine miles, when we were very much interrupted by drifting ice, and with fome difficulty reached an ifland, where we landed at feven. I immediately proceeded to

the

the further part of it, in order to difcover if there was any probability of our being able to get from thence in the courfe of the day. It is about five miles in circumference, and I was very much furprized to find that the greater part of the wood with which it was formerly covered, had been cut down within twelve or fifteen years, and that the remaining ftumps were become altogether rotten. On making inquiry concerning the caufe of this extraordinary circumftance, the Englifh chief informed me, that feveral winters ago, many of the Slave Indians inhabited the iflands that were fcattered over the bay, as the furrounding waters abound with fifh throughout the year, but that they had been driven away by the Kniftenaux, who continually made war upon them. If an eftablifhment is to be made in this country, it muft be in the neighbourhood of this place on account of the wood and the fifhery.

At eleven we ventured to re-embark, as the wind had driven the greateft part of the ice paft the ifland, though we ftill had to encounter fome broken pieces of it, which threatened to damage our canoe. We fteered South-Eaft from point to point acrofs five bays, twenty-one miles. We took foundings feveral times, and found from fix to ten fathom water. I obferved that the country gradually defcended inland, and was ftill better covered with wood than in the higher parts. Wherever we approached the land, we perceived deferted lodges. The hunters killed two fwans and a beaver; and at length we landed at eight o'clock in the evening, when we unloaded and gummed our canoe.

Friday 26.   We continued our route at five o'clock, fteering South-Eaft for ten miles acrofs two deep bays: then South-South-Eaft, with iflands in fight

to

to the Eaftward. We then traverfed another bay in a courfe of three miles, then South one mile to a point which we named the Detour, and South-South-Weft four miles and an half, when there was an heavy fwell off the lake. Here I took an obfervation, when we were in 61. 40. North latitude. We then proceeded South-Weft four miles, and Weft-South-Weft among iflands: on one of which our Indians killed two rein-deer, but we loft three hours aft wind in going for them: this courfe was nine miles. About feven in the evening we were obliged to land for the night, as the wind became too ftrong from the South-Eaft. We thought we could obferve land in this direction when the wind was coming on from fome diftance. On the other fide of the Detour, the land is low, and the fhore is flat and dangerous, there being no fafe place to land in bad weather, except in the iflands which we had juft paffed. There feemed to be plenty of moofe and rein-deer in this country, as we faw their tracks wherever we landed. There were alfo great numbers of white partridges, which are at this feafon of a grey colour, like that of the moor-fowl. There was fome floating ice in the lake, and the Indians killed a couple of fwans.

At three this morning we were in the canoe, after having paffed a very reftlefs night from the perfecution of the mufquitoes. The weather was fine and calm, and our courfe Weft-South-Weft nine miles, when we came to the foot of a traverfe, the oppofite point in fight bearing South-Weft, diftance twelve miles. The bay is at leaft eight miles deep, and this courfe two miles more, in all ten miles. It now became very foggy, and as the bays were fo numerous, we landed for two hours, when the weather cleared up; and we took the advantage of fteering South thirteen miles,

and

1789.
June.
and paſſed ſeveral ſmall bays, when we came to the point of a very deep one, whoſe extremity was not diſcernible; the land bearing South from us, at the diſtance of about ten miles.   Our guide not having been here for eight winters, was at a loſs what courſe to take, though as well as he could recollect, this bay appeared to be the entrance of the river.   Accordingly, we ſteered down it, about Weſt-South-Weſt, till we were involved in a field of broken ice.   We ſtill could not diſcover the bottom of the bay, and a fog coming on, made it very difficult for us to get to an iſland to the South-Weſt, and it was nearly dark when we effected a landing.

Sunday 28.

At a quarter paſt three we were again on the water, and as we could perceive no current ſetting into this bay, we made the beſt of our way to the point that bore South from us yeſterday afternoon.   We continued our courſe South three miles more, South by Weſt ſeven miles, Weſt fifteen miles, when by obſervation we were in 61 degrees North latitude; we then proceeded Weſt-North-Weſt two miles.   Here we came to the foot of a traverſe, the oppoſite land bearing South-Weſt, diſtance fourteen miles, when we ſteered into a deep bay, about a Weſterly courſe; and though we had no land a head in ſight, we indulged the hope of finding a paſſage, which, according to the Indian, would conduct us to the entrance of the river.

Having a ſtrong wind aft, we loſt ſight of the Indians, nor could we put on ſhore to wait for them, without riſking material damage to the canoe, till we ran to the bottom of the bay, and were forced among the ruſhes; when we diſcovered that there was no paſſage there. In about two or three hours they joined us, but would not approach our

fire,

1789.
June.

fire, as there was no good ground for an encampment: they emptied their canoe of the water which it had taken in, and continued their route, but did not encamp till fun-fet. The Englifh chief was very much irritated againft the Red-Knife Indian, and even threatened to murder him, for having undertaken to guide us in a courfe of which he was ignorant; nor had we any reafon to be fatisfied with him, though he ftill continued to encourage us, by declaring that he recollected having paffed from the river, through the woods, to the place where he had landed. In the blowing weather to-day, we were obliged to make ufe of our large kettle, to keep our canoe from filling, although we did not carry above three feet fail. The Indians very narrowly efcaped.

Monday 29.

We embarked at four this evening, and fteered along the South-Weft fide of the bay. At half paft five we reached the extremity of the point, which we doubled, and found it to be the branch or paffage that was the object of our fearch, and occafioned by a very long ifland, which feparates it from the main channel of the river. It is about half a mile acrofs, and not more than fix feet in depth; the water appeared to abound in fifh, and was covered with fowl, fuch as fwans, geefe, and feveral kinds of ducks, particularly black ducks, that were very numerous, but we could not get within gun fhot of them.

The current, though not very ftrong, fet us South-Weft by Weft, and we followed this courfe fourteen miles, till we paffed the point of the long ifland, where the Slave Lake difcharges itfelf, and is ten miles in breadth. There is not more than from five to two fathom water, fo that when the lake is low, it may be prefumed the greateft part of

this

this channel muſt be dry. The river now turns to the weſtward, becoming gradually narrower for twenty-four miles, till it is not more than half a mile wide; the current, however, is then much ſtronger, and the ſoundings were three fathom and a half. The land on the North ſhore from the lake is low, and covered with trees; that to the South is much higher, and has alſo an abundance of wood. The current is very ſtrong, and the banks are of an equal height on both ſides, conſiſting of a yellow clay, mixed with ſmall ſtones; they are covered with large quantities of burned wood, lying on the ground, and young poplar trees, that have ſprung up ſince the fire that deſtroyed the larger wood. It is a very curious and extraordinary circumſtance, that land covered with ſpruce pine, and white birch, when laid waſte by fire, ſhould ſubſequently produce nothing but poplars, where none of that ſpecies of tree were previouſly to be found.

A ſtiff breeze from the Eaſtward drove us on at a great rate under ſail, in the ſame courſe, though obliged to wind among iſlands. We kept the North channel for about ten miles, whoſe current is much ſtronger than that of the South; ſo that the latter is conſequently the better road to come up. Here the river widened, and the wind dying away, we had recourſe to our paddles. We kept our courſe to the North-Weſt, on the North ſide of the river, which is here much wider, and aſſumes the form of a ſmall lake; we could not, however, diſcover an opening in any direction, ſo that we were at a loſs what courſe to take, as our Red-Knife Indian had never explored beyond our preſent ſituation. He at the ſame time informed us that a river falls in from the North, which takes its riſe in the Horn Mountain, now in ſight, which is the country of the Beaver Indians;

and

and that he and his relations frequently meet on that river. He alfo added, that there are very extenfive plains on both fides of it, which abound in buffaloes and moofe deer.

By keeping this courfe, we got into fhallows, fo that we were forced to fteer to the left, till we recovered deep water, which we followed, till the channel of the river opened on us to the fouthward. we now made for the fhore, and encamped foon after funfet. Our courfe ought to have been Weft fifteen miles, fince we took to the paddle, the Horn Mountains bearing from us North-Weft, and running North-North-Eaft and South-South-Weft. Our foundings, which were frequent during the courfe of the day, were from three to fix fathoms water. The hunters killed two geefe and a fwan: it appeared, indeed, that great numbers of fowls breed in the iflands which we had paffed.

At four this morning we got under way, the weather being fine and calm. Our courfe was South-Weft by South thirty-fix miles. On the South fide of the river is a ridge of low mountains, running Eaft and Weft by compafs. The Indians picked up a white goofe, which appeared to have been lately fhot with an arrow, and was quite frefh. We proceeded South-Weft by South fix miles, and then came to a bay on our left, which is full of fmall iflands, and appeared to be the entrance of a river from the South. Here the ridge of mountains terminates. This courfe was fifteen miles.

At fix in the afternoon there was an appearance of bad weather; we landed, therefore, for the night; but before we could pitch our tents, a

violent

violent tempeft came on, with thunder, lightning, and rain, which, how-ever, foon ceafed, but not before we had fuffered the inconvenience of being drenched by it. The Indians were very much fatigued, having been employed in running after wild fowl, which had lately caft their feathers; they, however, caught five fwans, and the fame number of geefe. I founded feveral times in the courfe of the day, and found from four to fix fathoms water

CHAP.

CHAPTER III.

Continue our courfe. The river narrows. Loft the lead. Paffed a fmall river. Violent rain. Land on a fmall ifland. Expect to arrive at the rapids. Conceal two bags of pemican in an ifland. A view of mountains. Pafs feveral encampments of the natives. Arrive among the iflands. Afcend an high hill. Violence of the current. Ice feen along the banks of the river. Land at a village of the natives. Their conduct and appearance, Their fabulous ftories. The Englifh Chief and Indians difcontented. Obtain a new guide. Singular cuftoms of the natives. An account of their dances. Defcription of their perfons, drefs, orna-ments, buildings, army for war and hunting, canoes, &c. Paffed on among iflands. Encamped beneath an hill, and prevented from afcending by the mufquitoes. Landed at an encampment. Conduct of the inha-bitants. They abound in fabulous accounts of dangers. Land at other encampments. Procure plenty of hares and partridges. Our guide anxious to return. Land and alarm the natives, called the Hare Indians, &c. Exchange our guide. State of the weather.

1789.
July.
Wednef. 1.

AT half paft four in the morning we continued our voyage, and in a fhort time found the river narrowed to about half a mile. Our courfe was Wefterly among iflands, with a ftrong current. Though the land is high on both fides, the banks are not perpendicular. This

courfe

courfe was twenty-one miles; and on founding we found nine fathoms water. We then proceeded Weft-North-Weft nine miles, and paffed a river upon the South-Eaft fide; we founded, and found twelve fathoms; and then we went North-Weft by Weft three miles. Here I loft my lead, which had faftened at the bottom, with part of the line, the current running fo ftrong that we could not clear it with eight paddles, and the ftrength of the line, which was equal to four paddles. Continued North by Weft five miles, and faw an high mountain, bearing South from us; we then proceeded North-Weft by North four miles. We now paffed a fmall river on the North fide, then doubled a point to Weft-South-Weft. At one o'clock there came on lightning and thunder, with wind and rain, which ceafed in about half an hour, and left us almoft deluged with wet, as we did not land. There were great quantities of ice along the banks of the river.

We landed upon a fmall ifland, where there were the poles of four lodges ftanding, which we concluded to have belonged to the Knifti-neaux, on their war excurfions, fix or feven years ago. This courfe was fifteen miles Weft, to where the river of the Mountain falls in from the Southward. It appears to be a very large river, whofe mouth is half a mile broad. About fix miles further a fmall river flows in the fame direction; and our whole courfe was twenty-four miles. We landed oppofite to an ifland, the mountains to the Southward being in fight. As our canoe was deeply laden, and being alfo in daily expectation of coming to the rapids or fall, which we had been taught to confider with apprehenfion, we concealed two bags of pemican in the oppofite ifland, in the hope that they would be of future fervice to us.

The

The Indians were of a different opinion, as they entertained no expectation of returning that feafon, when the hidden provifions would be fpoiled. Near us were two Indian encampments of the laft year. By the manner in which thefe people cut their wood, it appears that they have no iron tools. The current was very ftrong during the whole of this day's voyage; and in the article of provifions two fwans were all that the hunters were able to procure.

The morning was very foggy; but at half paft five we embarked; it cleared up, however, at feven, when we difcovered that the water, from being very limpid and clear, was become dark and muddy. This alteration muft have proceeded from the influx of fome river to the Southward, but where thefe ftreams firft blended their waters the fog had prevented us from obferving. At nine we perceived a very high mountain a-head, which appeared, on our nearer approach, to be rather a clufter of mountains, ftretching as far as our view could reach to the Southward, and whofe tops were loft in the clouds. At noon there was lightning, thunder, and rain, and at one, we came abreaft of the mountains: their fummits appeared to be barren and rocky, but their declivities were covered with wood: they appeared alfo to be fprinkled with white ftones, which gliftened in the fun, and were called by the Indians *manetoe afeniah,* or fpirit ftones. I fufpected that they were Talc, though they poffeffed a more brilliant whitenefs: on our return, however, thefe appearances were diffolved, as they were nothing more than patches of fnow.

Our courfe had been Weft-South-Weft thirty miles, and we proceeded

ceeded with great caution, as we continually expected to approach some great rapid or fall. This was such a prevalent idea, that all of us were occasionally persuaded that we heard those sounds which betokened a fall of water. Our course changed to West by North, along the mountains, twelve miles, North by West twenty-one miles, and at eight o'clock in the evening we went on shore for the night on the North side of the river. We saw several encampments of the natives, some of which had been erected in the present spring, and others at some former period. The hunters killed only one swan and a beaver: the latter was the first of its kind which we had seen in this river. The Indians complained of the perseverance with which we pushed forward, and that they were not accustomed to such severe fatigue as it occasioned.

Friday 3.   The rain was continual through the night, and did not subside till seven this morning, when we embarked and steered North-North-West for twelve miles, the river being enclosed by high mountains on either side. We had a strong head-wind, and the rain was so violent as to compel us to land at ten o'clock. According to my reckoning, since my last observation, we had run two hundred and seventeen miles West, and forty-four miles North. At a quarter past two the rain subsided, and we got again under way, our former course continuing for five miles. Here a river fell in from the North, and in a short time the current became strong and rapid, running with great rapidity among rocky islands, which were the first that we had seen in this river, and indicated our near approach to rapids and falls. Our present course was North-West by North ten miles, North-West three miles, West-North-West twelve miles, and North-West three miles, when we encamped at eight

in

in the evening, at the foot of an high hill, on the north fhore, which in fome parts rofe perpendicular from the river. I immediately afcended it, accompanied by two men and fome Indians, and in about an hour and an half, with very hard walking, we gained the fummit, when I was very much furprized to find it crowned by an encampment. The Indians informed me, that it is the cuftom of the people who have no arms to choofe thefe elevated fpots for the places of their refidence, as they can render them inacceffible to their enemies, particularly the Knifteneaux, of whom they are in continual dread. The profpect from this height was not fo extenfive as we expected, as it was terminated by a circular range of hills, of the fame elevation as that on which we ftood. The intervals between the hills were covered with fmall lakes, which were inhabited by great numbers of fwans. We faw no trees but the pine and the birch, which were fmall in fize and few in number.

We were obliged to fhorten our ftay here, from the fwarms of mufquitoes which attacked us on all fides, and were, indeed, the only inhabitants of the place. We faw feveral encampments of the natives in the courfe of the day, but none of them were of this year's eftablifhment. Since four in the afternoon the current had been fo ftrong that it was, at length, in an actual ebullition, and produced an hiffing noife like a kettle of water in a moderate ftate of boiling. The weather was now become extremely cold, which was the more fenfibly felt, as it had been very fultry fome time before and fince we had been in the river.

At five in the morning the wind and weather having undergone no alteration from yefterday, we proceeded North-Weft by Weft twenty-two miles,

miles, North-Weft fix miles, North-Weft by North four miles, and Weft North-Weft five miles: we then paffed the mouth of a fmall river from the North, and after doubling a point, South-Weft one mile, we paffed the influx of another river from the South. We then continued our courfe North-North-Weft, with a mountain a-head, fifteen miles, when the opening of two rivers appeared oppofite to each other: we then proceeded Weft four miles, and North-Weft thirteen miles. At eight in the evening, we encamped on an ifland. The current was as ftrong through the whole of this day as it had been the preceding afternoon; neverthelefs, a quantity of ice appeared along the banks of the river. The hunters killed a beaver and a goofe, the former of which funk before they could get to him: beavers, otters, bears, &c. if fhot dead at once, remain like a bladder, but if there remains enough of life for them to ftruggle, they foon fill with water and go to the bottom.

Sunday 5.   The fun fet laft night at fifty-three minutes paft nine, by my watch, and rofe at feven minutes before two this morning: we embarked foon after, fteering North-North-Weft, through iflands for five miles, and Weft four miles. The river then encreafed in breadth, and the current began to flacken in a fmall degree; after the continuation of our courfe, we perceived a ridge of high mountains before us, covered with fnow, Weft-South-Weft ten miles, and at three-quarters paft feven o'clock, we faw feveral fmokes on the North fhore, which we made every exertion to approach. As we drew nearer, we difcovered the natives running about in great apparent confufion; fome were making to the woods, and others hurrying to their canoes. Our hunters landed before us, and addreffed the few that had not efcaped, in the Chipewyan language, which, fo great was

their

their confusion and terror, they did not appear to understand. But when they perceived that it was impossible to avoid us, as we were all landed, they made us signs to keep at a distance, with which we complied, and not only unloaded our canoe, but pitched our tents, before we made any attempt to approach them. During this interval, the English chief and his young men were employed in reconciling them to our arrival: and when they had recovered from their alarm, of hostile intention, it appeared that some of them perfectly comprehended the language of our Indians; so that they were at length persuaded, though not without evident signs of reluctance and apprehension, to come to us. Their reception, however, soon dissipated their fears, and they hastened to call their fugitive companions from their hiding places.

There were five families, consisting of twenty-five or thirty persons, and of two different tribes, the Slave and Dog-rib Indians. We made them smoke, though it was evident they did not know the use of tobacco; we likewise supplied them with grog; but I am disposed to think, that they accepted our civilities rather from fear than inclination. We acquired a more effectual influence over them by the distribution of knives, beads, awls, rings, gartering, fire-steels, flints, and hatchets; so that they became more familiar even than we expected, for we could not keep them out of our tents: though I did not observe that they attempted to purloin any thing.

The information which they gave respecting the river, had so much of the fabulous, that I shall not detail it: it will be sufficient just

to

to mention their attempts to perfuade us, that it would require feveral winters to get to the fea, and that old age would come upon us before the period of our return: we were alfo to encounter monfters of fuch horrid fhapes and deftructive powers as could only exift in their wild imaginations. They added, befides, that there were two impaffable falls in the river, the firft of which was about thirty days march from us.

Though I placed no faith in thefe ftrange relations, they had a very different effect upon our Indians, who were already tired of the voyage. It was their opinion and anxious wifh, that we fhould not hefitate to return. They faid that, according to the information which they had received, there were very few animals in the country beyond us, and that as we proceeded, the fcarcity would increafe, and we fhould abfolutely perifh from hunger, if no other accident befel us. It was with no fmall trouble that they were convinced of the folly of thefe reafonings; and, by my defire, they induced one of thofe Indians to accompany us, in confideration of a fmall kettle, an axe, a knife, and fome other articles.

Though it was now three o'clock in the afternoon, the canoe was ordered to be reloaded, and as we were ready to embark our new recruit was defired to prepare himfelf for his departure, which he would have declined; but as none of his friends would take his place, we may be faid, after the delay of an hour, to have compelled him to embark. Previous to his departure a ceremony took place, of which I could not learn the meaning: he cut off a lock of his hair, and having divided it into three parts, he faftened one of them to the hair on the

upper

upper part of his wife's head, blowing on it three times with the utmoſt violence in his power, and uttering certain words. The other two he faſtened with the ſame formalities, on the heads of his two children.

During our ſhort ſtay with theſe people, they amuſed us with dancing, which they accompanied with their voices; but neither their ſong or their dance poſſeſſed much variety. The men and women formed a promiſcuous ring. The former have a bone dagger or piece of ſtick between the fingers of the right hand, which they keep extended above the head, in continual motion: the left they ſeldom raiſe ſo high, but work it backwards and forwards in an horizontal direction; while they leap about and throw themſelves into various antic poſtures, to the meaſure of their muſic, always bringing their heels cloſe to each other at every pauſe. The men occaſionally howl in imitation of ſome animal, and he who continues this violent exerciſe for the longeſt period, appears to be conſidered as the beſt performer. The women ſuffer their arms to hang as without the power of motion. They are a meagre, ugly, ill-made people, particularly about the legs, which are very clumſy and covered with ſcabs. The latter circumſtance proceeds probably from their habitually roaſting them before the fire. Many of them appeared to be in a very unhealthy ſtate, which is owing, as I imagine, to their natural filthineſs. They are of a moderate ſtature, and as far as could be diſcovered, through the coat of dirt and greaſe that covers them, are of a fairer complexion than the generality of Indians who are the natives of warmer climates.

Some of them have their hair of a great length; while others ſuffer a long treſs to fall behind, and the reſt is cut ſo ſhort as to expoſe
their

their ears, but no other attention whatever is paid to it. The beards of some of the old men were long, and the reſt had them pulled out by the roots, ſo that not an hair could be ſeen on their chins. The men have two double lines, either black or blue, tattooed upon each cheek, from the ear to the noſe. The griſtle of the latter is perforated ſo as to admit a gooſe-quill or a ſmall piece of wood to be paſſed through the orifice. Their clothing is made of the dreſſed ſkins of the rein or mooſe-deer, though more commonly of the former. Theſe they prepare in the hair for winter, and make ſhirts of both, which reach to the middle of their thighs. Some of them are decorated with an embroidery of very neat workmanſhip with porcupine quills and the hair of the mooſe, coloured red, black, yellow, and white. Their upper garments are ſuf-ficiently large to cover the whole body, with a fringe round the bottom, and are uſed both ſleeping and awake. Their leggins come half way up the thigh, and are ſewed to their ſhoes: they are embroidered round the ancle, and upon every ſeam. The dreſs of the women is the ſame as that of the men. The former have no covering on their private parts, except a taſſel of leather which dangles from a ſmall cord, as it appears, to keep off the flies, which would otherwiſe be very troubleſome. Whether circumciſion be praćtiſed among them, I cannot pretend to ſay, but the appearance of it was general among thoſe whom I ſaw.

Their ornaments conſiſt of gorgets, bracelets for the arms and wriſts, made of wood, horn, or bone, belts, garters, and a kind of band to go round the head, compoſed of ſtrips of leather of one inch and an half broad, embroidered with porcupine·quills, and ſtuck round with the claws of bears or wild fowl inverted, to which are ſuſpended a few ſhort thongs of the ſkin of an animal that reſembles the ermine, in the form

of

of a taffel. Their cinctures and garters are formed of porcupine quills
woven with finews, in a ftyle of peculiar fkill and neatnefs : they have others of different materials, and more ordinary workmanfhip ; and to both they attach a long fringe of ftrings of leather, worked round with hair of various colours. Their mittens are alfo fufpended from the neck in a pofition convenient for the reception of the hands.

Their lodges are of a very fimple ftructure : a few poles fupported by a fork, and forming a femicircle at the bottom, with fome branches or a piece of bark as a covering, conftitutes the whole of their native architecture. They build two of thefe huts facing each other, and make the fire between them. The furniture harmonifes with the buildings : they have a few difhes of wood, bark, or horn; the veffels in which they cook their victuals, are in the fhape of a gourd, narrow at the top and wide at the bottom, and of watape*, fabricated in fuch a manner as to hold water, which is made to boil by putting a fucceffion of red-hot ftones into it. Thefe veffels contain from two to fix gallons. They have a number of fmall leather bags to hold their embroidered work, lines, and nets. They always keep a large quantity of the fibres of willow bark, which they work into thread on their thighs. Their nets are from three to forty fathoms in length, and from thirteen to thirty-fix mefhes in depth. The fhort deep ones they fet in the eddy current of rivers, and the long ones in the lakes. They likewife make lines of the finews of the rein-deer, and manufacture their hooks from wood, horn, or bone. Their arms and weapons for hunting, are bows and arrows, fpears, daggers, and poga-

---

* Watape is the name given to the divided roots of the fpruce-fir, which the natives weave into a degree of compactnefs that renders it capable of containing a fluid. The different parts of the bark canoes are alfo fewed together with this kind of filament.

magans,

magans, or clubs. The bows are about five or six feet in length, and the strings are of finews or raw skins. The arrows are two feet and an half long, including the barb, which is varioufly formed of bone, horn, flint, iron, or copper, and are winged with three feathers. The pole of the spears is about six feet in length, and pointed with a barbed bone of ten inches. With this weapon they strike the rein-deer in the water. The daggers are flat and sharp-pointed, about twelve inches long, and made of horn or bone. The pogamagon is made of the horn of the rein-deer, the branches being all cut off, except that which forms the extremity. This instrument is about two feet in length, and is employ-ed to dispatch their enemies in battle, and such animals as they catch in snares placed for that purpose. These are about three fathom long, and are made of the green skin of the rein or moose-deer, but in such small strips, that it requires from ten to thirty strands to make this cord, which is not thicker than a cod-line; and strong enough to resist any animal that can be entangled in it. Snares or nooses are also made of sinews to take lesser animals, such as hares and white partridges, which are very numerous. Their axes are manufactured of a piece of brown or grey stone from six to eight inches long, and two inches thick. The inside is flat, and the outside round and tapering to an edge, an inch wide. They are fastened by the middle with the flat side inwards to an handle two feet long, with a cord of green skin. This is the tool with which they split their wood, and we believe, the only one of its kind among them. They kindle fire, by striking together a piece of white or yellow pyrites and a flint stone, over a piece of touchwood. They are univerfally provided with a small bag containing these materials, so that they are in a continual state of preparation to produce fire. From the ad-

joining

joining tribes, the Red-Knives and Chepewyans, they procure, in barter for marten fkins and a few beaver, fmall pieces of iron, of which they manufacture knives, by fixing them at the end of a fhort ftick, and with them and the beaver's teeth, they finifh all their work. They keep them in a fheath hanging to their neck, which alfo contains their awls both of iron and horn.

Their canoes are fmall, pointed at both ends, flat-bottomed and co-vered in the fore part. They are made of the bark of the birch-tree and fir-wood, but of fo flight a conftruction, that the man whom one of thefe light veffels bears on the water, can, in return, carry it over land with-out any difficulty. It is very feldom that more than one perfon embarks in them, nor are they capable of receiving more than two. The paddles are fix feet long, one half of which is occupied by a blade, of about eight inches wide. Thefe people informed us, that we had paffed large bodies of Indians who inhabit the mountains on the Eaft fide of the river.

At four o'clock in the afternoon we embarked, and our Indian ac-quaintance promifed to remain on the bank of the river till the fall, in cafe we fhould return. Our courfe was Weft-South-Weft, and we foon paffed the Great Bear Lake River, which is of a confiderable depth, and an hundred yards wide: its water is clear, and has the greenifh hue of the fea. We had not proceeded more than fix miles when we were obliged to land for the night, in confequence of an heavy guft of wind, accom-panied with rain. We encamped beneath a rocky hill, on the top of which, according to the information of our guide, it blew a ftorm every

day

day throughout the year. He found himfelf very uncomfortable in his new fituation, and pretended that he was very ill, in order that he might be permitted to return to his relations. To prevent his efcape, it became neceffary to keep a ftrict watch over him during the night.

Monday 6.

At three o'clock, in a very raw and cloudy morning, we embarked, and fteered Weft-South-Weft four miles, Weft four miles, Weft-North-Weft five miles, Weft eight miles, Weft by South fixteen miles, Weft twenty-feven miles, South-Weft nine miles, then Weft fix miles, and encamped at half paft feven. We paffed through numerous iflands, and had the ridge of fnowy mountains always in fight. Our conductor informed us that great numbers of bears, and fmall white buffaloes, frequent thofe mountains, which are alfo inhabited by Indians. We encamped in a fimilar fituation to that of the preceding evening, beneath another high rocky hill, which I attempted to afcend, in company with one of the hunters, but before we had got half way to the fummit, we were almoft fuffocated by clouds of mufquitoes, and were obliged to return. I obferved, however, that the mountains terminated here, and that a river flowed from the Weftward: I alfo difcovered a ftrong ripling current, or rapid, which ran clofe under a fteep precipice of the hill.

Tuefday 7.

We embarked at four in the morning, and croffed to the oppo-fite fide of the river, in confequence of the rapid; but we might have fpared ourfelves this trouble, as there would have been no dan-ger in continuing our courfe, without any circuitous deviation what-ever. This circumftance convinced us of the erroneous account given by the natives of the great and approaching dangers of our navigation,

as

as this rapid was ſtated to be one of them. Our courſe was now North-North-Weſt three miles, Weſt-North-Weſt four miles, North-Weſt ten miles, North two miles, when we came to a river that flowed from the Eaſtward. Here we landed at an encampment of four fires, all the inhabitants of which ran off with the utmoſt ſpeed, except an old man and an old woman. Our guide called aloud to the fugitives, and entreated them to ſtay, but without effect: the old man, however, did not heſitate to approach us, and repreſented himſelf as too far advanced in life, and too indifferent about the ſhort time he had to remain in the world, to be very anxious about eſcaping from any danger that threatened him; at the ſame time he pulled his grey hairs from his head by handfulls to diſtribute among us, and implored our favour for himſelf and his relations. Our guide, however, at length removed his fears, and perſuaded him to recall the fugitives, who conſiſted of eighteen people; whom **I** reconciled to me on their return with preſents of beads, knives, awls, &c. with which they appeared to be greatly delighted. They differed in no reſpect from thoſe whom we had already ſeen; nor were they deficient in hoſpitable attentions; they provided us with fiſh, which was very well boiled, and cheerfully accepted by us. Our guide ſtill ſickened after his home, and was ſo anxious to return thither, that we were under the neceſſity of forcing him to embark.

Theſe people informed us that we were cloſe to another great rapid, and that there were ſeveral lodges of their relations in its vicinity. Four canoes, with a man in each, followed us, to point out the particular channels we ſhould follow for the ſecure paſſage of the rapid. They alſo abounded in diſcouraging ſtories concerning the dangers and difficulties which we were to encounter.

From

From hence our courfe was North-North-Eaft two miles, when the river appeared to be enclofed, as it were, with lofty, perpendicular, white rocks, which did not afford us a very agreeable profpect. We now went on fhore in order to examine the rapid, but did not perceive any figns of it, though the Indians ftill continued to magnify its dangers: however, as they ventured down it, in their fmall canoes, our apprehenfions were confequently removed, and we followed them at fome diftance, but did not find any increafe in the rapidity of the current; at length the Indians informed us that we fhould find no other rapid but that which was now bearing us along. The river at this place is not above three hundred yards in breadth, but on founding I found fifty fathoms water. At the two rivulets that offer their tributary ftreams from either fide, we found fix families, confifting of about thirty-five perfons, who gave us an ample quantity of excellent fifh, which were, however, confined to white fifh, the poiffon inconnu, and another of a round form and greenifh colour, which was about fourteen inches in length. We gratified them with a few prefents, and continued our voyage. The men, however, followed us in fifteen canoes.

This narrow channel is three miles long, and its courfe North-North-Eaft. We then fteered North three miles, and landed at an encampment of three or more families, containing twenty-two perfons, which was fituated on the bank of a river, of a confiderable appearance, which came from the Eaftward. We obtained hares and partridges from thefe people, and prefented in return fuch articles as greatly delighted them. They very much regretted that they had no goods or merchandize to exchange with us, as they had left them at a lake, from whence the river

issued,

issued, and in whose vicinity some of their people were employed in setting snares for rein deer. They engaged to go for their articles of trade, and would wait our return, which we assured them would be within two months. There was a youth among them in the capacity of a slave, whom our Indians understood much better than any of the natives of this country, whom they had yet seen: he was invited to accompany us, but took the first opportunity to conceal himself, and we saw him no more.

We now steered West five miles, when we again landed, and found two families, containing seven people, but had reason to believe that there were others hidden in the woods. We received from them two dozen of hares, and they were about to boil two more, which they also gave us. We were not ungrateful for their kindness, and left them. Our course was now North-West four miles, and at nine we landed and pitched our tents, when one of our people killed a grey crane. Our conductor renewed his complaints, not, as he assured us, from any apprehension of our ill-treatment, but of the Esquimaux, whom he represented as a very wicked and malignant people; who would put us all to death. ·He added, also, that it was but two summers since a large party of them came up this river, and killed many of his relations. Two Indians followed us from the last lodges.

At half past two in the morning we embarked, and steered a Westerly course, and soon after put ashore at two lodges of nine Indians. We made them a few trifling presents, but without disembarking, and had proceeded but a small distance from thence, when we observed several

smokes

fmokes beneath an hill, on the North fhore, and on our approach we perceived the natives climbing the afcent to gain the woods. The Indians, however, in the two fmall canoes which were ahead of us, having affured them of our friendly intentions, they returned to their fires, and we difembarked. Several of them were clad in hare-fkins, but in every other circumftance they refembled thofe whom we had already feen. We were, however, informed that they were of a different tribe, called the Hare Indians, as hares and fifh are their principal fupport, from the fcarcity of rein-deer and beaver, which are the only animals of the larger kind that frequent this part of the country. They were twenty-five in number; and among them was a woman who was afflicted with an abcefs in the belly, and reduced, in confequence, to a mere fkeleton: at the fame time feveral old women were finging and howling around her; but whether thefe noifes were to operate as a charm for her cure, or merely to amufe and confole her, I do not pretend to determine. A fmall quantity of our ufual prefents were received by them with the greateft fatisfaction.

Here we made an exchange of our guide, who had become fo troublefome that we were obliged to watch him night and day, except when he was upon the water. The man, however, who had agreed to go in his place foon repented of his engagement, and endeavoured to perfuade us that fome of his relations further down the river, would readily accompany us, and were much better acquainted with the river than himfelf. But, as he had informed us ten minutes before that we fhould fee no more of his tribe, we paid very little attention to his remonftrances, and compelled him to embark.

In

In about three hours a man overtook us in a fmall canoe, and we fufpected that his object was to facilitate, in fome way or other, the efcape of our conductor. About twelve we alfo obferved an Indian walking along the North-Eaft fhore, when the fmall canoes paddled towards him. We accordingly followed, and found three men, three women, and two children, who had been on an hunting expedition. They had fome flefh of the rein-deer, which they offered to us, but it was fo rotten, as well as offenfive to the fmell, that we excufed our-felves from accepting it. They had alfo their wonderful ftories of danger and terror, as well as their countrymen, whom we had already feen; and we were now informed, that behind the oppofite ifland there was a Manitoe or fpirit, in the river, which fwallowed every perfon that approached it. As it would have employed half a day to have indulged our curiofity in proceeding to examine this phænomenon, we did not deviate from our courfe, but left thefe people with the ufual prefents, and proceeded on our voyage. Our courfe and diftance this day were Weft twenty-eight miles, Weft-North-Weft twenty-three miles, Weft-South-Weft fix miles, Weft by North five miles, South-Weft four miles, and encamped at eight o'clock. A fog prevailed the greater part of the day, with frequent fhowers of fmall rain.

CHAP.

CHAPTER IV.

The new guide makes his escape. Compel another to supply his place. Land at an encampment of another tribe of Indians. Account of their manners, dreſs, weapons, &c. Traffic with them. Deſcription of a beautiful fiſh. Engage another guide. His curious behaviour. Kill a fox and ground-hog. Land at an encampment of a tribe called the Deguthee Denees, or Quarellers. Saw flax growing wild. The varying character of the river and its banks. Diſtant mountains. Perplexity from the numerous channels of the river. Determined to proceed. Land where there had been an encampment of the Eſquimaux. Saw large flocks of wild fowl. View of the ſun at midnight. Deſcription of a place lately deſerted by the Indians. Houſes of the natives deſcribed. Frequent ſhowers. Saw a black fox. The diſcontents of our hunters renewed, and pacified. Face of the country. Land at a ſpot lately inhabited. Peculiar circumſtances of it. Arrive at the entrance of the lake Proceed to an iſland. Some account of it.

1789.
July.
Thurſday 9.

THUNDER and rain prevailed during the night, and, in the courſe of it, our guide deſerted; we therefore compelled another of theſe people, very much againſt his will, to ſupply the place of his fugitive countryman. We alſo took away the paddles of one of them who

remained

remained behind, that he might not follow us on any fcheme of promoting the efcape of his companion, who was not eafily pacified. At
length, however, we fucceeded in the act of conciliation, and at half
paft three quitted our ftation. In a fhort time we faw a fmoke on the
Eaft fhore, and directed our courfe towards it. Our new guide began
immediately to call to the people that belonged to it in a particular
manner, which we did not comprehend. He informed us that they
were not of his tribe, but were a very wicked, malignant people, who
would beat us cruelly, pull our hair with great violence from our heads,
and mal-treat us in various other ways.

The men waited our arrival, but the women and children took to the
woods. There were but four of thefe people, and previous to our landing, they all harangued us at the fame moment, and apparently with
violent anger and refentment. Our hunters did not underftand them,
but no fooner had our guide addreffed them, than they were appeafed.
I prefented them with beads, awls, &c. and when the women and children returned from the woods, they were gratified with fimilar articles.
There were fifteen of them; and of a more pleafing appearance than
any which we had hitherto feen, as they were healthy, full of flefh,
and clean in their perfons. Their language was fomewhat different,
but I believe chiefly in the accent, for they and our guide converfed
intelligibly with each other; and the Englifh chief clearly comprehended
one of them, though he was not himfelf underftood.

Their arms and utenfils differ but little from thofe which have been
defcribed in a former chapter. The only iron they have is in fmall pieces,
which

which ferve them for knives. They obtain this metal from the Efqui-maux Indians. Their arrows are made of very light wood, and are winged only with two feathers; their bows differed from any which we had feen, and we underftood that they were furnifhed by the Efquimaux, who are their neighbours: they confift of two pieces, with a very ftrong cord of finews along the back, which is tied in feveral places, to preferve its fhape; when this cord becomes wet, it requires a ftrong bow-ftring, and a powerful arm to draw it. The veffel in which they prepare their food, is made of a thin frame of wood, and of an oblong fhape; the bottom is fixed in a curve, in the fame manner as a cafk. Their fhirts are not cut fquare at the bottom, but taper to a point, from the belt downwards as low as the knee, both before and behind, with a border, embellifhed with a fhort fringe. They ufe alfo another fringe, fimilar to that which has been already defcribed, with the addition of the ftone of a grey farinaceous berry, of the fize and fhape of a large barley-corn: it is of a brown colour, and fluted, and being bored is run on each ftring of the fringe; with this they decorate their fhirts, by fewing it in a femicircle on the breaft and back, and croffing over both fhoulders; the fleeves are wide and fhort, but the mittens fupply their deficiency, as they are long enough to reach over a part of the fleeve, and are commodioufly fufpended by a cord from the neck. If their leggins were made with waiftbands, they might with great propriety be denominated trowfers: they faften them with a cord round the middle, fo that they appear to have a fenfe of decency which their neighbours cannot boaft. Their fhoes are fewed to their leggins, and decorated on every feam. One of the men was clad in a fhirt made of the fkins of the mufk-rat. The drefs of the women is the fame as that of the men, except

in

in their fhirts, which are longer, and without the finifhing of a fringe on their breaft. Their peculiar mode of tying the hair is as follows:—that which grows on the temples, or the fore part of the fkull, is formed into two queues, hanging down before the ears; that of the fcalp or crown is fafhioned in the fame manner to the back of the neck, and is then tied with the reft of the hair, at fome diftance from the head. A thin cord is employed for thefe purpofes, and very neatly worked with hair, artificially coloured. The women, and, indeed, fome of the men, let their hair hang loofe on their fhoulders, whether it be long or fhort.

We purchafed a couple of very large moofe fkins from them, which were very well dreffed; indeed we did not fuppofe that there were any of thofe animals in the country; and it appears from the accounts of the natives themfelves, that they are very fcarce. As for the beaver, the exiftence of fuch a creature does not feem to be known by them. Our people bought fhirts of them, and many curious articles, &c. They prefented us with a moft delicious fifh, which was lefs than an herring, and very beautifully fpotted with black and yellow: its dorfal fin reached from the head to the tail; in its expanded ftate takes a triangular form, and is variegated with the colours that enliven the fcales: the head is very fmall, and the mouth is armed with fharp-pointed teeth.

We prevailed on the native, whofe language was moft intelligible, to accompany us. He informed us that we fhould fleep ten nights more before we arrived at the fea; that feveral of his relations refided in the immediate vicinity of this part of the river, and that in three nights we

fhould

fhould meet with the Efquimaux, with whom they had formerly made war, but were now in a ftate of peace and amity. He mentioned the laft Indians whom we had feen in terms of great derifion; defcribing them as being no better than old women, and as abominable liars; which coincided with the notion we already entertained of them.

As we pufhed off, fome of my men difcharged their fowling pieces, that were only loaded with powder, at the report of which the Indians were very much alarmed, as they had not before heard the dif-charge of fire arms. This circumftance had fuch an effect upon our guide, that we had reafon to apprehend he would not fulfil his promife. When, however, he was informed that the noife which he had heard was a fignal of friendfhip, he was perfuaded to embark in his own fmall canoe, though he had been offered a feat in ours.

Two of his companions, whom he reprefented as his brothers, followed us in their canoes; and they amufed us not only with their native fongs, but with others, in imitation of the Efquimaux; and our new guide was fo enlivened by them, that the antics he performed, in keeping time to the finging, alarmed us with continual apprehenfion that his boat muft upfet: but he was not long content with his confined fituation, and paddling up along-fide our canoe, requefted us to receive him in it, though but a fhort time before he had refolutely refufed to accept our invitation. No fooner had he entered our canoe, than he began to perform an Efquimaux dance, to our no fmall alarm. He was, how-ever, foon prevailed upon to be more tranquil; when he began to difplay various indecencies, according to the cuftoms of the Efquimaux, of which

which he boafted an intimate acquaintance. On our putting to fhore, in order to leave his canoe, he informed us, that on the oppofite hill the Efquimaux, three winters before, killed his grandfather. We faw a fox, and a ground hog on the hill, the latter of which the brother of our guide fhot with his bow and arrow.

About four in the afternoon we perceived a fmoke on the Weft fhore, when we traverfed and landed. The natives made a moft terrible uproar, talking with great vociferation, and running about as if they were deprived of their fenfes, while the greater part of the women, with the children, fled away. Perceiving the diforder which our appearance occafioned among thefe people, we had waited fome time before we quitted the canoe; and I have no doubt, if we had been without people to introduce us, that they would have attempted fome violence againft us; for when the Indians fend away their women and children, it is always with an hoftile defign. At length we pacified them with the ufual prefents, but they preferred beads to any of the articles that I offered them; particularly fuch as were of a blue colour; and one of them even requefted to exchange a knife which I had given him for a fmall quantity of thofe ornamental baubles. I purchafed of them two fhirts for my hunters; and at the fame time they prefented me with fome arrows, and dried fifh. This party confifted of five families, to the amount, as I fuppofe, of forty men, women, and children; but I did not fee them all, as feveral were afraid to venture from their hiding-places. They are called *Deguthee Dinees*, or the *Quarrellers*.

Our guide, like his predeceffors, now manifefted his wifh to leave us,

and

and entertained fimilar apprehenfions that we fhould not return by this paffage. He had his alarms alfo refpecting the Efquimaux, who might kill us, and take away the women. Our Indians, however, affured him that we had no fears of any kind, and that he need not be alarmed for himfelf. They alfo convinced him that we fhould return by the way we were going, fo that he confented to re-embark without giving us any further trouble; and eight fmall canoes followed us. Our courfes this day were South-Weft by Weft fix miles, South-Weft by South thirty miles, South-Weft three miles, Weft by South twelve miles, Weft by North two miles, and we encamped at eight in the evening on the Eaftern bank of the river.

The Indians whom I found here, informed me, that from the place where I this morning met the firft of their tribe, the diftance overland, on the Eaft fide, to the fea, was not long; and that from hence, by proceeding to the Weftward, it was ftill fhorter. They alfo reprefented the land on both fides as projecting to a point. Thefe people do not appear to harbour any thievifh difpofitions; at leaft we did not perceive that they took, or wanted to take, any thing from us by ftealth or artifice. They enjoyed the amufements of dancing and jumping in common with thofe we had already feen; and, indeed, thefe exercifes feem to be their favourite diverfions. About mid-day the weather was fultry, but in the afternoon it became cold. There was a large quantity of wild flax, the growth of the laft year, laying on the ground, and the new plants were fprouting up through it. This circumftance I did not obferve in any other part.

At

At four in the morning we embarked, at a fmall diftance from the place of our encampment; the river, which here becomes narrower, flows between high rocks; and a meandring courfe took us North-Weft four miles. At this fpot the banks became low; indeed, from the firft rapid, the country does not wear a mountainous appearance; but the banks of the river are generally lofty, in fome places perfectly naked, and in others well covered with fmall trees, fuch as the fir and the birch. We continued our laft courfe for two miles, with mountains before us, whofe tops were covered with fnow.

The land is low on both fides of the river, except thefe mountains, whofe bafe is diftant about ten miles: here the river widens, and runs through various channels, formed by iflands, fome of which are without a tree, and little more than banks of mud and fand; while others are covered with a kind of fpruce fir, and trees of a larger fize than we had feen for the laft ten days. Their banks, which are about fix feet above the furface of the water, difplay a face of folid ice, intermixed with veins of black earth and as the heat of the fun melts the ice, the trees frequently fall into the river.

So various were the channels of the river at this time, that we were at a lofs which to take. Our guide preferred the Eafternmoft, on account of the Efquimaux, but I determined to take the middle channel, as it appeared to be a larger body of water, and running North and South: befides, as there was a greater chance of feeing them I concluded, that we could always go to the Eaftward, whenever we might prefer it. Our courfe

was

was now Weſt by North ſix miles, North-Weſt by Weſt, the ſnowy mountains being Weſt by South from us, and ſtretching to the Northward as
far as we could ſee.   According to the information of the Indians, they
are part of the chain of mountains which we approached on the third
of this month.   I obtained an obſervation this day that gave me 67. 47.
North latitude, which was farther North than I expeſted, according to the
courſe I kept; but the difference was owing to the variation of the compaſs, which was more Eaſterly than I imagined.   From hence it was
evident that theſe waters emptied themſelves into the Hyperborean
Sea; and though it was probable that, from the want of proviſion, we
could not return to Athabaſca in the courſe of the ſeaſon, I nevertheleſs, determined to penetrate to the diſcharge of them.

My new conduſtor being very much diſcouraged and quite tired of
his ſituation, uſed his influence to prevent our proceeding.   He had
never been, he ſaid, at the *Benahulla Toe*, or White Man's Lake; and
that when he went to the Eſquimaux Lake, which is at no great diſtance,
he paſſed over land from the place where we found him, and to that part
where the Eſquimaux paſs the ſummer.   In ſhort, my hunters alſo became ſo diſheartened from theſe accounts, and other circumſtances, that
I was confident they would have left me, if it had been in their power.
I, however, ſatisfied them, in ſome degree, by the aſſurance, that I would
proceed onwards but ſeven days more, and if I did not then get to the
ſea, I would return.   Indeed, the low ſtate of our proviſions, without
any other conſideration, formed a very ſufficient ſecurity for the main-

tenance

tenance of my engagement. Our laſt courſe was thirty-two miles, with a ſtronger current than could be expected in ſuch a low country.

We now proceeded North-North-Weſt four miles, North-Weſt three miles, North-Eaſt two miles, North-Weſt by Weſt three miles, and North-Eaſt two miles. At half paſt eight in the evening we landed and pitched our tents, near to where there had been three encampments of the Eſquimaux, ſince the breaking up of the ice. The natives, who followed us yeſterday, left us at our ſtation this morning. In the courſe of the day we ſaw large flocks of wild fowl.

I ſat up all night to obſerve the ſun. At half paſt twelve I called up one of the men to view a ſpectacle which he had never before ſeen; when, on ſeeing the ſun ſo high, he thought it was a ſignal to embark, and began to call the reſt of his companions, who would ſcarcely be perſuaded by me, that the ſun had not deſcended nearer to the horizon, and that it was now but a ſhort time paſt midnight.

We repoſed, however, till three quarters after three, when we entered the canoe, and ſteered about North-Weſt, the river taking a very ſerpentine courſe. About ſeven we ſaw a ridge of high land: at twelve we landed at a ſpot where we obſerved that ſome of the natives had lately been. I counted thirty places where there had been fires; and ſome of the men who went further, ſaw as many more. They muſt have been here for a conſiderable time, though it does not appear that they had erected any huts. A great number of poles, however, were ſeen fixed in the river, to which they had attached their nets, and there ſeemed

to

to be an excellent fiſhery. One of the fiſh, of the many which we ſaw leap out of the water, fell into our canoe; it was about ten inches long, and of a round ſhape. About the places where they had made their fires were ſcattered pieces of whalebone, and thick burned leather, with parts of the frames of three canoes; we could alſo obſerve where they had ſpilled train oil; and there was the ſingular appearance of a ſpruce fir, ſtripped of its branches to the top like an Engliſh may-pole. The weather was cloudy, and the air cold and unpleaſant. From this place for about five miles, the river widens, it then flows in a variety of narrow, meandering channels, amongſt low iſlands, enlivened with no trees, but a few dwarf willows.

At four, we landed, where there were three houſes, or rather huts, belonging to the natives. The ground-plot is of an oval form, about fifteen feet long, ten feet wide in the middle, and eight feet at either end: the whole of it is dug about twelve inches below the ſurface of the ground, and one half of it is covered over with willow branches; which probably ſerves as a bed for the whole family. A ſpace, in the middle of the other part, of about four feet wide, is deepened twelve inches more, and is the only ſpot in the houſe where a grown perſon can ſtand upright. One ſide of it is covered, as has been already deſcribed, and the other is the hearth or fire-place, of which, however, they do not make much uſe. Though it was cloſe to the wall, the latter did not appear to be burned. The door or entrance is in the middle of one end of the houſe, and is about two feet and an half high and two feet wide, and has a covered way or porch five feet in length; ſo that it is abſolutely neceſſary to creep on all fours

in

in order to get into, or out of, this curious habitation. There is an hole of about eighteen inches fquare on the top of it, which ferves the three-fold purpofe of a window, an occafional door, and a chimney. The under-ground part of the floor is lined with fplit wood. Six or eight ftumps of fmall trees driven into the earth, with the root upwards, on which are laid fome crofs pieces of timber, fupport the roof of the building, which is an oblong fquare of ten feet by fix. The whole is made of drift-wood covered with branches and dry grafs; over which is laid a foot deep of earth. On each fide of thefe houfes are a few fquare holes in the ground of about two feet in depth, which are covered with fplit wood and earth, except in the middle. Thefe appeared to be contrived for the prefervation of the winter ftock of provifions. In and about the houfes we found fledge runners and bones, pieces of whalebone, and poplar bark cut in circles, which are ufed as corks to buoy the nets, and are fixed to them by pieces of whalebone. Before each hut a great number of ftumps of trees were fixed in the ground, upon which it appeared that they hung their fifh to dry.

We now continued our voyage, and encamped at eight o'clock. I calculated our courfe at about North-Weft, and, allowing for the wind-ings, that we had made fifty-four miles. We expected, throughout the day, to meet with fome of the natives. On feveral of the iflands we per-ceived the print of their feet in the fand, as if they had been there but a few days before, to procure wild fowl. There were frequent fhowers of rain in the afternoon, and the weather was raw and difagreeable. We faw a black fox; but trees were now become very rare objects, except a few dwarf willows, of not more than three feet in height.

The

The difcontents of our hunters were now renewed by the accounts which our guide had been giving of that part of our voyage that was approaching. According to his information, we were to fee a larger lake on the morrow. Neither he nor his relations, he faid, knew any thing about it, except that part which is oppofite to, and not far from, their country. The Efquimaux alone, he added, inhabit its fhores, and kill a large fifh that is found in it, which is a principal part of their food; this, we prefumed, muft be the whale. He alfo mentioned white bears and another large animal which was feen in thofe parts, but our hunters could not underftand the defcription which he gave of it. He alfo re-prefented their canoes as being of a large conftruction, which would com-modioufly contain four or five families. However, to reconcile the Englifh chief to the neceffary continuance in my fervice, I prefented him with one of my capots or travelling coats; at the fame time, to fatisfy the guide, and keep him, if poffible, in good humour, I gave him a fkin of the moofe-deer, which, in his opinion, was a valuable prefent.

Sunday 12.   It rained with violence throughout the night, and till two in the morn-ing; the weather continuing very cold. We proceeded on the fame meandering courfe as yefterday, the wind North-North-Weft, and the country fo naked that fcarce a fhrub was to be feen. At ten in the morn-ing, we landed where there were four huts, exactly the fame as thofe which have been fo lately defcribed. The adjacent land is high and covered with fhort grafs and flowers, though the earth was not thawed above four inches from the furface; beneath which was a folid body of ice. This beautiful appearance, however, was ftrangely contrafted with the ice and fnow that are feen in the vallies. The foil,
                                                                    where

where there is any, is a yellow clay mixed with ftones. Thefe huts appear to have been inhabited during the laft winter; and we had reafon to think, that fome of the natives had been lately there, as the beach was covered with the track of their feet. Many of the runners and bars of their fledges were laid together, near the houfes, in a manner that feemed to denote the return of the proprietors. There were alfo pieces of netting made of finews, and fome bark of the willow. The thread of the former was plaited, and no ordinary portion of time muft have been employed in manufacturing fo great a length of cord. A fquare ftone-kettle, with a flat bottom, alfo occupied our attention, which was capable of containing two gallons; and we were puzzled as to the means thefe people muft have employed to have chifelled it out of a folid rock into its prefent form. To thefe articles may be added, fmall pieces of flint fixed into handles of wood, which, probably, ferve as knives; feveral wooden difhes; the ftern and part of a large canoe; pieces of very thick leather, which we conjectured to be the covering of a canoe; feveral bones of large fifh, and two heads; but we could not determine the animal to which they belonged, though we conjectured that it muft be the fea-horfe.

When we had fatisfied our curiofity we re-embarked, but we were at a lofs what courfe to fteer, as our guide feemed to be as ignorant of this country as ourfelves. Though the current was very ftrong, we appeared to have come to the entrance of the lake. The ftream fet to the Weft, and we went with it to an high point, at the diftance of about eight miles, which we conjectured to be an ifland; but, on approaching it, we perceived it to be connected with the fhore by a low neck of land. I now

took

took an obfervation which gave 69. 1. North latitude.   From the point
that has been juft mentioned, we continued the fame courfe for the
Wefternmoft point of an high ifland, and the Wefternmoft land in fight,
at the diftance of fifteen miles.

The lake was quite open to us to the Weftward, and out of the channel
of the river there was not more than four feet water, and in fome places
the depth did not exceed one foot.   From the fhallownefs of the
water it was impoffible to coaft to the Weftward.   At five o'clock
we arrived at the ifland, and during the laft fifteen miles, five feet was
the deepeft water.   The lake now appeared to be covered with ice, for
about two leagues diftance, and no land ahead, fo that we were prevented
from proceeding in this direction by the ice, and the fhallownefs of the
water along the fhore.

We landed at the boundary of our voyage in this direction, and as
foon as the tents were pitched I ordered the nets to be fet, when I proceeded with the Englifh chief to the higheft part of the ifland, from
which we difcovered the folid ice, extending from the South-Weft by
compafs to the Eaftward.   As far as the eye could reach to the South-
Weftward, we could dimly perceive a chain of mountains, ftretching
further to the North than the edge of the ice, at the diftance of upwards
of twenty leagues.   To the Eaftward we faw many iflands, and in our
progrefs we met with a confiderable number of white partridges, now
become brown.   There were alfo flocks of very beautiful plovers,
and I found the neft of one of them with four eggs.   White owls,
likewife, were among the inhabitants of the place: but the dead, as
well

well as the living, demanded our attention, for we came to the grave of one of the natives, by which lay a bow, a paddle, and a fpear. The Indians informed me that they landed on a fmall ifland, about four leagues from hence, where they had feen the tracks of two men, that were quite frefh; they had alfo found a fecret ftore of train oil, and feveral bones of white bears were fcattered about the place where it was hid. The wind was now fo high that it was impracticable for us to vifit the nets.

My people could not, at this time, refrain from expreffions of real concern, that they were obliged to return without reaching the fea: indeed the hope of attaining this object encouraged them to bear, without repining, the hardfhips of our unremitting voyage. For fome time paft their fpirits were animated by the expectation that another day would bring them to the *Mer d'ouest*: and even in our prefent fituation they declared their readinefs to follow me wherever I fhould be pleafed to lead them. We faw feveral large white gulls, and other birds, whofe back, and upper feathers of the wing, are brown; and whofe belly, and under feathers of the wing are white.

CHAP.

CHAPTER V.

The baggage removed from the rising of the water. One of the nets driven away by the wind and current. Whales are seen. Go in pursuit of them, but prevented from continuing it by the fog. Proceed to take a view of the ice. Canoe in danger from the swell. Examine the islands. Describe one of them. Erect a post to perpetuate our visit there. The rising of the water appears to be the tide. Successful fishing. Uncertain weather. Sail among the islands. Proceed to a river. Temperature of the air improves. Land on a small island, which is a place of sepulture. Description of it. See a great number of wild fowl. Fine view of the river from the high land. The hunters kill rein-deer. Cranberries, &c. found in great plenty. The appearance and state of the country. Our guide deserts. Large flight of geese: kill many of them. Violent rain. Return up the river. Leave the channels for the main stream. Obliged to tow the canoe. Land among the natives. Circumstances concerning them. Their account of the Esquimaux Indians. Accompany the natives to their huts. Account of our provisions.

1789.
July.
Monday 13.

WE had no sooner retired to rest last night, if I may use that expression, in a country where the sun never sinks beneath the horizon, than some of the people were obliged to rise and remove the baggage, on account

of

of the rifing of the water. At eight in the morning the weather was
fine and calm, which afforded an opportunity to examine the nets, one of which had been driven from its pofition by the wind and current. We caught feven poiffons inconnus, which were unpalatable; a white fifh, that proved delicious; and another about the fize of an herring, which none of us had ever feen before, except the Englifh chief, who recognized it as being of a kind that abounds in Hudfon's Bay. About noon the wind blew hard from the Weftward, when I took an obfervation, which gave 69. 14. North latitude, and the meridian variation of the compafs was thirty-fix degrees Eaftward*.

This afternoon I re-afcended the hill, but could not difcover that the ice had been put in motion by the force of the wind. At the fame time I could juft diftinguifh two fmall iflands in the ice, to the North-Weft by compafs. I now thought it neceffary to give a new net to my men to mount, in order to obtain as much provifion as poffible from the water, our ftores being reduced to about five hundred weight, which, without any other fupply, would not have fufficed for fifteen people above twelve days. One of the young Indians, however, was fo fortunate as to find the net that had been miffing, and which contained three of the poiffons inconnus.

It blew very hard from the North-Weft fince the preceding evening. Tuefday 14. Having fat up till three in the morning, I flept longer than ufual; but about eight one of my men faw a great many animals in the water, which

---

* The longitude has fince been difcovered by the dead reckoning to be 135. Weft.

he

he at firſt ſuppoſed to be pieces of ice. About nine, however, I was awakened to reſolve the doubts which had taken place reſpecting this extraordinary appearance. I immediately perceived that they were whales; and having ordered the canoe to be prepared, we embarked in purſuit of them. It was, indeed, a very wild and unreflecting enterpriſe, and it was a very fortunate circumſtance that we failed in our attempt to overtake them, as a ſtroke from the tail of one of theſe enormous fiſh would have daſhed the canoe to pieces. We may, perhaps, have been indebted to the foggy weather for our ſafety, as it prevented us from continuing our purſuit. Our guide informed us that they are the ſame kind of fiſh which are the principal food of the Eſquimaux, and they were frequently ſeen as large as our canoe. The part of them which appeared above the water was altogether white, and they were much larger than the largeſt porpoiſe.

About twelve the fog diſperſed, and being curious to take a view of the ice, I gave orders for the canoe to be got in readineſs. We accordingly embarked, and the Indians followed us. We had not, however, been an hour on the water, when the wind roſe on a ſudden from the North-Eaſt, and obliged us to tack about, and the return of the fog prevented us from aſcertaining our diſtance from the ice; indeed, from this circumſtance, the iſland which we had ſo lately left was but dimly ſeen. Though the wind was cloſe, we ventured to hoiſt the ſail, and from the violence of the ſwell it was by great exertions that two men could bale out the water from our canoe. We were in a ſtate of actual danger, and felt every correſponding emotion of pleaſure when we reached the land. The Indians had fortunately got more to windward, fo that the fwell in fome meafure drove them on fhore, though their canoes were nearly filled with water; and had they been laden, we fhould have feen them no more. As I did not propofe to fatisfy my curiofity at the rifk of fimilar dangers, we continued our courfe along the iflands, which fcreened us from the wind. I was now determined to take a more particular examination of the iflands, in the hope of meeting with parties of the natives, from whom I might be able to obtain fome interefting intelligence, though our conductor difcouraged my expectations by reprefenting them as very fhy and inacceffible people. At the fame time he informed me that we fhould probably find fome of them, if we navigated the channel which he had originally recommended us to enter.

At eight we encamped on the Eaftern end of the ifland, which I had named the Whale Ifland. It is about feven leagues in length, Eaft and Weft by compafs; but not more than half a mile in breadth. We faw feveral red foxes, one of which was killed. There were alfo five or fix very old huts on the point where we had taken our ftation. The nets were now fet, and one of them in five fathom water, the current fetting North-Eaft by compafs. This morning I ordered a poft to be erected clofe to our tents, on which I engraved the latitude of the place, my own name, the number of perfons which I had with me, and the time we remained there.

Being awakened by fome cafual circumftance, at four this morning, I was furprifed on perceiving that the water had flowed under our baggage. As the wind had not changed, and did not blow with greater violence than

when

when we went to reſt, we were all of opinion that this circumſtance proceeded from the tide. We had, indeed, obſerved at the other end of the iſland that the water roſe and fell; but we then imagined that it muſt have been occaſioned by the wind. The water continued to riſe till about ſix, but I could not aſcertain the time with the re-quiſite preciſion, as the wind then began to blow with great vio-lence; I therefore determined, at all events, to remain here till the next morning, though, as it happened, the ſtate of the wind was ſuch as to render my ſtay here an act of neceſſity. Our nets were not very ſuc-ceſsful, as they preſented us with only eight fiſh. From an obſervation which I obtained at noon, we were in 69. 7. North latitude. As the evening approached, the wind increaſed, and the weather became cold. Two ſwans were the only proviſion which the hunters procured for us.

Thurſday 16.   The rain did not ceaſe till ſeven this morning, the weather being at intervals very cold and unpleaſant. Such was its inconſtancy, that I could not make an accurate obſervation; but the tide appeared to riſe ſixteen or eighteen inches.

We now embarked, and ſteered under ſail among the iſlands, where I hoped to meet with ſome of the natives, but my expectation was not gratified. Our guide imagined that they were gone to their diſtant haunts, where they fiſh for whales and hunt the rein-deer, that are oppoſite to his country. His relations, he ſaid, ſee them every year, but he did not encourage us to expect that we ſhould find any of them, unleſs it were at a ſmall river that falls into the great one, from the Eaſtward, at a conſider-able diſtance from our immediate ſituation. We accordingly made for the

river,

river, and ſtemmed the current. At two in the afternoon the water was quite ſhallow in every part of our courſe, and we could always find the bottom with the paddle. At ſeven we landed, encamped, and ſet the nets. Here the Indians killed two geeſe, two cranes, and a white owl. Since we entered the river, we experienced a very agreeable change in the temperature of the air; but this pleaſant circumſtance was not without its inconvenience, as it ſubjected us to the perſecution of the muſquitoes.

On taking up the nets, they were found to contain but ſix fiſh. We embarked at four in the morning, and paſſed four encampments, which appeared to have been very lately inhabited. We then landed upon a ſmall round iſland, cloſe to the Eaſtern ſhore, which poſſeſſed ſomewhat of a ſacred character, as the top of it ſeemed to be a place of ſepulture, from the numerous graves which we obſerved there. We found the frame of a ſmall canoe, with various diſhes, troughs, and other utenſils, which had been the living property of thoſe who could now uſe them no more, and form the ordinary accompaniments of their laſt abodes. As no part of the ſkins that muſt have covered the canoe was remaining, we concluded that it had been eaten by wild animals that inhabit, or occaſionally frequent, the iſland. The frame of the canoe, which was entire, was put together with whalebone: it was ſewed in ſome parts, and tied in others. The ſledges were from four to eight feet long; the length of the bars was upwards of two feet; the runners were two inches thick and nine inches deep; the prow was two feet and an half high, and formed of two pieces, ſewed with whalebone; to three other thin ſpars of wood, which were of the ſame height, and fixed in the runners by means

of

of mortifes, were fewed two thin broad bars lengthways, at a fmall dif-tance from each other; thefe frames were fixed together with three or four crofs bars, tied faft upon the runners; and on the lower edge of the latter, fmall pieces of horn were faftened by wooden pegs, that they might flide with greater facility. They are drawn by fhafts, which I imagine are applied to any particular fledge as they are wanted, as I faw no more than one pair of them.

About half paft one we came oppofite to the firft fpruce-tree that we had feen for fome time: there are but very few of them on the main land, and they are very fmall; thofe are larger which are found on the iflands, where they grow in patches, and clofe together. It is, indeed, very extraordinary that there fhould be any wood whatever in a country where the ground never thaws above five inches from the furface. We landed at feven in the evening. The weather was now very pleafant, and in the courfe of the day we faw great numbers of wild fowl, with their young ones, but they were fo fhy that we could not approach them. The Indians were not very fuccefsful in their foraging party, as they killed only two grey cranes, and a grey goofe. Two of them were employed on the high land to the Eaftward, through the greater part of the day, in fearch of rein-deer, but they could difcover nothing more than a few tracks of that animal. I alfo afcended the high land, from whence I had a delightful view of the river, divided into innumerable ftreams, mean-dering through iflands, fome of which were covered with wood, and others with grafs. The mountains, that formed the oppofite horizon, were at the diftance of forty miles. The inland view was neither fo extenfive nor agreeable, being terminated by a near range of bleak,

barren

barren hills, between which are fmall lakes or ponds, while the furrounding country is covered with tufts of mofs, without the fhade of a
fingle tree. Along the hills is a kind of fence, made with branches,
where the natives had fet fnares to catch white partridges.

The nets did not produce a fingle fifh, and at three o'clock in the morning we took our departure. The weather was fine and clear, and we paffed
feveral encampments. As the prints of human feet were very frefh in
the fand, it could not have been long fince the natives had vifited the
fpot. We now proceeded in the hope of meeting with fome of them at
the river, whither our guide was conducting us with that expectation.
We obferved a great number of trees, in different places, whofe branches
had been lopped off to the tops. They denote the immediate abode of
the natives, and probably ferve for fignals to direct each other to their refpective winter quarters. Our hunters, in the courfe of the day killed two
rein-deer, which were the only large animals that we had feen fince we had
been in this river, and proved a very feafonable fupply, as our Pemmican
had become mouldy for fome time paft; though in that fituation we
were under the neceffity of eating it.

In the vallies and low lands near the river, cranberries are found
in great abundance, particularly in favourable afpects. It is a fingular
circumftance, that the fruit of two fucceeding years may be gathered at
the fame time, from the fame fhrub. Here was alfo another berry, of
a very pale yellow colour, that refembles a rafpberry, and is of a very
agreeable flavour. There is a great variety of other plants and herbs,
whofe names and properties are unknown to me.

The

The weather became cold towards the afternoon, with the appearance of rain, and we landed for the night at feven in the evening   The Indians killed eight geefe.   During the greater part of the day I walked with the Englifh chief, and found it very difagreeable and fatiguing.   Though the country is fo elevated, it was one continual morafs, except on the fummits of fome barren hills.   As I carried my hanger in my hand, I frequently examined if any part of the ground was in a ftate of thaw, but could never force the blade into it, beyond the depth of fix or eight inches.   The face of the high land, towards the river, is in fome places rocky, and in others a mixture of fand and ftone, veined with a kind of red earth, with which the natives bedaub themfelves.

Sunday 19.   It rained, and blew hard from the North, till eight in the morning, when we difcovered that our conductor had efcaped.   I was, indeed, furprifed at his honefty, as he left the moofe-fkin which I had given him for a covering, and went off in his fhirt, though the weather was very cold.   I inquired of the Indians if they had given him any caufe of offence, or had obferved any recent difpofition in him to defert us, but they affured me that they had not in any inftance difpleafed him: at the fame time they recollected that he had expreffed his apprehenfions of being taken away as a flave; and his alarms were probably increafed on the preceding day, when he faw them kill the two rein-deer with fo much readinefs.   In the afternoon the weather became fine and clear, when we faw large flights of geefe with their young ones, and the hunters killed twenty-two of them.   As they had at this time caft their feathers, they could not fly.   They were of a fmall kind, and much inferior in fize to thofe that frequent the vicinity of Athabafca.   At eight, we took

our

our ſtation near an Indian encampment, and, as we had obſerved in
ſimilar ſituations, pieces of bone, rein-deer's horn, &c. were ſcattered about it. It alſo appeared, that the natives had been employed here in working wood into arms, utenſils, &c.

We embarked at three this morning, when the weather was cloudy, with ſmall rain and aft wind. About twelve the rain became ſo violent as to compel us to encamp at two in the afternoon. We ſaw great num_ bers of fowl, and killed among us fifteen geeſe and four ſwans. Had the weather been more favourable, we ſhould have added conſiderably to our booty. We now paſſed the river, where we expected to meet ſome of the natives, but diſcovered no ſigns of them. The ground cloſe to the river does not riſe to any conſiderable height, and the hills, which are at a ſmall diſtance, are covered with the ſpruce fir and ſmall birch trees, to their very ſummits.

We embarked at half paſt one this morning, when the weather was cold and unpleaſant, and the wind South-Weſt. At ten, we left the channels formed by the iſlands for the uninterrupted channel of the river, where we found the current ſo ſtrong, that it was abſolutely neceſſary to tow the canoe with a line. The land on both ſides was elevated, and almoſt perpendicular, and the ſhore beneath it, which is of no great breadth, was covered with a grey ſtone that falls from the precipice. We made much greater expedition with the line, than we could have done with the paddles. The men in the canoe relieved two of thoſe on ſhore every two hours, ſo that it was very hard and fatiguing duty, but it ſaved a great deal of that time which was ſo precious to us. At half

paſt

paſt eight, we landed at the ſame ſpot where we had already encamped on the ninth inſtant.

In about an hour after our arrival, we were joined by eleven of the natives, who were ſtationed further up the river, and there were ſome among them whom we had not ſeen during our former viſit to this place. The brother of our late guide, however, was of the party, and was eager in his inquiries after him; but our account did not prove ſatisfactory. They all gave evident tokens of their ſuſpicion, and each of them made a diſtinct harangue on the occaſion. Our Indians, indeed, did not underſtand their eloquence, though they conjectured it to be very unfavourable to our aſſertions. The brother, nevertheleſs, propoſed to barter his credulity for a ſmall quantity of beads, and promiſed to believe every thing I ſhould ſay, if I would gratify him with a few of thoſe baubles: but he did not ſucceed in his propoſition, and I contented myſelf with giving him the bow and arrows which our conductor had left with us.

My people were now neceſſarily engaged in putting the fire-arms in order, after the violent rain of the preceding day; an employment which very much attracted the curioſity, and appeared, in ſome degree to awaken the apprehenſions, of the natives. To their inquiries concerning the motives of our preparation, we anſwered by ſhewing a piece of meat and a gooſe, and informing them, that we were preparing our arms to procure ſimilar proviſions: at the ſame time we aſſured them, though it was our intention to kill any animals we might find, there was no intention to hurt or injure them. They, however, entreated us not to diſcharge our pieces in their preſence. I requeſted the Engliſh chief to aſk them ſome

queſtions,

queftions, which they either did not or would not underftand; fo that I failed in obtaining any information from them.

All my people went to reft; but I thought it prudent to fit up, in order to watch the motions of the natives. This circumftance was a fubject of their inquiry; and their curiofity was ftill more excited, when they faw me employed in writing. About twelve o'clock I perceived four of their women coming along the fhore; and they were no fooner feen by their friends, than they ran haftily to meet them, and perfuaded two of them, who, I fuppofe, were young, to return, while they brought the other two who were very old, to enjoy the warmth of our fire; but, after ftaying there for about half an hour, they alfo retreated. Thofe who remained, immediately kindled a fmall fire, and laid themfelves down to fleep round it, like fo many whelps, having neither fkins or garments of any kind to cover them, notwithftanding the cold that prevailed. My people having placed their kettle of meat on the fire, I was obliged to guard it from the natives, who made feveral attempts to poffefs themfelves of its contents; and this was the only inftance I had hitherto difcovered, of their being influenced by a pilfering difpofition. It might, perhaps, be a general opinion, that provifions were a common property. I now faw the fun fet for the firft time fince I had been here before. During the preceding night, the weather was fo cloudy, that I could not obferve its defcent to the horizon. The water had funk, at this place, upward of three feet fince we had paffed down the river.

We began our march at half paft three this morning, the men being
employed

employed to tow the canoe. I walked with the Indians to their huts, which were at a greater diftance than I had any reafon to expect, for it occupied three hours in hard walking to reach them. We paffed a narrow and deep river in our way, at the mouth of which the natives had fet their nets. They had hid their effects, and fent their young women into the woods, as we faw but very few of the former, and none of the latter. They had large huts built with drift wood on the declivity of the beach, and in the infide the earth was dug away, fo as to form a level floor. At each end was a ftout fork, whereon was laid a ftrong ridge-pole, which formed a fupport to the whole ftructure, and a covering of fpruce bark preferved it from the rain. Various fpars of different heights were fixed within the hut, and covered with fplit fifh that hung on them to dry; and fires were made in different parts to accelerate the operation. There were rails alfo on the outfide of the building, which were hung around with fifh, but in a frefher ftate than thofe within. The fpawn is alfo carefully preferved and dried in the fame manner. We obtained as many fifh from them as the canoe could conveniently contain, and fome ftrings of beads were the price paid for them, an article which they preferred to every other. Iron they held in little or no eftimation.

During the two hours that I remained here, I employed the Englifh chief in a continual ftate of inquiry concerning thefe people. The information that refulted from this conference was as follows.

This nation or tribe is very numerous, with whom the Efquimaux had been continually at variance, a people who take every advantage of attacking thofe who are not in a ftate to defend themfelves; and though

they

they had promifed friendfhip, had lately, and in the moft treacherous manner, butchered fome of their people. As a proof of this circum-ftance, the relations of the deceafed fhewed us, that they had cut off their hair on the occafion. They alfo declared their determination to withdraw all confidence in future from the Efquimaux, and to collect themfelves in a formidable body, that they might be enabled to revenge the death of their friends.

From their account, a ftrong party of Efquimaux occafionally afcends this river, in large canoes, in fearch of flint ftones, which they employ to point their fpears and arrows. They were now at their lake due Eaft from the fpot where we then were, which was at no great diftance over land, where they kill the rein-deer, and that they would foon begin to catch big fifh for the winter ftock. We could not, however, obtain any information refpecting the lake in the direction in which we were. To the Eaftward and Weftward where they faw it, the ice breaks up, but foon freezes again.

The Efquimaux informed them that they faw large canoes full of white men to the Weftward, eight or ten winters ago, from whom they obtained iron in exchange for leather. The lake where they met thefe canoes, is called by them *Belhoullay Toe*, or White Man's Lake. They alfo reprefented the Efquimaux as dreffing like themfelves. They wear their hair fhort, and have two holes perforated, one on each fide of the mouth, in a line with the under lip, in which they place long beads that they find in the lake. Their bows are fomewhat different from thofe ufed by the natives we had feen, and they employ flings from

whence

whence they throw ftones with fuch dexterity that they prove very formidable weapons in the day of battle.

We alfo learned in addition from the natives, that we fhould not fee any more of their relations, as they had all left the river to go in purfuit of rein-deer for their provifions, and that they themfelves fhould engage in a fimilar expedition in a few days. Rein-deer, bears, wolvereens, martens, foxes, hares, and white buffaloes are the only quadrupeds in their country ; and that the latter were only to be found in the mountains to the Weftward.

We proceeded with the line throughout the day, except two hours, when we employed the fail. We encamped at eight in the evening. From the place we quitted this morning, the banks of the river are well covered with fmall wood, fpruce, firs, birch, and willow. We found it very warm during the whole of our progrefs.

Thurfday 23.   At five in the morning we proceeded on our voyage, but found it very difficult to travel along the beach. We obferved feveral places where the natives had ftationed themfelves and fet their nets fince our paffage downwards. We paffed a fmall river, and at five o'clock our Indians put to fhore in order to encamp, but we proceeded onwards, which difpleafed them very much, from the fatigue they fuffered, and at eight we encamped at our pofition of the 8th inftant. The day was very fine, and we employed the towing line throughout the courfe of it.   At ten, our hunters returned, fullen and diffatisfied. We had not touched any of our provifion ftores for fix days, in which time we had confumed two

rein

rein-deer, four fwans, forty-five geefe, and a confiderable quantity of fifh : but it is to be confidered, that we were ten men, and four women. I have always obferved, that the north men poffeffed very hearty appetites, but they were very much exceeded by thofe with me, fince we entered this river. I fhould really have thought it abfolute gluttony in my people, if my own appetite had not increafed in a fimilar proportion.

CHAP.

CHAPTER VI.

Employ the towing line. Defcription of a place where the Indians come to collect flint. Their fhynefs and fufpicions. Current leffens. Appearance of the country. Abundance of hares. Violent ftorm. Land near three lodges. Alarm of the Indians. Supply of fifh from them. Their fabulous accounts. Continue to fee Indian lodges. Treatment of a difeafe. Mifunderftanding with the natives. The interpreter harangues them. Their accounts fimilar to thofe we have already received. Their curious conduct. Purchafe fome beaver fkins. Shoot one of their dogs. The confequence of that act. Apprehenfions of the women. Large quantities of liquorice. Swallow's nefts feen in the precipices. Fall in with a party of natives killing geefe. Circumftances concerning them. Hurricane. Variation of the weather. Kill great numbers of geefe. Abundance of feveral kinds of berries. State of the river and its bank

---

1789.
July.

Friday 24.

AT five we continued our courfe, but, in a very fhort time, were under the neceffity of applying to the aid of the line, the ftream being fo ftrong as to render all our attempts unavailing to ftem it with the paddles. We paffed a fmall river, on each fide of which the natives and Efquimaux collect flint. The bank is an high, fteep, and foft rock, variegated with red,

red, green, and yellow hues. From the continual dripping of water, parts of it frequently fall and break into fmall ftony flakes like flate, but not fo hard. Among them are found pieces of *Petrolium,* which bears a refemblance to yellow wax, but is more friable. The Englifh chief informed me, that rocks of a fimilar kind are fcattered about the country, at the back of the Slave Lake, where the Chepewyans collect copper.

At ten, we had an aft wind, and the men who had been engaged in towing, re-embarked. At twelve we obferved a lodge on the fide of the river, and its inhabitants running about in great confufion, or hurrying to the woods. Three men waited our arrival, though they remained at fome diftance from us, with their bows and arrows ready to be employed; or at leaft, that appeared to be the idea they wifhed to convey to us, by continually fnapping the ftrings of the former, and the figns they made to forbid our approach. The Englifh chief, whofe language they, in fome degree, underftood, endeavoured to remove their diftruft of us; but till I went to them with a prefent of beads, they refufed to have any communication with us.

When they firft perceived our fail, they took us for the Efquimaux Indians, who employ a fail in their canoes. They were fufpicious of our defigns, and queftioned us with a view to obtain fome knowledge of them. On feeing us in poffeffion of fome of the clothes, bows, &c. which muft have belonged to fome of the Deguthee Denees, or Quarrellers, they imagined, that we had killed fome of them, and were bearing away the fruits of our victory. They appeared, indeed, to be of the fame
tribe,

tribe, though they were afraid of acknowledging it. From their quef-tions, it was evident that they had not received any notice of our being in thofe parts.

They would not acknowledge that they had any women with them, though we had feen them running to the woods; but pretended that they had been left at a confiderable diftance from the river, with fome relations, who were engaged in killing rein-deer. Thefe people had been here but a fhort time, and their lodge was not yet completed; nor had they any fifh in a ftate of preparation for their provifion. I gave them a knife and fome beads for an horn-wedge or chifel, with which they fplit their canoe-wood. One of my Indians having broken his paddle, attempted to take one of theirs, which was immediately con-tefted by its owner, and on my interfering to prevent this act of injuftice, he manifefted his gratitude to me on the occafion. We loft an hour and a half in this conference.

The Englifh chief was during the whole of the time in the woods, where fome of the hidden property was difcovered, but the women con-trived to elude the fearch that was made after them. Some of thefe articles were purloined, but I was ignorant of this circumftance till we had taken our departure, or I fhould certainly have given an ample re-muneration. Our chief expreffed his difpleafure at their running away to conceal themfelves, their property, and their young women, in very bitter terms. He faid his heart was fet againft thofe flaves; and com-plained aloud of his difappointment in coming fo far without feeing the natives, and getting fomething from them.

We

We employed the fail and the paddle fince ten this morning, and pitched our tents at feven in the evening. We had no fooner encamped than we were vifited by an Indian whom we had feen before, and whofe family was at a fmall diftance up the river: at nine he left us. The weather was clear and ferene.

We embarked this morning at a quarter paft three, and at feven we paffed the lodge of the Indian who had vifited us the preceding evening. There appeared to have been more than one family, and we naturally concluded that our vifitor had made fuch an unfavourable report of us, as to induce his companions to fly on our approach. Their fire was not extinguifhed, and they had left a confiderable quantity of fifh fcattered about their dwelling.

The weather was now very fultry; but the current had relaxed of its force, fo that the paddle was fufficient for our progrefs during the greateft part of the day. The inland part of the country is mountainous and the banks of the river low, but covered with wood, among which is the poplar, but of fmall growth, and the firft which we had feen on our return. A pigeon alfo flew by us, and hares appeared to be in great plenty. We paffed many Indian encampments which we did not fee in our paffage down the river. About feven the fky, to the Weftward, became of a fteel-blue colour, with lightning and thunder. We accordingly landed to prepare ourfelves againft the coming ftorm; but before we could erect our tents, it came on with fuch violence, that we expected it to carry every thing before it. The ridge-pole of my tent was broken in the middle, where it was found, and nine inches and an half in

circumference;

circumference; and we were obliged to throw ourfelves flat on the ground to efcape being wounded by the ftones that were hurled about in the air like fand. The violence of the ftorm, however, fubfided in a fhort time, but left the fky overcaft with the appearance of rain.

Sunday 26.   It rained from the preceding evening to this morning, when we embarked at four o'clock. At eight we landed at three large Indian lodges. Their inhabitants, who were afleep, expreffed uncommon alarm and agitation when they were awakened by us, though moft of them had feen us before. Their habitations were crowded with fifh, hanging to dry in every part; but as we wanted fome for prefent ufe, we fent their young men to vifit the nets, and they returned with abundance of large white fifh, to which the name has been given of *poiffon inconnu*; fome of a round fhape, and green colour; and a few white ones; all which were very agreeable food. Some beads, and a few other trifles, were gratefully received in return. Thefe people are very fond of iron work of any kind, and my men purchafed feveral of their articles for fmall pieces of tin.

There were five or fix perfons whom we had not feen before; and among them was a Dog-rib Indian, whom fome private quarrel had driven from his country. The Englifh chief underftood him as well as one of his own nation, and gave the following account of their converfation:—

He had been informed by the people with whom he now lives, the Hare Indians, that there is another river on the other fide of the mountains

tains to the South-Weft, which falls into the *Belhoullay Toe*, or Whiteman's Lake, in comparifon of which that on whofe banks we then were, was but a fmall ftream; that the natives were very large, and very wicked, and kill common men with their eyes; that they make canoes larger than ours; that thofe who inhabit the entrance of it kill a kind of beaver, the fkin of which is almoft red; and that large canoes often frequent it. As there is no known communication by water with this river, the natives who faw it went over the mountains.

As he mentioned that there were fome beavers in this part of the country, I told him to hunt it, and defire the others to do the fame, as well as the martens, foxes, beaver-eater or wolvereen, &c. which they might carry to barter for iron with his own nation, who are fupplied with goods by us, near their country. He was anxious to know whether we fhould return that way: at the fame time he informed us that we fhould fee but few of the natives along the river, as all the young men were engaged in killing rein-deer, near the Efquimaux Lake, which, he alfo faid, was at no great diftance. The latter he reprefented as very treacherous, and added, that they had killed one of his people. He told us likewife, that fome plan of revenge was meditating, unlefs the offending party paid a fufficient price for the body of the murdered perfon.

My Indians were very anxious to poffefs themfelves of a woman that was with the natives, but as they were not willing to part with her, I interfered, to prevent her being taken by force: indeed I was obliged to exercife the utmoft vigilance, as the Indians who accompanied me were ever ready to take what they could from the natives, without making them any
return.

return. About twelve we paffed a river of fome appearance, flowing from the Eaftward. One of the natives who followed us, called it the Winter Road River. We did not find the ftream ftrong to-day along the fhore, as there were many eddy currents: we therefore employed the fail during fome hours of it, and went on fhore for the night at half paft feven.

Monday 27. The weather was now fine, and we renewed our voyage at half paft two. At feven we landed where there were three families, fituated clofe to the rapids. We found but few people; for as the Indian who followed us yefterday had arrived here before us, we fuppofed that the greater part had fled, on the intelligence which he gave of our approach. Some of thefe people we had feen before, when they told us that they had left their property at a lake in the neighbourhood, and had promifed to fetch it before our return; but we now found them as unprovided as when we left them. They had plenty of fifh, fome of which was packed up in birch bark.

During the time we remained with them, which was not more than two hours, I endeavoured to obtain fome additional intelligence refpecting the river which had been mentioned on the preceding day; when they declared their total ignorance of it, but from the reports of others, as they had never been beyond the mountains, on the oppofite fide of their own river: they had, however, been informed that it was larger than that which wafhed the banks whereon they lived, and that its courfe was towards the mid-day fun. They added, that there were people at a fmall diftance up the river, who inhabited the oppofite mountains, and had lately defcended from them to obtain fupplies of fifh. Thefe people, they fuggefted,

gested, must be well acquainted with the other river, which was the object of my inquiry. I engaged one of them, by a bribe of some beads, to describe the circumjacent country upon the sand. This singular map he immediately undertook to delineate, and accordingly traced out a very long point of land between the rivers, though without paying the least attention to their courses, which he represented as running into the great lake, at the extremity of which, as he had been told by Indians of other nations, there was a Belhoullay Couin, or White Man's Fort. This I took to be Unalascha Fort, and consequently the river to the West to be Cook's River; and that the body of water or sea into which this river discharges itself at Whale Island, communicates with Norton Sound. I made an advantageous proposition to this man to accompany me across the mountains to the other river, but he refused it. At the same time he recommended me to the people already mentioned, who were fishing in the neighbourhood, as better qualified to assist me in the undertaking which I had proposed.

One of this small company of natives was grievously afflicted with ulcers in his back; and the only attention which was paid to his miserable condition, as far at least as we could discover, proceeded from a woman, who carefully employed a bunch of feathers in preventing the flies from settling upon his sores.

At ten this morning we landed near the lodges which had already been mentioned to us, and I ordered my people to make preparation for passing the remaining part of the day here, in order to obtain that familiarity with the natives which might induce them to afford me, without reserve, the
information

information that I fhould require from them. This objeƈt, however, was in danger of being altogether fruftrated, by a mifunderftanding that had taken place between the natives and my young Indians, who were already arrived there. Before the latter could difembark, the former feized the canoe, and dragged it on fhore, and in this aƈt of violence the boat was broken, from the weight of the perfons in it. This infult was on the point of being ferioufly revenged, when I arrived, to prevent the confequences of fuch a difpofition. The variation of the compafs was about twenty-nine degrees to the Eaft.

At four in the afternoon I ordered my interpreter to harangue the natives, affembled in council; but his long difcourfe obtained little fatif-faƈtory intelligence from them. Their account of the river to the Weft-ward, was fimilar to that which we had already received; and their defcription of the inhabitants of that country, was ftill more abfurd and ridiculous. They reprefented them as being of a gigantic ftature, and adorned with wings; which, however, they never employed in flying. That they fed on large birds, which they killed with the greateft eafe, though common men would be certain viƈtims of their voracity if they ventured to approach them. They alfo defcribed the people that inha-bited the mouth of the river as poffeffing the extraordinary power of kill-ing with their eyes, and devouring a large beaver at a fingle meal. They added that canoes of very large dimenfions vifited that place. They did not, however, relate thefe ftrange circumftances from their own knowledge, but on the reports of other tribes, as they themfelves never ventured to proceed beyond the firft mountains, where they went in fearch of the fmall white buffaloes, as the inhabitants of the other fide

endeavour

endeavour to kill them whenever they meet.   They likewife mentioned
that the fources of thofe ftreams which are tributary to both the great
rivers, are feparated by the mountains.   It appeared to us, however, that
thefe people knew more about the country than they chofe to communicate, or at leaft reached me, as the interpreter, who had long been tired
of the voyage, might conceal fuch a part of their communications as, in
in his opinion, would induce me to follow new routes, or extend my
excurfions.   No fooner was the conference concluded, than they began
to dance, which is their favourite, and, except jumping, their only amufement.   In this paftime old and young, male and female, continued their
exertions, till their ftrength was exhaufted.   This exercife was accompanied by loud imitations of the various noifes produced by the rein-
deer, the bear, and the wolf.

When they had finifhed their antics, I defired the Englifh chief to
renew the former fubjects; which he did without fuccefs.   I therefore
affumed an angry air, expreffed my fufpicions that they withheld their
information, and concluded with a menace, that if they did not give me
all the fatisfaction in their power, I would force one of them along with
me to-morrow, to point out the road to the other river.   On this declaration, they all, at one and the fame moment, became fick, and anfwered
in a very faint tone, that they knew no more than they had already communicated, and that they fhould die if I took any of them away.   They
began to perfuade my interpreter to remain with them, as they loved him
as well as they did themfelves, and that he would be killed if he continued with me.   Nor did this propofition, aided as it was by the folicitation of his women, fail of producing a confiderable effect upon him,
though he endeavoured to conceal it from me.

I now

I now found that it would be fruitlefs for me to expect any accounts of the country, or the other great river, till I got to the river of the Bear Lake, where I expected to find fome of the natives, who promifed to wait for us there. Thefe people had actually mentioned this river to me when we paffed them, but I then paid no attention to that circumflance, as I imagined it to be either a mifunderflanding of my interpreter, or that it was an invention which, with their other lies, might tend to prevent me from proceeding down their river.

We were plentifully fupplied with fifh, as well dry as frefh, by thefe people; they alfo gathered as many whirtle berries as we chofe, for which we paid with the ufual articles of beads, awls, knives, and tin. I purchafed a few beaver-fkins of them, which, according to their accounts, are not very numerous in this country; and that they do not abound in moofe-deer and buffaloes. They were alarmed for fome of their young men, who were killing geefe higher up the river, and entreated us to do them no harm. About fun-fet I was under the neceffity of fhooting one of their dogs, as we could not keep thofe animals from our baggage. It was in vain that I had remonflrated on this fubject, fo that I was obliged to commit the act which has been juft mentioned. When thefe people heard the report of the piftol, and faw the dog dead, they were feized with a very general alarm, and the women took their children on their backs and ran into the woods. I ordered the caufe of this act of feverity to be explained, with the affurance that no injury would be offered to themfelves. The woman, however, to whom the dog belonged, was very much affected, and declared that the lofs of five children, during the preceding winter, had not affected her fo much as the death of

this

this animal. But her grief was not of very long duration; and a few beads, &c. foon affuaged her forrow. But as they can without difficulty get rid of their affliction, they can with equal eafe affume it, and feign ficknefs if it be neceffary with the fame verfatility. When we arrived this morning, we found the women in tears, from an apprehenfion that we were come to take them away. To the eye of an European they certainly were objects of difguft; but there were thofe among my party who obferved fome hidden charms in thefe females which rendered them objects of defire, and means were found, I believe, that very foon diffipated their alarms and fubdued their coynefs.

On the upper part of the beach, liquorice grew in great abundance and it was now in bloffom. I pulled up fome of the roots, which were large and long; but the natives were ignorant of its qualities, and confidered it as a weed of no ufe or value.

At four this morning I ordered my people to prepare for our depar- ture; and while they were loading the canoe, I went with the Englifh chief to vifit the lodges, but the greater part of their inhabitants had quitted them during the night, and thofe that remained pretended ficknefs, and refufed to rife. When, however, they were convinced that we did not mean to take any of them with us, their ficknefs abandoned them, and when we had embarked, they came forth from their huts, to defire that we would vifit their nets, which were at a fmall diftance up the river, and take all the fifh we might find in them. We accordingly availed ourfeves of this permiffion, and took as many as were neceffary for our own fupply.

We

We landed fhortly after where there were two more lodges, which were full of fifh, but without any inhabitants, who were probably with the natives whom we had juft left. My Indians, in rummaging thefe places, found feveral articles which they propofed to take; I therefore gave beads and awls, to be left as the purchafe of them; but this act of juftice they were not able to comprehend, as the people themfelves were not prefent. I took up a net and left a large knife in the place of it. It was about four fathoms long, and thirty-two mefhes in depth: thefe nets are much more convenient to fet in the eddy current than our long ones. This is the place that the Indians call a rapid though we went up it all the way with the paddle; fo that the current could not be fo ftrong here, as in many other parts of the river; indeed if it were fo, the difficulty of towing would be almoft infuperable, as in many parts the rocks, which are of a great height and rather project over the water, leave no fhore between them and the ftream. Thefe precipices abound in fwallows' nefts. The weather was now very fultry, and at eleven we were under the neceffity of landing to gum our canoe.

In about an hour we fet forward, and at one in the afternoon, went on fhore at a fire, which we fuppofed to have been kindled by the young men, who, as we had been already informed, were hunting geefe. Our hunters found their canoe and the fowl they had got, fecreted in the woods; and foon after, the people themfelves, whom they brought to the waterfide. Out of two hundred geefe we picked thirty-fix which were eatable; the reft were putrid and emitted an horrid ftench. They had been killed fome time without having been gutted, and in this ftate

of

of loathfome rottennefs, we have every reafon to fuppofe they are eaten by the natives. We paid for thofe which we had taken, and departed. At feven in the evening, the weather became cloudy and overcaft; at eight we encamped; at nine, it began to thunder with great violence; an heavy rain fucceeded, accompanied with an hurricane, that blew down our tents, and threatened to carry away the canoe, which had been faftened to fome trees with a cod-line. The ftorm lafted two hours and deluged us with wet.

Yefterday the weather was cloudy and the heat infupportable; and now we could not put on clothes enough to keep us warm. We embarked at a quarter paft four with an aft wind, which drove us on at a great rate, though the current is very ftrong. At ten we came to the other rapid which we got up with the line on the Weft fide, where we found it much ftronger than when we went down; the water had alfo fallen at leaft five feet fince that time, fo that feveral fhoals appeared in the river which we had not feen before. One of my hunters narrowly efcaped being drowned in croffing a river that falls in from the Weftward, and is the moft confiderable, except the mountain river, that flows in this direction. We had ftrong Northerly and cold wind throughout the whole of the day, and took our ftation for the night at a quarter paft eight. We killed a goofe and caught fome young ones.

We renewed our voyage at four this morning after a very rainy night. The weather was cloudy, but the cold had moderated, and the wind was

North-

North-Weſt. We were enabled to employ the ſail during part of the day, and encamped at about ſeven in the evening. We killed eleven old geeſe and forty young ones which had juſt begun to fly. The Engliſh chief was very much irritated againſt one of his young men: that jealouſy occaſioned this uneaſineſs, and that it was not without very ſuf-ficient cauſe, was all I could diſcover. For the laſt two or three days we had eaten the liquorice root, of which there is great abundance on the banks of the river. We found it a powerful aſtringent.

Friday 31.   The rain was continual throughout the night, and did not ſubſide till nine this morning, when we renewed our progreſs. The wind and weather the ſame as yeſterday. About three in the afternoon it cleared up and the wind died away, when it became warm. At five the wind veered to the Eaſt, and brought cold along with it. There were plenty of whirtle berries, raſpberries, and a berry called *Poire*, which grows in the greateſt abundance. We were very much impeded in our way by ſhoals of ſand and ſmall ſtones, which render the water ſhallow at a diſtance from the ſhore. In other places the bank of the river is lofty: it is formed of black earth and ſand, and, as it is conti-nually falling, diſplayed to us, in ſome parts, a face of ſolid ice, to within a foot of the ſurface. We finiſhed this day's voyage at a quarter before eight, and in the courſe of it killed ſeven geeſe.

We now had recourſe to our corn, for we had only conſumed three days of our original proviſion ſince we began to mount the current. It was my intention to have aſcended the river on the South ſide from

the

the laft rapid, to difcover if there were any rivers of confequence that flow from the Weftward: but the fand-banks were fo numerous and the current fo ftrong, that I was compelled to traverfe to the oppofite fide, where the eddy currents are very frequent, which gave us an opportunity of fetting our nets and making much more head-way.

CHAP.

CHAPTER VII.

Voyage continued. Suspect the integrity of the interpreter. Stars visible. Springs of mineral water, and lumps of iron ore. Arrive at the river of the Bear Lake. Coal mine in a state of combustion. Water of the river diminished. Continue to see Indian encampments, and kill geese, &c. Hunting excursions. A canoe found on the edge of a wood. Attempt to ascend a mountain. Account of the passage to it. See a few of the natives. Kill a beaver and some hares. Design of the English chief. Kill a wolf. Changeable state of the weather. Recover the Pemmican, which had been hidden in an island. Natives fly at our approach. Meet with dogs. Altercation with the English chief. Account of the articles left by the fugitives. Shoals of the river covered with saline matter. Encamp at the mouth of the river of the mountain. The ground on fire on each side of it. Continue to see encampments of the natives. Various kinds of berries. Kill geese, swans, &c. &c. &c. Corroding quality of the water. Weather changeable. Reach the entrance of the Slave Lake. Dangers encountered on entering it. Caught pike and trout. Met M. Le Roux on the lake. Further circumstances till our return to Fort Chepewyan. Conclusion of the voyage.

1789.
August.
Saturday 1.

WE embarked at three this morning, the weather being clear and cold, with the wind at South-East. At three in the afternoon we traversed and landed to take the canoe in tow: here was an encampment

of

of the natives, which we had reafon to fuppofe they had quitted the preceding day. At five we perceived a family, confifting of a man, two women, and as many children, ftationed by the fide of the water, whom we had not feen before. They informed us, that they had but few fifh, and that none of their friends were in the neighbourhood, except the inhabitants of one lodge on the other fide of the river, and a man who belonged to them, and who was now occupied in hunting. I now found my interpreter very unwilling to afk fuch queftions as were dictated to him, from the apprehenfion, as I imagined, that I might obtain fuch intelligence as would prevent him from feeing Athabafca this feafon. We left him with the Indian, and pitched our tents at the fame place where we had paffed the night on the fifth of laft month. The Englifh chief came along with the Indian to our fire; and the latter informed us that the native who went down part of the river with us had paffed there, and that we fhould meet with three lodges of his tribe above the river of the Bear Lake. Of the river to the Weftward he knew nothing but from the relation of others. This was the firft night fince our departure from Athabafca, when it was fufficiently dark to render the ftars vifible.

We fet off at three this morning with the towing-line. I walked with my Indians, as they went fafter than the canoe, and particularly as I fufpected that they wanted to arrive at the huts of the natives before me. In our way, I obferved feveral fmall fprings of mineral water running from the foot of the mountain, and along the beach I faw feveral lumps of iron ore. When we came to the river of the Bear Lake, I ordered one of the young Indians to wait for my canoe, and I took my

place

place in their ſmall canoe.   This river is about two hundred and fifty yards broad at this place, the water clear and of a greeniſh colour. When I landed on the oppoſite ſhore, I diſcovered that the natives had been there very lately from the print of their feet in the ſand.   We continued walking till five in the afternoon, when we ſaw ſeveral ſmokes along the ſhore.   As we naturally concluded, that theſe were certain indications where we ſhould meet the natives who were the objeᶜts of our ſearch, we quickened our pace; but, in our progreſs, experienced a very ſulphurous ſmell, and at length diſcovered that the whole bank was on fire for a very conſiderable diſtance.   It proved to be a coal mine, to which the fire had communicated from an old Indian encampment. The beach was covered with coals, and the Engliſh chief gathered ſome of the ſofteſt he could find, as a black dye; it being the mineral, as he informed me, with which the natives render their quills black.

Here we waited for the large canoe, which arrived an hour after us. At half paſt ten we ſaw ſeveral Indian marks, which conſiſted of pieces of bark fixed on poles, and pointing to the woods, oppoſite to which is an old beaten road, that bore the marks of being lately frequented; the beach alſo was covered with tracks.   At a ſmall diſtance were the poles of five lodges ſtanding; where we landed and unloaded our canoe.   I then diſpatched one of my men and two young Indians to ſee if they could find any natives within a day's march of us.   I wanted the Engliſh chief to go, but he pleaded fatigue, and that it would be of no uſe.   This was the firſt time he had refuſed to comply with my deſire, and jealouſy, I believe, was the cauſe of it in the preſent inſtance; though I had taken every precaution that he ſhould not have cauſe to be jealous of the Canadians.   There

was

was not, at this time, the leaſt appearance of ſnow on the oppoſite mountains, though they were almoſt covered with it when we paſſed before. Set two nets, and at eleven o'clock at night the men and Indians returned, They had been to their firſt encampment, where there were four fires, and which had been quitted a ſhort time before; ſo that they were obliged to make the circuit of ſeveral ſmall lakes, which the natives croſs with their canoes. This encampment was on the borders of a lake which was too large for them to venture round it, ſo that they did not proceed any further. They ſaw ſeveral beavers and beaver lodges in thoſe ſmall lakes. They killed one of theſe animals whoſe fur began to get long, a ſure indication that the fall of the year approaches. They alſo ſaw many old tracks of the mooſe and rein deer. This is the time when the rein-deer leave the plains to come to the woods, as the muſquitoes begin to diſappear; I, therefore, apprehended that we ſhould not find a ſingle Indian on the river ſide, as they would be in or about the mountains ſetting ſnares to take them.

We proceeded with a ſtrong Weſterly wind, at four this morning, the weather being cloudy and cold. At twelve it cleared up and became fine: the current alſo increaſed. The water had fallen ſo much ſince our paſſage down the river, that here, as in other places, we diſcovered many ſhoals which were not then viſible. We killed ſeveral geeſe of a larger ſize than thoſe which we had generally ſeen. Several Indian encampments were ſeen along the river, and we landed at eight for the night. Monday 3.

At four in the morning we renewed our courſe, when it was fine and calm. Tueſday 4.

calm.   The night had been cold and a very heavy dew had fallen.   At nine we were obliged to land in order to gum the canoe, when the weather became extremely warm.   Numerous tracks of rein deer appeared on the fide of the river.   At half paft five we took our ftation for the night, and fet the nets.   The current was very ftrong all day, and we found it very difficult to walk along the beach, from the large ftones which were fcattered over it.

Wednef. 5.   We raifed our nets but had not the good fortune to take a fingle fifh. The water was now become fo low that the eddy currents would not admit of fetting them.   The current had not relaxed its ftrength; and the difficulty of walking along the beach was continued.   The air was now become fo cold, that our exercife, violent as it was, fcarce kept us warm. We paffed feveral points which we fhould not have accomplifhed, if the canoe had been loaded.   We were very much fatigued, and at fix were glad to conclude our toilfome march.   The Indians killed two geefe. The women who did not quit the canoe, were continually employed in making fhoes of moofe-fkin, for the men, as a pair did not laft more than a day.

Thurfday 6.   The rain prevented us from proceeding till half paft fix, when we had a ftrong aft wind, which, aided by the paddles, drove us on at a great rate.   We encamped at fix to wait for our Indians, whom we had not feen fince the morning; and at half paft feven they arrived very much diffatisfied with their day's journey.   Two days had now elapfed fince we had feen the leaft appearance of Indian habitations.

Friday 7.   We embarked at half paft three, and foon after perceived two rein-

deer

deer on the beach before us. We accordingly checked our courfe; but our Indians, in contending who fhould be the firft to get near thefe animals, alarmed and loft them. We, however, killed a female rein-deer, and from the wounds in her hind-legs, it was fuppofed that fhe had been purfued by wolves, who had devoured her young one: her udder was full of milk, and one of the young Indians poured it among fome boiled corn, which he ate with great delight, efteeming it a very delicious food. At five in the afternoon we faw an animal running along the beach, but could not determine, whether it was a grey fox or a dog. In a fhort time we went afhore for the night, at the entrance of a fmall river, as I thought there might be fome natives in the vicinity of the place. I ordered my hunters to put their fuzees in order, and gave them ammunition to proceed on an hunting party the next day; they were alfo inftrubed to difcover if there were any natives in the neighbouring mountains. I found a fmall canoe at the edge of the woods, which contained a paddle and a bow: it had been repaired this fpring, and the workmanfhip of the bark excelled any that I had yet feen. We faw feveral encampments in the courfe of the day. The current of the river was very ftrong, and along the points equal to rapids.

The rain was very violent throughout the night, and continued till the afternoon of this day, when the weather began to clear, with a ftrong, cold, and Wefterly wind. At three the Indians proceeded on the hunting expedition, and at eight they returned without having met with the leaft fuccefs; though they faw numerous tracks of the reindeer. They came to an old beaten road, which one of them followed

for

for ſome time; but it did not appear to have been lately frequented. The rain now returned and continued till the morning.

Sunday 9.   We renewed our voyage at half paſt three, the weather being cold and cloudy; but at ten it became clear and moderate. We ſaw another canoe at the outſide of the wood, and one of the Indians killed a dog, which was in a meagre, emaciated condition. We perceived various places where the natives had made their fires; for theſe people reſide but a ſhort time near the river, and remove from one bank to the other, as it ſuits their purpoſes. We ſaw a path which was con- nected with another on the oppoſite ſide of the river. The water had riſen conſiderably ſince laſt night, and there had been a ſtrong current throughout the day. At ſeven we made to the ſhore and encamped.

Monday 10.   At three this morning we returned to our canoe; the weather fine and clear, with a light wind from the South-Eaſt. The Indians were be- fore us in purſuit of game. At ten we landed oppoſite to the mountains which we had paſſed on the ſecond of the laſt month, in order to aſcer- tain the variation of the compaſs at this place; but this was accom- pliſhed in a very imperfect manner, as I could not depend on my watch. One of the hunters joined us here, fatigued and unſucceſsful. As theſe mountains are the laſt of any conſiderable magnitude on the South-Weſt ſide of the river, I ordered my men to croſs to that ſide of it, that I might aſcend one of them. It was near four in the afternoon when I landed, and I loſt no time in proceeding to the attainment of my ob- ject. I was accompanied only by a young Indian, as the curioſity of

my

my people was fubdued by the fatigue they had undergone; and we
foon had reafon to believe that we fhould pay dearly for the indulgence of our own. The wood, which was chiefly of fpruce firs, was fo thick that it was with great difficulty we made our way through it. When we had walked upwards of an hour, the under-wood decreafed, while the white birch and poplar were the largeft and talleft of their kind that I had ever feen. The ground now began to rife, and was covered with fmall pines, and at length we got the firft view of the mountains fince we had left the canoe; as they appeared to be no nearer to us, though we had been walking for three hours, than when we had feen them from the river, my companion expreffed a very great anxiety to return; his fhoes and leggins were torn to pieces, and he was alarmed at the idea of paffing through fuch bad roads during the night. I perfifted, however, in proceeding, with a determination to pafs the night on the mountains and return on the morrow. As we approached them, the ground was quite marfhy, and we waded in water and grafs up to the knees, till we came within a mile of them, when I fuddenly funk up to my arm-pits, and it was with fome difficulty that I extricated myfelf from this difagreeable fituation. I now found it impoffible to proceed: to crofs this marfhy ground in a ftraight line was impracticable; and it extended fo far to the right and left, that I could not attempt to make the circuit: I therefore determined to return to the canoe, and arrived there about midnight, very much fatigued with this fruitlefs journey.

We obferved feveral tracks along the beach, and an encampment at the edge of the woods, which appeared to be five or fix days old. We
fhould

ſhould have continued our route along this ſide of the river, but we had not ſeen our hunters ſince yeſterday morning. We accordingly embarked before three, and at five traverſed the river, when we ſaw two of them coming down in ſearch of us. They had killed no other animals than one beaver, and a few hares. According to their account, the woods were ſo thick that it was impoſſible to follow the game through them. They had ſeen ſeveral of the natives encampments, at no great diſtance from the river; and it was their opinion that they had diſcovered us in our paſſage down it, and had taken care to avoid us; which accounted for the ſmall number we had ſeen on our return.

I requeſted the Engliſh chief to return with me to the other ſide of the river, in order that he might proceed to diſcover the natives, whoſe tracks and habitations we had ſeen there; but he was backward in complying with my deſire, and propoſed to ſend the young men; but I could not truſt to them, and at the ſame time was become rather doubtful of him. They were ſtill afraid leſt I ſhould obtain ſuch accounts of the other river as would induce me to travel overland to it, and that they ſhould be called upon to accompany me. I was, indeed, informed by one of my own people, that the Engliſh chief, his wives and companions, had determined to leave me on this ſide of the Slave Lake, in order to go to the country of the Beaver Indians; and that about the middle of the winter he would return to that lake, where he had appointed to meet ſome of his relations, who, during the laſt ſpring, had been engaged in war.

We now traverſed the river, and continued to track the Indians till paſt twelve, when we loſt all traces of them; in conſequence, as we imagined,

gined, of their having croffed to the Eaftern fide. We faw feveral dogs on both fhores; and one of the young Indians killed a wolf, which the men ate with great fatisfaction: we fhot, alfo, fifteen young geefe that were now beginning to fly. It was eight when we took our evening ftation, having loft four hours in making our traverfes. There was no interruption of the fine weather during the courfe of this day.

We proceeded on our voyage at three this morning, and difpatched the two young Indians acrofs the river, that we might not mifs any of the natives that fhould be on the banks of it. We faw many places where fires had been lately made along the beach, as well as fire running in the woods. At four we arrived at an encampment which had been left this morning. Their tracks were obfervable in feveral places in the woods, and as it might be prefumed that they could not be at any great diftance, it was propofed to the chief to accompany me in fearch of them. We accordingly, though with fome hefitation on his part, pene-trated feveral miles into the woods, but without difcovering the objects of our refearch. The fire had fpread all over the country, and had burned about three inches of the black, light foil, which covered a body of cold clay, that was fo hard as not to receive the leaft impreffion of our feet. At ten we returned from our unfuccefsful excurfion. In the mean time the hunters had killed feven geefe. There were feveral fhowers of rain, accompanied with gufts of wind and thunder. The nets had been fet during our abfence.

The nets were taken up, but not one fifh was found in them; and at half

half paſt three we continued our route, with very favourable weather. We paſſed ſeveral places, where fires had been made by the natives, and many tracks were perceptible along the beach. At ſeven we were oppo-ſite the iſland where our Pemmican had been concealed: two of the Indians were accordingly diſpatched in ſearch of it, and it proved very acceptable, as it rendered us more independent of the proviſions which were to be obtained by our fowling pieces, and qualified us to get out of the river without that delay which our hunters would other-wiſe have required. In a ſhort time we perceived a ſmoke on the ſhore to the South-Weſt, at the diſtance of three leagues, which did not appear to proceed from any running fire. The Indians, who were a little way ahead of us, did not diſcover them, being engaged in the purſuit of a flock of geeſe, at which they fired ſeveral ſhots, when the ſmoke imme-diately diſappeared; and in a ſhort time we ſaw ſeveral of the natives run along the ſhore, ſome of whom entered their canoes. Though we were almoſt oppoſite to them, we could not croſs the river without going further up it, from the ſtrength of the current; I therefore or-dered our Indians to make every poſſible exertion, in order to ſpeak with them, and wait our arrival. But as ſoon as our ſmall canoe ſtruck off, we could perceive the poor affrighted people haſten to the ſhore, and after drawing their canoes on the beach, hurry into the woods. It was paſt ten before we landed at the place where they had deſerted their canoes, which were four in number. They were ſo terrified that they had left ſeveral articles on the beach. I was very much diſpleaſed with my Indians, who inſtead of ſeeking the natives, were dividing their pro-perty. I rebuked the Engliſh chief with ſome ſeverity for his conduct, and immediately ordered him, his young men, and my own people, to

go

go in fearch of the fugitives, but their fears had made them too nimble
for us, and we could not overtake them. We faw feveral dogs in the woods, and fome of them followed us to our canoe.

The Englifh chief was very much difpleafed at my reproaches, and exprefled himfelf to me in perfon to that effect. This was the very opportunity which I wanted, to make him acquainted with my diffatis-faction for fome time paft. I ftated to him that I had come a great way, and at a very confiderable expence, without having obtained the object of my wifhes, and that I fufpected he had concealed from me a principal part of what the natives had told him refpecting the country, left he fhould be obliged to follow me: that his reafon for not killing game, &c. was his jealoufy, which likewife prevented him from looking after the na-tives as he ought; and that we had never given him any caufe for any fuf-picions of us. Thefe fuggeftions irritated him in a very high degree, and he accufed me of fpeaking ill words to him; he denied the charge of jealoufy, and declared that he did not conceal any thing from us; and that as to the ill fuccefs of their hunting, it arofe from the nature of the country, and the fcarcity, which had hitherto appeared, of animals in it. He con-cluded by informing me that he would not accompany me any further; that though he was without ammunition, he could live in the fame man-ner as the flaves, (the name given to the inhabitants of that part of the country), and that he would remain among them. His harangue was fucceeded by a loud and bitter lamentation; and his relations affifted the vociferations of his grief; though they faid that their tears flowed for their dead friends. I did not interrupt their grief for two hours, but as I could not well do without them, I was at length obliged to footh it, and

induce

induce the chief to change his refolution, which he did, but with great apparent reluctance; when we embarked as we had hitherto done.

The articles which the fugitives had left behind them, on the prefent occafion, were bows, arrows, fnares for moofe and rein-deer, and for hares; to thefe may be added a few difhes, made of bark, fome fkins of the marten and the beaver, and old beaver robes, with a fmall robe made of the fkin of the lynx. Their canoes were coarfely made of the bark of the fpruce-fir, and will carry two or three people. I ordered my men to remove them to the fhade, and gave moft of the other articles to the young Indians. The Englifh chief would not accept of any of them. In the place, and as the purchafe of them, I left fome cloth, fome fmall knives, a file, two fire-fteels, a comb, rings, with beads and awls. I alfo ordered a marten fkin to be placed on a proper mould, and a beaver fkin to be ftretched on a frame, to which I tied a fcraper. The Indians were of opinion that all thefe articles would be loft, as the natives were fo much frightened that they would never return. Here we loft fix hours; and on our quitting the place, three of the dogs which I have already mentioned followed us along the beach.

We pitched our tents at half paft eight, at the entrance of the river of the mountain; and while the people were unloading the canoe, I took a walk along the beach, and on the fhoals, which being uncovered fince we paffed down, by the finking of the waters, were now white with a faline fubftance. I fent for the Englifh chief to fup with me, and a dram or two difpelled all his heart-burning and difcontent. He informed me that it was a cuftom with the Chepewyan chiefs to go to war after they

had

had ſhed tears, in order to wipe away the diſgrace attached to ſuch **a**
feminine weakneſs, and that in the enſuing ſpring he ſhould not fail **to**
execute his deſign; at the ſame time he declared his intention to continue with us as long as I ſhould want him. I took care that he ſhould
carry ſome liquid conſolation to his lodge, to prevent the return of his
chagrin. The weather was fine, and the Indians killed three geeſe.

At a quarter before four this morning, we returned to our canoe, and
went about two miles up the river of the mountains. Fire was in the
ground on each ſide of it. In traverſing, I took ſoundings, and found
five, four and an half, and three and an half fathoms water. Its ſtream
was very muddy, and formed a cloudy ſtreak along the water of the great
river, on the Weſt ſide to the Eaſtern rapid, where the waters of the two
rivers at length blend in one. It was impoſſible not to conſider it as an
extraordinary circumſtance, that the current of the former river ſhould
not incorporate with that of the latter, but flow, as it were, in diſtinƈt
ſtreams at ſo great a diſtance, and till the contraƈted ſtate of the channel
unites them. We paſſed ſeveral encampments of the natives, and a river
which flowed in from the North, that had the appearance of being navigable. We concluded our voyage of this day at half paſt five in the
afternoon. There were plenty of berries, which my people called *poires*;
they are of a purple hue, ſomewhat bigger than a pea, and of a luſcious
taſte; there were alſo gooſeberries, and a few ſtrawberries.

We continued our courſe from three in the morning till half paſt five
in the afternoon. We ſaw ſeveral encampments along the beach, till it
became too narrow to admit them; when the banks roſe into a conſiderable

able degree of elevation, and there were more eddy currents.   The Indians killed twelve geefe, and berries were collected in great abundance.   The weather was fultry throughout the day.

Sunday 16.   We continued our voyage at a quarter before four, and in five hours paffed the place where we had been ftationed on the 13th of June.   Here the river widened, and its fhores became flat.   The land on the North fide is low, compofed of a black foil, mixed with ftones, but agreeably covered with the afpen, the poplar, the white birch, the fpruce fir, &c. The current was fo moderate, that we proceeded upon it almoft as faft as in dead water.   At twelve we paffed an encampment of three fires, which was the only one we faw in the courfe of the day.   The weather was the fame as yefterday.

Monday 17.   We proceeded at half paft three; and faw three fucceffive encampments. From the peculiar ftructure of the huts, we imagined that fome of the Red-Knife Indians had been in this part of the country, though it is not ufual for them to come this way.   I had laft night ordered the young Indians to precede us, for the purpofe of hunting, and at ten we overtook them.   They had killed five young fwans; and the Englifh chief prefented us with an eagle, three cranes, a fmall beaver, and two geefe. We encamped at feven this evening on the fame fpot which had been our refting-place on the 29th of June.

Tuefday 18.   At four this morning I equipped all the Indians for an hunting excurfion, and fent them onward, as our ftock of provifion was nearly exhaufted.   We followed at half paft fix, and croffed over to the North fhore,

fhore, where the land is low and fcarcely vifible in the horizon. It was near twelve when we arrived. I now got an obfervation, when it was 61. 33. North latitude. We were near five miles to the North of the main channel of the river. The frefh tracks and beds of buffaloes were very perceptible. Near this place a river flowed in from the Horn mountains which are at no great diftance. We landed at five in the afternoon, and before the canoe was unloaded, the Englifh chief arrived with the tongue of a cow, or female buffalo, when four men and the Indians were difpatched for the flefh; but they did not return till it was dark, with five geefe. They informed me, that they had feen feveral human tracks in the fand on the oppofite ifland. The fine weather continued without interruption.

The Indians were again fent forward in purfuit of game: and fome time being employed in gumming the canoe, we did not embark till half paft five, and at nine we landed to wait the return of the hunters. I here found the variation of the compafs to be about twenty degrees Eaft.

The people made themfelves paddles and repaired the canoe. It is an extraordinary circumftance for which I do not pretend to account, that there is fome peculiar quality in the water of this river, which corrodes wood, from the deftructive effect it had on the paddles. The hunters arrived at a late hour without having feen any large animals. Their booty confifted only of three fwans and as many geefe. The women were employed in gathering cranberries and crowberries, which were found in great abundance.

We

We embarked at four o'clock, and took the North ſide of the channel, though the current was on that ſide much ſtronger, in order to take a view of the river, which had been mentioned to me in our paſſage downwards, as flowing from the country of the Beaver Indians, and which fell in hereabouts. We could not, however, diſcover it, and it is probable that the account was referable to the river which we had paſſed on Tueſday. The current was very ſtrong, and we croſſed over to an iſland oppoſite to us; here it was ſtill more impetuous, and aſſumed the hurry of a rapid. We found an awl and a paddle on the ſide of the water; the former we knew to belong to the Kniſtineaux: I ſuppoſed it to be the chief Merde-d'ours and his party, who went to war laſt ſpring, and had taken this route on their return to Athabaſca. Nor is it improbable that they may have been the cauſe that we ſaw ſo few of the natives on the banks of this river. The weather was raw and cloudy, and formed a very unpleaſant contraſt to the warm, ſunny days which immediately preceded it. We took up our abode for the night at half paſt ſeven, on the Northern ſhore, where the adjacent country is both low and flat-The Indians killed five young ſwans, and a beaver. There was an appearance of rain.

The weather was cold, with a ſtrong Eaſterly wind and frequent ſhowers, ſo that we were detained in our ſtation. In the afternoon the Indians got on the track of a mooſe-deer, but were not ſo fortunate as to overtake it.

The wind veered round to the Weſtward, and continued to blow ſtrong and cold. We, however, renewed our voyage, and, in three

hours

hours reached the entrance of the Slave Lake, under half ſail; with the paddle, it would have taken us at leaſt eight hours. The Indians did not arrive till four hours after us; but the wind was ſo violent, that it was not expedient to venture into the lake; we therefore ſet a net and encamped for the night. The women gathered large quantities of the fruit, already mentioned, called Pathagomenan, and cranberries, crow-berries, mooſeberries, &c. The Indians killed two ſwans and three geeſe.

The net produced but five ſmall pike, and at five we embarked, and entered the lake by the ſame channel through which we had paſſed from it. The South-Weſt ſide would have been the ſhorteſt, but we were not certain of there being plenty of fiſh along the coaſt, and we were ſure of finding abundance of them in the courſe we preferred. Beſides, I expected to find my people at the place where I left them, as they had received orders to remain there till the fall.

We paddled a long way into a deep bay to get the wind, and having left our maſt behind us, we landed to cut another. We then hoiſted ſail and were driven on at a great rate. At twelve the wind and ſwell were augmented to ſuch a degree, that our under yard broke, but luckily the maſt thwart reſiſted, till we had time to faſten down the yard with a pole, without lowering ſail. We took in a large quantity of water, and had our maſt given way, in all probability, we ſhould have filled and ſunk. Our courſe continued to be very dangerous, along a flat lee-ſhore, without being able to land till three in the afternoon. Two men were continually employed in bailing out the water which we took in on all ſides. We fortunately doubled a point that ſcreened us from the

wind

1789.
Auguft.

wind and fwell, and encamped for the night, in order to wait for our Indians. We then fet our nets, made a yard and maft, and gummed the canoe. On vifiting the nets, we found fix white fifh, and two pike. The women gathered cranberries and crowberries in great plenty ; and as the night came on the weather became more moderate.

Monday 24.   Our nets this morning produced fourteen white fifh, ten pikes, and a couple of trouts. At five we embarked with a light breeze from the South, when we hoifted fail, and proceeded flowly, as our Indians had not come up with us. At eleven we went on fhore to prepare the kettle, and dry the nets; at one we were again on the water. At four in the afternoon we perceived a large canoe with a fail, and two fmall ones ahead ; we foon came up with them, when they proved to be M. Le Roux and an Indian, with his family, who were on an hunting party, and had been out twenty five days. It was his intention to have gone as far as the river, to leave a letter for me, to inform me of his fituation. He had feen no more Indians where I had left him ; but had made a voyage to Lac la Marte, where he met eighteen fmall canoes of the Slave Indians, from whom he obtained five packs of fkins, which were principally thofe of the marten. There were four Beaver Indians among them, who had bartered the greateft part of the abovementioned articles with them, before his arrival. They informed him that their relations had more fkins, but that they were afraid to venture with them, though they had been informed that people were to come with goods to barter for them. He gave thefe people a pair of ice chifels each, and other articles, and fent them away to conduct their friends to the Slave Lake, where he was to remain during the fucceeding winter.

We

We fet three nets, and in a fhort time caught twenty fifh of different kinds. In the dufk of the evening the Englifh chief arrived with a moft pitiful account that he had like to have been drowned in trying to follow us; and that the other men had alfo a very narrow efcape. Their canoe, he faid, had broken on the fwell, at fome diftance from the fhore, but as it was flat, they had with his affiftance been able to fave themfelves. He added, that he left them lamenting, left they fhould not overtake me, if I did not wait for them: he alfo exprefled his apprehenfions that they would not be able to repair their canoe. This evening I gave my men fome rum to cheer them after their fatigues

1789. Auguft.

We rofe this morning at a late hour, when we vifited the nets, which produced but few fifh: my people, indeed, partook of the ftores of M. Le Roux. At eleven the young Indians arrived, and reproached me for having left them fo far behind. They had killed two fwans, and brought me one of them. The wind was Southerly throughout the day, and too ftrong for us to depart, as we were at the foot of a grand traverfe. At noon I had an obfervation, which gave 61. 29. North latitude. Such was the ftate of the weather, that we could not vifit our nets. In the afternoon the fky darkened, and there was lightning, accompanied with loud claps of thunder. The wind alfo veered round to the Weftward, and blew an hurricane.

Tuefday 25.

It rained throughout the night, and till eight in the morning, without any alteration in the wind. The Indians went on an hunting excurfion, but returned altogether without fuccefs in the evening. One of them was fo unfortunate as to mifs a moofe-deer. In the afternoon there were heavy fhowers, with thunder, &c.

Wednef. 26.

We

We embarked before four, and hoiſted ſail. At nine we landed to dreſs victuals, and wait for M. Le Roux and the Indians. At eleven we proceeded with fine and calm weather. At four in the afternoon a light breeze ſprang up to the Southward, to which we ſpread our ſail, and at half paſt five in the afternoon went on ſhore for the night. We then ſet our nets. The Engliſh chief and his people being quite exhauſted with fatigue, he this morning expreſſed his deſire to remain behind, in order to proceed to the country of the Beaver Indians, engaging at the ſame time that he would return to Athabaſca in the courſe of the winter.

It blew very hard throughout the night, and this morning, ſo that we found it a buſineſs of ſome difficulty to get to our nets; our trouble, however, was repaid by a conſiderable quantity of white fiſh, trout, &c. Towards the afternoon the wind increaſed. Two of the men who had been gathering berries ſaw two mooſe-deer, with the tracks of buffaloes and rein-deer. About ſun-ſet we heard two ſhots, and ſaw a fire on the oppoſite ſide of the bay; we accordingly made a large fire alſo, that our poſition might be determined. When we were all gone to bed, we heard the report of a gun very near us, and in a very ſhort time the Engliſh chief preſented himſelf drenched with wet, and in much apparent confuſion informed me that the canoe with his companions was broken to pieces; and that they had loſt their fowling pieces, and the fleſh of a rein-deer, which they had killed this morning. They were, he ſaid, at a very ſhort diſtance from us; and at the ſame time requeſted that fire might be ſent to them, as they were ſtarving with cold. They and his women, however, ſoon joined us, and were immediately accommodated with dry clothes.

I ſent

I ſent the Indians on an hunting party, but they returned without ſuc-ceſs; and they expreſſed their determination not to follow me any further, from their apprehenſion of being drowned.

We embarked at one this morning, and took from the nets a large trout, and twenty white fiſh. At ſun-riſe a ſmart aft breeze ſprang up, which wafted us to M. Le Roux's houſe by two in the afternoon. It was late before he and our Indians arrived; when, according to a promiſe which I had made the latter, I gave them a plentiful equipment of iron ware, ammunition, tobacco, &c. as a recompence for the toil and inconveni-ence they had ſuſtained with me.

I propoſed to the Engliſh chief to proceed to the country of the Beaver Indians, and bring them to diſpoſe of their peltries to M. Le Roux, whom I intended to leave there the enſuing winter. He had already engaged to be at Athabaſca, in the month of March next, with plenty of furs.

I ſat up all night to make the neceſſary arrangements for the embarka-tion of this morning, and to prepare inſtruƈtions for M. Le Roux. We obtained ſome proviſions here, and parted from him at five, with fine calm weather. It ſoon, however, became neceſſary to land on a ſmall iſland, to ſtop the leakage of the canoe, which had been occaſioned by the ſhot of an arrow under the water mark, by ſome Indian children. While this buſineſs was proceeding, we took the opportunity of dreſſing ſome fiſh. At twelve the wind ſprang up from the South-Eaſt, which was in the teeth of our direƈtion, ſo that our progreſs was greatly impeded. I had an obſervation,

which

which gave 62. 15. North latitude.   We landed at feven in the evening, and pitched our tents.

Tuefday 1.

We continued our voyage at five in the morning, the weather calm and fine, and paffed the Ifle à la Cache about twelve, but could not perceive the land, which was feen in our former paffage.   On paffing the Carreboeuf Iflands, at five in the afternoon, we faw land to the South by Weft, which we thought was the oppofite fide of the lake, ftretching away to a great diftance.   We landed at half paft fix in the evening, when there was thunder, and an appearance of change in the weather.

Wednef. 2.

It rained and blew hard the latter part of the night.   At half paft five the rain fubfided, when we made a traverfe of twelve miles, and took in a good deal of water.   At twelve it became calm, when I had an obfervation, which gave 61. 36. North latitude.   At three in the afternoon there was a flight breeze from the Weftward, which foon increafed, when we hoifted fail, and took a traverfe of twenty-four miles for the point of the old Fort, where we arrived at feven and ftopped for the night.   This traverfe fhortened our way three leagues; indeed we did not expect to have cleared the lake in fuch a fhort time.

Thurfday 3.

It blew with great violence throughout the night, and at four in the morning we embarked, when we did not make more than five miles in three hours without ftopping; notwithftanding we were fheltered from the fwell by a long bank.   We now entered the fmall river, where the wind could have no effect upon us.   There were frequent fhowers in the courfe of the day, and we encamped at fix in the evening.

The

The morning was dark and cloudy, neverthelefs we embarked at five; but at ten it cleared up. We faw a few fowl, and at feven in the evening went on fhore for the night.

The weather continued to be cloudy. At five we proceeded, and at eight it began to rain very hard. In about half an hour we put to fhore, and were detained for the remaining part of the day.

It rained throughout the night, with a ftrong North wind. Numerous flocks of wild fowl paffed to the Southward: at fix in the afternoon, the rain, in fome meafure, fubfided, and we embarked, but it foon returned with renewed violence; we neverthelefs took the advantage of an aft wind, though it coft us a complete drenching. The hunters killed feven geefe, and we pitched our tents at half paft fix in the evening.

We were on the water at five this morning, with an head-wind, accompanied by fucceffive fhowers. At three in the afternoon we ran the canoe on a ftump, and it filled with water before fhe could be got to land. Two hours were employed in repairing her, and at feven in the evening we took our ftation for the night.

We renewed our voyage at half paft four in a thick mift which lafted till nine, when it cleared away, and fine weather fucceeded. At three in the afternoon we came to the firft carrying-place, *Portage des Noyes*, and encamped at the upper end of it to dry our clothes, fome of which were almoft rotten.

We

We embarked at five in the morning, and our canoe was damaged on the mens' fhoulders who were bearing it over the carrying-place, called *Portage du Chetique*. The guide repaired her, however, while the other men were employed in carrying the baggage. The canoe was gummed at the carrying-place, named the *Portage de la Montagne*. After having paffed the carrying places, we encamped at the Dog River, at half paft four in the afternoon, in a ftate of great fatigue. The canoe was again gummed, and paddles were made to replace thofe that had been broken in afcending the rapids. A fwan was the only animal we killed throughout the day.

Thurfday 10. There was rain and violent wind during the night: in the morning the former fubfided and the latter increafed. At half paft five we continued our courfe with a North-Wefterly wind. At feven we hoifted fail: in the forenoon there were frequent fhowers of rain and hail, and in the afternoon two fhowers of fnow: the wind was at this time very ftrong, and at fix in the evening we landed at a lodge of Knifteneaux, confifting of three men and five women and children. They were on their return from war, and one of them was very fick: they feparated from the reft of their party in the enemy's country, from abfolute hunger. After this feparation, they met with a family of the hoftile tribe, whom they deftroyed. They were entirely ignorant of the fate of their friends, but imagined, that they had returned to the Peace River, or had perifhed for want of food. I gave medicine to the fick,*

and

---

* This man had conceived an idea, that the people with whom he had been at war, had thrown medicine at him, which had caufed his prefent complaint, and that he defpaired of recovery. The natives are fo fuperftitious, that this idea alone was fufficient to kill him. Of this weaknefs I took advantage;

and a fmall portion of ammunition to the healthy; which, indeed, they very much wanted, as they had entirely lived for the laft fix months on the produce of their bows and arrows. They appeared to have been great fufferers by their expedition.

It froze hard during the night, and was very cold throughout the day, with an appearance of fnow. We embarked at half paft four in the morning, and continued our courfe till fix in the evening, when we landed for the night at our encampment of the third of June.

The weather was cloudy and alfo very cold. At eight we em- barked with a North-Eaft wind, and entered the Lake of the Hills. About ten, the wind veered to the Weftward, and was as ftrong as we could bear it with the high fail, fo that we arrived at Chepewyan fort by three o'clock in the afternoon, where we found Mr. Macleod, with five men, bufily employed in building a new houfe. Here, then, we concluded this voyage, which had occupied the confiderable fpace of one hundred and two days.

---

vantage; and affured him, that if he would never more go to war with fuch poor defencelefs people, that I would cure him. To this propofition he readily confented, and on my giving him medicine, which confifted of Turlington's balfam, mixed in water, I declared, that it would lofe its effect, if he was not fincere in the promife that he made me. In fhort, he actually recovered, was true to his engagements, and on all occafions manifefted his gratitude to me.

JOURNAL

OF A

SECOND VOYAGE, &c.

CHAPTER I.

Leave Fort Chepewyan. Proceed to the Peace River. State of the Lakes. Arrive at Peace Point. The reason affigned for its name. The weather cold. Arrive at the Falls. Defcription of the country. Land at the Fort, called The Old Eftablifhment. The principal building deftroyed by fire. Courfe of the river. Arrive at another fort. Some account of the natives. Depart from thence. Courfe of the river continued. It divides into two branches. Proceed along the principal one. Land at the place of our winter's refidence. Account of its circumftances and inhabitants, &c. Preparations for erecting a fort, &c. &c. Table of the weather. Broke the thermometer. Froft fets in. Defcription of birds.

H AVING made every neceffary preparation, I left Fort Chepewyan, _{1792.} 1792.
October 10. to proceed up the Peace River. I had refolved to go as far as our moft diftant fettlement, which would occupy the remaining part of the feafon,

it

it being the route by which I propofed to attempt my next difcovery, acrofs the mountains from the fource of that river; for whatever diftance I could reach this fall, would be a proportionate advancement of my voyage.

In confequence of this defign, I left the eftablifhment of Fort Chepe-wyan, in charge of Mr. Roderic Mackenzie, accompanied by two canoes laden with the neceffary articles for trade: we accordingly fteered Weft for one of the branches that communicates with the Peace River, called the Pine River; at the entrance of which we waited for the other canoes, in order to take fome fupplies from them, as I had reafon to apprehend they would not be able to keep up with us. We entered the Peace River at feven in the morning of the 12th, taking a Wefterly courfe. It is evident, that all the land between it and the Lake of the Hills, as far as the Elk River, is formed by the quantity of earth and mud, which is carried down by the ftreams of thofe two great rivers. In this fpace there are feveral lakes. The lake, Clear Water, which is the deepeft, Lake Vaffieu, and the Athabafca Lake, which is the largeft of the three, and whofe denomination in the Kniftineaux language, implies, a flat low, fwampy country, fubject to inundations. The two laft lakes are now fo fhallow, that, from the caufe juft mentioned, there is every reafon to expect, that in a few years, they will have exchanged their character and become extenfive forefts.

This country is fo level, that, at fome feafons, it is entirely overflowed, which accounts for the periodical influx and reflux of the waters between the Lake of the Hills and the Peace River.

On

On the 13th at noon we came to the Peace Point; from which, according to the report of my interpreter, the river derives its name; it was the fpot where the Knifteneaux and Beaver Indians fettled their difpute; the real name of the river and point being that of the land which was the object of contention.

When this country was formerly invaded by the Knifteneaux, they found the Beaver Indians inhabiting the land about Portage la Loche; and the adjoining tribe were thofe whom they called flaves. They drove both thefe tribes before them; when the latter proceeded down the river from the Lake of the Hills, in confequence of which that part of it obtained the name of the Slave River. The former proceeded up the river; and when the Knifteneaux made peace with them, this place was fettled to be the boundary.

We continued our voyage, and I did not find the current fo ftrong in this river as I had been induced to believe, though this, perhaps, was not the period to form a correct notion of that circumftance, as well as of the breadth, the water being very low; fo that the ftream has not appeared to me to be in any part that I have feen, more than a quarter of a mile wide.

The weather was cold and raw, fo as to render our progrefs unpleafant; at the fame time we did not relax in our expedition, and, at three on the afternoon of the 17th we arrived at the falls. The river at this place is about four hundred yards broad, and the fall about twenty feet high: the firft carrying place is eight hundred paces in length, and the

laft,

laſt, which is about a mile onwards, is ſomething more than two thirds of that diſtance. Here we found ſeveral fires, from which circumſtance we concluded, that the canoes deſtined for this quarter, which left the fort ſome days before us, could not be far a-head. The weather continued to be very cold, and the ſnow that fell during the night was ſeveral inches deep.

On the morning of the 18th, as ſoon as we got out of the draught of the fall, the wind being at North-Eaſt, and ſtrong in our favour, we hoiſted ſail, which carried us on at a conſiderable rate againſt the current, and paſſed the Loon River before twelve o'clock; from thence we ſoon came along the Grande Iſle, at the upper end of which we encamped for the night. It now froze very hard: indeed, it had ſo much the appearance of winter, that I began to entertain ſome alarm leſt we might be ſtopped by the ice: we therefore ſet off at three o'clock in the morning of the 19th, and about eight we landed at the Old Eſtabliſhment.

The paſſage to this place from Athabaſca having been ſurveyed by M. Vandrieul, formerly in the Company's ſervice, I did not think it ne- ceſſary to give any particular attention to it; I ſhall, however, juſt ob- ſerve, that the courſe in general from the Lake of the Hills to the falls, is Weſterly, and as much to the North as the South of it, from thence it is about Weſt-South-Weſt to this fort.

The country in general is low from our entrance of the river to the falls, and with the exception of a few open parts covered with graſs, it is clothed with wood. Where the banks are very low the

the foil is good, being compofed of the fediment of the river and putrefied leaves and vegetables. Where they are more elevated, they difplay a face of yellowifh clay, mixed with fmall ftones. On a line with the falls, and on either fide of the river, there are faid to be very extenfive plains, which afford pafture to numerous herds of buffaloes. Our people a-head flept here laft night, and, from their careleffnefs, the fire was communicated to and burned down, the large houfe, and was proceeding faft to the fmaller buildings when we arrived to extinguifh it.

We continued our voyage, the courfe of the river being South-Weft by Weft one mile and a quarter, South by Eaft one mile, South-Weft by South three miles, Weft by South one mile, South-South-Weft two miles, South four miles, South-Weft feven miles and an half, South by Weft one mile, North-North-Weft two miles and an half, South five miles and a quarter, South-Weft one mile and an half, North-Eaft by Eaft three miles and an half, and South-Eaft by Eaft one mile.

We overtook Mr. Finlay, with his canoes, who was encamped near the fort of which he was going to take the charge, during the enfuing winter, and made every neceffary preparative for a becoming appearance on our arrival the following morning. Although I had been fince the year 1787 in the Athabafca country, I had never yet feen a fingle native of that part of it which we had now reached.

At fix o'clock in the morning of the 20th, we landed before the houfe amidft the rejoicing and firing of the people, who were animated with the profpect of again indulging themfelves in the luxury of rum, of which

they

they had been deprived fince the beginning of May; as it is a practice throughout the North-Weft, neither to fell or give any rum to
the natives during the fummer.   There was at this time only one chief
with his people, the other two being hourly expected with their bands;
and on the 21ft and 22d they all arrived except the war chief and
fifteen men.   As they very foon expreffed their defire of the expected regale, I called them together, to the number of forty-two hunters,
or men capable of bearing arms, to offer fome advice, which would
be equally advantageous to them and to us, and I ftrengthened my
admonition with a nine gallon cafk of reduced rum and a quantity of
tobacco.   At the fame time I obferved, that as I fhould not often vifit
them, I had inftanced a greater degree of liberality than they had been
accuftomed to.

The number of people belonging to this eftablifhment amounts to about
three hundred, of which, fixty are hunters.   Although they appear from
their language to be of the fame flock as the Chepewyans, they differ
from them in appearance, manners, and cuftoms, as they have adopted
thofe of their former enemies, the Knifteneaux: they fpeak their language, as well as cut their hair, paint, and drefs like them, and poffefs
their immoderate fondnefs for liquor and tobacco.   This defcription,
however, can be applied only to the men, as the women are lefs
adorned even than thofe of the Chepewyan tribes.   We could not obferve, without fome degree of furprize, the contraft between the neat and
decent appearance of the men, and the naftinefs of the women.   I am
difpofed, however, to think that this circumftance is generally owing to
the extreme fubmiffion and abafement of the latter: for I obferved, that
one

one of the chiefs allowed two of his wives more liberty and familiarity than were accorded to the others, as well as a more becoming exterior, and their appearance was proportionably pleafing. I fhall, however, take a future opportunity to fpeak more at large on this fubject.

There were frequent changes of the weather in the courfe of the day, and it froze rather hard in the night. The thicknefs of the ice in the morning was a fufficient notice for me to proceed. I accordingly gave the natives fuch good counfel as might influence their behaviour, communicated my directions to Mr. Findlay for his future conduct, and took my leave under feveral vollies of mufketry, on the morning of the 23d. I had already difpatched my loaded canoes two days before, with directions to continue their progrefs without waiting for me. Our courfe was South-South-Eaft one mile and an half, South three quarters; Eaft feven miles and an half, veering gradually to the Weft four miles and an half. South-Eaft by South three miles, South-Eaft three miles and an half, Eaft-South-Eaft to Long Point three miles, South-Weft one mile and a quarter, Eaft by North four miles and three quarters, Weft three miles and an half, Weft-South-Weft one mile, Eaft by South five miles and and an half, South three miles and three quarters, South-Eaft by South three miles, Eaft-South-Eaft three miles, Eaft-North-Eaft one mile, when there was a river that flowed in on the right, Eaft two miles and an half, Eaft-South-Eaft half a mile, South-Eaft by South feven miles and an half, South two miles, South-South-Eaft three miles and an half; in the courfe of which we paffed an ifland South by Weft, where a rivulet flowed in on the right, one mile, Eaft one mile and an half, South five miles, South-Eaft by South four miles and an half, South-Weft one

mile

mile, South-Eaft by Eaft four miles and an half, Weft-South-Weft half a mile, South-Weft fix miles and three quarters, South-Eaft by South one mile and an half, South one mile and an half, South-Eaft by South two miles, South-Weft three quarters of a mile, South-Eaft by South two miles and an half, Eaft by South one mile and three quarters, South two miles, South-Eaft one mile and an half, South-South-Eaft half a mile, Eaft by South two miles and an half, North-Eaft three miles, South-Weft by Weft fhort diftance to the eftablifhment of laft year, Eaft-North-Eaft four miles, South-South-Eaft one mile and three quarters, South half a mile, South-Eaft by South three quarters of a mile, North-Eaft by Eaft one mile, South three miles, South-South-Eaft one mile and three quarters, South by Eaft four miles and an half, South-Weft three miles, South by Eaft two miles, South by Weft one mile and an half, South-Weft two miles, South by Weft four miles and an half, South-Weft one mile and an half, and South by Eaft three miles. Here we arrived at the forks of the river; the Eaftern branch appearing to be not more than half the fize of the Weftern one. We purfued the latter, in a courfe South-Weft by Weft fix miles, and landed on the firft of November at the place which was defigned to be my winter refidence: indeed, the weather had been fo cold and difagreeable, that I was more than once apprehenfive of our being flopped by the ice, and, after all, it required the utmoft exertions of which my men were capable to prevent it; fo that on their arrival they were quite exhaufted. Nor were their labours at an end, for there was not a fingle hut to receive us: it was, however, now in my power to feed and fuftain them in a more comfortable manner.

We

We found two men here who had been fent forward laft fpring, for the purpofe of fquaring timber for the erection of an houfe, and cutting pallifades, &c. to furround it. With them was the principal chief of the place, and about feventy men, who had been anxioufly waiting for our arrival, and received us with every mark of fatisfaction and regard which they could exprefs. If we might judge from the quantity of powder that was wafted on our arrival, they certainly had not been in want of ammunition, at leaft during the fummer.

The banks of the river, from the falls, are in general lofty, except at low woody points, accidentally formed in the manner I have already mentioned: they alfo difplayed, in all their broken parts, a face of clay, intermixed with ftone; in fome places there likewife appeared a black mould.

In the fummer of 1788, a fmall fpot was cleared at the Old Eftablifhment, which is fituated on a bank thirty feet above the level of the river, and was fown with turnips, carrots, and parfnips. The firft grew to a large fize, and the others thrived very well. An experiment was alfo made with potatoes and cabbages, the former of which were fuccefsful; but for want of care the latter failed. The next winter the perfon who had undertaken this cultivation, fuffered the potatoes, which had been collected for feed, to catch the froft, and none had been fince brought to this place. There is not the leaft doubt but the foil would be very productive, if a proper attention was given to its preparation. In the fall of the year 1787, when I firft arrived at Athabafca, Mr. Pond was fettled on the banks of the Elk River, where he remained for three years, and had formed as fine a kitchen garden as I ever faw in Canada.

In

In addition to the wood which flourifhed below the fall, thefe banks produce the cyprefs tree, arrow-wood, and the thorn. On either fide of the river, though invifible from it, are extenfive plains, which abound in buffaloes, elks, wolves, foxes, and bears. At a confiderable diftance to the Weftward, is an immenfe ridge of high land or mountains, which take an oblique direction from below the falls, and are inhabited by great numbers of deer, who are feldom difturbed, but when the Indians go to hunt the beaver in thofe parts; and, being tired of the flefh of the latter, vary their food with that of the former. This ridge bears the name of the Deer Mountain. Oppofite to our prefent fituation, are beautiful meadows, with various animals grazing on them, and groves of poplars irregularly fcattered over them.

My tent was no fooner pitched, than I fummoned the Indians together, and gave each of them about four inches of Brazil tobacco, a dram of fpirits, and lighted the pipe. As they had been very troublefome to my predeceffor, I informed them that I had heard of their mifconduct, and was come among them to inquire into the truth of it. I added alfo that it would be an eftablifhed rule with me to treat them with kindnefs, if their behaviour fhould be fuch as to deferve it; but, at the fame time, that I fhould be equally fevere if they failed in thofe returns which I had a right to expect from them. I then prefented them with a quantity of rum, which I recommended to be ufed with difcretion; and added fome tobacco, as a token of peace. They, in return, made me the faireft promifes; and, having expreffed the pride they felt on beholding me in their country, took their leave.

I now

I now proceeded to examine my fituation; and it was with great fatisfaction I obferved that the two men who had been fent hither fome time before us, to cut and fquare timber for our future operations, had employed the intervening period with activity and fkill. They had formed a fufficient quantity of pallifades of eighteen feet long, and feven inches in diameter, to inclofe a fquare fpot of an hundred and twenty feet; they had alfo dug a ditch of three feet deep to receive them; and had prepared timber, planks, &c. for the erection of an houfe.

I was, however, fo much occupied in fettling matters with the Indians, and equipping them for their winter hunting, that I could not give my attention to any other object, till the 7th, when I fet all hands at work to conftruct the fort, build the houfe, and form ftore-houfes. On the pre-ceding day the river began to run with ice, which we call the laft of the navigation. On the 11th we had a South-Weft wind, with fnow. On the 16th the ice ftopped in the other fork, which was not above a league from us, acrofs the intervening neck of land. The water in this branch continued to flow till the 22d, when it was arrefted alfo by the froft, fo that we had a paffage acrofs the river, which would laft to the latter end of the fucceeding April. This was a fortunate circumftance, as we de-pended for our fupport upon what the hunters could provide for us, and they had been prevented by the running of the ice from croffing the river. They now, however, very fhortly procured us as much frefh meat as we required, though it was for fome time a toilfome bufinefs to my people, for as there was not yet a fufficient quantity of fnow to run fledges, they were under the neceffity of loading themfelves with the fpoils of the chafe.

On

On the 27th the froſt was ſo ſevere that the axes of the workmen became almoſt as brittle as glaſs. The weather was very various until the 2d of December, when my Farenheit's thermometer was injured by an accident, which rendered it altogether uſeleſs. The following table, therefore, from the 16th of November, to this unfortunate circumſtance, is the only correct account of the weather which I can offer.

Month and Year	Date	Hours A.M.	below 0	above 0	Wind	Weather	Hour	below 0	above 0	Wind	Weather	Hour P.M.	below 0	above 0	Wind	Weather	
1792 Nov	16	8½		10			12	0	14			6		15		cloudy	
	17	8½		17		clear	12		20		clear	6		23		ditto	
	18	9		19	ESE		12		21	ESE		6		14	ESE	clear	
	19	8		5	NW		12		12	NW		6		9	NW	ditto	Strong wind.
	20	8½		4	——	ditto	12		14	——	ditto	6		19	——	cloudy	at 10 laſt night 1 below 0.
	21	8		19	——		12		25	——		6		23	——		Rsver ſtopped.
	22	9		27	——	cloudy	12		29	——	cloudy	6		28	——	cloudy	Ice drove, and water riſes.
	23	8½		2	N.	clear	12		23	——	clear	6		15	N.		Ice drove again.
	24	8	3		——	ditto	12	0	0	NE.		6	1		N E.	cloudy	
	25	8	14		——	ditto	12	4		——		6	2		——	clear	Snowed laſt night 2 inches.
	26	0	10		N.	ditto	12		2	N.		6	0	0	N.	ditto	
	27	8	2		——	ditto	12		2	——		6		1	S W	ditto	
	28	8	16		——	ditto	12	3		——		6	7		S.	ditto	After dark, over caſt.
	29	7½		4	——	cloudy	12		13			6		7	——	ditto	Ditto, a little wind S. W.
	30	9		4	S.		12		13	S.	cloudy	5		16	S.	cloudy	
Dec.	1	9		10	——		12		19	S. E.		5		24	S. E.	ditto	Fell 3 inches ſnow laſt night
	2	9		27	E.												

In this ſituation, removed from all thoſe ready aids which add ſo much to the comfort, and indeed is a principal characteriſtic of civilized life, I was under the neceſſity of employing my judgment and experience in acceſſory circumſtances, by no means connected with the habits of my life, or the enterpriſe in which I was immediately engaged. I was now among a people who had no knowledge whatever of remedial application

tion to thofe diforders and accidents to which man is liable in every part of the globe, in the diftant wildernefs, as in the peopled city. Thev had not the leaft acquaintance with that primitive medicine which confifts in an experience of the healing virtues of herbs and plants, and is frequently found among uncivilifed and favage nations. This circumftance now obliged me to be their phyfician and furgeon, as a woman with a fwelled breaft, which had been lacerated with flint ftones for the cure of it, prefented herfelf to my attention, and by cleanlinefs, poultices, and healing falve, I fucceeded in producing a cure. One of thefe people alfo, who was at work in the woods, was attacked with a fudden pain near the firft joint of his thumb, which difabled him from holding an axe. On examining his arm, I was aftonifhed to find a narrow red ftripe, about half an inch wide, from his thumb to his fhoulder; the pain was violent, and accompanied with chillinefs and fhivering. This was a cafe that appeared to be beyond my fkill, but it was neceffary to do fomething towards relieving the mind of the patient, though I might be unfuccefsful in removing his complaint. I accordingly prepared a kind of volatile liniment of rum and foap, with which I ordered his arm to be rubbed, but with little or no effect. He was in a raving ftate throughout the night, and the red ftripe not only encreafed, but was alfo accompanied with the appearance of feveral blotches on his body, and pains in his ftomach: the propriety of taking fome blood from him now occurred to me, and I ventured, from abfolute neceffity, to perform that operation for the firft time, and with an effect that juftified the treatment. The following night afforded him reft, and in a fhort time he regained his former health and activity.

I was

I was very much furprifed on walking in the woods at fuch an incle-ment period of the year, to be faluted with the finging of birds, while they feemed by their vivacity to be actuated by the invigorating power of a more genial feafon. Of thefe birds the male was fomething lefs than the robin; part of his body is of a delicate fawn colour, and his neck, breaft, and belly, of a deep fcarlet; the wings are black, edged with fawn colour, and two white ftripes running acrofs them; the tail is variegated, and the head crowned with a tuft. The female is fmaller than the male, and of a fawn colour throughout, except on the neck, which is enlivened by an hue of gloffy yellow. I have no doubt but they are conftant inhabitants of this climate, as well as fome other fmall birds which we faw, of a grey colour.

CHAP.

CHAPTER II.

Removed from the tent to the houfe. Build habitations for the people. The hardfhips they fuffer. Violent hurricane. Singular circumftances attending it. The commencement of the new year. An Indian cured of a dangerous wound. State of the weather. Curious cuftoms among the Indians, on the death of a relation. Account of a quarrel. An Indian's reafoning on it. Murder of one of the Indians. The caufe of it. Some account of the Rocky Mountain Indians. Curious circumftance refpecting a woman in labour, &c. A difpute between two Indians, which arofe from gaming. An account of one of their games. Indian fuperftition. Mildnefs of the feafon. The Indians prepare fnow fhoes. Singular cuftoms. Further account of their manners. The flavifh ftate of the women. Appearance of fpring. Difpatch canoes with the trade to Fort Chepewyan. Make preparations for the voyage of difcovery.

I THIS day removed from the tent into the houfe which had been erected for me, and fet all the men to begin the buildings intended for their own habitation. Materials fufficient to erect a range of five houfes for them, of about feventeen by twelve feet, were already collected. It would be confidered by the inhabitants of a milder climate, as a great evil, to be expofed to the weather at this rigorous feafon of the year, but thefe people are inured to it, and it is neceffary to defcribe in fome mea-

1792.
Decemb. 23.

fure

sure the hardships which they undergo without a murmur, in order to convey a general notion of them.

The men who were now with me, left this place in the beginning of last May, and went to the Rainy Lake in canoes, laden with packs of fur, which, from the immense length of the voyage, and other concurring circumstances, is a most severe trial of patience and perseverance: there they do not remain a sufficient time for ordinary repose, when they take a load of goods in exchange, and proceed on their return, in a great measure, day and night. They had been arrived near two months, and, all that time, had been continually engaged in very toilsome labour, with nothing more than a common shed to protect them from the frost and snow. Such is the life which these people lead; and is continued with unremitting exertion, till their strength is lost in premature old age.

The Canadians remarked, that the weather we had on the 25th, 26th, and 27th of this month, denoted such as we might expect in the three succeeding months. On the 29th, the wind being at North-East, and the weather calm and cloudy, a rumbling noise was heard in the air like distant thunder, when the sky cleared away in the South-West; from whence there blew a perfect hurricane, which lasted till eight. Soon after it commenced, the atmosphere became so warm that it dissolved all the snow on the ground; even the ice was covered with water, and had the same appearance as when it is breaking up in the spring. From eight to nine the weather became calm, but immediately after a wind arose from the North-East with equal violence,

with

with clouds, rain, and hail, which continued throughout the night and till the evening of the next day, when it turned to fnow. One of the people who wintered at Fort Dauphin in the year 1780, when the fmall-pox firft appeared there, informed me, that the weather there was of a fimilar defcription.

On the firft day of January, my people, in conformity to the ufual cuftom, awoke me at the break of day with the difcharge of fire-arms, with which they congratulated the appearance of the new year. In return, they were treated with plenty of fpirits, and when there is any flour, cakes are always added to their regales, which was the cafe on the prefent occafion.

On my arrival here laft fall, I found that one of the young Indians had loft the ufe of his right hand by the burfting of a gun, and that his thumb had been maimed in fuch a manner as to hang only by a fmall ftrip of flefh. Indeed, when he was brought to me, his wound was in fuch an offenfive ftate, and emitted fuch a putrid fmell, that it required all the refolution I poffeffed to examine it. His friends had done every thing in their power to relieve him; but as it confifted only in finging about him, and blowing upon his hand, the wound, as may be well imagined, had got into the deplorable ftate in which I found it. I was rather alarmed at the difficulty of the cafe, but as the young man's life was in a ftate of hazard, I was determined to rifk my furgical reputation, and accordingly took him under my care. I immediately formed a poultice of bark, ftripped from the roots of the fpruce-fir, which I applied to the wound, having firft wafhed it with the juice of the

bark:

bark: this proved a very painful dreſſing: in a few days, however, the wound was clean, and the proud fleſh around it deſtroyed. I wiſhed very much in this ſtate of the buſineſs to have ſeparated the thumb from the hand, which I well knew muſt be effected before the cure could be performed; but he would not conſent to that operation, till, by the application of vitriol, the fleſh by which the thumb was ſuſpended, was ſhrivelled almoſt to a thread. When I had ſucceeded in this object, I perceived that the wound was cloſing rather faſter than I deſired. The ſalve I applied on the occaſion was made of the Canadian balſam, wax, and tallow dropped from a burning candle into water. In ſhort, I was ſo ſucceſsful, that about Chriſtmas my patient engaged in an hunting party, and brought me the tongue of an elk: nor was he finally ungrateful. When he left me I received the warmeſt acknowledgments, both from himſelf, and the relations with whom he departed, for my care of him. I certainly did not ſpare my time or attention on the occaſion, as I regularly dreſſed his wound three times a day, during the courſe of a month.

On the 5th in the morning the weather was calm, clear, and very cold; the wind blew from the South-Weſt, and in the courſe of the afternoon it began to thaw. I had already obſerved at Athabaſca, that this wind never failed to bring us clear mild weather, whereas, when it blew from the oppoſite quarter, it produced ſnow. Here it is much more perceptible, for if it blows hard South-Weſt for four hours, a thaw is the conſequence, and if the wind is at North-Eaſt it brings ſleet and ſnow To this cauſe it may be attributed, that there is now ſo little ſnow in this part of the world. Theſe warm winds come off the Pacific Ocean,
which

which cannot, in a direct line, be very far from us; the diftance being fo fhort, that though they pafs over mountains covered with fnow, there is not time for them to cool.

There being feveral of the natives at the houfe at this time, one of them, who had received an account of the death of his father, proceeded in filence to his lodge, and began to fire off his gun. As it was night, and fuch a noife being fo uncommon at fuch an hour, efpecially when it was fo often repeated, I fent my interpreter to inquire into the caufe of it, when he was informed by the man himfelf, that this was a common cuftom with them on the death of a near relation, and was a warning to their friends not to approach, or intrude upon them, as they were, in confequence of their lofs, become carelefs of life. The chief, to whom the deceafed perfon was alfo related, appeared with his war-cap on his head, which is only worn on thefe folemn occafions, or when preparing for battle, and confirmed to me this fingular cuftom of firing guns, in order to exprefs their grief for the death of relations and friends.* The women alone indulge in tears on fuch occafions; the men confidering it as a mark of pufillanimity and a want of fortitude to betray any per-fonal tokens of fenfibility or forrow.

The Indians informed me, that they had been to hunt at a large lake, called by the Knifteneaux, the Slave Lake, which derived its name from that of its original inhabitants, who were called Slaves. They repre-

---

* When they are drinking together, they frequently prefent their guns to each other, when any of the parties have not other means of procuring rum. On fuch an occafion they always difcharge their pieces, as a proof, I imagine, of their being in good order, and to determine the quantity of liquor the may propofe to get in exchange for them.

fented

fented it as a large body of water, and that it lies about one hundred
and twenty miles due Eaft from this place. It is well known to the
Knifteneaux, who are among the inhabitants of the plains on the banks
of the Safkatchiwine river; for formerly, when they ufed to come to
make war in this country, they came in their canoes to that lake, and
left them there; from thence there is a beaten path all the way to the
Fork, or Eaft branch of this river, which was their war-road.

January 10.   Among the people who were now here, there were two Rocky Mountain Indians, who declared, that the people to whom we had given that
denomination, are by no means entitled to it, and that their country has
ever been in the vicinity of our prefent fituation. They faid, in fupport
of their affertion, that thefe people were entirely ignorant of thofe parts
which are adjacent to the mountain, as well as the navigation of the
river; that the Beaver Indians had greatly encroached upon them, and
would foon force them to retire to the foot of thefe mountains. They
reprefented themfelves as the only real natives of that country then
with me: and added, that the country, and that part of the river that
intervenes between this place and the mountains, bear much the fame
appearance as that around us; that the former abounds with animals,
but that the courfe of the latter is interrupted, near, and in the mountains, by fucceffive rapids and confiderable falls. Thefe men alfo informed me, that there is another great river towards the mid-day fun,
whofe current runs in that direction, and that the diftance from it is not
great acrofs the mountains.

The natives brought me plenty of furs. The fmall quantity of
fnow, at this time, was particularly favourable for hunting the beaver, as
from

from this circumſtance, thoſe animals could, with the greater facility, be traced from their lodges to their lurking-places.

On the 12th the hunter arrived, having left his mother-in-law, who was lately become a widow with three ſmall children, and in actual labour of a fourth.   Her daughter related this circumſtance to the women here, without the leaſt appearance of concern, though ſhe repreſented her as in a ſtate of great danger, which probably might proceed from her being abandoned in this unnatural manner.   At the ſame time without any apparent conſciouſneſs of her own barbarous negligence; if the poor abandoned woman ſhould die, ſhe would moſt probably lament her with great outcries, and, perhaps, cut off one or two joints of her fingers as tokens of her grief.   The Indians, indeed, conſider the ſtate of a woman in labour as among the moſt trifling occurrences of corporal pain to which human nature is ſubject, and they may be, in ſome meaſure, juſtified in this apparent inſenſibility from the circumſtances of that ſituation among themſelves.   It is by no means uncommon in the haſty removal of their camps from one poſition to another, for a woman to be taken in labour, to deliver herſelf in her way, without any aſſiſtance or notice from her aſſociates in the journey, and to overtake them before they complete the arrangements of their evening ſtation, with her new-born babe on her back.

I was this morning threatened with a very unpleaſant event, which, however, I was fortunately enabled to control.   Two young Indians being engaged in one of their games, a diſpute enſued, which roſe to ſuch an height, that they drew their knives, and if I had not happened

to

to have appeared, they would, I doubt not, have employed them to very bloody purpofes. So violent was their rage, that after I had turned them both out of the houfe, and feverely reprimanded them, they ftood in the fort for at leaft half an hour, looking at each other with a moft vindictive afpect, and in fullen filence.

The game which produced this ftate of bitter enmity, is called that of the Platter, from a principal article of it. The Indians play at it in the following manner.

The inftruments of it confift of a platter, or difh, made of wood or bark, and fix round, or fquare, but flat pieces of metal, wood, or ftone, whofe fides or furfaces are of different colours. Thefe are put into the difh, and after being for fome time fhaken together, are thrown into the air, and received again in the difh with confiderable dexterity; when, by the number that are turned up of the fame mark or colour, the game is regulated. If there fhould be equal numbers, the throw is not reckoned; if two or four, the platter changes hands.

On the 13th, one of thefe people came to me, and prefented in himfelf a curious example of Indian fuperftition. He requefted me to furnifh him with a remedy that might be applied to the joints of his legs and thighs, of which he had, in a great meafure loft the ufe for five winters. This affliction he attributed to his cruelty about that time, when having found a wolf with two whelps in an old Beaver lodge, he fet fire to it and confumed them.

The

The winter had been fo mild, that the fwans had but lately left us, and at this advanced period there was very little fnow on the ground: it was, however, at this time a foot and a half in depth, in the environs of the eftablifhment below this, which is at the diftance of about feventy leagues.

On the 28th the Indians were now employed in making their fnow-fhoes, as the fnow had not hitherto fallen in fufficient quantity to render them neceffary.

The weather now became very cold, and it froze fo hard in the night that my watch ftopped; a circumftance that had never happened to this watch fince my refidence in the country.

There was a lodge of Indians here, who were abfolutely ftarving with cold and hunger. They had lately loft a near relation, and had, according to cuftom, thrown away every thing belonging to them, and even exchanged the few articles of raiment which they poffeffed, in order, as I prefume, to get rid of every thing that may bring the deceafed to their remembrance. They alfo deftroy every thing belonging to any deceafed perfon, except what they confign to the grave with the late owner of them. We had fome difficulty to make them comprehend that the debts of a man who dies fhould be difcharged, if he left any furs behind him: but thofe who underftand this principle of juftice, and profefs to adhere to it, never fail to prevent the appearance of any fkins beyond fuch as may be neceffary to fatisfy the debts of their dead relation.

On the 8th I had an obfervation for the longitude. In the courfe of this

this day one of my men, who had been fome time with the Indians, came to inform me that one of them had threatened to ftab him; and on his preferring a complaint to the man with whom he now lived, and to whom I had given him in charge, he replied, that he had been very imprudent to play and quarrel with the young Indians out of his lodge, where no one would dare to come and quarrel with him; but that if he had loft his life where he had been, it would have been the confequence of his own folly. Thus, even among thefe children of nature, it appears that a man's houfe is his caftle, where the protection of hofpitality is rigidly maintained.

The hard froft which had prevailed from the beginning of February continued to the 16th of March, when the wind blowing from the South-Weft, the weather became mild.

On the 22d a wolf was fo bold as to venture among the Indian lodges, and was very near carrying off a child.

I had another obfervation of Jupiter and his fatellites for the longitude. On the 13th fome geefe were feen, and thefe birds are always confidered as the harbingers of fpring. On the 1ft of April my hunters fhot five of them. This was a much earlier period than I ever remember to have obferved the vifits of wild fowl in this part of the world. The weather had been mild for the laft fortnight, and there was a promife of its continuance. On the 5th the fnow had entirely difappeared.

At half paft four this morning I was awakened to be informed that an Indian had been killed. I accordingly haftened to the camp, where
I found

I found two women employed in rolling up the dead body of a man, called the White Partridge, in a beaver robe, which I had lent him. He had received four mortal wounds from a dagger, two within the collar-bone, one in the left breaſt, and another in the ſmall of the back, with two cuts acroſs his head. The murderer, who had been my hunter through-out the winter, had fled; and it was pretended that ſeveral relations of the deceaſed were gone in purſuit of him. The hiſtory of this un-fortunate event is as follows:—

Theſe two men had been comrades for four years; the murderer had three wives; and the young man who was killed, becoming enamoured of one of them, the huſband conſented to yield her to him, with the reſerved power of claiming her as his property, when it ſhould be his pleaſure. This connection was uninterrupted for near three years, when, whimſical as it may appear, the huſband became jealous, and the public amour was ſuſpended. The parties, however, made their private aſſig-nations, which cauſed the woman to be ſo ill treated by her huſband, that the paramour was determined to take her away by force; and this project ended in his death. This is a very common practice among the Indians, and generally terminates in very ſerious and fatal quarrels. In conſequence of this event all the Indians went away in great apparent hurry and con-fuſion, and in the evening not one of them was to be ſeen about the fort.

The Beaver and Rocky Mountain Indians, who traded with us in this river, did not exceed an hundred and fifty men, capable of bearing arms; two thirds of whom call themſelves Beaver Indians. The latter differ only from the former, as they have, more or leſs, imbibed the cuſ-

toms

toms and manners of the Knifteneaux. As I have already obferved, they are paffionately fond of liquor, and in the moments of their feftivity will barter any thing they have in their poffeffion for it.

Though the Beaver Indians made their peace with the Knifteneaux, at Peace Point, as already mentioned, yet they did not fecure a ftate of amity from others of the fame nation, who had driven away the natives of the Safkatchiwine and Miffinipy Rivers, and joined at the head water of the latter, called the Beaver River: from thence they proceeded Weft by the Slave Lake juft defcribed, on their war excurfions, which they often repeated, even till the Beaver Indians had procured arms, which was in the year 1782. If it fo happened that they miffed them, they proceeded Weftward till they were certain of wreaking their vengeance on thofe of the Rocky Mountain, who being without arms, became an eafy prey to their blind and favage fury. All the European articles they poffeffed, previous to the year 1780, were obtained from the Knifteneaux and Chepewyans, who brought them from Fort Churchill, and for which they were made to pay an extravagant price.

As late as the year 1786, when the firft traders from Canada arrived on the banks of this river, the natives employed bows and fnares, but at prefent very little ufe is made of the former, and the latter are no longer known. They ftill entertain a great dread of their natural enemies, but they are fince become fo well armed, that the others now call them their allies. The men are in general of a comely appearance, and fond of perfonal decoration. The women are of a contrary difpofition, and the flaves of the men: in common with all the Indian tribes polygamy is allowed

among

among them. They are very fubject to jealoufy, and fatal confequences frequently refult from the indulgence of that paffion. But notwithftanding the vigilance and feverity which is exercifed by the hufband, it feldom happens that a woman is without her favourite, who,
in the abfence of the hufband, exacts the fame fubmiffion, and practifes
the fame tyranny. And fo premature is the tender paffion, that it is
fometimes known to invigorate fo early a period of life as the age of
eleven or twelve years. The women are not very prolific; a circumftance which may be attributed, in a great meafure, to the hardfhips that
they fuffer, for except a few fmall dogs, they alone perform that labour
which is allotted to beafts of burthen in other countries. It is not uncommon, while the men carry nothing but a gun, that their wives and daughters follow with fuch weighty burdens, that if they lay them down they
cannot replace them, and that is a kindnefs which the men will not deign
to perform; fo that during their journeys they are frequently obliged to
lean againft a tree for a fmall portion of temporary relief. When they
arrive at the place which their tyrants have chofen for their encampment, they arrange the whole in a few minutes, by forming a curve of
poles, meeting at the top, and expanding into circles of twelve or fifteen
feet diameter at the bottom, covered with dreffed fkins of the moofe
fewed together. During thefe preparations, the men fit down quietly to
the enjoyment of their pipes, if they happen to have any tobacco. But
notwithftanding this abject ftate of flavery and fubmiffion, the women
have a confiderable influence on the opinion of the men in every thing
except their own domeftic fituation.

Thefe Indians are excellent hunters, and their exercife in that capacity

is

is fo violent as to reduce them in general to a very meagre appearance. Their religion is of a very contracted nature, and I never witneffed any ceremony of devotion which they had not borrowed from the Knifteneaux, their feafts and fafts being in imitation of that people. They are more vicious and warlike than the Chepewyans, from whence they fprang, though they do not poffefs their felfifhnefs, for while they have the means of purchafing their neceffaries, they are liberal and generous, but when thofe are exhaufted they become errant beggars: they are, however, remarkable for their honefty, for in the whole tribe there were only two women and a man who had been known to have fwerved from that virtue, and they were confidered as objects of difregard and reprobation. They are afflicted with but few difeafes, and their only remedies confift in binding the temples, procuring perfpiration, finging, and blowing on the fick perfon, or affected part. When death overtakes any of them, their property, as I have before obferved, is facrificed and deftroyed; nor is there any failure of lamentation or mourning on fuch occafion: they who are more nearly related to the departed perfon, black their faces, and fometimes cut off their hair; they alfo pierce their arms with knives and arrows. The grief of the females is carried to a ftill greater excefs; they not only cut their hair, and cry and howl, but they will fometimes, with the utmoft deliberation, employ fome fharp inftrument to feparate the nail from the finger, and then force back the flefh beyond the firft joint, which they immediately amputate. But this extraordinary mark of affliction is only difplayed on the death of a favourite fon, an hufband, or a father. Many of the old women have fo often repeated this ceremony, that they have not a complete finger remaining on either hand. The women renew their lamentations
tations

tations at the graves of their departed relatives for a long fucceffion of years. They appear, in common with all the Indian tribes, to be very fond of their children, but they are as carelefs in their mode of fwadling them in their infant ftate, as they are of their own drefs: the child is laid down on a board, of about two feet long, covered with a bed of mofs, to which it is faftened by bandages, the mofs being changed as often as the occafion requires. The chief of the nation had no lefs than nine wives, and children in proportion.

When traders firft appeared among thefe people, the Canadians were treated with the utmoft hofpitality and attention; but they have, by their fubfequent conduct, taught the natives to withdraw that refpect from them, and fometimes to treat them with indignity. They differ very much from the Chepewyans and Knifteneaux, in the abhorrence they profefs of any carnal communication between their women and the white people. They carry their love of gaming to excefs; they will purfue it for a fucceffion of days and nights, and no apprehenfion of ruin, nor influence of domeftic affection, will reftrain them from the indulgence of it. They are a quick, lively, active people, with a keen, penetrating, dark eye; and though they are very fufceptible of anger, are as eafily appeafed. The males eradicate their beards, and the females their hair in every part, except their heads, where it is ftrong and black, and without a curl. There are many old men among them, but they are in general ignorant of the fpace in which they have been inhabitants of the earth, though one of them told me that he recollected fixty winters.

An Indian in fome meafure explained his age to me, by relating that
he

he remembered the oppofite hills and plains, now interfperfed with groves of poplars, when they were covered with mofs, and without any animal inhabitant but the rein-deer. By degrees, he faid, the face of the country changed to its prefent appearance, when the elk came from the Eaft, and was followed by the buffalo; the rein-deer then retired to the long range of high lands that, at a confiderable diftance, run parallel with this river.

On the 20th of April I had an obfervation of Jupiter and his fatellites, for the longitude, and we were now vifited by our fummer companions the gnats and mofquitoes. On the other fide of the river, which was yet covered with ice, the plains were delightful; the trees were budding, and many plants in bloffom. Mr. Mackay brought me a bunch of flowers of a pink colour, and a yellow button, encircled with fix leaves of a light purple. The change in the appearance of nature was as fudden as it was pleafing, for a few days only were paffed away fince the ground was covered with fnow. On the 25th the river was cleared of the ice.

I now found that the death of the man called the White Partridge, had deranged all the plans which I had fettled with the Indians for the fpring hunting. They had affembled at fome diftance from the fort, and fent an embaffy to me, to demand rum to drink, that they might have an opportunity of crying for their deceafed brother. It would be con- fidered as an extreme degradation in an Indian to weep when fober, but a ftate of intoxication fanctions all irregularities. On my refufal, they threatened to go to war, which, from motives of intereft as well as humanity, we did our utmoft to difcourage; and as a fecond meffage

was

was brought by perfons of fome weight among thefe people, and on whom I could depend, I thought it prudent to comply with the demand, on an exprefs condition, that they would continue peaceably at home.

The month of April being now paft, in the early part of which I was moft bufily employed in trading with the Indians, I ordered our old canoes to be repaired with bark, and added four new ones to them, when with the furs and provifions I had purchafed, fix canoes were loaded and difpatched on the 8th of May for Fort Chepewyan. I had, however, retained fix of the men who agreed to accompany me on my projected voyage of difcovery. I alfo engaged my hunters, and clofed the bufinefs of the year for the company by writing my public and private difpatches.

Having afcertained, by various obfervations, the latitude of this place to be 56. 9. North, and longitude 117. 35. 15. Weft:—on the 9th day of May, I found, that my acrometer was one hour forty-fix minutes flow to apparent time; the mean going of it I had found to be twenty-two feconds flow in twenty-four hours. Having fettled this point, the canoe was put into the water: her dimenfions were twenty-five feet long within, exclufive of the curves of ftem and ftern, twenty-fix inches hold, and four feet nine inches beam. At the fame time fhe was fo light, that two men could carry her on a good road three or four miles without refting. In this flender veffel, we fhipped provifions, goods for prefents, arms, ammunition, and baggage, to the weight of three thoufand pounds, and an equipage of ten people; viz. Alexander Mackay, Jofeph Landry,

Charles

Charles Ducette,* François Beaulieux, Baptift Biffon, Francois Courtois, and Jacques Beauchamp, with two Indians as hunters and interpreters. One of them, when a boy, was ufed to be fo idle, that he obtained the reputable name of Cancre, which he ftill poffeffes. With thefe perfons I embarked at feven in the evening. My winter interpreter, with another perfon, whom I left here to take care of the fort, and fupply the natives with ammunition during the fummer, fhed tears on the reflection of thofe dangers which we might encounter in our expedition, while my own people offered up their prayers that we might return in fafety from it.

---

* Jofeph Landry and Charles Ducette were with me in my former voyage.

CHAP.

CHAPTER III.

Proceed on the voyage of discovery. Beautiful scenery. The canoe too heavily laden. The country in a state of combustion. Meet with an hunting party. State of the river, &c. Meet with Indians. See the tracks of bears, and one of their dens. Sentiment of an Indian. Junction of the Bear River. Appearance of the country. State of the river. Observe a fall of timber. Abundance of animals. See some bears. Come in sight of the rocky mountains. The canoe receives an injury and is repaired. Navigation dangerous. Rapids and falls. Succession of difficulties and dangers.

——————

1793.
May.
Thursday 9.

WE began our voyage with a course South by West against a strong current one mile and three quarters, South-West by South one mile, and landed before eight on an island for the night.

Friday 10.

The weather was clear and pleasant, though there was a keenness in the air; and at a quarter past three in the morning we continued our voyage, steering South-West three quarters of a mile, South-West by South one mile and a quarter, South three quarters of a mile, South-West by South one quarter of a mile, South-West by West one mile, South-West by South three miles, South by West three quarters of a mile,

mile, and South-Weſt one mile. The canoe being ſtrained from its having
been very heavily laden, became ſo leaky, that we were obliged to land,
unload, and gum it. As this circumſtance took place about twelve, I had
an opportunity of taking an altitude, which made our latitude 55. 58. 48.

When the canoe was repaired we continued our courſe, ſteering South-
Weſt by Weſt one mile and an half, when I had the misfortune to drop
my pocket-compaſs into the water; Weſt half a mile, Weſt-South-Weſt
four miles and an half. Here, the banks are ſteep and hilly, and in ſome
parts undermined by the river. Where the earth has given way, the face
of the cliffs diſcovers numerous ſtrata, conſiſting of reddiſh earth and
ſmall ſtones, bitumen, and a greyiſh earth, below which, near the water-
edge, is a red ſtone. Water iſſues from moſt of the banks, and the ground
on which it ſpreads is covered with a thin white ſcurf, or particles of
a ſaline ſubſtance: there are ſeveral of theſe ſalt ſprings. At half paſt
ſix in the afternoon the young men landed, when they killed an elk
and wounded a buffalo. In this ſpot we formed our encampment for
the night.

From the place which we quitted this morning, the Weſt ſide of the
river diſplayed a ſucceſſion of the moſt beautiful ſcenery I had ever beheld. The ground riſes at intervals to a conſiderable height, and ſtretching inwards to a conſiderable diſtance: at every interval or pauſe in the
riſe, there is a very gently-aſcending ſpace or lawn, which is alternate
with abrupt precipices to the ſummit of the whole, or, at leaſt as far as
the eye could diſtinguiſh. This magnificent theatre of nature has all
the decorations which the trees and animals of the country can afford it:
groves

groves of poplars in every fhape vary the fcene; and their intervals are enlivened with vaft herds of elks and buffaloes: the former choofing the fteeps and uplands, and the latter preferring the plains. At this time the buffaloes were attended with their young ones who were frifking about them; and it appeared that the elks would foon exhibit the fame enlivening circumftance. The whole country difplayed an exuberant verdure; the trees that bear a bloffom were advancing faft to that de-lightful appearance, and the velvet rind of their branches reflecting the oblique rays of a rifing or fetting fun, added a fplendid gaiety to the fcene, which no expreffions of mine are qualified to defcribe. The Eaft fide of the river confifts of a range of high land covered with the white fpruce and the foft birch, while the banks abound with the alder and the willow. The water continued to rife, and the current being proportionably ftrong, we made a greater ufe of fetting poles than paddles.

The weather was overcaft. With a ftrong wind a-head, we embarked at four in the morning, and left all the frefh meat behind us, but the portion which had been affigned to the kettle; the canoe being already too heavily laden. Our courfe was Weft-South-Weft one mile, where a fmall river flowed in from the Eaft, named *Quifcatina Sepy*, or River with the High Banks; Weft half a mile, South half a mile, South-Weft by Weft three quarters of a mile, Weft one mile and a quarter, South-Weft a quarter of a mile, South-South-Weft half a mile, and Weft by South a mile and an half. Here I took a meridian altitude, which gave 55. 56. 3. North latitude. We then proceeded Weft three miles and an half, Weft-South-Weft, where the whole plain was on fire, one mile,

Weft

Weſt one mile, and the wind ſo ſtrong a-head, that it occaſioned the canoe to take in water, and otherwiſe impeded our progreſs. Here we landed to take time, with the mean of three altitudes, which made the watch ſlow, 1. 42. 10. apparent time.

We now proceeded Weſt-South-Weſt, one mile and a quarter, where we found a chief of the Beaver Indians on an hunting party. I remained, however, in my canoe, and though it was getting late, I did not chooſe to encamp with theſe people, leſt the friends of my hunters might diſcourage them from proceeding on the voyage. We, therefore, continued our courſe, but ſeveral Indians kept company with us, running along the bank and converſing with my people, who were ſo attentive to them, that they drove the canoe on a ſtony flat, ſo that we were under the neceſſity of landing to repair the damages, and put up for the night, though very contrary to my wiſhes. My hunters obtained permiſſion to proceed with ſome of theſe people to their lodges, on the promiſe of being back by the break of day; though I was not without ſome apprehenſion reſpecting them. The chief, however, and another man, as well as ſeveral people from the lodges, joined us, before we had completed the repair of the canoe; and they made out a melancholy ſtory, that they had neither ammunition or tobacco ſufficient for their neceſſary ſupply during the ſummer. I accordingly referred him to the Fort, where plenty of thoſe articles were left in the care of my interpreter, by whom they would be abundantly furniſhed, if they were active and induſtrious in purſuing their occupations. I did not fail, on this occaſion, to magnify the advantages of the preſent expedition; obſerving, at the ſame time, that its ſucceſs would depend on the fidelity and

conduct

conduct of the young men who were retained by me to hunt. The
chief alfo propofed to borrow my canoe, in order to tranfport himfelf
and family acrofs the river: feveral plaufible reafons, it is true, fuggefted themfelves for refifting his propofition; but when I ftated to him,
that, as the canoe was intended for a voyage of fuch confequence, no
woman could be permitted to be embarked in it, he acquiefced in the refufal. It was near twelve at night when he took his leave, after I had
gratified him with a prefent of tobacco.

Some of the Indians paffed the night with us, and I was informed by
them, that, according to our mode of proceeding, we fhould, in ten days,
get as far as the rocky mountains. The young men now returned, to
my great fatisfaction, and with the appearance of contentment: though
I was not pleafed when they dreffed themfelves in the clothes which I
had given them before we left the Fort, as it betrayed fome latent defign.

At four in the morning we proceeded on our voyage, fteering Weft
three miles, including one of our courfe yefterday, North-Weft by North
four miles, Weft two miles and an half, North-Weft by Weft a mile and
an half, North by Eaft two miles, North-Weft by Weft one mile, and
North-North-Weft three miles. After a continuation of our courfe
where to the North for a mile and an half, we landed for the night on an
ifland feveral of the Indians vifited us, but unattended by their women,
who remained in their camp, which was at fome diftance from us.

The land on both fides of the river, during the two laft days, is very
much elevated, but particularly in the latter part of it, and, on the Weftern
side,

fide, prefents in different places, white, fteep, and lofty cliffs. Our view being confined by thefe circumftances, we did not fee fo many animals as on the 10th. Between thefe lofty boundaries, the river becomes narrow, and in a great meafure free from iflands; for we had paffed only four: the ftream, indeed, was not more than from two hundred to three hundred yards broad; whereas before thefe cliffs preffed upon it, its breadth was twice that extent and befprinkled with iflands. We killed an elk, and fired feveral fhots at animals from the canoe.

The greater part of this band being Rocky Mountain Indians, I endeavoured to obtain fome intelligence of our intended route, but they all pleaded ignorance, and uniformly declared, that they knew nothing of the country beyond the firft mountain: at the fame time they were of opinion, that, from the ftrength of the current and the rapids, we fhould not get there by water; though they did not hefitate to exprefs their furprife at the expedition we had already made.

I inquired, with fome anxiety, after an old man who had already given me an account of the country beyond the limits of his tribe, and was very much difappointed at being informed, that he had not been feen for upwards of a moon. This man had been at war on another large river beyond the Rocky Mountain, and defcribed to me a fork of it between the mountains; the Southern branch of which he directed me to take: from thence, he faid, there was a carrying-place of about a day's march for a young man to get to the other river. To prove the truth of his relation, he confented, that his fon, who had been with

him

him in thofe parts, fhould accompany me; and he accordingly fent him to the Fort fome days before my departure; but the preceding night he deferted with another young man, whofe application to attend me as a hunter, being refufed, he perfuaded the other to leave me. I now thought it right to repeat to them what I had faid to the chief of the firft band, refpecting the advantages which would be derived from the voyage, that the young men might be encouraged to remain with me; as without them I fhould not have attempted to proceed.

The firft object that prefented itfelf to me this morning was the young man whom I have already mentioned, as having feduced away my intended guide. At any other time or place I fhould have chaftifed him for his paft conduct, but in my fituation it was neceffary to pafs over his offence, left he fhould endeavour to exercife the fame influence over thofe who were fo effential to my fervice. Of the deferter he gave no fatisfactory account, but continued to exprefs his wifh to attend me in his place, for which he did not poffefs any neceffary qualifications.

The weather was cloudy, with an appearance of rain; and the Indians preffed me with great earneftnefs to pafs the day with them, and hoped to prolong my ftay among them by affuring me that the winter yet lingered in the rocky mountains: but my object was to lofe no time, and having given the chief fome tobacco for a fmall quantity of meat, we embarked at four, when my young men could not conceal their chagrin at parting with their friends, for fo long a period as the voyage threatened to occupy. When I had affured them that in three moons we fhould return to them, we proceeded on our courfe,
Weft

West-North-West half a mile, West-South-West one mile and an half, West by North three miles, North-West by West two miles and an half, South-West by West half a mile, South-South-West a mile and an half, and South-West a mile and a half. Here I had a meridian altitude, which gave 56. 17. 44. North latitude.

The last course continued a mile and an half, South by West three quarters of a mile, South-West by South three miles and an half, and West-South-West two miles and an half. Here the land lowered on both sides, with an increase of wood, and displayed great numbers of animals. The river also widened from three to five hundred yards, and was full of islands and flats. Having continued our course three miles, we made for the shore at seven, to pass the night.

At the place from whence we proceeded this morning, a river falls in from the North; there are also several islands, and many rivulets on either side, which are too small to deserve particular notice. We perceived along the river tracks of large bears, some of which were nine inches wide, and of a proportionate length. We saw one of their dens, or winter quarters, called *watee*, in an island, which was ten feet deep, five feet high, and six feet wide; but we had not yet seen one of those animals. The Indians entertain great apprehension of this kind of bear, which is called the grisly bear, and they never venture to attack it but in a party of at least three or four. Our hunters, though they had been much higher than this part of our voyage, by land, knew nothing of the river. One of them mentioned, that having been engaged in a war expedition, his party on their return made their canoes at some distance

below

below us. The wind was North throughout the day, and at times blew with confiderable violence.

The apprehenfions which I had felt refpecting the young men were not altogether groundlefs, for the eldeft of them told me that his uncle had laft night addreffed him in the following manner:—" My nephew, your departure makes my heart painful. The white people may be faid to rob us of you. They are about to conduct you into the midft of our enemies, and you may never more return to us. Were you not with the Chief*, I know not what I fhould do, but he requires your attendance, and you muft follow him."

The weather was clear, and the air fharp, when we embarked at half paft four. Our courfe was South by Weft one mile and an half, South-Weft by South half a mile, South-Weft. We here found it neceffary to unload, and gum the canoe, in which operation we loft an hour; when we proceeded on the laft courfe one mile and an half. I now took a meridian altitude, which gave 56. 11. 19. North latitude, and continued to proceed Weft-South-Weft two miles and an half. Here the Bear River, which is of a large appearance, falls in from the Eaft; Weft three miles and an half, South-South-Weft one mile and an half, and South-Weft four miles and an half, when we encamped upon an ifland about feven in the evening.

During the early part of the day, the current was not fo ftrong as we

---

* Thefe people, as well as all the natives on this fide of Lake Winipic, give the mercantile agent that diftinguifhed appellation.

had

had generally found it, but towards the evening it became very rapid, and was broken by numerous iflands. We were gratified, as ufual, with the fight of animals. The land on the Weft fide is very irregular, but has the appearance of being a good beaver country; indeed we faw fome of thofe animals in the river. Wood is in great plenty, and feveral rivulets added their ftreams to the main river. A goofe was the only article of provifion which we procured to day. Smoke was feen, but at a great diftance before us.

The rain prevented us from continuing our route till paft fix in the morning, when our courfe was South-Weft by Weft three quarters of a mile; at which time we paffed a river on the left, Weft by South two miles and an half. The bank was fteep, and the current ftrong. The laft courfe continued one mile and an half, Weft-South-Weft two miles, where a river flowed in from the right, Weft by South one mile and an half, Weft-North-Weft one mile, and Weft by North two miles. Here the land takes the form of an high ridge, and cut our courfe, which was Weft for three miles, at right angles. We now completed the voyage of this day.

In the preceding night the water rofe upwards of two inches, and had rifen in this proportion fince our departure. The wind, which was Weft-South-Weft, blew very hard throughout the day, and with the ftrength of the current, greatly impeded our progrefs. The river, in this part of it, is full of iflands; and the land, on the South or left fide, is thick with wood. Several rivulets alfo fall in from that quarter. At the entrance of the laft river which we paffed, there was a quantity of

wood,

wood, which had been cut down by axes, and fome by the beaver. This fall, however, was not made, in the opinion of my people, by any of the Indians with whom we were acquainted.

The land to the right is of a very irregular elevation and appearance, compofed in fome places of clay, and rocky cliffs, and others exhibiting ftratas of red, green, and yellow colours. Some parts, indeed, offer a beautiful fcenery, in fome degree fimilar to that which we paffed on the fecond day of our voyage, and equally enlivened with the elk and the buffalo, who were feeding in great numbers, and unmolefted by the hunter. In an ifland which we paffed, there was a large quantity of white birch, whofe bark might be employed in the conftruction of canoes.

The weather being clear, we reimbarked at four in the morning, and proceeded Weft by North three miles. Here the land again appeared as if it run acrofs our courfe, and a confiderable river difcharged itfelf by various ftreams. According to the Rocky Mountain Indian, it is called the Sinew River. This fpot would be an excellent fituation for a fort or factory, as there is plenty of wood, and every reafon to believe that the country abounds in beaver. As for the other animals, they are in evident abundance, as in every direction the elk and the buffalo are feen in poffeffion of the hills and the plains. Our courfe continued Weft-North-Weft three miles and an half, North-Weft one mile and an half, South-Weft by Weft two miles; (the latitude was by obfervation 56. 16. 54.) North, Weft by North half a mile, Weft-North-Weft three quarters of a mile; a fmall river appearing on the right, North-Weft one mile and an half, Weft by North half a mile, Weft by South one mile and an half, Weft one mile; and at feven we formed our encampment.

Mr. Mackay,

Mr. Mackay, and one of the young men, killed two elks, and mortally wounded a buffalo, but we only took a part of the flesh of the former. The land above the spot where we encamped, spreads into an extensive plain, and stretches on to a very high ridge, which, in some parts, prefents a face of rock, but is principally covered with verdure, and varied with the poplar and white birch tree. The country is so crowded with animals as to have the appearance, in some places, of a stall-yard, from the state of the ground, and the quantity of dung which is scattered over it. The soil is black and light. We this day saw two grisly and hideous bears.

Friday 17.

It froze during the night, and the air was sharp in the morning, when we continued our course West-North-West three miles and an half, South-West by South two miles and an half, South-West by West one mile and an half, West three quarters of a mile, West-South-West one mile and a quarter, and South-West by South one mile and an half. At two in the afternoon the rocky mountains appeared in fight, with their summits covered with snow, bearing South-West by South: they formed a very agreeable object to every person in the canoe, as we attained the view of them much sooner than we expected. A small river was seen on our right, and we continued our progress South-West by South six miles, when we landed at seven, which was our usual hour of encampment.

Mr. Mackay, who was walking along the side of the river, discharged his piece at a buffalo, when it burst near the muzzle, but without any mischievous consequences. On the high grounds, which were on the opposite side of the river, we saw a buffalo tearing up and down with great fury, but could not discern the cause of his impetuous motions; my hunters

hunters conjectured that he had been wounded with an arrow by some of the natives. We afcended feveral rapids in the courfe of the day, and faw one bear.

It again froze very hard during the night, and at four in the morning we continued our voyage, but we had not proceeded two hundred yards, before an accident happened to the canoe, which did not, however, employ more than three quarters of an hour to complete the repair. We then fteered South by Weft one mile and three quarters, South-Weft by South three miles, South-Weft by Weft one mile and a quarter, Weft by South three quarters of a mile, South-Weft half a mile, Weft by South one mile, South by Weft one mile and an half, South-South-Weft, where there is a fmall run of water from the right, three miles and an half, when the canoe ftruck on the ftump of a tree, and unfortunately where the banks were fo fteep that there was no place to unload, except a fmall fpot, on which we contrived to difpofe the lading in the bow, which lightened the canoe fo as to raife the broken part of it above the furface of the water; by which contrivance we reached a convenient fituation. It required, however, two hours to complete the repair, when the weather became dark and cloudy, with thunder, lightning, and rain; we, however, continued the laft courfe half a mile, and at fix in the evening we were compelled by the rain to land for the night.

About noon we had landed on an ifland where there were eight lodges of laft year. The natives had prepared bark here for five canoes, and there is a road along the hills where they had paffed. Branches were cut and broken along it; and they had alfo ftripped off the bark of the trees, to get the interior rind, which forms a part of their food.

The

The current was very ftrong through the whole of the day, and the coming up along fome of the banks was rendered very dangerous, from the continual falling of large ftones, from the upper parts of them. This place appears to be a particular pafs for animals acrofs the river, as there are paths leading to it on both fides, every ten yards.

In the courfe of the day we faw a ground hog, and two cormorants. The earth alfo appeared in feveral places to have been turned up by the bears, in fearch of roots.

Sunday 19.   It rained very hard in the early part of the night, but the weather became clear towards the morning, when we embarked at our ufual hour. As the current threatened to be very ftrong, Mr. Mackay, the two hunters, and myfelf, went on fhore, in order to lighten the canoe, and afcended the hills, which are covered with cyprefs, and but little encumbered with underwood. We found a beaten path, and before we had walked a mile fell in with an herd of buffaloes, with their young ones; but I would not fuffer the Indians to fire on them, from an apprehenfion that the report of their fowling pieces would alarm the natives that might be in the neighbourhood; for we were at this time fo near the mountains, as to juftify our expectation of feeing fome of them. We, however, fent our dog after the herd, and a calf was foon fecured by him. While the young men were fkinning the animal, we heard two reports of firearms from the canoe, which we anfwered, as it was a fignal for my return: we then heard another, and immediately haftened down the hill, with our veal, through a very clofe wood. There we met one of the men, who

informed

informed us that the canoe was at a fmall diftance below, at the foot of a very ftrong rapid, and that as feveral waterfalls appeared up the river, we fhould be obliged to unload and carry. I accordingly haftened to the canoe, and was greatly difpleafed that fo much time had been loft, as I had given previous directions that the river fhould be followed as long as it was practicable. The laft Indians whom we faw had informed us that at the firft mountain there was a confiderable fucceffion of rapids, cafcades, and falls, which they never attempted to afcend; and where they always paffed over land the length of a day's march. My men imagined that the carrying place was at a fmall diftance below us, as a path appeared to afcend an hill, where there were feveral lodges, of the laft year's conftruction. The account which had been given me of the rapids, was perfectly correct: though by croffing to the other fide, I muft acknowledge with fome rifk, in fuch an heavy-laden canoe, the river appeared to me to be practicable, as far as we could fee: the traverfe, therefore, was attempted, and proved fuccefsful. We now towed the canoe along an ifland, and proceeded without any confiderable difficulty till we reached the extremity of it, when the line could be no longer employed; and in endeavouring to clear the point of the ifland, the canoe was driven with fuch violence on a ftony fhore, as to receive confiderable injury. We now employed every exertion in our power to repair the breach that had been made, as well as to dry fuch articles of our loading as more immediately required it: we then tranfported the whole acrofs the point, when we reloaded, and continued our courfe about three quarters of a mile. We could now proceed no further on this fide of the water, and the traverfe was rendered extremely dangerous, not only from the ftrength of the current, but by the cafcades juft

below

below us, which, if we had got among them, would have involved us and the canoe in one common deftruction. We had no other alternative than to return by the fame courfe we came, or to hazard the traverfe, the river on this fide being bounded by a range of fteep, over-hanging rocks, beneath which the current was driven on with refiftlefs impetuofity from the cafcades. Here are feveral iflands of folid rock, covered with a fmall portion of verdure, which have been worn away by the conftant force of the current, and occafionally, as I prefume, of ice, at the water's edge, fo as to be reduced in that part to one fourth the extent of the upper furface; prefenting, as it were, fo many large tables, each of which was fupported by a pedeftal of a more circumfcribed projection. They are very elevated for fuch a fituation, and afford an afylum for geefe, which were at this time breeding on them. By croffing from one to the other of thefe iflands, we came at length to the main traverfe, on which we ventured, and were fuccefsful in our paffage. Mr. Mackay, and the Indians, who obferved our manœuvres from the top of a rock, were in continual alarm for our fafety, with which their own, indeed, may be faid to have been nearly connected: however, the dangers that we encountered were very much augmented by the heavy loading of the canoe.

When we had effected our paffage, the current on the Weft fide was almoft equally violent with that from whence we had juft efcaped, but the craggy bank being fomewhat lower, we were enabled, with a line of fixty fathoms, to tow the canoe, till we came to the foot of the moft rapid cafcade we had hitherto feen. Here we unloaded, and carried every thing over a rocky point of an hundred and twenty paces. When the

canoe

canoe was reloaded, I, with thofe of my people who were not immediately employed, afcended the bank, which was there, and indeed, as far as we could fee it, compofed of clay, ftone, and a yellow gravel. My prefent fituation was fo elevated, that the men, who were coming up a ftrong point could not hear me, though I called to them with the utmoft ftrength of my voice, to lighten the canoe of part of its lading. And here I could not but reflect, with infinite anxiety, on the hazard of my enterprize: one falfe ftep of thofe who were attached to the line, or the breaking of the line itfelf, would have at once configned the canoe, and every thing it contained, to inftant deftruction: it, however, afcended the rapid in perfect fecurity, but new dangers immediately prefented themfelves, for ftones, both fmall and great, were continually rolling from the bank, fo as to render the fituation of thofe who were dragging the canoe beneath it extremely perilous; befides, they were at every ftep in danger, from the fteepnefs of the ground, of falling into the water: nor was my folicitude diminifhed by my being neceffarily removed at times from the fight of them.

In our paffage through the woods, we came to an inclofure, which had been formed by the natives for the purpofe of fetting fnares for the elk, and of which we could not difcover the extent. After we had travelled for fome hours through the foreft, which confifted of the fpruce, birch, and the largeft poplars I had ever feen, we funk down upon the river, where the bank is low, and near the foot of a mountain; between which, and an high ridge, the river flows in a channel of about one hundred yards broad; though, at a fmall diftance below, it rufhes on between perpendicular rocks, where it is not much more than half that breadth.

breadth.   Here I remained, in great anxiety, expecting the arrival of
the canoe, and after some time I sent Mr. Mackay with one of the Indians down the river in search of it, and with the other I went up it to
examine what we might expect in that quarter.   In about a mile and
a half I came to a part where the river washes the feet of lofty precipices,
and prefented, in the form of rapids and cafcades, a fucceffion of difficulties to our navigation.   As the canoe did not come in fight we returned, and from the place where I had feparated with Mr. Mackay, we
faw the men carrying it over a fmall rocky point.   We met them at the
entrance of the narrow channel already mentioned; their difficulties had
been great indeed, and the canoe had been broken, but they had per-
fevered with fuccefs, and having paffed the carrying-place, we proceeded
with the line as far as I had already been, when we croffed over and
encamped on the oppofite beach; but there was no wood on this fide
of the water, as the adjacent country had been entirely overrun by fire.
We faw feveral elks feeding on the edge of the oppofite precipice, which
was upwards of three hundred feet in height.

Our courfe to-day was about South-South-Weft two miles and an half,
South-Weft half a mile, South-Weft by South one mile and an half, South-
by Weft half a mile, South-Weft half a mile, and Weft one mile and an half.
There was a fhower of hail, and fome rain from flying clouds.   I now difpatched a man with an Indian to vifit the rapids above, when the latter
foon left him to purfue a beaver, which was feen in the fhallow water on
the infide of a ftony ifland; and though Mr. Mackay, and the other
Indian joined him, the animal at length efcaped from their purfuit.
Several others were feen in the courfe of the day, which I by no means
                                                                  expected,

expected, as the banks are almoſt every where ſo much elevated **above**
the channel of the river. Juſt as the obſcurity of the night drew on,
the man returned with an account that it would be impracticable to
paſs ſeveral points, as well as the ſuper-impending promontories.

The weather was clear with a ſharp air, and we renewed our voyage
at a quarter paſt four, on a courſe South-Weſt by Weſt three quarters
of a mile. We now, with infinite difficulty paſſed along the foot of a
rock, which, fortunately, was not an hard ſtone, ſo that we were enabled
to cut ſteps in it for the diſtance of twenty feet; from which, at the
hazard of my life, I leaped on a ſmall rock below, where I received thoſe
who followed me on my ſhoulders. In this manner four of us paſſed
and dragged up the canoe, in which attempt we broke her. Very
luckily, a dry tree had fallen from the rock above us, without which we
could not have made a fire, as no wood was to be procured within a
mile of the place. When the canoe was repaired, we continued towing
it along the rocks to the next point, when we embarked, as we could
not at preſent make any further uſe of the line, but got along the rocks
of a round high iſland of ſtone, till we came to a ſmall ſandy bay. As
we had already damaged the canoe, and had every reaſon to think that
ſhe ſoon would riſk much greater injury, it became neceſſary for us to
ſupply ourſelves with bark, as our proviſion of that material article was
almoſt exhauſted; two men were accordingly ſent to procure it, who
ſoon returned with the neceſſary ſtore.

Mr. Mackay, and the Indians who had been on ſhore, ſince we broke
the canoe, were prevented from coming to us by the rugged and impaſſable

paffable ftate of the ground. We, therefore, again refumed our courfe
with the affiftance of poles, with which we pufhed onwards till we came
beneath a precipice, where we could not find any bottom ; fo that we were
again obliged to have recourfe to the line, the management of which
was rendered not only difficult but dangerous, as the men employed in
towing were under the neceffity of paffing on the outfide of trees that
grew on the edge of the precipice. We, however, furmounted this difficulty, as we had done many others, and the people who had been
walking over land now joined us. They alfo had met with their obftacles in paffing the mountain.

It now became neceffary for us to make a traverfe, where the water
was fo rapid, that fome of the people ftripped themfelves to their fhirts
that they might be the better prepared for fwimming, in cafe any accident happened to the canoe, which they ferioufly apprehended; but we
fucceeded in our attempt without any other inconvenience, except that
of taking in water. We now came to a cafcade, when it was thought
neceffary to take out part of the lading. At noon we ftopped to take an
altitude, oppofite to a fmall river that flowed in from the left: while I
was thus engaged, the men went on fhore to faften the canoe, but as the
current was not very ftrong, they had been negligent in performing
this office; it proved, however, fufficiently powerful to fheer her off,
and if it had not happened that one of the men, from abfolute fatigue
had remained and held the end of the line, we fhould have been deprived of every means of profecuting our voyage, as well as of prefent fubfiftence. But notwithftanding the ftate of my mind on fuch
an alarming circumftance, and an intervening cloud that interrupted
me,

me, the altitude which I took has been fince proved to be tolerably correct, and gave 56. North latitude. Our laft courfe was South-South-Weft two miles and a quarter.

We now continued our toilfome and perilous progrefs with the line Weft by North, and as we proceeded the rapidity of the current increafed, fo that in the diftance of two miles we were obliged to unload four times, and carry every thing but the canoe : indeed, in many places, it was with the utmoft difficulty that we could prevent her from being dafhed to pieces againft the rocks by the violence of the eddies. At five we had proceeded to where the river was one continued rapid. Here we again took every thing out of the canoe, in order to tow her up with the line, though the rocks were fo fhelving as greatly to increafe the toil and hazard of that operation. At length, however, the agitation of the water was fo great, that a wave ftriking on the bow of the canoe broke the line, and filled us with inexpreffible difmay, as it appeared impoffible that the veffel could efcape from being dafhed to pieces, and thofe who were in her from perifhing. Another wave, however, more propitious than the former, drove her out of the tumbling water, fo that the men were enabled to bring her afhore, and though fhe had been carried over rocks by thefe fwells which left them naked a moment after, the canoe had received no material injury. The men were, however, in fuch a ftate from their late alarm, that it would not only have been unavailing but imprudent to have propofed any further progrefs at prefent, particularly as the river above us, as far as we could fee, was one white fheet of foaming water.

CHAP.

CHAPTER IV.

Continuation of difficulties and dangers. Discontents among the people. State of the river and its banks. Volcanic chasms in the earth. Dispatch various persons to discover ways across the mountain. Obstacles present themselves on all sides. Preparations made to attempt the mountain. Account of the ascent with the canoe and baggage. The trees that are found there. Arrive at the river. Extraordinary circumstances of it. Curious hollows in the rocks. Prepare the canoe. Renew our progress up the river. The state of it. Leave some tokens of amity for the natives. The weather very cold. Lost a book of my observations for several days. Continue to proceed up the river. Send a letter down the current in a rum-keg. Came to the forks, and proceed up the Eastern branch. Circumstances of it.

1793.
May.

THAT the discouragements, difficulties, and dangers, which had hitherto attended the progress of our enterprize, should have excited a wish in several of those who were engaged in it to discontinue the pursuit, might be naturally expected; and indeed it began to be muttered on all sides that there was no alternative but to return.

Instead of paying any attention to these murmurs, I desired those who had uttered them to exert themselves in gaining an ascent of the

hill,

hill, and encamp there for the night. In the mean time I set off with one of the Indians, and though I continued my examination of the river almost as long as there was any light to assist me, I could see no end of the rapids and cascades : I was, therefore, perfectly satisfied, that it would be impracticable to proceed any further by water. We returned from this reconnoitring excursion very much fatigued, with our shoes worn out and wounded feet; when I found that, by felling trees on the declivity of the first hill, my people had contrived to ascend it.

From the place where I had taken the altitude at noon, to the place where we made our landing, the river is not more than fifty yards wide, and flows between stupendous rocks, from whence huge fragments sometimes tumble down, and falling from such an height, dash into small stones, with sharp points, and form the beach between the rocky projections. Along the face of some of these precipices, there appears a stratum of a bitumenous substance which resembles coal; though while some of the pieces of it appeared to be excellent fuel, others resisted, for a considerable time, the action of fire, and did not emit the least flame. The whole of this day's course would have been altogether impracticable, if the water had been higher, which must be the case at certain seasons. We saw also several encampments of the Knisteneaux along the river, which must have been formed by them on their war excursions : a decided proof of the savage, blood-thirsty disposition of that people; as nothing less than such a spirit could impel them to encounter the difficulties of this almost inaccessible country, whose natives are equally unoffending and defenceless.

Mr.

Mr. Mackay informed me, that in paffing over the mountains, he ob-ferved feveral chafms in the earth that emitted heat and fmoke, which diffufed a ftrong fulphureous ftench.   I fhould certainly have vifited this phænomenon, if I had been fufficiently qualified as a naturalift, to have offered fcientific conjectures or obfervations thereon.

Tuefday 21.

It rained in the morning, and did not ceafe till about eight, and as the men had been very fatigued and difheartened, I fuffered them to con-tinue their reft till that hour.   Such was the ftate of the river, as I have already obferved, that no alternative was left us; nor did any means of proceeding prefent themfelves to us, but the paffage of the mountain over which we were to carry the canoe as well as the baggage.   As this was a very alarming enterprize, I difpatched Mr. Mackay with three men and the two Indians to proceed in a ftraight courfe from the top of the mountain, and to keep the line of the river till they fhould find it na-vigable.   If it fhould be their opinion, that there was no practicable paf-fage in that direction, two of them were inftructed to return in order to make their report; while the others were to go in fearch of the Indian carrying-place.   While they were engaged in this excurfion, the people who remained with me were employed in gumming the canoe, and making handles for the axes.   At noon I got an altitude, which made our latitude 56. 0. 8.   At three o'clock had time, when my watch was flow 1. 31. 32. apparent time.

At fun-fet, Mr. Mackay returned with one of the men, and in about two hours was followed by the others.   They had penetrated thick woods, afcended hills and funk into vallies, till they got beyond the

rapids,

rapids, which, according to their calculation, was a diftance of three leagues. The two parties returned by different routes, but they both agreed, that with all its difficulties, and they were of a very alarming nature, the outward courfe was that which muft be preferred. Unpromifing, however, as the account of their expedition appeared, it did not fink them into a ftate of difcouragement; and a kettle of wild rice, fweetened with fugar, which had been prepared for their return, with their ufual regale of rum, foon renewed that courage which difdained all obftacles that threatened our progrefs: and they went to reft, with a full determination to furmount them on the morrow. I fat up, in the hope of getting an obfervation of Jupiter and his firft fatellite, but the cloudy weather prevented my obtaining it.

At break of day we entered on the extraordinary journey which was to occupy the remaining part of it. The men began, without delay, to cut a road up the mountain, and as the trees were but of fmall growth, I ordered them to fell thofe which they found convenient, in fuch a manner, that they might fall parallel with the road, but, at the fame time, not feparate them entirely from the ftumps, fo that they might form a kind of railing on either fide. The baggage was now brought from the waterfide to our encampment. This was likewife from the fteep fhelving of the rocks, a very perilous undertaking, as one falfe ftep of of any of the people employed in it, would have been inftantly followed by falling headlong into the water. When this important object was attained, the whole of the party proceeded with no fmall degree of apprehenfion, to fetch the canoe, which, in a fhort time, was alfo brought to the encampment; and, as foon as we had recovered from our fatigue, we

advanced

advanced with it up the mountain, having the line doubled and faftened fucceffively as we went on to the ftumps; while a man at the end of it, hauled it round a tree, holding it on and fhifting it as we proceeded; fo that we may be faid, with ftriƈt truth, to have warped the canoe up the mountain: indeed by a general and moft laborious exertion, we got every thing to the fummit by two in the afternoon. At noon, the latitude was 56. 0. 47 North. At five, I fent the men to cut the road onwards, which they effeƈted for about a mile, when they returned.

The weather was cloudy at intervals, with fhowers and thunder. At about ten, I obferved an emerfion of Jupiter's fecond fatellite; time by the achrometer 8. 32. 20. by which I found the longitude to be 120. 29. 30. Weft from Greenwich.

Thurfday 23.   The weather was clear at four this morning, when the men began to carry. I joined Mr. Mackay, and the two Indians in the labour of cutting a road. The ground continued rifing gently till noon, when it began to decline; but though on fuch an elevated fituation, we could fee but little, as mountains of a ftill higher elevation and covered with fnow, were feen far above us in every direƈtion. In the afternoon the ground became very uneven; hills and deep defiles alternately prefented themfelves to us. Our progrefs, however, exceeded my expectation, and it was not till four in the afternoon that the carriers overtook us. At five, in a ftate of fatigue that may be more readily conceived than expreffed, we encamped near a rivulet or fpring that iffued from beneath a large mafs of ice and fnow.

Our

Our toilſome journey of this day I compute at about three miles; along the firſt of which the land is covered with plenty of wood, conſiſting of large trees, encumbered with little underwood, through which it was by no means difficult to open a road, by following a well-beaten elk path: for the two ſucceeding miles we found the country overſpread with the trunks of trees, laid low by fire ſome years ago; among which large copſes had ſprung up of a cloſe growth, and intermixed with briars, ſo as to render the paſſage through them painful and tedious. The ſoil in the woods is light and of a duſky colour; that in the burned country is a mixture of ſand and clay with ſmall ſtones. The trees are ſpruce, red-pine, cypreſs, poplar, white birch, willow, alder, arrow-wood, red-wood, liard, ſervice-tree, bois-picant, &c. I never ſaw any of the laſt kind before. It riſes to about nine feet in height, grows in joints without branches, and is tufted at the extremity. The ſtem is of an equal ſize from the bottom to the top, and does not exceed an inch in diameter; it is covered with ſmall prickles, which caught our trowſers, and working through them, ſometimes found their way to the fleſh. The ſhrubs are, the gooſeberry, the currant, and ſeveral kinds of briars.

We continued our very laborious journey, which led us down ſome ſteep hills, and through a wood of tall pines. After much toil and trouble in bearing the canoe through the difficult paſſages which we encountered, at four in the afternoon we arrived at the river, ſome hundred yards above the rapids or falls, with all our baggage. I compute the diſtance of this day's progreſs to be about four miles; indeed I ſhould have meaſured the whole of the way, if I had not been obliged to engage perſonally

Friday 24.

fonally in the labour of making the road. But after all, the Indian carry-ing way, whatever may be its length, and I think it cannot exceed ten miles, will always be found more fafe and expeditious than the paffage which our toil and perfeverance formed and furmounted.

Thofe of my people who vifited this place on the 21ft, were of opinion that the water had rifen very much fince that time. About two hundred yards below us the ftream rufhed with an aftonifhing but filent velocity, between perpendicular rocks, which are not more than thirty-five yards afunder: when the water is high, it runs over thofe rocks, in a channel three times that breadth, where it is bounded by far more elevated precipices. In the former are deep round holes, fome of which are full of water, while others are empty, in whofe bottom are fmall round ftones, as fmooth as marble. Some of thefe natural cylinders would contain two hundred gallons. At a fmall diftance below the firft of thefe rocks, the channel widens in a kind of zig-zag progreffion; and it was really awful to behold with what infinite force the water drives againft the rocks on one fide, and with what impetuous ftrength it is repelled to the other: it then falls back, as it were, into a more ftrait but rugged paffage, over which it is toffed in high, foaming, half-formed billows, as far as the eye could follow it.

The young men informed me that this was the place where their relations had told me that I fhould meet with a fall equal to that of Niagara: to ex-culpate them, however, from their apparent mifinformation, they declared that their friends were not accuftomed to utter falfehoods, and that the fall had probably been deftroyed by the force of the water. It is, how-ever,

ever, very evident that thofe people had not been here, or did not adhere to the truth. By the number of trees which appeared to have been felled with axes, we difcovered that the Knifteneaux, or fome tribes who are known to employ that inftrument, had paffed this way. We paffed through a fnare enclofure, but faw no animals, though the country was very much interfeded by their tracks.

It rained throughout the night, and till twelve this day; while the bufi- nefs of preparing great and fmall poles, and putting the canoe in order, &c. caufed us to remain here till five in the afternoon. I now attached a knife, with a fteel, flint, beads, and other trifling articles to a pole, which I erected, and left as a token of amity to the natives. When I was making this arrangement, one of my attendants, whom I have already defcribed under the title of the Cancre, added to my affortment a fmall round piece of green wood, chewed at one end in the form of a brufh, which the Indians ufe to pick the marrow out of bones. This he informed me was an emblem of a country abounding in animals. The water had rifen during our ftay here one foot and an half perpendicular height.

We now embarked, and our courfe was North-Weft one mile and three quarters. There were mountains on all fides of us, which were covered with fnow: one in particular, on the South fide of the river, rofe to a great height. We continued to proceed Weft three quarters of a mile, North-Weft one mile, and Weft-South-Weft a quarter of a mile, when we encamped for the night. The Cancre killed a fmall elk.

The

The weather was clear and sharp, and between three and four in the morning we renewed our voyage, our first course being West by South three miles and an half, when the men complained of the cold in their fingers, as they were obliged to push on the canoe with the poles. Here a small river flowed in from the North. We now continued to steer West-South-West a quarter of a mile, West-North-West a mile and an half, and West two miles, when we found ourselves on a parallel with a chain of mountains on both sides the river, running South and North. The river, both yesterday and the early part of to-day, was from four to eight hundred yards wide, and full of islands, but was at this time diminished to about two hundred yards broad, and free from islands, with a smooth but strong current. Our next course was South-West two miles, when we encountered a rapid, and saw an encampment of the Knisteneaux. We now proceeded North-West by West one mile, among islands, South-West by West three quarters of a mile, South-South-East one mile, veered to South-West through islands three miles and an half, and South by East half a mile. Here a river poured in on the left, which was the most considerable that we had seen since we had passed the mountain. At seven in the evening we landed and encamped.

Though the sun had shone upon us throughout the day, the air was so cold that the men, though actively employed, could not resist it without the aid of their blanket coats. This circumstance might in some degree be expected from the surrounding mountains, which were covered with ice and snow; but as they are not so high as to produce the extreme cold which we suffered, it must be more particularly attri-

buted

buted to the high fituation of the country itfelf, rather than to the local elevation of the mountains, the greateft height of which does not exceed fifteen hundred feet; though in general they do not rife to half that altitude. But as I had not been able to take an exact meafurement, I do not prefume upon the accuracy of my conjecture. Towards the bottom of thefe heights, which were clear of fnow, the trees were putting forth their leaves, while thofe in their middle region ftill retained all the characteriftics of winter, and on their upper parts there was little or no wood.

* The weather was clear, and we continued our voyage at the ufual Monday 27. hour, when we fuccelfively found feveral rapids and points to impede our progrefs. At noon our latitude was 56. 5. 54. North. The Indians killed a ftag; and one of the men who went to fetch it was very much endangered by the rolling down of a large ftone from the heights above him.

The day was very cloudy. The mountains on both fides of the river Tuefday 28. feemed to have funk, in their elevation, during the voyage of yefterday. To-day they refumed their former altitude, and run fo clofe on either fide of the channel, that all view was excluded of every thing but themfelves. This part of the current was not broken by iflands; but in the afternoon we approached fome cafcades, which obliged us to carry our canoe and its lading for feveral hundred yards. Here we obferved an encampment

---

* From this day, to the 4th of June the courfes of my voyage are omitted, as I loft the book that contained them. I was in the habit of fometimes indulging myfelf with a fhort doze in the canoe, and I imagine that the branches of the trees brufhed my book from me, when I was in fuch a fituation, which renders the account of thefe few days lefs diftinct than ufual.

of

of the natives, though fome time had elapfed fince it had been inhabited. The greater part of the day was divided between heavy fhowers and fmall rain; and we took our ftation on the fhore about fix in the evening, about three miles above the laft rapid.

Wednef. 29.   The rain was fo violent throughout the whole of this day, that we did not venture to proceed. As we had almoft expended the contents of a rum-keg, and this being a day which allowed of no active employment, I amufed myfelf with the experiment of enclofing a letter in it, and dif-patching it down the ftream, to take its fate. I according introduced a written account of all our hardfhips, &c. carefully enclofed in bark, into the fmall barrel by the bung-hole, which being carefully fecured, I con-figned this epiftolatory cargo to the mercy of the current.

Thurfd. 30.   We were alarmed this morning at break of day, by the continual bark-ing of our dog, who never ceafed from running backwards and forwards in the rear of our fituation: when, however, the day advanced, we dif-covered the caufe of our alarm to proceed from a wolf, who was parad-ing a ridge a few yards behind us, and had been moft probably allured by the fcent of our fmall portion of frefh meet. The weather was cloudy, but it did not prevent us from renewing our progrefs at a very early hour. A confiderable river appeared from the left, and we continued our courfe till feven in the evening, when we landed at night where there was an Indian encampment.

Friday 31.   The morning was clear and cold, and the current very powerful. On croffing the mouth of a river that flowed in from the right of us, we were

were very much endangered; indeed all the rivers which I have lately feen, appear to overflow their natural limits, as it may be fuppofed, from the melting of the mountain fnow. The water is almoft white, the bed of the river being of lime-ftone. The mountains are one folid mafs of the fame materials, but without the leaft fhade of trees, or decoration of foliage. At nine the men were fo cold that we landed, in order to kindle a fire, which was confidered as a very uncommon circumftance at this feafon; a fmall quantity of rum, however, ferved as an adequate fub-ftitute; and the current being fo fmooth as to admit of the ufe of pad-dles, I encouraged them to proceed without any further delay. In a fhort time an extenfive view opened upon us, difplaying a beautiful fheet of water, that was heightened by the calmnefs of the weather, and a fplendid fun. Here the mountains, which were covered with wood, opened on either fide, fo that we entertained the hope of foon leaving them behind us. When we had got to the termination of this profpect, the river was barred with rocks, forming cafcades and fmall iflands. To pro-ceed onwards, we were under the neceffity of clearing a narrow paffage of the drift wood, on the left fhore. Here the view convinced us that our late hopes were without foundation, as there appeared a ridge or chain of mountains, running South and North as far as the eye could reach.

On advancing two or three miles, we arrived at the fork, one branch running about Weft-North-Weft, and the other South-South-Eaft. If I had been governed by my own judgment, I fhould have taken the former, as it appeared to me to be the moft likely to bring us neareft to the part where I wifhed to fall on the Pacific Ocean, but the old man, whom

whom I have already mentioned as having been frequently on war expeditions in this country, had warned me not, on any account, to follow
it, as it was foon loft in various branches among the mountains, and that
there was no great river that ran in any direction near it; but by following the latter, he faid, we fhould arrive at a carrying-place to another large
river, that did not exceed a day's march, where the inhabitants build
houfes, and live upon iflands.   There was fo much apparent truth in the
old man's narrative, that I determined to be governed by it; for I did not
entertain the leaft doubt, if I could get into the other river, that I
fhould reach the ocean.

I accordingly ordered my fteerfman to proceed at once to the
Eaft branch, which appeared to be more rapid than the other, though
it did not poffefs an equal breadth.   Thefe circumftances difpofed
my men and Indians, the latter in particular being very tired of the
voyage, to exprefs their wifhes that I fhould take the Weftern branch,
efpecially when they perceived the difficulty of ftemming the current, in the direction on which I had determined.   Indeed the rufh of
water was fo powerful, that we were the greateft part of the afternoon
in getting two or three miles—a very tardy and mortifying progrefs, and
which, with the voyage, was openly execrated by many of thofe who
were engaged in it: and the inexpreffible toil thefe people had endured,
as well as the dangers they had encountered, required fome degree of
confideration; I therefore employed thofe arguments which were the beft
calculated to calm their immediate difcontents, as well as to encourage
their future hopes, though, at the fame, time I delivered my fentiments in
fuch a manner as to convince them that I was determined to proceed.

On

On the 1ft of June we embarked at fun-rife, and towards noon the current began to flacken; we then put to fhore, in order to gum the canoe, when a meridian altitude gave me 55. 42. 16. North latitude. We then continued our courfe, and towards the evening the current began to recover its former ftrength. Mr. Mackay and the Indians had already difembarked, to walk and lighten the boat. At fun-fet we encamped on a point, being the firft dry land which had been found on this fide the river, that was fit for our purpofe, fince our people went on fhore. In the morning we paffed a large rapid river, that flowed in from the right.

In no part of the North-Weft did I fee fo much beaver-work, within an equal diftance, as in the courfe of this day. In fome places they had cut down feveral acres of large poplars; and we faw alfo a great number of thefe active and fagacious animals. The time which thefe wonderful creatures allot for their labours, whether in erecting their curious habitations, or providing food, is the whole of the interval between the fetting and the rifing fun.

Towards the dufky part of the evening we heard feveral difcharges from the fowling pieces of our people, which we anfwered, to inform them of our fituation; and fome time after it was dark, they arrived in an equal ftate of fatigue and alarm: they were alfo obliged to fwim acrofs a channel in order to get to us, as we were fituated on an ifland, though we were ignorant of the circumftance, till they came to inform us. One of the Indians was pofitive that he heard the difcharge of fire-arms above our encampment; and on comparing the number of our difcharges with theirs, there appeared to be fome foundation for his
alarm,

alarm, as we imagined that we had heard two reports more than they acknowledged; and, in their turn, they declared that they had heard twice the number of thofe which we knew had proceeded from us. The Indians were therefore certain, that the Knifteneaux muft be in our vicinity, on a war expedition, and confequently, if they were numerous, we fhould have had no reafon to expect the leaft mercy from them in this diftant country. Though I did not believe that circumftance, or that any of the natives could be in poffeffion of fire-arms, I thought it right, at all events, we fhould be prepared. Our fufees were, therefore, primed and loaded, and having extinguifhed our fire, each of us took his ftation at the foot of a tree, where we paffed an uneafy and reftlefs night.

The fucceeding morning being clear and pleafant, we proceeded at an early hour againft a rapid current, interfected by iflands. About eight we paffed two large trees, whofe roots having been undermined by the current, had recently fallen into the river; and, in my opinion, the crafh of their fall had occafioned the noife which caufed our late alarm. In this manner the water ravages the iflands in thefe rivers, and by driving down great quantities of wood, forms the foundations of others. The men were fo oppreffed with fatigue, that it was neceffary they fhould encamp at fix in the afternoon. We, therefore, landed on a fandy ifland, which is a very uncommon object, as the greater part of the iflands confift of a bottom of round ftones and gravel, covered from three to ten feet with mud and old drift-wood. Beaver-work was as frequently feen as on the preceding day.

On the 3d of June we renewed our voyage with the rifing fun. At noon

noon I obtained a meridian altitude, which gave 55. 22. 3. North lati-
tude. I alſo took time, and the watch was ſlow 1. 30. 14. apparent time.
According to my calculation, this place is about twenty-five miles South-
Eaſt of the fork.*

* I ſhall now proceed with my uſual regularity, which, as I have already mentioned, has been, for ſome days, ſuſpended, from the loſs of my book of obſervation.

CHAP.

CHAPTER V.

Continue our voyage. Heavy fog. The water rifes. Succeſſion of courſes.
Progreſſive account of this branch. Leave the canoe to proceed, and
aſcend an hill to reconnoitre. Climb a tree to extend my view of the
country. Return to the river. The canoe not arrived. Go in ſearch of
it. Extreme heat, muſquitoes, &c. Increaſing anxiety reſpecting the
canoe. It at length appears. Violent ſtorm. Circumſtances of our pro-
greſs. Forced to haul the canoe up the ſtream by the branches of trees.
Succeſſion of courſes. Wild parſnips along the river. Expect to meet
with natives. Courſes continued. Fall in with ſome natives. Our inter-
courſe with them. Account of their dreſs, arms, utenſils, and manners,
&c. New diſcouragements and difficulties preſent themſelves.

1793.
June.
Tueſday 4.

WE embarked this morning at four in a very heavy fog. The water
had been continually riſing, and, in many places, overflowed its banks.
The current alſo was ſo ſtrong, that our progreſs was very tedious, and
required the moſt laborious exertions. Our courſe was this day, South-
South-Eaſt one mile, South-South-Weſt half a mile, South-Eaſt three
quarters of a mile, North-Eaſt by Eaſt three quarters of a mile, South-
Eaſt half a mile, South-Eaſt by South one mile, South-South-Eaſt one
mile three quarters, South-Eaſt by South half a mile, Eaſt by South a
quarter

quarter of a mile, South-Eaft three quarters of a mile, North-Eaft by Eaft half a mile, Eaft by North a quarter of a mile, South-Eaft half a mile, South-Eaft by South a quarter of a mile, South-Eaft by Eaft half a mile, North-Eaft by Eaft half a mile, North-North-Eaft three quarters of a mile, to South by Eaft one mile and an half. We could not find a place fit for an encampment, till nine at night, when we landed on a bank of gravel, of which little more appeared above water than the fpot we occupied.

This morning we found our canoe and baggage in the water, which had continued rifing during the night. We then gummed the canoe, as we arrived at too late an hour to perform that operation on the preceding evening. This neceffary bufinefs being completed, we traverfed to the North fhore, where I difembarked with Mr. Mackay, and the hunters, in order to afcend an adjacent mountain, with the hope of obtaining a view of the interior part of the country. I directed my people to proceed with all poffible diligence, and that, if they met with any accident, or found my return neceffary, they fhould fire two guns. They alfo underftood, that when they fhould hear the fame fignal from me, they were to anfwer, and wait for me, if I were behind them.

When we had afcended to the fummit of the hill, we found that it extended onwards in an even, level country; fo that, encumbered as we were, with the thick wood, no diftant view could be obtained; I therefore climbed a very lofty tree, from whofe top I difcerned on the right a ridge of mountains covered with fnow, bearing about North-Weft; from thence another ridge of high land, whereon no fnow was
visible,

vifible, ftretched towards the South ; between which and the fnowy hills on the Eaft fide, there appeared to be an opening, which we determined to be the courfe of the river.

Having obtained all the fatisfaction that the nature of the place would admit, we proceeded forward to overtake the canoe, and after a warm walk came down upon the river, when we difcharged our pieces twice, but received no anfwering fignal. I was of opinion, that the canoe was before us, while the Indians entertained an oppofite notion. I, however, croffed another point of land, and came again to the waterfide about ten. Here we had a long view of the river, which circumftance excited in my mind, fome doubts of my former fentiments. We repeated our fignals, but without any return ; and as every moment now increafed my anxiety, I left Mr. Mackay and one of the Indians at this fpot to make a large fire, and fend branches adrift down the current as notices of our fituation, if the canoe was behind us ; and proceeded with the other Indian acrofs a very long point, where the river makes a confiderable bend, in order that I might be fatisfied if the canoe was a-head. Having been accuftomed, for the laft fortnight to very cold weather, I found the heat of this day almoft infupportable, as our way lay over a dry fand, which was relieved by no fhade, but fuch as a few fcattered cypreffes could afford us. About twelve we arrived once more at the river, and the difcharge of our pieces was as unfuccefsful as it had hitherto been. The water rufhed before us with uncommon velocity ; and we alfo tried the experiment of fending frefh branches down it. To add to the difagreeablenefs of our fituation, the gnats and mufquitoes appeared in fwarms to torment us. When we returned to our companions, we found that they had not been

contented

contented with remaining in the pofition where I had left them, but had been three or four miles down the river, but were come back to their ftation, without having made any difcovery of the people on the water.

Various very unpleafing conjectures at once perplexed and diftreffed us: the Indians, who are inclined to magnify evils of any and every kind, had at once configned the canoe and every one on board it to the bottom; and were already fettling a plan to return upon a raft, as well as calculating the number of nights that would be required to reach their home. As for myfelf, it will be eafily believed, that my mind was in a ftate of extreme agitation; and the imprudence of my conduct in leaving the people, in fuch a fituation of danger and toilfome exertion, added a very painful mortification to the fevere apprehenfions I already fuffered: it was an act of indifcretion which might have put an end to the voyage that I had fo much at heart, and compelled me at length to fubmit to the fcheme which my hunters had already formed for our return.

At half paft fix in the evening, Mr. Mackay and the Cancre fet off to proceed down the river, as far as they could before the night came on, and to continue their journey in the morning to the place where we had encamped the preceding evening. I alfo propofed to make my ex-curfion upwards; and, if we both failed of fuccefs in meeting the canoe, it was agreed that we fhould return to the place where we now feparated.

In

In this fituation we had wherewithal to drink in plenty, but with folid food we were totally unprovided. We had not feen even a partridge throughout the day, and the tracks of rein-deer that we had difcovered, were of an old date. We were, however, preparing to make a bed of the branches of trees, where we fhould have had no other canopy than that afforded us by the heavens, when we heard a fhot, and foon after another, which was the notice agreed upon, if Mr. Mackay and the Indian fhould fee the canoe: that fortunate circumftance was alfo confirmed by a return of the fignal from the people. I was, however, fo fatigued from the heat and exercife of the day, as well as incommoded from drinking fo much cold water, that I did not wifh to remove till the following morning; but the Indian made fuch bitter complaints of the cold and hunger which he fuffered, that I complied with his folicitations to depart; and it was almoft dark when we reached the canoe, barefooted, and drenched with rain. But thefe inconveniences affected me very little, when I faw myfelf once more furrounded with my people. They informed me, that the canoe had been broken; and that they had this day experienced much greater toil and hardfhips than on any former occafion. I thought it prudent to affect a belief of every reprefentation that they made, and even to comfort each of them with a confolatory dram: for, however difficult the paffage might have been, it was too fhort to have occupied the whole day, if they had not relaxed in their exertions. The rain was accompanied with thunder and lightning.

It appeared from the various encampments which we had feen, and from feveral paddles we had found, that the natives frequent this part of

the

1793.
June.

the country at the latter end of the fummer and the fall. The courfe to day was nearly Eaft-South-Eaft two miles and an half, South by Weft one mile, South-South-Eaft one mile and an half, Eaft two miles, and South-Eaft by South one mile.

At half paft four this morning we continued our voyage, our courfes Thurfday 6. being South-Eaft by South one mile, Eaft by South three quarters of a mile, South-Eaft by Eaft two miles. The whole of this diftance we proceeded by hauling the canoe from branch to branch. The current was fo ftrong, that it was impoffible to ftem it with the paddles; the depth was too great to receive any affiftance from the poles, and the bank of the river was fo clofely lined with willows and other trees, that it was impoffible to employ the line. As it was paft twelve before we could find a place that would allow of our landing, I could not get a meridian altitude. We occupied the reft of the day in repairing the canoe, drying our cloaths, and making paddles and poles to replace thofe which had been broken or loft.

The morning was clear and calm; and fince we had been at this Friday 7. ftation the water had rifen two inches; fo that the current became ftill ftronger; and its velocity had already been fo great as to juf-tify our defpair in getting up it, if we had not been fo long accuf-tomed to furmount it. I laft night obferved an emerfion of Jupiter's firft fatellite, but inadvertently went to bed, without committing the exact time to writing: if my memory is correct, it was 8. 18. 10. by the time-piece. The canoe, which had been little better than a wreck, being now repaired, we proceeded Eaft two miles and a quarter.

quarter, South-South-Eaſt half a mile, South-Eaſt a quarter of a mile, when we landed to take an altitude for time. We continued our route at South-Eaſt by Eaſt three quarters of a mile, and landed again to determine the latitude, which is 55. 2. 51. To this I add, 2. 45. Southing, which will make the place of taking altitude for time 55. 5. 36. with which I find that my time-piece was ſlow 1. 32. 23. apparent time; and made the longitude obtained 122. 35. 50. Weſt of Greenwich.

From this place we proceeded Eaſt by South four miles and an half, Eaſt-South-Eaſt one mile and an half, in which ſpace there falls in a ſmall river from the Eaſt; Eaſt half a mile, South-Eaſt a mile and an half, Eaſt a quarter of a mile, and encamped at ſeven o'clock. Mr. Mackay and the hunters walked the greateſt part of the day, and in the courſe of their excurſion killed a porcupine.* Here we found the bed of a very large bear quite freſh. During the day ſeveral Indian encampments were ſeen, which were of a late erection. The current had alſo loſt ſome of its impetuoſity during the greater part of the day.

Saturday 8.　　It rained and thundered through the night, and at four in the morning we again encountered the current. Our courſe was Eaſt a quarter of a mile, round to South by Eaſt along a very high white ſandy bank on the Eaſt ſhore, three quarters of a mile, South-South-Eaſt a quarter of a mile, South-South-Weſt a quarter of a mile, South-South-Eaſt one mile and a quarter, South-Eaſt two miles, with a ſlack current; South-Eaſt by

---

* We had been obliged to indulge our hunters with ſitting idle in the canoe, leſt their being compelled to ſhare in the labour of navigating it ſhould diſguſt and drive them from us. We, therefore, employed them as much as poſſible on ſhore, as well to procure proviſions as to lighten the canoe.

Eaſt

Eaſt two miles and a quarter, Eaſt a quarter of a mile, South-South-Eaſt a quarter of a mile, South-Eaſt by South four miles and an half, South-Eaſt one mile and an half, South-South-Weſt half a mile, Eaſt-North-Eaſt half a mile, Eaſt-South-Eaſt a quarter of a mile, South-Eaſt by South one mile, South-Eaſt by Eaſt half a mile, Eaſt by South three quarters of a mile, when the mountains were in full view in this direction, and Eaſtward. For the three laſt days we could only ſee them at ſhort intervals and long diſtances; but till then, they were continually in ſight on either ſide, from our entrance into the fork. Thoſe to the left were at no great diſtance from us.

For the laſt two days we had been anxiouſly looking out for the carrying-place, but could not diſcover it, and our only hope was in ſuch information as we ſhould be able to procure from the natives. All that remained for us to do, was to puſh forwards till the river ſhould be no longer navigable: it had now, indeed, overflowed its banks, ſo that it was eight at night before we could diſcover a place to encamp. Having found plenty of wild parſneps, we gathered the tops, and boiled them with pemmican for our ſupper.

The rain of this morning terminated in an heavy miſt at half paſt Sunday 9. five, when we embarked and ſteered South-Eaſt one mile and an half, when it veered North-North-Eaſt half a mile, South-Eaſt three quarters of a mile, Eaſt by South three quarters of a mile, Eaſt-South-Eaſt a quarter of a mile, South-South-Eaſt a quarter of a mile, South-Eaſt by Eaſt one mile, North-Eaſt by Eaſt half a mile, South-Eaſt by Eaſt half a mile, South-Eaſt by South three quarters of a mile, South-Eaſt three

quarters

quarters of a mile, Eaſt by South half a mile, South-Eaſt by Eaſt half a mile, Eaſt-North-Eaſt three quarters of a mile, when it veered to South-South-Eaſt half a mile, then back to Eaſt (when a blue mountain, clear of ſnow, appeared a-head) one mile and an half; North-Eaſt by Eaſt half a mile, Eaſt by North one mile, when it veered to South-Eaſt half a mile, then on to North-Weſt three quarters of a mile, and back to North-Eaſt by Eaſt half a mile, South by Weſt a quarter of a mile, North-Eaſt by Eaſt to North-North-Eaſt half a mile, South-South-Eaſt a quarter of a mile. and Eaſt by North half a mile: here we perceived a ſmell of fire; and in a ſhort time heard people in the woods, as if in a ſtate of great confuſion, which was occaſioned, as we afterwards underſtood, by their diſcovery of us. At the ſame time this unexpected circumſtance produced ſome little diſcompoſure among ourſelves, as our arms were not in a ſtate of preparation, and we were as yet unable to aſcertain the number of the party. I conſidered, that if there were but few it would be needleſs to purſue them, as it would not be probable that we ſhould overtake them in theſe thick woods; and if they were numerous, it would be an act of great imprudence to make the attempt, at leaſt during their preſent alarm. I therefore ordered my people to ſtrike off to the oppoſite ſide, that we might ſee if any of them had ſufficient courage to remain; but, before we were half over the river, which, in this part, is not more than an hundred yards wide, two men appeared on a riſing ground over againſt us, brandiſhing their ſpears, diſplaying their bows and arrows, and accompanying their hoſtile geſtures with loud vociferations. My interpreter did not heſitate to aſſure them, that they might diſpel their apprehenſions, as we were white people, who meditated no injury, but were, on the contrary, deſirous of demonſtrating

every

every mark of kindneſs and friendſhip. They did not, however, ſeem diſpoſed to confide in our declarations, and actually threatened, if we came over before they were more fully ſatisfied of our peaceable intentions, that they would diſcharge their arrows at us. This was a decided kind of conduct which I did not expect; at the ſame time I readily complied with their propoſition, and after ſome time had paſſed in hearing and anſwering their queſtions, they conſented to our landing, though not without betraying very evident ſymptoms of fear and diſtruſt. They, however, laid aſide their weapons, and when I ſtepped forward and took each of them by the hand, one of them, but with a very tremulous action, drew his knife from his ſleeve, and preſented it to me as a mark of his ſubmiſſion to my will and pleaſure. On our firſt hearing the noiſe of theſe people in the woods, we diſplayed our flag, which was now ſhewn to them as a token of friendſhip. They examined us, and every thing about us, with a minute and ſuſpicious attention. They had heard, indeed, of white men, but this was the firſt time that they had ever ſeen an human being of a complexion different from their own. The party had been here but a few hours; nor had they yet erected their ſheds; and, except the two men now with us, they had all fled, leaving their little property behind them. To thoſe which had given us ſuch a proof of their confidence, we paid the moſt conciliating attentions in our power. One of them I ſent to recal his people, and the other, for very obvious reaſons, we kept with us. In the mean time the canoe was unloaded, the neceſſary baggage carried up the hill, and the tents pitched.

Here I determined to remain till the Indians became ſo familiarized with us, as to give all the intelligence which we imagined might be obtained

tained from them.   In fact, it had been my intention to land where I might moſt probably diſcover the carrying-place, which was our more immediate object, and undertake marches of two or three days, in different directions, in ſearch of another river.   If unſucceſsful in this attempt, it was my purpoſe to continue my progreſs up the preſent river, as far as it was navigable, and if we did not meet with natives to inſtruct us in our further progreſs, I had determined to return to the fork, and take the other branch, with the hope of better fortune.

It was about three in the afternoon when we landed, and at five the whole party of Indians were aſſembled.   It conſiſted only of three men, three women, and ſeven or eight boys and girls.   With their ſcratched legs, bleeding feet, and diſhevelled hair, as in the hurry of their flight they had left their ſhoes and leggins behind them, they diſplayed a moſt wretched appearance : they were conſoled, however, with beads, and other trifles, which ſeemed to pleaſe them ; they had pemmican alſo given them to eat, which was not unwelcome, and in our opinion, at leaſt, ſuperior to their own proviſion, which conſiſted entirely of dried fiſh.

When I thought that they were ſufficiently compoſed, I ſent for the men to my tent, to gain ſuch information reſpecting the country as I concluded it was in their power to afford me.   But my expectations were by no means ſatisfied : they ſaid that they were not acquainted with any river to the Weſtward, but that there was one from whence they were juſt arrived, over a carrying-place of eleven days march, which they repreſented as being a branch only of the river before us.   Their iron-

work

work they obtained from the people who inhabit the bank of that river, and an adjacent lake, in exchange for beaver fkins, and dreffed moofe fkins. They reprefented the latter as travelling, during a moon, to get to the country of other tribes, who live in houfes, with whom they traffic for the fame commodities; and that thefe alfo extend their journies in the fame manner to the fea coaft, or, to ufe their expreffion, the Stinking Lake, where they trade with people like us, that come there in veffels as big as iflands. They added, that the people to the Weftward, as they have been told, are very numerous. Thofe who inhabit the other branch they flated as confifting of about forty families, while they themfelves did not amount to more than a fourth of that number; and were almoft continually compelled to remain in their ftrong holds, where they fometimes perifhed with cold and hunger, to fecure themfelves from their enemies, who never failed to attack them whenever an opportunity prefented itfelf.

This account of the country, from a people who I had every reafon to fuppofe were well acquainted with every part of it, threatened to difcon-cert the projeƈt on which my heart was fet, and in which my whole mind was occupied. It occurred to me, however, that from fear, or other motives, they might be tardy in their communication; I therefore affured them that, if they would direƈt me to the river which I defcribed to them, I would come in large veffels, like thofe that their neighbours had defcribed, to the mouth of it, and bring them arms and ammunition in exchange for the produce of their country; fo that they might be able to defend themfelves againft their enemies, and no longer remain in that abjeƈt, diftreffed, and fugitive ftate in which they then lived. I

added

added alſo, that in the mean time, if they would, on my return, accompany me below the mountains, to a country which was very abundant in animals, I would furniſh them, and their companions, with every thing they might want; and make peace between them and the Beaver Indians. But all theſe promiſes did not appear to advance the object of my inquiries, and they ſtill perſiſted in their ignorance of any ſuch river as I had mentioned, that diſcharged itſelf into the ſea.

In this ſtate of perplexity and diſappointment, various projects preſented themſelves to my mind, which were no ſooner formed than they were diſcovered to be impracticable, and were conſequently abandoned. At one time I thought of leaving the canoe, and every thing it contained, to go over land, and purſue that chain of connexion by which theſe people obtain their iron-work; but a very brief courſe of reflection convinced me that it would be impoſſible for us to carry proviſions for our ſupport through any conſiderable part of ſuch a journey, as well as preſents, to ſecure us a kind reception among the natives, and ammunition for the ſervice of the hunters, and to defend ourſelves againſt any act of hoſtility. At another time my ſolicitude for the ſucceſs of the expedition incited a wiſh to remain with the natives, and go to the ſea by the way they had deſcribed; but the accompliſhment of ſuch a journey, even if no accident ſhould interpoſe, would have required a portion of time which it was not in my power to beſtow. In my preſent ſtate of information, to proceed further up the river was conſidered as a fruitleſs waſte of toilſome exertion; and to return unſucceſsful, after all our labour, ſufferings, and dangers, was an idea too painful to indulge. Beſides, I could not yet abandon the hope that the Indians might not yet be ſufficiently

ficiently compofed and confident, to difclofe their real knowledge of the country freely and fully to me. Nor was I altogether without my doubts refpecting the fidelity of my interpreter, who being very much tired of the voyage, might be induced to withhold thofe communications which would induce me to continue it. I therefore continued my attentions to the natives, regaled them with fuch provifions as I had, indulged their children with a tafte of fugar, and determined to fufpend my converfation with them till the following morning. On my expreffing a defire to partake of their fifh, they brought me a few dried trout, well cured, that had been taken in the river which they lately left. One of the men alfo brought me five beaver fkins, as a prefent.

The folicitude that poffeffed my mind interrupted my repofe; when the dawn appeared I had already quitted my bed, and was waiting with impatience for another conference with the natives. The fun, however, had rifen before they left their leafy bowers, whither they had retired with their children, having moft hofpitably refigned their beds, and the partners of them, to the folicitations of my young men.

I now repeated my inquiries, but my perplexity was not removed by any favourable variation in their anfwers. About nine, however, one of them, ftill remaining at my fire, in converfation with the interpreters, I underftood enough of his language to know that he mentioned fomething about a great river, at the fame time pointing fignificantly up that which was before us. On my inquiring of the interpreter refpecting that expreffion, I was informed that he knew of a large river that runs towards the midday fun, a branch of which flowed near the fource of that which we

were

were now navigating; and that there were only three fmall lakes, and as many carrying-places, leading to a fmall river, which difcharges itfelf into the great river, but that the latter did not empty itfelf into the fea. The inhabitants, he faid, built houfes, lived on iflands, and were a numerous and warlike people. I defired him to defcribe the road to the other river, by delineating it with a piece of coal, on a ftrip of bark, which he accomplifhed to my fatisfaction. The opinion that the river did not difcharge itfelf into the fea, I very confidently imputed to his ignorance of the country.

My hopes were now renewed, and an object prefented itfelf which awakened my utmoft impatience. To facilitate its attainment, one of the Indians was induced, by prefents, to accompany me as a guide to the firft inhabitants, which we might expect to meet on the fmall lakes in our way. I accordingly refolved to depart with all expedition, and while my people were making every neceffary preparation, I employed myfelf in writing the following defcription of the natives around me:

They are low in ftature, not exceeding five feet fix or feven inches; and they are of that meagre appearance which might be expected in a people whofe life is one fucceffion of difficulties, in procuring fubfiftence. Their faces are round, with high cheek bones; and their eyes, which are fmall, are of a dark brown colour; the cartilage of their nofe is perforated, but without any ornaments fufpended from it; their hair is of a dingy black, hanging loofe and in diforder over their fhoulders, but irregularly cut in the front, fo as not to obftruct the fight; their beards are eradicated, with the exception of a few ftraggling hairs, and their complexion is a fwarthy yellow.

Their

Their dreſs conſiſts of robes made of the ſkins of the beaver, the ground hog, and the rein-deer, dreſſed in the hair, and of the mooſe-ſkin without it. All of them are ornamented with a fringe, while ſome of them have taſſels hanging down the ſeams; thoſe of the ground hog are decorated on the fur ſide with the tails of the animal, which they do not ſeparate from them. Their garments they tie over the ſhoulders, and faſten them round the middle with a belt of green ſkin, which is as ſtiff as horn. Their leggins are long, and, if they were topped with a waiſtband, might be called trowſers: they, as well as their ſhoes, are made of dreſſed mooſe, elk, or rein-deer ſkin. The organs of generation they leave uncovered.

The women differ little in their dreſs from the men, except in the addition of an apron, which is faſtened round the waiſt, and hangs down to the knees. They are in general of a more luſty make than the other ſex, and taller in proportion, but infinitely their inferiors in cleanlineſs. A black artificial ſtripe croſſes the face beneath the eye, from ear to ear, which I firſt took for ſcabs, from the accumulation of dirt on it. Their hair, which is longer than that of the men, is divided from the forehead to the crown, and drawn back in long plaits behind the ears. They have alſo a few white beads, which they get where they procure their iron: they are from a line to an inch in length, and are worn in their ears, but are not of European manufacture. Theſe, with bracelets made of horn and bone, compoſe all the ornaments which decorate their perſons. Necklaces of the griſly or white bear's claws, are worn excluſively by the men.

Their

Their arms confift of bows made of cedar, fix feet in length, with a fhort iron fpike at one end, and ferve occafionally as a fpear. Their arrows are well made, barbed, and pointed with iron, flint, ftone, or bone; they are feathered, and from two to two feet and an half in length. They have two kinds of fpears, but both are double edged, and of well polifhed iron; one of them is about twelve inches long, and two wide; the other about half the width, and two thirds of the length; the fhafts of the firft are eight feet in length, and the latter fix. They have alfo fpears made of bone. Their knives confift of pieces of iron, fhaped and handled by themfelves. Their axes are fomething like our adze, and they ufe them in the fame manner as we employ that inftrument. They were, indeed, furnifhed with iron in a manner that I could not have fuppofed, and plainly proved to me that their communication with thofe, who communicate with the inhabitants of the fea coaft, cannot be very difficult, and from their ample provifion of iron weapons, the means of procuring it muft be of a more diftant origin than I had at firft conjectured.

They have fnares made of green fkin, which they cut to the fize of fturgeon twine, and twift a certain number of them together; and though when completed they do not exceed the thicknefs of a cod-line, their ftrength is fufficient to hold a moofe deer: they are from one and an half to two fathoms in length. Their nets and fifhing lines are made of willow-bark and nettles; thofe made of the latter are finer and fmoother than if made with hempen thread. Their hooks are fmall bones, fixed in pieces of wood fplit for that purpofe, and tied round with fine watape, which has been particularly defcribed in the former voyage.

Their

Their kettles are alſo made of watape, which is ſo cloſely woven that they never leak, and they heat water in them, by putting red-hot ſtones into it. There is one kind of them, made of ſpruce-bark, which they hang over the fire, but at ſuch a diſtance as to receive the heat without being within reach of the blaze; a very tedious operation. They have various diſhes of wood and bark ; ſpoons of horn and wood, and buckets; bags of leather and net-work, and baſkets of bark, ſome of which hold their fiſhing-tackle, while others are contrived to be carried on the back. They have a brown kind of earth in great abundance, with which they rub their clothes, not only for ornament but utility, as it prevents the leather from becoming hard after it has been wetted. They have ſpruce bark in great plenty, with which they make their canoes, an operation that does not require any great portion of ſkill or ingenuity, and is managed in the following manner.—The bark is taken off the tree the whole length of the intended canoe, which is commonly about eighteen feet, and is ſewed with watape at both ends; two laths are then laid, and fixed along the edge of the bark which forms the gunwale ; in theſe are fixed the bars, and againſt them bear the ribs or timbers, that are cut to the length to which the bark can be ſtretched; and, to give additional ſtrength, ſtrips of wood are laid between them: to make the whole water-tight, gum is abundantly employed. Theſe veſſels carry from two to five people. Canoes of a ſimilar conſtruction were uſed by the Beaver Indians within theſe few years, but they now very generally employ thoſe made of the bark of the birch tree, which are by far more durable. Their paddles are about ſix feet long, and about one foot is occupied by the blade, which is in the ſhape of an heart.

Previous

Previous to our departure, the natives had caught a couple of trout, of about fix pounds weight, which they brought me, and I paid them with beads. They likewife gave me a net, made of nettles, the fkin of a moofe-deer, dreffed, and a white horn in the fhape of a fpoon, which refembles the horn of the buffalo of the Copper-Mine River; but their defcription of the animal to which it belongs does not anfwer to that. My young men alfo got two quivers of excellent arrows, a collar of white bear's claws, of a great length, horn bracelets, and other articles, for which they received an ample remuneration.

CHAP.

CHAPTER VI.

Continue the voyage. State of the river. Succeſſion of courſes. Sentiment of the guide. Conical mountain. Continuation of courſes. Leave the main branch. Enter another. Deſcription of it. Saw beaver. Enter a lake. Arrive at the upper ſource of the Unjigah, or Peace River. Land, and croſs to a ſecond lake. Local circumſtances. Proceed to a third lake. Enter a river. Encounter various difficulties. In danger of being loſt. The circumſtances of that ſituation deſcribed. Alarm and diſſatisfaction among the people. They are at length compoſed. The canoe repaired. Roads cut through woods. Paſs moraſſes. The guide deſerts. After a ſucceſſion of difficulties, dangers, and toilſome marches, we arrive at the great river.

1793.
June.
Monday 10,

AT ten we were ready to embark. I then took leave of the Indians, but encouraged them to expect us in two moons, and expreſſed an hope that I ſhould find them on the road with any of their relations whom they might meet. I alſo returned the beaver ſkins to the man who had preſented them to me, deſiring him to take care of them till I came back, when I would purchaſe them of him. Our guide expreſſed much leſs concern about the undertaking in which he had engaged, than his companions, who appeared to be affected with great ſolicitude for his ſafety.

We

We now pufhed off the canoe from the bank, and proceeded Eaft half a mile, when a river flowed in from the left, about half as large as that which we were navigating. We continued the fame courfe three quarters of a mile, when we miffed two of our fowling pieces, which had been forgotten, and I fent their owners back for them, who were abfent on this errand upwards of an hour. We now proceeded North-Eaft by Eaft half a mile, North-Eaft by North three quarters of a mile, when the current flackened: there was a verdant fpot on the left, where, from the remains of fome Indian timber-work, it appeared, that the natives have frequently encamped. Our next courfe was Eaft one mile, and we faw a ridge of mountains covered with fnow to the South-Eaft. The land on our right was low and marfhy for three or four miles, when it rofe into a range of heights that extended to the mountains. We proceeded Eaft-South-Eaft a mile and an half, South-Eaft by Eaft one mile, Eaft by South three quarters of a mile, South-Eaft by Eaft one mile, Eaft by South half a mile, North-Eaft by Eaft one mile, South-Eaft half a mile, Eaft-North-Eaft a mile and a quarter, South-South-Eaft half a mile, North-North-Eaft a mile and an half: here a river flowed in from the left, which was about one-fourth part as large as that which received its tributary waters. We then continued Eaft by South half a mile, to the foot of the mountain on the South of the above river. The courfe now veered fhort, South-Weft by Weft three quarters of a mile, Eaft by South a quarter of a mile, South half a mile, South-Eaft by South half a mile, South-Weft a quarter of a mile, Eaft by South a quarter of a mile, veered to Weft-North-Weft a quarter of a mile, South-Weft one eighth of a mile, Eaft South-Eaft one quarter of a mile, Eaft one fixth of a mile, South-South-Weft one twelfth of a mile,

Eaft

1793.
June.

Eaſt South-Eaſt one eighth of a mile, North-Eaſt by Eaſt one third of a mile, Eaſt by North one twelfth of a mile, North-Eaſt by Eaſt one third of a mile, Eaſt one ſixteenth of a mile, South-Eaſt one twelfth of a mile, North-Eaſt by Eaſt one twelfth of a mile, Eaſt one eighth of a mile, and Eaſt-South-Eaſt half a mile, when we landed at ſeven o'clock and encamped. During the greateſt part of the diſtance we came to-day, the river runs cloſe under the mountains on the left.

Tueſday 11.

The morning was clear and cold. On my interpreter's encouraging the guide to diſpel all apprehenſion, to maintain his fidelity to me, and not to deſert in the night, " How is it poſſible for me," he replied, " to " leave the lodge of the Great Spirit!—When he tells me that he has no " further occaſion for me, I will then return to my children." As we proceeded, however, he ſoon loſt, and with good reaſon, his exalted notions of me.

At four we continued our voyage, ſteering Eaſt by South a mile and an half, Eaſt by Eaſt half a mile. A river appeared on the left, at the foot of a mountain which, from its conical form, my young Indian called the Beaver Lodge Mountain. Having proceeded South-South-Eaſt half a mile, another river appeared from the right. We now came in a line with the beginning of the mountains we ſaw yeſter-day: others of the ſame kind ran parallel with them on the left ſide of the river, which was reduced to the breadth of fifteen yards, and with a moderate current.

We now ſteered Eaſt-North-Eaſt one eighth of a mile, South-Eaſt by South

South one eighth of a mile, Eaſt-South-Eaſt one ſixth of a mile, South-Weſt one eighth of a mile, Eaſt-South-Eaſt one eighth of a mile, South-South-Eaſt one ſixth of a mile, North-Eaſt by Eaſt one twelfth of a mile, Eaſt-South-Eaſt half a mile, South-Weſt by Weſt one third of a mile, South-South-Eaſt one eighth of a mile, South-South-Weſt one quarter of a mile, North-Eaſt one ſixth of a mile, South by Weſt one fourth of a mile, Eaſt three quarters of a mile, and North-Eaſt one quarter of a mile.   Here the mountain on the left appeared to be com-poſed of a ſucceſſion of round hills, covered with wood almoſt to their ſummits, which were white with ſnow, and crowned with withered trees. We now ſteered Eaſt, in a line with the high lands on the right five miles; North one twelfth of a mile, North-Eaſt by North one eighth of a mile, South by Eaſt one ſixteenth of a mile, North-Eaſt by North one fourth of a mile, where another river fell in from the right ; North-Eaſt by Eaſt one ſixth of a mile, Eaſt two miles and an half, South one twelfth of a mile, North-Eaſt half a mile, South-Eaſt one third of a mile, Eaſt one mile and a quarter, South-South-Weſt one ſixteenth of a mile, North-Eaſt by Eaſt half a mile, Eaſt one mile and three quarters, South and South-Weſt by Weſt half a mile, North-Eaſt half a mile, South one third of a mile, North-Eaſt by North one ſixth of a mile, Eaſt by South one fourth of a mile, South one eighth of a mile, South-Eaſt three quarters of a mile.   The canoe had taken in ſo much water, that it was neceſſary for us to land here, in order to ſtop the leakage, which occaſioned the delay of an hour and a quarter, North-Eaſt a quarter of a mile, Eaſt-North-Eaſt a quarter of a mile, South-Eaſt by South a ſixteenth of a mile, Eaſt by South a twelfth of a mile, North-Eaſt one ſixth of a mile, Eaſt-South-Eaſt one ſixteenth of a mile, South-Weſt half a mile, North-Eaſt a

quarter

quarter of a mile, Eaſt by South half a mile, South-South-Eaſt one twelfth of a mile, Eaſt half a mile, North Eaſt by North a quarter of a mile, South-South-Eaſt a quarter of a mile, North-Eaſt by North one twelfth of a mile, where a ſmall river flowed in from the left, South-Eaſt by Eaſt one twelfth of a mile, South by Eaſt a quarter of a mile, South-Eaſt one eighth of a mile, Eaſt one twelfth of a mile, North-Eaſt by North a quarter of a mile, South half a mile, South-Eaſt by South one eighth of a mile, North-Eaſt one fourth of a mile, South-Eaſt by Eaſt, and South-Eaſt by South one third of a mile, Eaſt-South-Eaſt, and North-North-Eaſt one third of a mile, and South by Weſt, Eaſt and Eaſt-North-Eaſt one eighth of a mile.

Here we quitted the main branch, which, according to the information of our guide, terminates at a ſhort diſtance, where it is ſupplied by the ſnow which covers the mountains. In the ſame direction is a valley which appears to be of very great depth, and is full of ſnow, that riſes nearly to the height of the land, and forms a reſervoir of itſelf ſufficient to furniſh a river, whenever there is a moderate degree of heat. The branch which we left was not, at this time, more than ten yards broad, while that which we entered was ſtill leſs. Here the current was very trifling, and the channel ſo meandering, that we ſometimes found it difficult to work the canoe forward. The ſtraight courſe from this to the entrance of a ſmall lake or pond, is about Eaſt one mile. This entrance by the river into the lake was almoſt choked up by a quantity of drift-wood, which appeared to me to be an extraordinary circumſtance; but I afterwards found that it falls down from the mountains. The water, however, was ſo high, that the country

was

was entirely overflowed, and we paffed with the canoe among the branches of trees. The principal wood along the banks is fpruce, intermixed with a few white birch, growing on detached fpots, the intervening fpaces being covered with willow and alder. We advanced about a mile in the lake, and took up our ftation for the night at an old Indian encampment. Here we expected to meet with natives, but were difappointed; but our guide encouraged us with the hope of feeing fome on the morrow. We faw beaver in the courfe of the afternoon, but did not difcharge our pieces, from the fear of alarming the inhabitants; there were alfo fwans in great numbers, with geefe and ducks, which we did not difturb for the fame reafon. We obferved alfo the tracks of moofe-deer that had croffed the river; and wild parfneps grew here in abundance, which have been already mentioned as a grateful vegetable. Of birds, we faw blue jays, yellow birds, and one beautiful humming-bird: of the firft and laft, I had not feen any fince I had been in the North-Weft.

The weather was the fame as yefterday, and we proceeded between three and four in the morning. We took up the net which we had fet the preceding evening, when it contained a trout, one white fifh, one carp, and three jub. The lake is about two miles in length, Eaft by South, and from three to five hundred yards wide. This I confider as the higheft and Southernmoft fource of the Unjigah, or Peace River, latitude, 54. 24. North, longitude 121. Weft of Greenwich, which, after a winding courfe through a vaft extent of country, receiving many large rivers in its progrefs, and paffing through the Slave Lake, empties itfelf into the Frozen Ocean, in 70. North latitude, and about 135 Weft longitude.

We

We landed and unloaded, where we found a beaten path leading over a low ridge of land of eight hundred and feventeen paces in length to another fmall lake. The diftance between the two mountains at this place is about a quarter of a mile, rocky precipices prefenting themfelves on both fides. A few large fpruce trees and liards were fcattered over the carrying-place. There were alfo willows along the fide of the water, with plenty of grafs and weeds. The natives had left their old canoes here, with bafkets hanging on the trees, which contained various articles. From the latter I took a net, fome hooks, a goat's-horn, and a kind of wooden trap, in which, as our guide informed me, the ground-hog is taken. I left, however, in exchange, a knife, fome fire-fteels, beads, awls, &c. Here two ftreams tumble down the rocks from the right, and lofe themfelves in the lake which we had left; while two others fall from the oppofite heights, and glide into the lake which we were approaching; this being the higheft point of land dividing thefe waters, and we are now going with the ftream. This lake runs in the fame courfe as the laft, but is rather narrower, and not more than half the length. We were obliged to clear away fome floating drift-wood to get to the carrying-place, over which is a beaten path of only an hundred and feventy-five paces long. The lake empties itfelf by a fmall river, which, if the channel were not interrupted by large trees that had fallen acrofs it, would have admitted of our canoe with all its lading: the impediment, indeed, might have been removed by two axe-men in a few hours. On the edge of the water, we obferved a large quantity of thick, yellow, fcum or froth, of an acrid tafte and fmell.

We

1793.
June.

We embarked on this lake, which is in the fame courfe, and about the fame fize as that which we had juft left, and from whence we paffed into a fmall river, that was fo full of fallen wood, as to employ fome time, and require fome exertion, to ᶠorce a paffage. At the entrance, it afforded no more water than was juft fufficient to bear the canoe; but it was foon increafed by many fmall ftreams which came in broken rills down the rugged fides of the mountains, and were furnifhed, as I fuppofe, by the melting of the fnow. Thefe acceffory ftreamlets had all the coldnefs of ice. Our courfe continued to be obftructed by banks of gravel, as well as trees which had fallen acrofs the river. We were obliged to force our way through the one, and to cut through the other, at a great expence of time and trouble. In many places the current was alfo very rapid and meandering. At four in the afternoon, we ftopped to unload and carry, and at five we entered a fmall round lake of about one third of a mile in diameter. From the laft lake to this is, I think, in a ftraight line, Eaft by South fix miles, though it is twice that diftance by the winding of the river. We again entered the river, which foon ran with great rapidity, and rufhed impetuoufly over a bed of flat ftones. At half paft fix we were ftopped by two large trees that lay acrofs the river, and it was with great difficulty that the canoe was prevented from driving againft them. Here we unloaded and formed our encampment.

The weather was cloudy and raw, and as the circumftances of this day's voyage had compelled us to be frequently in the water, which was cold as ice, we were almoft in a benumbed ftate. Some of the people who had gone afhore to lighten the canoe, experienced great difficulty

ficulty in reaching us, from the rugged ftate of the country; it was, in-deed, almoft dark when they arrived. We had no fooner landed than I fent two men down the river to bring me fome account of its circum-ftances, that I might form a judgment of the difficulties which might await us on the morrow; and they brought back a fearful detail of rapid currents, fallen trees, and large ftones. At this place our guide mani-fefted evident fymptoms of difcontent : he had been very much alarmed in going down fome of the rapids with us, and expreffed an anxiety to return. He fhewed us a mountain, at no great diftance, which he re-prefented as being on the other fide of a river, into which this empties itfelf.

At an early hour of this morning the men began to cut a road, in order to carry the canoe and lading beyond the rapid; and by feven they were ready. That bufinefs was foon effected, and the canoe reladen, to proceed with the current which ran with great rapidity. In order to lighten her, it was my intention to walk with fome of the people; but thofe in the boat with great earneftnefs requefted me to embark, de-claring, at the fame time, that, if they perifhed, I fhould perifh with them. I did not then imagine in how fhort a period their apprehenfion would be juftified. We accordingly pufhed off, and had proceeded but a very fhort way when the canoe ftruck, and notwithftanding all our ex-ertions, the violence of the current was fo great as to drive her fideways down the river, and break her by the firft bar, when I inftantly jumped into the water, and the men followed my example; but before we could fet her ftraight, or ftop her, we came to deeper water, fo that we were obliged to re-embark with the utmoft precipitation. One of the men

who

who was not fufficiently active, was left to get on fhore in the beft manner in his power. We had hardly regained our fituations when we
drove againft a rock which fhattered the ftern of the canoe in fuch a
manner, that it held only by the gunwales, fo that the fteerfman could
no longer keep his place. The violence of this ftroke drove us to the
oppofite fide of the river, which is but narrow, when the bow met with
the fame fate as the ftern. At this moment the foreman feized on fome
branches of a fmall tree in the hope of bringing up the canoe, but fuch
was their elafticity that, in a manner not eafily defcribed, he was jerked
on fhore in an inftant, and with a degree of violence that threatened his
deftruction. But we had no time to turn from our own fituation to inquire
what had befallen him; for, in a few moments, we came acrofs a cafcade
which broke feveral large holes in the bottom of the canoe, and ftarted
all the bars, except one behind the fcooping feat. If this accident, however, had not happened, the veffel muft have been irretrievably overfet.
The wreck becoming flat on the water, we all jumped out, while the
fteerfman, who had been compelled to abandon his place, and had not
recovered from his fright, called out to his companions to fave themfelves.
My peremptory commands fuperfeded the effects of his fear, and they all
held faft to the wreck; to which fortunate refolution we owed our fafety,
as we fhould otherwife have been dafhed againft the rocks by the force
of the water, or driven over the cafcades. In this condition we were
forced feveral hundred yards, and every yard on the verge of deftruction;
but, at length, we moft fortunately arrived in fhallow water and a fmall
eddy, where we were enabled to make a ftand, from the weight of the canoe
refting on the ftones, rather than from any exertions of our exhaufted
ftrength. For though our efforts were fhort, they were pufhed to the

utmoft,

utmoſt, as life or death depended on them. This alarming ſcene, with all its terrors and dangers, occupied only a few minutes ; and in the preſent ſuſpenſion of it, we called to the people on ſhore to come to our aſſiſtance, and they immediately obeyed the ſummons. The foreman, however, was the firſt with us ; he had eſcaped unhurt from the extraordinary jerk with which he was thrown out of the boat, and juſt as we were beginning to take our effects out of the water, he appeared to give his aſſiſtance. The Indians, when they ſaw our deplorable ſituation, inſtead of making the leaſt effort to help us, ſat down and gave vent to their tears. I was on the outſide of the canoe, where I remained till every thing was got on ſhore, in a ſtate of great pain from the extreme cold of the water; ſo that at length, it was with difficulty I could ſtand, from the benumbed ſtate of my limbs.

The loſs was conſiderable and important, for it conſiſted of our whole ſtock of balls, and ſome of our furniture ; but theſe conſiderations were forgotten in the impreſſions of our miraculous eſcape. Our firſt inquiry was after the abſent man, whom in the firſt moment of danger, we had left to get on ſhore, and in a ſhort time his appearance removed our anxiety. We had, however, ſuſtained no perſonal injury of conſequence, and my bruiſes ſeemed to be in the greater proportion.

All the different articles were now ſpread out to dry. The powder had fortunately received no damage, and all my inſtruments had eſcaped. Indeed, when my people began to recover from their alarm, and to enjoy a ſenſe of ſafety, ſome of them, if not all, were by no means ſorry for

our

our late misfortune, from the hope that it muſt put a period to our voyage, particularly as we were without a canoe, and all the bullets funk in the river.   It did not, indeed, feem poſſible to them that we could proceed under thefe circumſtances.   I liſtened, however, to the obfervations that were made on the occafion without replying to them, till their panic was difpelled, and they had got themfelves warm and comfortable, with an hearty meal, and rum enough to raife their fpirits.

I then addreſſed them, by recommending them all to be thankful for their late very narrow efcape.   I alfo ſtated, that the navigation was not impracticable in itfelf, but from our ignorance of its courfe; and that our late experience would enable us to purfue our voyage with greater fecurity.   I brought to their recollection, that I did not deceive them, and that they were made acquainted with the difficulties and dangers they muſt expect to encounter, before they engaged to accompany me.   I alfo urged the honour of conquering difaſters, and the difgrace that would attend them on their return home, without having attained the object of the expedition.   Nor did I fail to mention the courage and refolution which was the peculiar boaſt of the North men; and that I depended on them, at that moment, for the maintenance of their character.   I quieted their apprehenfion as to the lofs of the bullets, by bringing to their recollection that we ſtill had ſhot from which they might be manufactured.   I at the fame time acknowledged the difficulty of reſtoring the wreck of the canoe, but confided in our ſkill and exertion to put it in fuch a ſtate as would carry us on to where we might procure bark, and build a new one.   In ſhort, my harangue

rangue produced the defired effect, and a very general affent appeared to go wherever I fhould lead the way.

Various opinions were offered in the prefent pofture of affairs, and it was rather a general wifh that the wreck fhould be abandoned, and all the lading carried to the river, which our guide informed us was at no great diftance, and in the vicinity of woods where he believed there was plenty of bark. This project feemed not to promife that certainty to which I looked in my prefent operations; befides, I had my doubts refpecting the views of my guide, and confequently could not confide in the reprefentation he made to me. I therefore difpatched two of the men at nine in the morning, with one of the young Indians, for I did not venture to truft the guide out of my fight, in fearch of bark, and to endeavour, if it were poffible, in the courfe of the day, to penetrate to the great river, into which that before us difcharges itfelf in the direction which the guide had communicated. I now joined my people in order to repair, as well as circumftances would admit, our wreck of a canoe, and I began to fet them the example.

At noon I had an altitude, which gave 54. 23. North latitude. At four in the afternoon I took time, with the hope that in the night I might obtain an obfervation of Jupiter, and his fatellites, but I had not a fufficient horizon, from the propinquity of the mountains. The refult of my calculation for time was 1. 38. 28. flow apparent time.

It now grew late, and the people who had been fent on the excurfion already mentioned, were not yet returned; about ten o'clock, however,

however, I heard a man halloo, and I very gladly returned the fignal. In a fhort time our young Indian arrived with a fmall roll of indifferent bark: he was oppreffed with fatigue and hunger, and his clothes torn to rags: he had parted with the other two men at fun-fet, who had walked the whole day, in a dreadful country, without procuring any good bark, or being able to get to the large river. His account of the river, on whofe banks we were, could not be more unfavourable or difcouraging; it had appeared to him to be little more than a fucceffion of falls and rapids, with occafional interruptions of fallen trees.

Our guide became fo diffatisfied and troubled in mind, that we could not obtain from him any regular account of the country before us. All we could collect from him was, that the river into which this empties itfelf is but a branch of a large river, the great fork being at no great dif-tance from the confluence of this; and that he knew of no lake, or large body of ftill water, in the vicinity of thefe rivers. To this account of the country, he added fome ftrange, fanciful, but terrifying defcrip-tions of the natives, fimilar to thofe which were mentioned in the former voyage.

We had an efcape this day, which I muft add to the many inftances of good fortune which I experienced in this perilous expedition. The powder had been fpread out, to the amount of eighty pounds weight, to receive the air; and, in this fituation, one of the men carelefsly and compofedly walked acrofs it with a lighted pipe in his mouth, but with-out any ill confequence refulting from fuch an act of criminal negligence. I need not add that one fpark might have put a period to all my anxiety and ambition.

I obferved

I obferved feveral trees and plants on the banks of this river, which I
had not feen to the North of the latitude 52. fuch as the cedar, maple, hemlock, &c. At this time the water rofe faft, and paffed on with the rapidity of an arrow fhot from a bow.

The weather was fine, clear, and warm, and at an early hour of the morning we refumed our repair of the canoe. At half paft feven our two men returned hungry and cold, not having tafted food, or enjoyed the leaft repofe for twenty-four hours, with their clothes torn into tatters, and their fkin lacerated, in paffing through the woods. Their account was the fame as that brought by the Indian, with this exception, that they had reafon to think they faw the river, or branch which our guide had mentioned; but they were of opinion that from the frequent obftructions in this river, we fhould have to carry the whole way to it, through a dreadful country, where much time and labour would be required to open a paffage through it.

Difcouraging as thefe accounts were, they did not, however, interrupt for a moment the tafk in which we were engaged, of repairing the canoe; and this work we contrived to complete by the conclufion of the day. The bark which was brought by the Indian, with fome pieces of oil-cloth, and plenty of gum, enabled us to put our fhattered veffel in a condition to anfwer our prefent purpofes. The guide, who has been mentioned as manifefting continual figns of diffatisfaction, now affumed an air of contentment, which I attributed to a fmoke that was vifible in the direction of the river; as he naturally expected, if we fhould fall in with any natives, which was now very probable, from fuch a circumftance, that

that he fhould be releafed from a fervice which he had found fo irkfome and full of danger. I had an obfervation at noon, which made our latitude 54. 23. 43. North. I alfo took time, and found it flow apparent time 1. 38. 44.

Saturday 15. The weather continued the fame as the preceding day, and according to the directions which I had previoufly given, my people began at a very early hour to open a road, through which we might carry a part of our lading ; as I was fearful of rifquing the whole of it in the canoe, in its prefent weak flate, and in a part of the river which is full of fhoals and rapids. Four men were employed to conduct her, lightened as fhe was of twelve packages. They paffed feveral dangerous places, and met with various obftructions, the current of the river being frequently ftopped by rafts of drift wood, and fallen trees, fo that after fourteen hours hard labour we had not made more than three miles. Our courfe was South-Eaft by Eaft, and as we had not met with any accident, the men appeared to feel a renewed courage to continue their voyage. In the morning, however, one of the crew, whofe name was Beauchamp, peremptorily refufed to embark in the canoe. This being the firft example of abfolute difobedience which had yet appeared during the courfe of our expedition, I fhould not have paffed it over without taking fome very fevere means to prevent a repetition of it ; but as he had the general character of a fimple fellow, among his companions, and had been frightened out of what little fenfe he poffeffed, by our late dangers, I rather preferred to confider him as unworthy of accompanying us, and to reprefent him as an object of ridicule and contempt for his pufillanimous behaviour; though, in fact, he was a very ufeful, active, and laborious man.

At

At the clofe of the day we affembled round a blazing fire ; and the whole party, being enlivened with the ufual beverage which I fupplied on thefe occafions, forgot their fatigues and apprehenfions ; nor did they fail to anticipate the pleafure they fhould enjoy in getting clear of their prefent difficulties, and gliding onwards with a ftrong and fteady ftream, which our guide had defcribed as the characteriftic of the large river we foon expected to enter.

The fine weather continued, and we began our work, as we had done the preceding day; fome were occupied in opening a road, others were carrying, and the reft employed in conducting the canoe. I was of the firft party, and foon difcovered that we had encamped about half a mile above feveral falls, over which we could not attempt to run the canoe, lightened even as fhe was. This circumftance rendered it necef-fary that the road fhould be made fufficiently wide to admit the canoe to pafs; a tedious and toilfome work. In running her down a rapid above the falls, an hole was broken in her bottom, which occafioned a confi-derable delay, as we were deftitute of the materials neceffary for her effectual reparation. On my being informed of this misfortune, I re-turned, and ordered Mr. Mackay, with two Indians, to quit their occu-pation in making the road, and endeavour to penetrate to the great river, according to the direction which the guide had communicated, without paying any attention to the courfe of the river before us.

When the people had repaired the canoe in the beft manner they were able, we conducted her to the head of the falls; fhe was then unloaded and taken out of the water, when we carried her for a confiderable dif-

tance

tance through a low, fwampy country. I appointed four men to this laborious office, which they executed at the peril of their lives, for the canoe was now become fo heavy, from the additional quantity of bark and gum neceffary to patch her up, that two men could not carry her more than an hundred yards, without being relieved; and as their way lay through deep mud, which was rendered more difficult by the roots and proftrate trunks of trees, they were every moment in danger of falling; and beneath fuch a weight, one falfe ftep might have been attended with fatal confequences. The other two men and myfelf followed as faft as we could, with the lading. Thus did we toil till feven o'clock in the evening, to get to the termination of the road that had been made in the morning. Here Mr. Mackay and the Indian joined us, after having been at the river, which they reprefented as rather large. They had alfo obferved, that the lower part of the river before us was fo full of fallen wood, that the attempt to clear a paffage through it, would be an unavailing labour. The country through which they had paffed was morafs, and almoft impenetrable wood. In paffing over one of the embarras, our dog, which was following them, fell in, and it was with very great difficulty that he was faved, as the current had carried him under the drift. They brought with them two geefe, which had been fhot in the courfe of their expedition. To add to our perplexities and embarraffments, we were perfecuted by mufquitoes and fand-flies, through the whole of the day.

The extent of our journey was not more than two miles South-Eaft; and fo much fatigue and pain had been fuffered in the courfe of it, that my people, as might be expeƈted, looked forward to a continuance of it with difcouragement and difmay. I was, indeed, informed that murmurs

murs prevailed among them, of which, however, I took no notice. When we were affembled together for the night, I gave each of them a dram, and in a fhort time they retired to the repofe which they fo much required. We could difcover the termination of the mountains at a confiderable diftance on either fide of us, which, according to my conjecture, marked the courfe of the great river. On the mountains to the Eaft there were feveral fires, as their fmokes were very vifible to us. Exceffive heat prevailed throughout the day.

Having fat up till twelve laft night, which had been my conftant practice fince we had taken our prefent guide, I awoke Mr. Mackay to watch him in turn. I then laid down to reft, and at three I was awakened to be informed that he had deferted. Mr. Mackay, with whom I was difpleafed on this occafion, and the Cancre, accompanied by the dog, went in fearch of him, but he had made his efcape: a defign which he had for fome time meditated, though I had done every thing in my power to induce him to remain with me.

This misfortune did not produce any relaxation in our exertions. At an early hour of the morning we were all employed in cutting a paffage of three quarters of a mile, through which we carried our canoe and cargo, when we put her into the water with her lading, but in a very fhort time were ftopped by the drift-wood, and were obliged to land and carry. In fhort, we purfued our alternate journies, by land and water, till noon, when we could proceed no further, from the various fmall unnavigable channels into which the river branched in every direction; and no other mode of getting forward now remained for us, but

by

by cutting a road acrofs a neck of land. I accordingly difpatched two men to afcertain the exact diftance, and we employed the interval of their abfence in unloading and getting the canoe out of the water. It was eight in the evening when we arrived at the bank of the great river. This journey was three quarters of a mile Eaft-North-Eaft, through a continued fwamp, where, in many places, we waded up to the middle of our thighs. Our courfe in the fmall river was about South-Eaft by Eaft three miles. At length we enjoyed, after all our toil and anxiety, the inexpreffible fatisfaction of finding ourfelves on the bank of a navigable river, on the Weft fide of the firft great range of mountains.

CHAP.

CHAPTER VII.

Rainy night. Proceed on the great river. Circumftances of it. Account of courfes. Come to rapids. Obferve feveral fmokes. See a flight of white ducks. Pafs over a carrying-place with the canoe, &c. The difficulties of that paffage. Abundance of wild onions. Re-embark on the river. See fome of the natives. They defert their camp and fly into the woods. Courfes continued. Kill a red deer, &c. Circumftances of the river. Arrive at an Indian habitation. Defcription of it. Account of a curious machine to catch fifh. Land to procure bark for the purpofe of conftructing a new canoe. Conceal a quantity of pemmican for provifion on our return. Succeffion of courfes. Meet with fome of the natives. Our intercourfe with them. Their information refpecting the river, and the country. Defcription of thofe people.

1793.
June.
Tuefday 18.

IT rained throughout the night and till feven in the morning; nor was I forry that the weather gave me an excufe for indulging my people with that additional reft, which their fatigues, during the laft three days, rendered fo comfortable to them. Before eight, however, we were on the water, and driven on by a ftrong current, when we fteered Eaft-South-Eaft half a mile, South-Weft by South half a mile, South-South-Eaft half a mile, South-Weft half a mile, went round to North-Weft half a mile,

mile, backed South-South-Eaft three quarters of a mile, South-South-West half a mile, South by Eaft a quarter of a mile, and South-Weft by South three quarters of a mile.   Here the water had fallen confiderably, fo that feveral mud and fand-banks were vifible.   There was alfo an hill ahead, Weft-South-Weft.

The weather was fo hazy that we could not fee acrofs the river, which is here about two hundred yards wide.   We now proceeded South by Weft one third of a mile, when we faw a confiderable quantity of beaver work along the banks, North-North-Weft half a mile, South-Weft by Weft one mile and an half, South-South-Weft one third of a mile, Weft by South one third of a mile, South by Eaft half a mile.   Mountains rofe on the left, immediately above the river, whofe fummits were covered with fnow; South-Weft half a mile, South a quarter of a mile, South-Eaft one third of a mile, South-South-Weft half a mile.   Here are feveral iflands, we then veered to Weft by South a third of a mile, South-South-Eaft a fixth of a mile.   On the right, the land is high, rocky, and covered with wood, Weft South-Weft one mile, a fmall river running in from the South-Eaft, South-Weft half a mile, South three quarters of a mile, South-Weft half a mile, South by Weft half a mile. Here a rocky point protrudes from the left, and narrows the river to an hundred yards; South-Eaft half a mile, Eaft by South one eighth of a mile.   The current now was very ftrong, but perfectly fafe, South-Eaft by South an eighth of a mile, Weft by North one third of a mile, South by Weft a twelfth of a mile, South-Weft one fourth of a mile.   Here the high land terminates on one fide of the river, while rocks rife to a confiderable height immediately above the other, and the channel widens

to

to an hundred and fifty yards, Weſt by South one mile. The river now narrows again between rocks of a moderate height, North-North-Eaſt an eighth of a mile, veered to South-Weſt an eighth of a mile, South and South-Weſt half a mile. The country appeared to be low, as far as I could judge of it from the canoe, as the view is confined by woods at the diſtance of about an hundred yards from the banks. Our courſe continued Weſt by North two miles, North half a mile, North-Weſt a quarter of a mile, South-Weſt two miles, North-Weſt three quarters of a mile; when a ridge of high land appeared in this direction, Weſt one mile. A ſmall river flowed in from the North, South a quarter of a mile, North-Weſt half a mile, South-South-Weſt two miles and an half, South-Eaſt three quarters of a mile; a rivulet loſt itſelf in the main ſtream, Weſt-North-Weſt half a mile. Here the current ſlackened, and we proceeded South-South-Weſt three quarters of a mile, South-Weſt three quarters of a mile, South by Eaſt three quarters of a mile, South-Eaſt by Eaſt one mile, when it veered gradually to Weſt North-Weſt half a mile; the river being full of iſlands. We proceeded due North, with little current, the river preſenting a beautiful ſheet of water for a mile and an half, South-Weſt by Weſt one mile, Weſt-North-Weſt one mile, when it veered round to South-Eaſt one mile, Weſt by North one mile, South-Eaſt one mile, Weſt by North three quarters of a mile, South one eighth of a mile, when we came to an Indian cabin of late erection. Here was the great fork, of which our guide had informed us, and it appeared to be the largeſt branch from the South-Eaſt. It is about half a mile in breadth, and aſſumes the form of a lake. The current was very ſlack, and we got into the middle of the channel, when we ſteered Weſt, and ſounded in ſixteen feet water. A ridge of high land now ſtretched on, as it were, acroſs our preſent direction:

direction: this courfe was three miles. We then proceeded Weft-South-Weft two miles, and founded in twenty-four feet water. Here the river narrowed and the current increafed. We then continued our courfe North-North-Weft three quarters of a mile, a fmall river falling in from the North-Eaft. It now veered to South by Weft one mile and a quarter, Weft-South-Weft four miles and an half, Weft by North one mile and a quarter, North-Weft by Weft one mile, Weft a mile and a quarter: the land was high on both fides, and the river narrowed to an hundred and fifty, or two hundred yards; North-Weft three quarters of a mile, South-Weft by South two miles and an half: here its breadth again increafed; South by Weft one mile, Weft-South-Weft half a mile, South-Weft by South three miles, South-South-Eaft one mile, with a fmall river running in from the left, South with a ftrong current one mile, then Eaft three quarters of a mile, South-Weft one mile, South-South-Eaft a mile and an half; the four laft diftances being a continual rapid; South-Weft by Weft one mile, Eaft-North-Eaft a mile and an half, Eaft-South-Eaft one mile, where a fmall river flowed in on the right; South-Weft by South two miles and an half, when another fmall river appeared from the fame quarter; South by Eaft half a mile, and South-Weft by Weft one mile and a quarter: here we landed for the night. When we had paffed the laft river we obferved fmoke rifing from it, as if produced by fires that had been frefh lighted; I therefore concluded that there were natives on its banks; but I was unwilling to fatigue my people, by pulling back againft the current in order to go in fearch of them.

This river appeared, from its high water-mark, to have fallen no more than one foot, while the fmaller branch, from a fimilar meafurement, had

funk

funk two feet and an half. On our entering it, we faw a flock of ducks
which were entirely white, except the bill and part of the wings. The weather was cold and raw throughout the day, and the wind South-Weft. We faw fmoke rifing in columns from many parts of the woods, and I fhould have been more anxious to fee the natives, if there had been any perfon with me who could have introduced me to them; but as that object could not be then attained without confiderable lofs of time, I determined to purfue the navigation while it continued to be fo favourable, and to wait till my return, if no very convenient opportunity offered in the mean time, to engage in an intercourfe with them.

The morning was foggy, and at three we were on the water. At half paft that hour, our courfe was Eaft by South three quarters of a mile, a fmall river flowing in from the right. We then proceeded South by Eaft half a mile, and South-South-Weft a mile and an half. During the laft diftance, clouds of thick fmoke rofe from the woods, that darkened the atmofphere, accompanied with a ftrong odour of the gum of cyprefs and the fpruce-fir. Our courfes continued to be South-Weft a mile and a quarter, North-Weft by Weft three quarters of a mile, South-South-Eaft a mile and a quarter, Eaft three quarters of a mile, South-Weft one mile, Weft by South three quarters of a mile, South-Eaft by South three quarters of a mile, South by Weft half a mile, Weft by South three quarters of a mile, South by Weft two miles and an half. In the laft courfe there was an ifland, and it appeared to me, that the main channel of the river had formerly been on the other fide of it. The banks were here compofed of high white cliffs, crowned with pinnacles in very grotefque fhapes. We continued to fteer South-Eaft by South a mile and an half, South by Eaft

half

half a mile, Eaſt one mile and a quarter, South-Eaſt by Eaſt one mile, South by Eaſt three quarters of a mile, South-Eaſt by Eaſt one mile, South-South-Eaſt half a mile, Eaſt one mile and a quarter, South by Eaſt half a mile, Eaſt a mile and an half, South-South-Eaſt three miles, and South-Weſt three quarters of a mile. In the laſt courſe the rocks con-tracted in ſuch a manner on both ſides of the river, as to afford the ap-pearance of the upper part of a fall or cataract. Under this apprehen-ſion we landed on the left ſhore, where we found a kind of foot-path, imperfectly traced, through which we conjectured that the natives occa-ſionally paſſed with their canoes and baggage. On examining the courſe of the river, however, there did not appear to be any fall as we expected; but the rapids were of a conſiderable length and impaſſable for a light canoe. We had therefore no alternative but to widen the road ſo as to admit the paſſage of our canoe, which was now carried with great diffi-culty; as from her frequent repairs, and not always of the uſual ma-terials, her weight was ſuch, that ſhe cracked and broke on the ſhoulders of the men who bore her. The labour and fatigue of this undertaking, from eight till twelve, beggars all deſcription, when we at length conquered this afflicting paſſage, of about half a mile, over a rocky and moſt rugged hill. Our courſe was South-South-Weſt. Here I took a meridian alti-tude which gave me 53. 42. 20. North latitude. We, however, loſt ſome time to put our canoe in a condition to carry us onwards. Our courſe was South a quarter of a mile to the next carrying-place; which was nothing more than a rocky point about twice the length of the canoe. From the extremity of this point to the rocky and almoſt perpendicular bank that roſe on the oppoſite ſhore, is not more than forty or fifty yards. The great body of water, at the ſame time tumbling in ſucceſſive caſcades along

the

the firſt carrying-place, rolls through this narrow paſſage in a very tur-bid current, and full of whirlpools. On the banks of the river there was great plenty of wild onions, which when mixed up with our pemmican was a great improvement of it; though they produced a phyſical effect on our appetites, which was rather inconvenient to the ſtate of our proviſions.

Here we embarked, and ſteered South-Eaſt by Eaſt three quarters of a mile. We now ſaw a ſmoke on the ſhore; but before we could reach land the natives had deſerted their camp, which appeared to be erected for no more than two families. My two Indians were inſtantly diſpatched in ſearch of them, and, by following their tracks, they ſoon overtook them; but their language was mutually unintelligible; and all attempts to produce a friendly communication were fruitleſs. They no ſooner perceived my young men than they prepared their bows and arrows, and made ſigns for them not to advance; and they thought it prudent to deſiſt from proceeding, though not before the natives had diſcharged five arrows at them, which, however, they avoided, by means of the trees. When they returned with this account, I very much re-gretted that I had not accompanied them; and as theſe people could not be at any very great diſtance, I took Mr. Mackay, and one of the Indians with me in order to overtake them; but they had got ſo far that it would have been imprudent in me to have followed them. My In-dians, who, I believe, were terrified at the manner in which theſe natives received them, informed me, that, beſides their bows, arrows, and ſpears, they were armed with long knives, and that they accompanied their ſtrange antics with menacing actions and loud ſhoutings. On my re-turn, I found my people indulging their curioſity in examining the bags and

and bafkets which the natives had left behind them. Some of them contained their fifhing tackle, fuch as nets, lines, &c. others of a fmaller fize were filled with a red earth, with which they paint themfelves. In feveral of the bags there were alfo fundry articles of which we did not know the ufe. I prevented my men from taking any of them ; and for a few articles of mere curiofity, which I took myfelf, I left fuch things in exchange as would be much more ufeful to their owners.

At four we left this place, proceeding with the ftream South-Eaft three quarters of a mile, Eaft-South-Eaft one mile, South three quarters of a mile, South-South-Weft one mile, South by Eaft three quarters of a mile, South-South-Eaft one mile, South-South-Weft two miles, South-South-Eaft three miles and a quarter, Eaft by North one mile, South-South-Eaft one mile and a quarter, with a rapid, South-South-Weft three quarters of a mile, South one mile and an half, South-Eaft one mile and a quarter, South three quarters of a mile, and South-South-Eaft one mile and an half. At half paft feven we landed for the night, where a fmall river flowed in from the right. The weather was fhowery, accompanied with feveral loud claps of thunder. The banks were overfhadowed by lofty firs, and wide-fpreading cedars.

Thurfday 20.   The morning was foggy, and at half paft four we proceeded with a South wind, South-Eaft by Eaft two miles, South-South-Eaft two miles and an half, and South-South-Weft two miles. The fog was fo thick, that we could not fee the length of our canoe, which rendered our progrefs dangerous, as we might have come fuddenly upon a cafcade or violent rapid. Our next courfe was Weft-North-Weft two miles and an half,

which

which comprehended a rapid. Being clofe in with the left bank of the river, we perceived two red deer at the very edge of the water: we killed one of them, and wounded the other, which was very fmall. We now landed, and the Indians followed the wounded animal, which they foon caught, and would have fhot another in the woods, if our dog, who followed them, had not difturbed it. From the number of their tracks it appeared that they abounded in this country. They are not fo large as the elk of the Peace River, but are the real red deer, which I never faw in the North, though I have been told that they are to be found in great numbers in the plains along the Red, or Affiniboin River. The bark had been ftripped off many of the fpruce trees, and carried away, as I prefumed, by the natives, for the purpofe of covering their cabins. We now got the venifon on board, and continued our voyage South-Weft one mile, South a mile and an half, and Weft one mile. Here the country changed its appearance; the banks were but of a moderate height, from whence the ground continued gradually rifing to a confiderable diftance, covered with poplars and cypreffes, but without any kind of underwood. There are alfo feveral low points which the river, that is here about three hundred yards in breadth, fometimes overflows, and are fhaded with the liard, the foft birch, the fpruce, and the willow. For fome diftance before we came to this part of the river, our view was confined within very rugged, irregular, and lofty banks, which were varied with the poplar, different kinds of fpruce fir, fmall birch trees, cedars, alders, and feveral fpecies of the willow. Our next courfe was South-Weft by Weft fix miles, when we landed at a deferted houfe, which was the only Indian habitation of this kind that I had feen on this fide of

Mechili-

Mechilimakina. It was about thirty feet long and twenty wide, with three doors, three feet high by one foot and an half in breadth. From this and other circumſtances, it appears to have been conſtructed for three families. There were alſo three fire-places, at equal diſtances from each other; and the beds were on either ſide of them. Behind the beds was a narrow ſpace, in the form of a manger, and ſomewhat elevated, which was appropriated to the purpoſe of keeping fiſh. The wall of the houſe, which was five feet in height, was formed of very ſtrait ſpruce timbers, brought cloſe together, and laid into each other at the corners. The roof was ſupported by a ridge pole, reſting on two upright forks of about ten feet high; that and the wall ſupport a certain number of ſpars, which are covered with ſpruce bark; and the whole attached and ſecured by the fibres of the cedar. One of the gable ends is cloſed with ſplit boards; the other with poles. Large rods are alſo fixed acroſs the upper part of the building, where fiſh may hang and dry. To give the walls additional ſtrength, upright poſts are fixed in the ground, at equal diſtances, both within and without, of the ſame height as the wall, and firmly attached with bark fibres. Openings appear alſo between the logs in the wall, for the purpoſe, as I con-jectured, of diſcharging their arrows at a beſieging enemy; they would be needleſs for the purpoſe of giving light, which is ſufficiently afforded by fiſſures between the logs of the building, ſo that it appeared to be con-ſtructed merely for a ſummer habitation. There was nothing further to attract our attention in or about the houſe, except a large machine, which muſt have rendered the taking off the roof abſolutely neceſ-ſary, in order to have introduced it. It was of a cylindrical form, fifteen feet long, and four feet and an half in diameter; one end was ſquare,

like

like the head of a cafk, and a conical machine was fixed inwards to the other end, of fimilar dimenfions: at the extremity of which was an opening of about feven inches diameter. This machine was certainly contrived to fet in the river, to catch large fifh; and very well adapted to that purpofe; as when they are once in, it muft be impoffible for them to get out, unlefs they fhould have ftrength fufficient to break through it. It was made of long pieces of fplit wood, rounded to the fize of a fmall finger, and placed at the diftance of an inch afunder, on fix hoops; to this was added a kind of boot of the fame materials, into which it may be fuppofed that the fifh are driven, when they are to be taken out. The houfe was left in fuch apparent order as to mark the defign of its owners to return thither. It anfwered in every particular the defcription given us by our late guide, except that it was not fituated on an ifland.

We left this place, and fteered South by Eaft one mile and a quarter when we paffed where there had been another houfe, of which the ridge-pole and fupporters alone remained: the ice had probably carried away the body of it. The bank was at this time covered with water, and a fmall river flowed in on the left. On a point we obferved an erection that had the appearance of a tomb; it was in an oblong form, covered, and very neatly walled with bark. A pole was fixed near it, to which, at the height of ten or twelve feet, a piece of bark was attached, which was probably a memorial, or fymbol of diftinction. Our next courfe was South by Weft two miles and an half, when we faw an houfe on an ifland, South-Eaft by Eaft one mile and three quarters, in which we obferved another ifland, with an houfe upon it. A river alfo flowed from the right, and the land was high and rocky, and wooded with the epinette.

Our

Our canoe was now become fo crazy, that it was a matter of abfolute neceffity to conftruct another; and as from the appearance of the country there was reafon to expect that bark was to be found, we landed at eight, with the hope of procuring it. I accordingly difpatched four men with that commiffion, and at twelve they returned with a fufficient quantity to make the bottom of a canoe of five fathom in length, and four feet and an half in height. At noon I had an obfervation, which gave me 53. 17. 28. North latitude.

We now continued our voyage South-Eaft by South one mile and an half, Eaft-South-Eaft one mile, Eaft-North-Eaft half a mile, South-Eaft two miles, South-Eaft by South one mile, South-Eaft fix miles, and Eaft-North-Eaft. Here the river narrows between fteep rocks, and a rapid fucceeded, which was fo violent that we did not venture to run it. I therefore ordered the loading to be taken out of the canoe, but fhe was now become fo heavy that the men preferred running the rapid to the carrying her overland. Though I did not altogether approve of their propofition, I was unwilling to oppofe it. Four of them undertook this hazardous expedition, and I haftened to the foot of the rapid with great anxiety, to wait the event, which turned out as I expected. The water was fo ftrong, that although they kept clear of the rocks, the canoe filled, and in this ftate they drove half way down the rapid, but fortunately fhe did not overfet; and having got her into an eddy, they emptied her, and in an half-drowned condition arrived fafe on fhore. The carrying-place is about half a mile over, with an Indian path acrofs it. Mr. Mackay, and the hunters, faw fome deer on an ifland above the rapid; and had that difcovery been made before the

departure

1793.
June.

departure of the canoe, there is little doubt but we fhould have added a confiderable quantity of venifon to our ftock of provifions. Our veffel was in fuch a wretched condition, as I have already obferved, that it occafioned a delay of three hours to put her in a condition to proceed. At length we continued our former courfe, Eaft-North-Eaft a mile and an half, when we paffed an extenfive Indian encampment; Eaft-South-Eaft one mile, where a fmall river appeared on the left; South-Eaft by South one mile and three quarters, Eaft by South half a mile, Eaft by North one mile, and faw another houfe on an ifland; South half a mile, Weft three quarters of a mile, South-Weft half a mile, where the cliffs of white and red clay appeared like the ruins of ancient caftles. Our canoe now veered gradually to Eaft-North-Eaft one mile and an half, when we landed in a ftorm of rain and thunder, where we perceived the remains of Indian houfes. It was impoffible to determine the wind in any part of the day, as it came a-head in all our directions.

Friday 21.

As I was very fenfible of the difficulty of procuring provifions in this country, I thought it prudent to guard againft any poffibility of diftrefs of that kind on our return; I therefore ordered ninety pounds weight of pemmican to be buried in an hole, fufficiently deep to admit of a fire over it without doing any injury to our hidden treafure, and which would, at the fame time, fecure it from the natives of the country, or the wild animals of the woods.

The morning was very cloudy, and at four o'clock we renewed our voyage, fteering South by Eaft one mile and a quarter, Eaft-South-Eaft half a mile, South by Eaft one mile and an half, Eaft half a mile, South-
Eaft

Eaſt two miles, where a large river flowed in from the left, and a ſmaller one from the right. We then continued South by Weſt three quarters of a mile, Eaſt by South a mile and an half, South three quarters of a mile, South-Eaſt by Eaſt one mile, South by Eaſt half a mile, South-Eaſt three quarters of a mile, South-Eaſt by South half a mile, South-Eaſt by Eaſt half a mile, the cliffs of blue and yellow clay, diſplaying the ſame groteſque ſhapes as thoſe which we paſſed yeſterday, South-South-Eaſt a mile and an half, South by Eaſt two miles. The latitude by obſervation was 52. 47. 51. North.

Here we perceived a ſmall new canoe, that had been drawn up to the edge of the woods, and ſoon after another appeared, with one man in it, which came out of a ſmall river. He no ſooner ſaw us than he gave the whoop, to alarm his friends, who immediately appeared on the bank, armed with bows and arrows, and ſpears. They were thinly habited, and diſplayed the moſt outrageous antics. Though they were certainly in a ſtate of great apprehenſion, they manifeſted by their geſtures that they were reſolved to attack us, if we ſhould venture to land. I therefore ordered the men to ſtop the way of the canoe, and even to check her drifting with the current, as it would have been extreme folly to have approached theſe ſavages before their fury had in ſome degree ſubſided. My interpreters, who underſtood their language, informed me that they threatened us with inſtant death if we drew nigh the ſhore; and they followed the menace by diſcharging a volley of arrows, ſome of which fell ſhort of the canoe, and others paſſed over it, ſo that they fortunately did us no injury. As we had been carried by the current below the ſpot where the Indians were, I ordered my people to paddle

to

to the oppofite fide of the river, without the leaft appearance of confufion, fo that they brought me abreaft of them. My interpreters, while
we were within hearing, had done every thing in their power to pacify
them, but in vain. We alfo obferved that they had fent off a canoe with
two men, down the river, as we concluded, to communicate their alarm,
and procure affiftance. This circumftance determined me to leave no
means untried that might engage us in a friendly intercourfe with them,
before they acquired additional fecurity and confidence, by the arrival
of their relations and neighbours, to whom their fituation would be
fhortly notified.

I therefore formed the following adventurous projeft, which was hap-
pily crowned with fuccefs. I left the canoe, and walked by myfelf along
the beach, in order to induce fome of the natives to come to me, which
I imagined they might be difpofed to do, when they faw me alone, without any apparent poffibility of receiving affiftance from my people, and
would confequently imagine that a communication with me was not
a fervice of danger. At the fame time, in order to poffefs the utmoft
fecurity of which my fituation was fufceptible, I direfted one of the
Indians to flip into the woods, with my gun and his own, and to conceal himfelf from their difcovery; he alfo had orders to keep as near
me as poffible, without being feen; and if any of the natives fhould
venture acrofs, and attempt to fhoot me from the water, it was his
inftruftions to lay him low: at the fame time he was particularly en-
joined not to fire till I had difcharged one or both of the piftols that I
carried in my belt. If, however, any of them were to land, and approach my perfon, he was immediately to join me. In the mean time

my

my other interpreter affured them that we entertained the moft friendly difpofition, which I confirmed by fuch fignals as I conceived would be comprehended by them. I had not, indeed, been long at my ftation, and my Indian in ambufh behind me, when two of the natives came off in a canoe, but ftopped when they had got within an hundred yards of me. I made figns for them to land, and as an inducement, difplayed looking glaffes, beads, and other alluring trinkets. At length, but with every mark of extreme apprehenfion, they approached the fhore, ftern foremoft, but would not venture to land. I now made them a pre-fent of fome beads, with which they were going to pufh off, when I renewed my entreaties, and, after fome time, prevailed on them to come afhore, and fit down by me. My hunter now thought it right to join me, and created fome alarm in my new acquaintance. It was, how-ever, foon removed, and I had the fatisfaction to find that he, and thefe people perfectly underftood each other. I inftructed him to fay every thing that might tend to footh their fears and win their confidence. I expreffed my wifh to conduct them to our canoe, but they declined my offer; and when they obferved fome of my people coming towards us, they requefted me to let them return; and I was fo well fatisfied with the progrefs I had made in my intercourfe with them, that I did not hefitate a moment in complying with their defire. During their fhort ftay, they obferved us, and every thing about us, with a mixture of admiration and aftonifhment. We could plainly diftinguifh that their friends received them with great joy on their return, and that the articles which they carried back with them were examined with a general and eager curiofity; they alfo appeared to hold a confultation, which lafted about a quarter of an hour, and the refult was, an invitation to

come

come over to them, which was cheerfully accepted. Neverthelefs, on our landing, they betrayed evident figns of confufion, which arofe, probably from the quicknefs of our movements, as the profpect of a friendly communication had fo cheered the fpirits of my people, that they paddled acrofs the river with the utmoft expedition. The two men, however, who had been with us, appeared, very naturally, to poffefs the greateft fhare of courage on the occafion, and were ready to receive us on our landing; but our demeanor foon difpelled all their apprehenfions, and the moft familiar communication took place between us. When I had fecured their confidence, by the diftribution of trinkets among them, and treated the children with fugar, I inftructed my interpreters to collect every neceffary information in their power to afford me.

According to their account, this river, whofe courfe is very extenfive, runs towards the mid-day fun; and that at its mouth, as they had been informed, white people were building houfes. They reprefented its current to be uniformly ftrong, and that in three places it was altogether impaffable, from the falls and rapids, which poured along between perpendicular rocks that were much higher, and more rugged, than any we had yet feen, and would not admit of any paffage over them. But befides the dangers and difficulties of the navigation, they added, that we fhould have to encounter the inhabitants of the country, who were very numerous. They alfo reprefented their immediate neighbours as a very malignant race, who lived in large fubterraneous receffes: and when they were made to underftand that it was our defign to proceed to the fea, they diffuaded us from profecuting our intention, as we

fhould

fhould certainly become a facrifice to the favage fpirit of the natives. Thefe people they defcribed as poffeffing iron, arms, and utenfils, which they procured from their neighbours to the Weftward, and were obtained by a commercial progrefs from people like ourfelves, who brought them in great canoes.

Such an account of our fituation, exaggerated as it might be in fome points, and erroneous in others, was fufficiently alarming, and awakened very painful reflections; neverthelefs it did not operate on my mind fo as to produce any change in my original determination. My firft object, therefore, was to perfuade two of thefe people to accompany me, that they might fecure for us a favourable reception from their neighbours. To this propofition they affented, but expreffed fome degree of diffatisfaction at the immediate departure, for which we were making preparation; but when we were ready to enter the canoe, a fmall one was feen doubling the point below, with three men in it. We thought it prudent to wait for their arrival, and they proved to be fome of their relations, who had received the alarm from the meffengers, which I have already mentioned as having been fent down the river for that purpofe, and who had paffed on, as we were afterwards informed, to extend the notice of our arrival. Though thefe people faw us in the midft of their friends, they difplayed the moft menacing actions, and hoftile poftures. At length, however, this wild, favage fpirit appeared to fubfide, and they were per-fuaded to land. One of them, who was a middle aged perfon, whofe agitations had been lefs frequent than thofe of his companions, and who was treated with particular refpect by them all, inquired who we were, whence we came, whither we were going, and what was the motive of

our

our coming into that country. When his friends had fatisfied him as far as they were able, refpecting us, he inftantly advifed us to delay our departure for that night, as their relations below, having been by this time alarmed by the meffengers, who had been fent for that purpofe, would certainly oppofe our paffage, notwithftanding I had two of their own people with me. He added, that they would all of them be here by fun-fet, when they would be convinced, as he was, that we were good people, and meditated no ill defigns againft them.

Such were the reafons which this Indian urged in favour of our remaining till the next morning; and they were too well founded for me to hefitate in complying with them; befides, by prolonging my ftay till the next morning, it was probable that I might obtain fome important intelligence refpecting the country through which I was to pafs, and the people who inhabited it. I accordingly ordered the canoe to be unloaded, taken out of the water, and gummed. My tent was alfo pitched, and the natives were now become fo familiar, that I was obliged to let them know my wifh to be alone and undifturbed.

My firft application to the native whom I have already particularly mentioned, was to obtain from him fuch a plan of the river as he fhould be enabled to give me; and he complied with this requeft with a degree of readinefs and intelligence that evidently proved it was by no means a new bufinefs to him. In order to acquire the beft information he could communicate, I affured him, if I found his account correct, that I fhould either return myfelf, or fend others to them, with fuch articles as they appeared to want: particularly arms and ammunition, with which they would be able to prevent their enemies from in-

vading

vading them.   I obtained, however, no addition to what I already knew, but that the country below us, as far as he was acquainted with it, abounded in animals, and that the river produced plenty of fiſh.

Our canoe was now become ſo weak, leaky, and unmanageable, that it became a matter of abſolute neceſſity to conſtruct a new one; and I had been informed, that if we delayed that important work till we got further down the river, we ſhould not be able to procure bark.   I therefore diſpatched two of my people, with an Indian, in ſearch of that neceſſary material.   The weather was ſo cloudy that I could not get an obſervation.*

I paſſed the reſt of the day in converſing with theſe people: they conſiſted of ſeven families, containing eighteen men; they were clad in leather, and had ſome beaver and rabbit-ſkin blankets.   They had not been long arrived in this part of the country, where they propoſed to paſs the ſummer, to catch fiſh for their winter proviſion: for this purpoſe they were preparing machines ſimilar to that which we found in the firſt Indian houſe we ſaw and deſcribed.   The fiſh which they take in them are large, and only viſit this part of the river at certain ſeaſons.   Theſe people differ very little, if at all, either in their appearance, language, or manners, from the Rocky-Mountain Indians.   The men whom I ſent in ſearch of bark, returned with a certain quantity of it, but of a very indifferent kind.   We were not gratified with the arrival of any of the natives whom we expected from a lower part of the river.

* The obſervation, already mentioned, I got on my return.

CHAP.

CHAPTER VIII.

Renew our voyage, accompanied by two of the natives. Account of courses. State of the river. Arrive at a subterranean house. See several natives. Brief description of them. Account of our conference with them. Saw other natives. Description of them. Their conduct, &c. The account which they gave of the country. The narrative of a female prisoner. The perplexities of my situation. Specimen of the language of two tribes. Change the plan of my journey. Return up the river. Succession of dangers and difficulties. Land on an island to build another canoe.

———

1793.
June.
Saturday 22.

AT six in the morning we proceeded on our voyage, with two of the Indians, one of them in a small pointed canoe, made after the fashion of the Esquimaux, and the other in our own. This precaution was necessary in a two-fold point of view, as the small canoe could be sent ahead to speak to any of the natives that might be seen down the river, and, thus divided, would not be easy for them both to make their escape. Mr. Mackay also embarked with the Indian, which seemed to afford him great satisfaction, and he was thereby enabled to keep us company with diminution of labour.

Our courses were South-South-East a mile and an half, South-East half

half a mile, South by Eaſt four miles and an half, South-Eaſt by South half a mile, South by Weſt half a mile, South-Eaſt by Eaſt one mile, South-South-Weſt a mile and an half, South by Eaſt one mile and a quarter. The country, on the right, preſented a very beautiful appearance: it roſe at firſt rather abruptly to the height of twenty-five feet, when the precipice was ſucceeded by an inclined plain to the foot of another ſteep; which was followed by another extent of gently-riſing ground: theſe objects, which were ſhaded with groves of fir, preſenting themſelves alternately to a conſiderable diſtance.

We now landed near an houſe, the roof of which alone appeared above ground; but it was deſerted by its inhabitants who had been alarmed at our approach. We obſerved ſeveral men in the ſecond ſteep, who diſplayed the ſame poſtures and menacing actions as thoſe which we have ſo lately deſcribed. Our conductors went to them immediately on an embaſſy of friendſhip, and, after a very vociferous diſcourſe, one of them was perſuaded to come to us, but preſented a very ferocious aſpect: the reſt, who were ſeven in number, ſoon followed his example. They held their bows and arrows in their hands, and appeared in their garments, which were faſtened round the neck, but left the right arm free for action. A cord faſtened a blanket or leather covering under the right armpit, ſo that it hung upon the left ſhoulder, and might be occaſionally employed as a target, that would turn an arrow which was nearly ſpent. As ſoon as they had recovered from their apprehenſions, ten women made their appearance, but without any children, whom, I imagine, they had ſent to a greater diſtance, to be out of the reach of all poſſible danger. I diſtributed a few preſents among them, and left my guides to

explain

explain to them the object of my journey, and the friendliness of my designs, with which they had themselves been made acquainted; their fears being at length removed, I gave them a specimen of the use to which we applied our fire-arms: at the same time, I calmed their astonishment, by the assurance, that, though we could at once destroy those who did us injury, we could equally protect those who shewed us kindness. Our stay here did not exceed half an hour, and we left these people with favourable impressions of us.

From this place we steered East by North half a mile, South by East three quarters of a mile, and South by West a mile and an half, when we landed again on seeing some of the natives on the high ground, whose appearance was more wild and ferocious than any whom we had yet seen. Indeed I was under some apprehension that our guides, who went to conciliate them to us, would have fallen a prey to their savage fury. At length, however, they were persuaded to entertain a more favourable opinion of us, and they approached us one after another, to the number of sixteen men, and several women, I shook hands with them all, and desired my interpreters to explain that salutation as a token of friendship. As this was not a place where we could remain with the necessary convenience, I proposed to proceed further, in search of a more commodious spot. They immediately invited us to pass the night at their lodges, which were at no great distance, and promised, at the same time, that they would, in the morning, send two men to introduce us to the next nation, who were very numerous, and illdisposed towards strangers. As we were pushing from the shore, we were very much surprised at hearing a woman pronounce several words

in

in the Knifteneaux language. She proved to be a Rocky-Mountain native, fo that my interpreters perfectly underftood her. She informed us that her country is at the forks of this river, and that fhe had been taken prifoner by the Knifteneaux, who had carried her acrofs the mountains. After having paffed the greateft part of the fummer with them, fhe had contrived to efcape, before they had reached their own country, and had re-croffed the mountains, when fhe expected to meet her own friends : but after fuffering all the hardfhips incident to fuch a journey, fhe had been taken by a war-party of the people with whom fhe then was, who had driven her relations from the river into the mountains. She had fince been detained by her prefent hufband, of whom fhe had no caufe to complain; neverthelefs fhe expreffed a ftrong defire to return to her own people. I prefented her with feveral ufeful articles, and defired her to come to me at the lodges, which fhe readily engaged to do. We arrived thither before the Indians, and landed, as we had pro-mifed. It was now near twelve at noon, but on attempting to take an altitude I found the angle too great for my fextant.

The natives whom we had already feen, and feveral others, foon joined us, with a greater number of women than I had yet feen; but I did not obferve the female prifoner among them. There were thirty-five of them, and my remaining ftore of prefents was not fufficient to enable me to be very liberal to fo many claimants. Among the men I found four of the adjoining nation, and a Rocky-Mountain Indian, who had been with them for fome time. As he was underftood by my inter-preters, and was himfelf well acquainted with the language of the ftrangers, I poffeffed the means of obtaining every information refpecting

the

the country, which it might be in their power to afford me. For this purpofe I felected an elderly man, from the four ftrangers, whofe countenance had prepoffeffed me in his favour. I ftated to thefe people, as I had already done to thofe from whom I had hitherto derived information, the objeĉts of my voyage, and the very great advantages which they would receive from my fuccefsful termination of it. They expreffed themfelves very much fatisfied at my communication, and affured me that they would not deceive me refpeĉting the fubjeĉt of my inquiry. An old man alfo, who appeared to poffefs the charaĉter of a chief, declared his wifh to fee me return to his land, and that his two young daughters fhould then be at my difpofal. I now proceeded to requeft the native, whom I had particularly feleĉted, to commence his information, by drawing a fketch of the country upon a large piece of bark, and he immediately entered on the work, frequently appealing to, and fometimes afking the advice of, thofe around him. He defcribed the river as running to the Eaft of South, receiving many rivers, and every fix or eight leagues encumbered with falls and rapids, fome of which were very dangerous, and fix of them impraĉticable. The carrying-places he reprefented as of great length, and paffing over hills and mountains. He depiĉted the lands of three other tribes, in fucceffion, who fpoke different languages. Beyond them he knew nothing either of the river or country, only that it was ftill a long way to the fea ; and that, as he had heard, there was a lake, before they reached the water, which the natives did not drink. As far as his knowledge of the river extended, the country on either fide was level, in many places without wood, and abounding in red deer, and fome of a fmall fallow kind. Few of the natives, he faid, would come to the banks for fome time ; but that at a certain feafon they would arrive there in great

numbers,

numbers, to fiſh.   They now procured iron, braſs, copper, and trinkets, from the Weſtward; but formerly theſe articles were obtained from the lower parts of the river, though in ſmall quantities.   A knife was produced which had been brought from that quarter.   The blade was ten inches long, and an inch and an half broad, but with a very blunted edge.   The handle was of horn.   We underſtood that this inſtrument had been obtained from white men, long before they had heard that any came to the Weſtward.   One very old man obſerved, that as long as he could remember, he was told of white people to the Southward; and that he had heard, though he did not vouch for the truth of the report, that one of them had made an attempt to come up the river, and was deſtroyed.

Theſe people deſcribe the diſtance acroſs the country as very ſhort to the Weſtern ocean; and, according to my own idea, it cannot be above five or ſix degrees.   If the aſſertion of Mr. Mears be correct, it cannot be ſo far, as the inland ſea which he mentions within Nootka, muſt come as far Eaſt as 126 Weſt longitude.   They aſſured us that the road was not difficult, as they avoided the mountains, keeping along the low lands between them, many parts of which are entirely free from wood.   According to their account, this way is ſo often travelled by them, that their path is viſible throughout the whole journey, which lies along ſmall lakes and rivers.   It occupied them, they ſaid, no more than ſix nights, to go to where they meet the people who barter iron, braſs, copper, beads, &c. with them, for dreſſed leather, and beaver, bear, lynx, fox, and marten ſkins.   The iron is about eighteen inches of two-inch bar.   To this they give an edge at one end, and fix it to an handle at right angles, which they employ as an axe.   When the iron is

worn

worn down, they fabricate it into points for their arrows and fpikes. Before they procured iron they employed bone and horn for thofe pur- pofes. The copper and brafs they convert into collars, arm-bands, bracelets, and other ornaments. They fometimes alfo point their arrows with thofe metals. They had been informed by thofe whom they meet to trade with, that the white people, from whom thefe articles are ob- tained, were building houfes at the diftance of three days, or two nights journey from the place where they met laft fall. With this route they all appeared to be well acquainted.

I now requefted that they would fend for the female prifoner whom I faw yefterday, but I received only vague and evafive anfwers : they probably apprehended, that it was our defign to take her from them. I was, however, very much difappointed at being prevented from having an interview with her, as fhe might have given me a correct account of the country beyond the forks of the river, as well as of the pafs, through the mountains, from them.

My people had liftened with great attention to the relation which had been given me, and it feemed to be their opinion, that it would be ab- folute madnefs to attempt a paffage through fo many favage and bar- barous nations. My fituation may, indeed, be more eafily conceived than expreffed : I had no more than thirty days provifion remaining, exclufive of fuch fupplies as I might obtain from the natives, and the toil of our hunters, which, however, was fo precarious as to be matter of little dependence : befides, our ammunition would foon be exhaufted, particularly our ball, of which we had not more than an hundred and
fifty,

fifty, and about thirty pounds weight of fhot, which, indeed, might be converted into bullets, though with great wafte.

The more I heard of the river, the more I was convinced it could not empty itfelf into the ocean to the North of what is called the River of the Weft, fo that with its windings, the diftance muft be very great. Such being the difcouraging circumftances of my fituation, which were now heightened by the difcontents of my people, I could not but be alarmed at the idea of attempting to get to the difcharge of fuch a rapid river, efpecially when I reflected on the tardy progrefs of my return up it, even if I fhould meet with no obftruction from the natives; a circumftance not very probable, from the numbers of them which would then be on the river; and whom I could have no opportunity of conciliating in my paffage down, for the reafons which have been altready mentioned. At all events, I muft give up every expectation of returning this feafon to Athabafca. Such were my reflections at this period; but inftead of continuing to indulge them, I determined to proceed with refolution, and fet future events at defiance. At the fame time I fuffered myfelf to nourifh the hope that I might be able to penetrate with more fafety, and in a fhorter period, to the ocean by the inland, weftern communication.

To carry this project into execution I muft have returned a confiderable diftance up the river, which would neceffarily be attended with a very ferious inconvenience, if I paffed over every other; as in a voyage of this kind, a retrograde motion could not fail to cool the ardour, flacken the zeal, and weaken the confidence of thofe, who have no greater inducement in the undertaking, than to follow the conductor of it. Such was the

ftate

ſtate of my mind at this period, and ſuch the circumſtances by which it was diſtreſſed and diſtracted.

To the people who had given me the foregoing information, I preſented ſome beads, which they preferred to any other articles in my poſſeſſion, and I recompenſed in the ſame manner two of them who communicated to me the following vocabulary in the languages of the Nagailer and Atnah tribes.

	The Nagailer, or Chin-Indians.	The Atnah. or Carrier-Indians.
Eye,	Nah,	Thlouſtin.
Hair,	Thigah,	Cahowdin.
Teeth,	Gough,	Chliough.
Noſe,	Nenzeh,	Piſax.
Head,	Thie,	Scapacay.
Wood,	Dekin,	Shedzay.
Hand,	Lah,	Calietha.
Leg,	Kin,	Squacht.
Tongue,	Thoula,	Dewhasjiſk.
Ear,	Zach,	Ithlinah.
Man,	Dinay,	Scuynlouch.
Woman,	Chiqoui,	Smoſledgenſk.
Beaver,	Zah,	Schugh,
Elk,	Yezey,	Oikoy-Beh.
Dog,	Sleing,	Scacah.
Ground-hog,	Thidnu,	Squaiquais.
Iron,	Thliſitch,	Soucoumang.

Fire,

	The Nagailer, or Chin-Indians.	The Atnah, or Carrier-Indians.
Fire,	Coun,	Teuck.
Water,	Tou,	Shaweliquoih.
Stone,	Zeh,	Ifhehoineah.
Bow,	Nettuny,	Ifquoinah.
Arrow,	Igah,	Squaili.
Yes,	Nefi,	Amaig.
Plains,	Thoughoud,	Spilela.
Come here,	Andezei,	Thla-elyeh.

The Atnah language has no affinity to any with which I am acquainted; but the Nagailer differs very little from that fpoken by the Beaver Indians, and is almoft the fame as that of the Chepewyans.

We had a thunder-ftorm with heavy rain; and in the evening when it had fubfided, the Indians amufed us with finging and dancing, in which they were joined by the young women. Four men now arrived whom we had not yet feen; they had left their families at fome diftance in the country, and expreffed a defire that we fhould vifit them there.

Sunday 23.   After a reftlefs night, I called the Indians together, from whom I yefterday received the intelligence which has been already mentioned, in the hope that I might obtain fome additional information. From their former account they did not make the leaft deviation; but they informed me further, that where they left this river, a fmall one from the Weftward falls into it, which was navigable for their canoes during four days,

and

and from thence they slept but two nights, to get to the people with whom they trade, and who have wooden canoes much larger than ours, in which they go down a river to the sea. They continued to inform me, that if I went that way we must leave our own canoe behind us; but they thought it probable that those people would furnish us with another. From thence they stated the distance to be only one day's voyage with the current to the lake whose water is nauseous, and where they had heard that great canoes came two winters ago, and that the people belonging to them, brought great quantities of goods and built houses.

At the commencement of this conversation, I was very much surprised by the following question from one of the Indians: " What," demanded he, " can be the reason that you are so particular and anxious in your inquiries of us respecting a knowledge of this country: do not you white men know every thing in the world?" This interrogatory was so very unexpected, that it occasioned some hesitation before I could answer it. At length, however, I replied, that we certainly were acquainted with the principal circumstances of every part of the world; that I knew where the sea is, and where I myself then was, but that I did not exactly understand what obstacles might interrupt me in getting to it; with which, he and his relations must be well acquainted, as they had so frequently surmounted them. Thus I fortunately preserved the impression in their minds, of the superiority of white people over themselves.

It was now, however, absolutely neeessary that I should come to a final
deter-

determination which route to take; and no long interval of reflection was employed, before I preferred to go over land: the comparative fhortnefs and fecurity of fuch a journey, were alone fufficient to determine me. I accordingly propofed to two of the Indians to accompany me, and one of them readily affented to my propofition.

I now called thofe of my people about me, who had not been prefent at my confultation with the natives; and after paffing a warm eulogium on their fortitude, patience, and perfeverance, I ftated the difficulties that threatened our continuing to navigate the river, the length of time it would require, and the fcanty provifion we had for fuch a voyage: I then proceeded for the foregoing reafons to propofe a fhorter route, by trying the over-land road to the fea. At the fame time, as I knew from experience, the difficulty of retaining guides, and as many circumftances might occur to prevent our progrefs in that direction, I declared my refolution not to attempt it, unlefs they would engage, if we could not after all proceed over land, to return with me, and continue our voyage to the difcharge of the waters, whatever the diftance might be. At all events, I declared, in the moft folemn manner, that I would not abandon my defign of reaching the fea, if I made the attempt alone, and that I did not defpair of returning in fafety to my friends.

This propofition met with the moft zealous return, and they unanimoufly affured me, that they were as willing now as they had ever been, to abide by my refolutions, whatever they might be, and to follow me wherever I fhould go. I therefore requefted them to prepare for an immediate departure, and at the fame time gave notice to the man who

had

had engaged to be our guide, to be in readiness to accompany us. When our determination to return up the river was made known, several of the natives took a very abrupt departure; but to those who remained, I gave a few useful articles, explaining to them at the same time, the advantages that would result to them, if their relations conducted me to the sea, along such a road as they had described. I had already given a moose skin to some of the women for the purpose of making shoes, which were now brought us; they were well sewed but ill shaped, and a few beads were considered as a sufficient remuneration for the skill employed on them. Mr. Mackay, by my desire, engraved my name, and the date of the year on a tree.

When we were ready to depart, our guide proposed, for the sake of expedition, to go over land to his lodge, that he might get there before us, to make some necessary preparation for his journey. I did not altogether relish his design, but was obliged to consent: I thought it prudent, however, to send Mr. Mackay, and the two Indians along with him. Our place of rendezvous, was the subterraneous house which we passed yesterday.

At ten in the morning we embarked, and went up the current much faster than I expected with such a crazy vessel as that which carried us. We met our people at the house as had been appointed; but the Indian still continued to prefer going on by land, and it would have been needless for me to oppose him. He proceeded, therefore, with his former companions, whom I desired to keep him in good humour by every reasonable

fonable gratification.   They were alfo furnifhed with a few articles that might be of ufe if they fhould meet with ftrangers.

In a fhort time after we had left the houfe, I faw a wooden canoe coming down the river, with three natives in it, who, as foon as they perceived us, made for the fhore, and hurried into the woods.   On paf-fing their veffel, we difcovered it to be one of thofe which we had feen at the lodges.   A fevere guft of wind, with rain, came from the South-South-Eaft.   This we found to be a very prevalent wind in thefe parts. We foon paffed another wooden canoe drawn ftern foremoft on the fhore; a circumftance which we had not hitherto obferved.   The men worked very hard, and though I imagined we went a-head very faft, we could not reach the lodges, but landed for the night at nine, clofe to the encampment of two families of the natives whom we had formerly feen at the lodges.   I immediately went and fat down with them, when they gave fome roafted fifh; two of my men who followed me were gratified alfo with fome of their provifions.   The youngeft of the two natives now quitted the fhed, and did not return during the time I remained there.   I endeavoured to explain to the other by figns, the caufe of my fudden return, which he appeared to underftand.   In the mean time my tent was pitched, and on my going to it, I was rather fur-prifed that he did not follow me, as he had been conftantly with me during the day and night I had paffed with his party on going down. We, however, went to reft in a ftate of perfect fecurity; nor had we the leaft apprehenfion for the fafety of our people who were gone by land.

We

We were in our canoe by four this morning, and paſſed by the Indian hut, which appeared in a ſtate of perfect tranquillity. We ſoon came in ſight of the point where we firſt ſaw the natives, and at eight were much ſurpriſed and diſappointed at ſeeing Mr. Mackay, and our two Indians coming alone from the ruins of an houſe that had been partly carried away by the ice and water, at a ſhort diſtance below the place where we had appointed to meet. Nor was our ſurpriſe and apprehenſion dimi-niſhed by the alarm which was painted in their countenances. When we had landed, they informed me that they had taken refuge in that place, with the determination to ſell their lives, which they conſidered in the moſt imminent danger, as dear as poſſible. In a very ſhort time after they had left us, they met a party of the Indians, whom we had known at this place, and were probably thoſe whom we had ſeen to land from their canoe. They appeared to be in a ſtate of extreme rage, and had their bows bent, with their arrows acroſs them. The guide ſtopped to aſk them ſome queſtions, which my people did not underſtand, and then ſet off with his utmoſt ſpeed. Mr. Mackay, however, did not leave him till they were both exhauſted with running. When the young man came up, he then ſaid, that ſome treacherous deſign was meditated againſt them, as he was induced to believe from the declaration of the natives, who told him that they were going to do miſchief, but refuſed to name the enemy. The guide then conducted them through very bad ways, as faſt as they could run; and when he was deſired to ſlacken his pace, he anſwered that they might follow him in any manner they pleaſed, but that he was impatient to get to his family, in order to prepare ſhoes, and other neceſſaries, for his journey. They did not, however, think it pru-dent to quit him, and he would not ſtop till ten at night. On paſſing a

track

1793.
June.
Monday 24.

track that was but lately made, they began to be ferioufly alarmed, and on inquiring of the guide where they were, he pretended not to underftand them.   They then all laid down, exhaufted with fatigue, and without any kind of covering: they were cold, wet, and hungry, but dared not light a fire, from the apprehenfion of an enemy.   This comfortlefs fpot they left at the dawn of day, and, on their arrival at the lodges, found them deferted; the property of the Indians being fcattered about, as if abandoned for ever.   The guide then made two or three trips into the woods, calling aloud, and bellowing like a madman.   At length he fet off in the fame direction as they came, and had not fince appeared. To heighten their mifery, as they did not find us at the place appointed, they concluded that we were all deftroyed, and had already formed their plan to take to the woods, and crofs in as a direct a line as they could proceed, to the waters of the Peace River, a fcheme which could only be fuggefted by defpair.   They intended to have waited for us till noon, and if we did not appear by that time, to have entered without further delay on their defperate expedition.

This alarm among the natives was a very unexpected as well as perilous event, and my powers of conjecture were exhaufted in fearching for the caufe of it.   A general panic feized all around me, and any further profecution of the voyage was now confidered by them as altogether hopelefs and impracticable.   But without paying the leaft attention to their opinions or furmifes, I ordered them to take every thing out of the canoe, except fix packages: when that was done, I left four men to take care of the lading, and returned with the others to our camp of laft night, where I hoped to find the two men, with their families, whom we

had

had feen there, and to be able to bring them to lodge with us, when I fhould wait the iffue of this myfterious bufinefs. This project, however, was difappointed, for thefe people had quitted their fheds in the filence of the night, and had not taken a fingle article of their little property with them.

Thefe perplexing circumftances made a deep impreffion on my mind, not as to our immediate fafety, for I entertained not the leaft apprehenfion of the Indians I had hitherto feen, even if their whole force fhould have been combined to attack us, but thefe untoward events feemed to threaten the profecution of my journey; and I could not reflect on the poffibility of fuch a difappointment but with fenfations little fhort of agony. Whatever might have been the wavering difpofition of the people on former occafions, they were now decided in their opinions as to the neceffity of returning without delay; and when we came back to them, their cry was—" Let us reimbark, and be gone." This, however, was not my defign, and in a more peremptory tone than I ufually employed, they were ordered to unload the canoe, and take her out of the water. On examining our property, feveral articles appeared to be miffing, which the Indians muft have purloined; and among them were an axe, two knives, and the young men's bag of medicines. We now took a pofition that was the beft calculated for defence, got our arms in complete order, filled each man's flafk of powder, and diftributed an hundred bullets, which were all that remained, while fome were employed in melting down fhot to make more. The weather was fo cloudy that I had not an opportunity of taking an obfervation.

While

While we were employed in making thefe preparations, we faw an Indian in a canoe come down the river, and land at the huts, which he began to examine. On perceiving us he ftood ftill, as if in a ftate of fufpenfe, when I inftantly difpatched one of my Indians towards him, but no perfuafions could induce him to have confidence in us; he even threatened that he would haften to join his friends, who would come and kill us. At the conclufion of this menace he difappeared. On the return of my young man, with this account of the interview, I pretended to difcredit the whole, and attributed it to his own apprehenfions and alarms. This, however, he denied, and afked with a look and tone of refentment, whether he had ever told me a lie? Though he was but a young man, he faid, he had been on war excurfions before he came with me, and that he fhould no longer confider me as a wife man, which he had hitherto done.

To add to our diftreffes we had not an ounce of gum for the reparation of the canoe, and not one of the men had fufficient courage to venture into the woods to collect it. In this perplexing fituation I entertained the hope that in the courfe of the night fome of the natives would return, to take away a part at leaft of the things which they had left behind them, as they had gone away without the covering neceffary to defend them from the weather and the flies. I therefore ordered the canoe to be loaded, and dropped to an old houfe, one fide of which, with its roof, had been carried away by the water; but the three remaining angles were fufficient to fhelter us from the woods. I then ordered two ftrong piquets to be driven into the ground, to which the canoe was faftened, fo that if we were hard preffed we had only to ftep on board

and

and puſh off. We were under the neceſſity of making a ſmoke to keep off the ſwarms of flies, which would have otherwiſe tormented us; but we did not venture to excite a blaze, as it would have been a mark for the arrows of the enemy. Mr. Mackay and myſelf, with three men kept alternate watch, and allowed the Indians to do as they fancied. I took the firſt watch, and the others laid down in their clothes by us. I alſo placed a centinel at a ſmall diſtance, who was relieved every hour. The weather was cloudy, with ſhowers of rain.

At one I called up the other watch, and laid down to a ſmall portion of broken reſt. At five I aroſe, and as the ſituation which we left yeſterday was preferable to that which we then occupied, I determined to return to it. On our arrival Mr. Mackay informed me that the men had ex-preſſed their diſſatisfaction to him in a very unreſerved manner, and had in very ſtrong terms declared their reſolution to follow me no further in my propoſed enterprize. I did not appear, however, to have received ſuch communications from him, and continued to employ my whole thoughts in contriving means to bring about a reconciliation with the natives, which alone would enable me to procure guides, without whoſe aſſiſtance it would be impoſſible for me to proceed, when my darling pro-ject would end in diſappointment.

At twelve we ſaw a man coming with the ſtream upon a raft, and he muſt have diſcovered us before we perceived him, as he was working very hard to get to the oppoſite ſhore, where he ſoon landed, and in-ſtantly fled into the woods. I now had a meridional altitude, which gave 60. 23. natural horizon, (the angle being more than the ſextant could

meaſure

1793.
June.
meafure with the artificial horizon,) one mile and an half diftant; and the eye five feet above the level of the water, gave 52. 47. 51. North latitude.

While I was thus employed, the men loaded the canoe without having received any orders from me, and as this was the firft time they had ventured to act in fuch a decided manner, I naturally concluded, that they had preconcerted a plan for their return. I thought it prudent, however, to take no notice of this tranfaction, and to wait the iffue of future circumftances. At this moment our Indians perceived a perfon in the edge of the woods above us, and they were immediately difpatched to difcover who it was. After a fhort abfence they returned with a young woman whom we had feen before: her language was not clearly comprehended by us, fo that we could not learn from her, at leaft with any degree of certainty, the caufe of this unfortunate alarm that had taken place among the natives. She told us that her errand was to fetch fome things which fhe had left behind her; and one of the dogs whom we found here, appeared to acknowledge her as his miftrefs. We treated her with great kindnefs, gave her fomething to eat, and added a prefent of fuch articles as we thought might pleafe her. On her expreffing a wifh to leave us, we readily confented to her departure, and indulged the hope that her reception would induce the natives to return in peace, and give us an opportunity to convince them, that we had no hoftile defigns whatever againft them. On leaving us, fhe went up the river without taking a fingle article of her own, and the dog fol-lowed. The wind was changeable throughout the day, and there were feveral fhowers in the courfe of it.

Though

Though a very apparent anxiety prevailed among the people for their departure, I appeared to be wholly inattentive to it, and at eight in the evening I ordered four men to ftep into the canoe, which had been loaded for feveral hours, and drop down to our guard-houfe, and my command was immediately obeyed: the reft of us proceeded there by land. When I was yet at a confiderable diftance from the houfe, and thought it im-poffible for an arrow to reach it, having a bow and quiver in my hand, I very imprudently let fly an arrow, when, to my aftonifhment and in-finite alarm, I heard it ftrike a log of the houfe. The men who had juft landed, imagined that they were attacked by an enemy from the woods. Their confufion was in proportion to their imaginary danger, and on my arrival I found that the arrow had paffed within a foot of one of the men; though it had no point, the weapon, incredible as it may appear, had entered an hard, dry log of wood upwards of an inch. But this was not all: for the men readily availed themfelves of this circumftance, to remark upon the danger of remaining in the power of a people pof-feffed of fuch means of deftruction. Mr. Mackay having the firft watch, I laid myfelf down in my cloak.

About midnight a ruftling noife was heard in the woods which created a general alarm, and I was awakened to be informed of the cir-cumftance, but heard nothing. At one I took my turn of the watch, and our dog continued unceafingly to run backwards and forwards along the fkirts of the wood in a ftate of reftlefs vigilance. At two in the morn-ing the centinel informed me, that he faw fomething like an human figure creeping along on all-fours about fifty paces above us. After fome time had paffed in our fearch, I at length difcovered that his infor-

mation

mation was true, and it appeared to me that a bear had occafioned the alarm; but when day appeared, it proved to be an old, grey-haired, blind man, who had been compelled to leave his hiding-place by extreme hunger, being too infirm to join in the flight of the natives to whom he belonged. When I put my hand on this objeᏩ of decaying nature, his alarm was fo great, that I expeᏩed it would have thrown him into convulfions. I immediately led him to our fire which had been juft lighted, and gave him fomething to eat, which he much wanted, as he had not tafted food for two days. When his hunger was fatisfied, and he had got warm and compofed, I requefted him to acquaint me with the caufe of that alarm which had taken place refpeᏩing us among his relations and friends, whofe regard we appeared to have conciliated but a few days paft, He replied, that very foon after we had left them, fome natives arrived from above, who informed them that we were enemies; and our unexpeᏩed return, in direᏩ contradiᏩion to our own declarations, confirmed them in that opinion. They were now, he faid, fo fcattered, that a confiderable time would elapfe, before they could meet again. We gave him the real hiftory of our return, as well as of the defertion of our guide, and, at the fame time, ftated the impoffibility of our proceeding, unlefs we procured a native to conduᏩ us. He replied, that if he had not loft his fight, he would with the greateft readinefs have accompanied us on our journey. He alfo confirmed the accounts which we had received of the country, and the route to the Weftward. I did not negleᏩ to employ every argument in my power, that he might be perfuaded of our friendly difpofitions to the inhabitants wherefoever we might meet them.

At

At fun-rife we perceived a canoe with one man in it on the oppofite fide of the river, and at our requeft, the blind man called to him to come to us, but he returned no anfwer, and continued his courfe as faft as he could paddle down the current. He was confidered as a fpy by my men, and I was confirmed in that opinion, when I faw a wooden canoe drifting with the ftream clofe in to the other fhore, where it was more than probable that fome of the natives might be concealed. It might, therefore, have been an ufelefs enterprife, or perhaps fatal to the future fuccefs of our undertaking, if we had purfued thefe people, as they might, through fear, have employed their arms againft us, and provoked us to retaliate.

The old man informed me, that fome of the natives whom I had feen here were gone up the river, and thofe whom I faw below had left their late ftation to gather a root in the plains, which, when dried, forms a confiderable article in their winter ftock of provifions. He had a woman, he faid, with him, who ufed to fee us walking along the fmall adjoining river, but when he called her he received no anfwer, fo that fhe had probably fled to join her people. He informed me, alfo, that he expefted a confiderable number of his tribe to come on the upper part of the river to catch fifh for their prefent fupport, and to cure them for their winter ftore; among whom he had a fon and two brothers.

In confequence of thefe communications, I deemed it altogether unneceffary to lofe any more time at this place, and I informed the old man that he muft accompany me for the purpofe of introducing us to his friends and relations, and that if we met with his fon or brothers, I depended upon him to perfuade them, or fome of their party, to attend us

as

as guides in our meditated expedition. He expreſſed his wiſhes to be excuſed from this ſervice, and in other circumſtances we ſhould not have infiſted on it, but, ſituated as we were, we could not yield to his requeſt.

At ſeven in the morning we left this place, which I named Deſerter's River or Creek. Our blind guide was, however, ſo averſe to continuing with us, that I was under the very diſagreeable neceſſity of ordering the men to carry him into the canoe; and this was the firſt act during my voyage, that had the ſemblance of violent dealing. He continued to ſpeak in a very loud tone, while he remained, according to his conjecture, near enough to the camp to be heard, but in a language that our interpreters did not underſtand. On aſking him what he ſaid, and why he did not ſpeak in a language known to us, he replied, that the woman underſtood him better in that which he ſpoke, and he requeſted her, if ſhe heard him, to come for him to the carrying-place, where he expected we ſhould leave him.

At length our canoe was become ſo leaky, that it was abſolutely unfit for ſervice; and it was the unremitting employment of one perſon to keep her clear of water: we, therefore, inquired of the old man where we could conveniently obtain the articles neceſſary to build a new one; and we underſtood from him that, at ſome diſtance up the river, we ſhould find plenty of bark and cedar.

At ten, being at the foot of a rapid, we ſaw a ſmall canoe coming down with two men in it. We thought it would be impoſſible for them to

eſcape,

efcape, and therefore ftruck off from the fhore with a defign to intercept them, directing the old man at the fame time to addrefs them; but they no fooner perceived us, than they fteered into the ftrength of the current, where I thought that they muft inevitably perifh; but their attention appeared to be engroffed by the fituation of their canoe, and they efcaped without making us the leaft reply.

About three in the afternoon we perceived a lodge at the entrance of a confiderable river on the right, as well as the tracks of people in the mud at the mouth of a fmall river on the left. As they appeared to be frefh, we landed, and endeavoured to trace them, but without fuccefs. We then croffed over to the lodge, which was deferted, but all the ufual furniture of fuch buildings remained untouched.

Throughout the whole of this day the men had been in a ftate of extreme ill-humour, and as they did not choofe openly to vent it upon me, they difputed and quarrelled among themfelves. About fun-fet the canoe ftruck upon the ftump of a tree, which broke a large hole in her bottom; a circumftance that gave them an opportunity to let loofe their difcontents without referve. I left them as foon as we had landed, and afcended an elevated bank, in a ftate of mind which I fcarce wifh to recollect, and fhall not attempt to defcribe. At this place there was a fubterraneous houfe, where I determined to pafs the night. The water had rifen fince we had paffed down, and it was with the utmoft exertion that we came up feveral points in the courfe of the day.

We

We embarked at half paſt four, with very favourable weather, and at eight we landed, where there was an appearance of our being able to procure bark ; we, however, obtained but a ſmall quantity. At twelve we went on ſhore again, and collected as much as was neceſſary for our purpoſe. It now remained for us to fix on a proper place for building another canoe, as it was impoſſible to proceed with our old one, which was become an abſolute wreck. At five in the afternoon we came to a ſpot well adapted to the buſineſs in which we were about to engage. It was on a ſmall iſland not much encumbered with wood, though there was plenty of the ſpruce kind on the oppoſite land, which was only divided from us by a ſmall channel. We now landed, but before the canoe was unloaded, and the tent pitched, a violent thunder-ſtorm came on, accompanied with rain, which did not ſubſide till the night had cloſed in upon us. Two of our men who had been in the woods for axe-handles, ſaw a deer, and one of them ſhot at it, but unluckily miſſed his aim. A net was alſo prepared and ſet in the eddy at the end of the iſland.

CHAP.

CHAPTER IX.

Make preparations to build a canoe. Engage in that important work. It proceeds with great expedition. The guide who had deferted arrives with another Indian. He communicates agreeable intelligence. They take an opportunity to quit the ifland. Complete the canoe. Leave the ifland, which was now named the Canoe Ifland. Obliged to put the people on fhort allowance. Account of the navigation. Difficult afcent of a rapid. Frefh perplexities. Continue our voyage up the river. Meet the guide and fome of his friends. Conceal fome pemmican and other articles. Make preparations for proceeding over land. Endeavour to fecure the canoe till our return. Proceed on our journey. Various circumftances of it.

1793.
June.

Friday 28.

AT a very early hour of the morning every man was employed in making preparations for building another canoe, and different parties went in fearch of wood, watape, and gum. At two in the afternoon they all returned fuccefsful, except the colleĉors of gum, and of that article it was feared we fhould not obtain here a fufficient fupply for our immediate wants. After a neceffary portion of time allotted for refrefh- ment, each began his refpeĉive work. I had an altitude at noon, which made us in 53. 2. 32. North latitude.

The

The weather continued to be fine. At five o'clock we renewed our labour, and the canoe was got in a ftate of confiderable forwardnefs. The conductor of the work, though a good man, was remarkable for the tardinefs of his operations, whatever they might be, and more difpofed to eat than to be active; I, therefore, took this opportunity of unfolding my fentiments to him, and thereby difcovering to all around me the real ftate of my mind, and the refolutions I had formed for my future conduct. After reproaching him for his general inactivity, but particularly on the prefent occafion, when our time was fo precious, I mentioned the apparent want of economy both of himfelf and his companions, in the article of provifions. I informed him that I was not altogether a ftranger to their late converfations, from whence I drew the conclufion that they wifhed to put an end to the voyage. If that were fo, I expreffed my wifh that they would be explicit, and tell me at once of their determination to follow me no longer. I concluded, however, by affuring him, that whatever plan they had meditated to purfue, it was my fixed and unalterable determination to proceed, in fpite of every difficulty that might oppofe, or danger that fhould threaten me. The man was very much mortified at my addreffing this remonftrance particularly to him; and replied, that he did not deferve my difpleafure more than the reft of them. My object being anfwered, the converfation dropped, and the work went on.

About two in the afternoon one of the men perceived a canoe with two natives in it, coming along the infide of the ifland, but the water being fhallow, it turned back, and we imagined that on perceiving us they had taken the alarm; but we were agreeably furprifed on feeing

them

them come up the outfide of the ifland, when we recognifed our guide, and one of the natives whom we had already feen. The former began immediately to apologize for his conduct, and affured me that fince he had left me, his whole time had been employed in fearching after his family, who had been feized with the general panic, that had been occafioned by the falfe reports of the people who had firft fled from us. He faid it was generally apprehended by the natives that we had been unfriendly to their relations above, who were expected upon the river in great numbers at this time; and that many of the Atnah or Chin nation, had come up the river to where we had been, in the hope of feeing us, and were very much difpleafed with him and his friends for having neglected to give them an early notice of our arrival there. He added, that the two men whom we had feen yefterday, or the day before, were juft returned from their rendezvous, with the natives of the fea coaft, and had brought a meffage from his brother-in-law, that he had a new axe for him, and not to forget to bring a moofe-fkin dreffed in exchange, which he actually had in his canoe. He expected to meet him, he faid, at the other end of the carrying-place.

This was as pleafing intelligence as we had reafon to expect, and it is almoft fuperfluous to obferve that we ftood in great need of it. I had a meridian altitude, which gave 53. 3. 7. North latitude. I alfo took time in the fore and afternoon, that gave a mean of 1. 37. 42. Achrometer flow apparent time, which, with an obferved immerfion of Jupiter's firft fatellite, made our longitude 122. 48. Weft of Greenwich.

The

The blind old man gave a very favourable account of us to his friends, and they all three were very merry together during the whole of the afternoon.   That our guide, however, might not efcape from us during the night, I determined to watch him.

Sunday 30.   Our ftrangers conducted themfelves with great good-humour through-out the day.   According to their information we fhould find their friends above and below the carrying-place.   They mentioned, alfo, that fome of them were not of their tribe, but are allied to the people of the fea coaft, who trade with the white men.   I had a meridian altitude, that gave 53. 3. 17. North latitude.

Laft night I had the firft watch, when one of my Indians propofed to fit up with me, as he underftood, from the old man's converfation, that he intended, in the courfe of the night, to make his efcape.   Accord-ingly at eleven I extinguifhed my light, and fat quietly in my tent, from whence I could obferve the motions of the natives.   About twelve, though the night was rather dark, I obferved the old man creeping on his hands and knees towards the water-fide.   We accordingly followed him very quietly to the canoe, and he would have gone away with it, if he had not been interrupted in his defign.   On upbraiding him for his treacherous conduct, when he had been treated with fo much kindnefs by us, he denied the intention of which we accufed him, and declared that his fole object was to affuage his thirft.   At length, however, he acknowledged the truth, and when we brought him to the fire, his friends, who now awoke, on being informed of what had paffed, repro-bated his conduct, and afked him how he could expect that the white

people

people would return to this country, if they experienced fuch ungrateful treatment. The guide faid, for his part, he was not a woman, and would never run away through fear. But notwithftanding this courageous declaration, at one I awakened Mr. Mackay, related to him what had paffed, and requefted him not to indulge himfelf in fleep till I fhould rife. It was feven before I awoke, and on quitting my tent I was furprifed at not feeing the guide and his companion, and my apprehenfions were increafed when I obferved that the canoe was removed from its late fituation. To my inquiries after them, fome of the men very compofedly anfwered that they were gone up the river, and had left the old man behind them. Mr. Mackay alfo told me, that while he was bufily employed on the canoe, they had got to the point before he had obferved their departure. The interpreter now informed me that at the dawn of day the guide had expreffed his defign, as foon as the fun was up, to go and wait for us, where he might find his friends. I hoped this might be true; but that my people fhould fuffer them to depart without giving me notice, was a circumftance that awakened very painful reflections in my breaft. The weather was clear in the forenoon. My obfervation this day gave 53. 3. 32. North latitude.

At five in the afternoon our veffel was completed, and ready for fervice. She proved a ftronger and better boat than the old one, though had it not been for the gum obtained from the latter, it would have been a matter of great difficulty to have procured a fufficiency of that article to have prevented her from leaking. The remainder of the day was employed by the people in cleaning and refrefhing themfelves, as they had enjoyed no relaxation from their labour fince we landed on this fpot.

The

The old man having manifefted for various and probably very falla-cious reafons, a very great averfion to accompany us any further, it did not appear that there was any neceffity to force his inclination. We now put our arms in order, which was foon accomplifhed, as they were at all times a general object of attention.

Tuefday 2.   It rained throughout the night, but at half paft three we were ready to embark, when I offered to conduct the old man where he had fuppofed we fhould meet his friends, but he declined the propofition. I therefore directed a few pounds of pemmican to be left with him, for his imme-diate fupport, and took leave of him and the place, which I named Canoe Ifland. During our ftay there we had been moft cruelly tormented by flies, particularly the fand-fly, which I am difpofed to confider as the moft tormenting infect of its fize in nature. I was alfo compelled to put the people upon fhort allowance, and confine them to two meals a-day, a regulation peculiarly offenfive to a Canadian voyager. One of thefe meals was compofed of the dried rows of fifh, pounded, and boiled in water, thickened with a fmall quantity of flour, and fattened with a bit of grian. Thefe articles, being brought to the confiftency of an hafty pudding, produced a fubftantial and not unpleafant difh. The natives are very careful of the rows of fifh, which they dry, and pre-ferve in bafkets made of bark. Thofe we ufed were found in the huts of the firft people who fled from us. During our abode in Canoe Ifland, the water funk three perpendicular feet. I now gave the men a dram each, which could not but be confidered, at this time, as a very comfortable treat. They were, indeed, in high fpirits, when they perceived the fuperior excellence of the new veffel, and reflected that it was the work of their own hands.

At

At eleven we arrived at the rapids, and the foreman, who had not forgotten the fright he fuffered on coming down it, propofed that the canoe and lading fhould be carried over the mountain. I threatened him with taking the office of foreman on myfelf, and fuggefted the evident change there was in the appearance of the water fince we paffed it, which upon examination had funk four feet and an half. As the water did not feem fo ftrong on the Weft fide, I determined to crofs over, having firft put Mr. Mackay, and our two hunters, on fhore, to try the woods for game. We accordingly traverfed, and got up clofe along the rocks, to a confiderable diftance, with the paddles, when we could proceed no further without affiftance from the line; and to draw it acrofs a perpendicular rock, for the diftance of fifty fathoms, appeared to be an infurmountable obftacle. The general opinion was to return, and carry on the other fide; I defired, however, two of the men to take the line, which was feventy fathoms in length, with a fmall roll of bark, and endeavour to climb up the rocks, from whence they were to defcend on the other fide of that which oppofed our progrefs; they were then to faften the end of the line to the roll of bark, which the current would bring to us; this being effected, they would be able to draw us up. This was an enterprife of difficulty and danger, but it was crowned with fuccefs; though to get to the water's edge above, the men were obliged to let themfelves down with the line, run round a tree, from the fummit of the rock. By a repetition of the fame operation, we at length cleared the rapid, with the additional trouble of carrying the canoe, and unloading at two cafcades. We were not more than two hours getting up this difficult part of the river, including the time employed in repairing an hole which had been broken in the canoe, by the negligence of the fteerfman.

Here

Here we expected to meet with the natives, but there was not the least appearance of them, except that the guide, his companion, and two others, had apparently paſſed the carrying-place. We ſaw ſeveral fiſh leap out of the water, which appeared to be of the ſalmon kind. The old man, indeed, had informed us that this was the ſeaſon when the large fiſh begin to come up the river. Our hunters returned, but had not ſeen the track of any animal. We now continued our journey; the current was not ſtrong, but we met with frequent impediments from the fallen trees, which lay along the banks. We landed at eight in the evening; and ſuffered indeſcribable inconveniences from the flies.

Wedneſ. 3.   It had rained hard in the night, and there was ſome ſmall rain in the morning. At four we entered our canoe, and at ten we came to a ſmall river, which anſwered to the deſcription of that whoſe courſe the natives ſaid, they follow in their journies towards the ſea coaſt; we therefore put into it, and endeavoured to diſcover if our guide had landed here; but there were no traces of him or of any others. My former perplexities were now renewed. If I paſſed this river, it was probable that I might miſs the natives; and I had reaſon to ſuſpect that my men would not conſent to return thither. As for attempting the woods, without a guide, to introduce us to the firſt inhabitants, ſuch a determination would be little ſhort of abſolute madneſs. At length, after much painful reflection, I reſolved to come at once to a full explanation with my people, and I experienced a conſiderable relief from this reſolution. Accordingly, after repeating the promiſe they had ſo lately made me, on our putting back up the river, I repreſented to them that this appeared to me to be the ſpot from which the natives took their departure for the

ſea

fea coaft, and added, withal, that I was determined to try it ; for though our guide had left us, it was poffible that, while we were making the neceffary preparations, he or fome others might appear, to relieve us from our prefent difficulties. I now found, to my great fatisfaction, that they had not come to any fixed determination among themfelves, as fome of them immediately affented to undertake the woods with me. Others, however, fuggefted that it might be better to proceed a few leagues further up the river, in expectation of finding our guide, or procuring another, and that after all we might return hither. This plan I very readily agreed to adopt, but before I left this place, to which I gave the name of the Weft-Road River, I fent fome of the men into the woods, in different directions, and went fome diftance up the river myfelf, which I found to be navigable only for fmall canoes. Two of the men found a good beaten path, leading up an hill juft behind us, which I imagined to be the great road.

At four in the afternoon we left this place, proceeding up the river; and had not been upon the water more than three quarters of an hour, when we faw two canoes coming with the ftream. No fooner did the people in them perceive us than they landed, and we went on fhore at the fame place with them. They proved to be our guide, and fix of his relations. He was covered with a painted beaver robe, fo that we fcarcely knew him in his fine habiliment. He inftantly defired us to acknowledge that he had not difappointed us, and declared, at the fame time, that it was his conftant intention to keep his word. I accordingly gave him a jacket, a pair of trowfers, and an handkerchief, as a reward for his honourable conduct. The ftrangers examined us with

the

the moſt minute attention, and two of them, as I was now informed, be-longed to the people whom we firſt ſaw, and who fled with ſo much alarm from us.   They told me, alſo, that they were ſo terrified on that occaſion, as not to approach their huts for two days; and that when they ventured thither, they found the greater part of their property de-ſtroyed, by the fire running in the ground.   According to their ac-count, they were of a different tribe, though I found no difference in their language from that of the Nagailas or Carriers.   They are called Naſcud Denee.   Their lodges were at ſome diſtance, on a ſmall lake, where they take fiſh, and if our guide had not gone for them there, we ſhould not have ſeen an human being on the river.   They informed me that the road by their habitation is the ſhorteſt, and they propoſed that we ſhould take it.

Tueſday 4.   At an early hour this morning, and at the ſuggeſtion of our guide, we proceeded to the landing-place that leads to the ſtrangers lodges. Our great difficulty here was to procure a temporary ſeparation from our company, in order to hide ſome articles we could not carry with us, and which it would have been imprudent to leave in the power of the natives.   Accordingly Mr. Mackay, and one of our Indians em-barked with them, and ſoon run out of our ſight.   At our firſt hiding-place we left a bag of pemmican, weighing ninety pounds, two bags of wild rice, and a gallon keg of gunpowder.   Previous to our putting theſe articles in the ground, we rolled them up in oil cloth, and dreſſed leather.   In the ſecond hiding-place, and guarded with the ſame rollers, we hid two bags of Indian corn, or maize, and a bale of different articles of merchandiſe.   When we had completed this important objeĉt, we

proceeded

proceeded till half paſt eight, when we landed at the entrance of a ſmall rivulet, where our friends were waiting for us.

Here it was neceſſary that we ſhould leave our canoe, and whatever we could not carry on our backs. In the firſt place, therefore, we prepared a ſtage, on which the canoe was placed bottom upwards, and ſhaded by a covering of ſmall trees and branches, to keep her from the ſun. We then built an oblong hollow ſquare, ten feet by five, of green logs, wherein we placed every article it was neceſſary for us to leave here, and covered the whole with large pieces of timber.

While we were eagerly employed in this neceſſary buſineſs, our guide and his companions were ſo impatient to be gone, that we could not per-ſuade the former to wait till we were prepared for our departure, and we had ſome difficulty in perſuading another of the natives to remain, who had undertook to conduct us-where the guide had promiſed to wait our arrival.

At noon we were in a ſtate of preparation to enter the woods, an undertaking of which I ſhall not here give any preliminary opinion, but leave thoſe who read it to judge for themſelves.

We carried on our backs four bags and an half of pemmican, weighing from eighty-five to ninety pounds each; a caſe with my inſtru-ments, a parcel of goods for preſents, weighing ninety pounds, and a par-cel containing ammunition of the ſame weight. Each of the Canadians had a burden of about ninety pounds, with a gun, and ſome ammuni-tion.

tion.   The Indians had about forty-five pounds weight of pemmican to carry, befides their gun, &c. with which they were very much diffatisfied, and if they had dared would have inftantly left us.   They had hitherto been very much indulged, but the moment was now arrived when indulgence was no longer practicable.   My own load, and that of Mr. Mackay, confifted of twenty-two pounds of pemmican, fome rice, a little fugar, &c. amounting in the whole to about feventy pounds each, befides our arms and ammunition.   I had alfo the tube of my telefcope fwung acrofs my fhoulder, which was a troublefome addition to my burthen.   It was determined that we fhould content ourfelves with two meals a-day, which were regulated without difficulty, as our provifions did not require the ceremony of cooking.

In this ftate of equipment we began our journey, as I have already mentioned, about twelve at noon, the commencement of which was a fteep afcent of about a mile; it lay along a well-beaten path, but the country through which it led was rugged and ridgy, and full of wood. When we were in a ftate of extreme heat, from the toil of our journey, the rain came on, and continued till the evening, and even when it ceafed the underwood continued its drippings upon us.

About half paft fix we arrived at an Indian camp of three fires, where we found our guide, and on his recommendation we determined to remain there for the night.   The computed diftance of this day's journey was about twelve geographical miles; the courfe about Weft.

At fun-fet an elderly man and three other natives joined us from the
Weftward.

1793.
July.

Weftward. The former bore a lance that very much refembled a fer-jeant's halberd. He had lately received it, by way of barter, from the natives of the Sea-Coaft, who procured it from the white men. We fhould meet, he faid, with many of his countrymen who had juft re-turned from thence. According to his report, it did not require more than fix days journey, for people who are not heavily laden, to reach the country of thofe with whom they bartered their fkins for iron, &c. and from thence it is not quite two day's march to the fea. They pro-pofed to fend two young men on before us, to notify to the different tribes that we were approaching, that they might not be furprifed at our appearance, and be difpofed to afford us a friendly reception. This was a meafure which I could not but approve, and endeavoured by fome fmall prefents to prepoffefs our couriers in our favour.

Thefe people live but poorly at this feafon, and I could procure no provifion from them, but a few fmall, dried fifh, as I think, of the carp kind. They had feveral European articles; and one of them had a ftrip of fur, which appeared to me to be of the fea otter. He obtained it from the natives of the coaft, and exchanged it with me for fome beads and a brafs crofs.

We retired to reft in as much fecurity as if we had been long habituated to a confidence in our prefent affociates: indeed, we had no alternative; for fo great were the fatigues of the day in our mode of travelling, that we were in great need of reft at night.

We had no fooner laid ourfelves down to reft laft night, than the Friday 5. natives

natives began to fing, in a manner very different from what I had been accuftomed to hear among favages. It was not accompanied either with dancing, drum, or rattle; but confifted of foft, plaintive tones, and a modulation that was rather agreeable: it had fomewhat the air of church mufic. As the natives had requefted me not to quit them at a very early hour in the morning, it was five before I defired that the young men, who were to proceed with us, fhould depart, when they prepared to fet off: but, on calling to our guide to conduct us, he faid, that he did not intend to accompany us any further, as the young men would anfwer our purpofe as well as himfelf. I knew it would be in vain to remonftrate with him, and therefore fubmitted to his caprice without a reply. However, I thought proper to inform him, that one of my people had loft his dag, or poignard, and requefted his affiftance in the recovery of it. He afked me what I would give him to conjure it back again; and a knife was agreed to be the price of his necromantic exertions. Accordingly, all the dags and knives in the place were gathered together, and the natives formed a circle round them; the conjurer alfo remaining in the middle. When this part of the ceremony was arranged, he began to fing, the reft joining in the chorus; and after fome time he produced the poignard which was ftruck in the ground, and returned it to me.

At feven we were ready to depart; when I was furprifed to hear our late guide propofe, without any folicitation on our part, to refume his office; and he actually conducted us as far as a fmall lake, where we found an encampment of three families. The young men who had undertaken to conduct us were not well underftood by my interpreters, who continued to be fo difpleafed with their journey, that they performed this part of their duty

duty with great reluctance. I endeavoured to perfuade an elderly man of this encampment to accompany us to the next tribe, but no inducement of mine could prevail on him to comply with my wifhes. I was, therefore, obliged to content myfelf with the guides I had already engaged, for whom we were obliged to wait fome time, till they had provided fhoes for their journey. I exchanged two halfpence here, one of his prefent Majefty, and the other of the State of Maffachufet's Bay, coined in 1787. They hung as ornaments in children's ears.

My fituation here was rendered rather unpleafant by the treatment which my hunters received from thefe people. The former, it appeared, were confidered as belonging to a tribe who inhabit the mountains, and are the natural enemies of the latter. We had alfo been told by one of the natives, of a very ftern afpect, that he had been ftabbed by a relation of theirs, and pointed to a fcar as the proof of it. I was, therefore, very glad to proceed on my journey.

Our guides conducted us along the lake through thick woods, and without any path, for about a mile and an half, when we loft fight of it. This piece of water is about three miles long and one broad. We then croffed a creek and entered upon a beaten track, through an open country, fprinkled with cyprefs trees. At twelve the fky became black, and an heavy guft with rain fhortly followed, which continued for upwards of an hour. When we perceived the approaching ftorm, we fixed our thin, light oil-cloth to fcreen us from it. On renewing our march, as the bufhes were very wet, I defired our guides, they having no burdens,

dens, to walk in front, and beat them as they went : this tafk they chofe to decline, and accordingly I undertook it.   Our road now lay along a lake, and acrofs a creek that ran into it.   The guides informed me, that this part of the country abounds in beaver : many traps were feen along the road which had been fet for lynxes and martens.   About a quarter of a mile from the place where we had been ftopped by the rain, the ground was covered with hail, and as we advanced, the hailftones in-creafed in fize, fome of them being as big as mufket-balls.   In this man-ner was the ground whitened for upwards of two miles.   At five in the afternoon we arrived on the banks of another lake, when it again threat-ened rain ; and we had already been fufficiently wetted in the courfe of the day, to look with complacency towards a repetition of it : we ac-cordingly fixed our fhed, the rain continuing with great violence through the remainder of the day : it was, therefore, determined, that we fhould ftop here for the night.

In the courfe of the day we paffed three winter huts ; they confifted of low walls, with a ridge-pole, covered with the branches of the Canadian balfam-tree.   One of my men had a violent pain in his knee, and I afked the guides to take a fhare of his burden, as they had nothing to carry but their beaver robes, and bows and arrows, but they could not be made to underftand a word of my requeft.

Saturday 6.   At four this morning I arofe from my bed, fuch as it was.   As we muft have been in a moft unfortunate predicament, if our guides fhould have deferted us in the night, by way of fecurity, I propofed to the youngeft of them to fleep with me, and he readily confented.   Thefe

people

people have no covering but their beaver garments, and that of my companions was a neft of vermin. I, however, fpread it under us, and having laid down upon it, we covered ourfelves with my camblet cloak. My companion's hair being greafed with fifh-oil, and his body fmeared with red earth, my fenfe of fmelling, as well as that of feeling, threatened to interrupt my reft; but thefe inconveniences yielded to my fatigue, and I paffed a night of found repofe.

I took the lead in our march, as I had done yefterday, in order to clear the branches of the wet which continued to hang upon them. We proceeded with all poffible expedition through a level country with but little under-wood; the larger trees were of the fir kind. At half paft eight we fell upon the road, which we firft intended to have taken from the Great River, and muft be fhorter than that which we had travelled. The Weft-road river was alfo in fight, winding through a valley. We had not met with any water fince our encampment of laft night, and though we were afflicted with violent thirft, the river was at fuch a diftance from us, and the defcent to it fo long and fteep, that we were compelled to be fatisfied with cafting our longing looks towards it. There appeared to be more water in the river here, than at its difcharge. The Indian account, that it is navigable for their canoes, is, I believe, perfectly correct.

Our guides now told us, that as the road was very good and well traced, they would proceed to inform the next tribe that we were coming. This information was of a very unpleafant nature; as it would have been eafy for them to turn off the road at an hundred yards from us, and, when

when we had paffed them, to return home. I propofed that óne of them
fhould remain with us, while two of my people fhould leave their loads
behind and accompany the other to the lodges. But they would not ftay
to hear our perfuafions, and were foon out of fight.

I now defired the Cancre to leave his burden, take a fmall quantity of provifion, with his arms and blanket, and follow me. I alfo
told my men to come on as faft as they could, and that I would wait for
them as foon as I had formed an acquaintance with the natives of the
country before us. We accordingly followed our guides with all the
expedition in our power, but did not overtake them till we came to a
family of natives, confifting of one man, two women, and fix children,
with whom we found them. Thefe people betrayed no figns of fear at
our appearance, and the man willingly converfed with my interpreter,
to whom he made himfelf more intelligible, than our guides had been
able to do. They, however, had informed him of the objeĉt of our
journey. He pointed out to us one of his wives, who was a native of the
fea coaft, which was not a very great diftance from us. This woman
was more inclined to corpulency than any we had yet feen, was of low
ftature, with an oblong face, grey eyes, and a flattifh nofe. She was decorated with ornaments of various kinds, fuch as large blue beads, either
pendant from her ears, encircling her neck, or braided in her hair: fhe
alfo wore bracelets of brafs, copper, and horn. Her garments confifted
of a kind of tunic, which was covered with a robe of matted bark,
fringed round the bottom with fkin of the fea otter. None of the women
whom I had feen fince we croffed the mountain wore this kind of tunic;
their blankets being merely girt round the waift. She had learned the

language

language of her hufband's tribe, and confirmed his account, that we were at no great diftance from the fea. They were on their way, fhe faid, to the great river to fifh. Age feemed to be an object of great veneration among thefe people, for they carried an old woman by turns on their backs who was quite blind and infirm from the very advanced period of her life.

Our people having joined us and refted themfelves, I requefted our guides to proceed, when the elder of them told me that he fhould not go any further, but that thefe people would fend a boy to accompany his brother, and I began to think myfelf rather fortunate, that we were not deferted by them all.

About noon we parted, and in two hours we came up with two men and their families: when we firft faw them they were fitting down, as if to reft themfelves; but no fooner did they perceive us than they rofe up and feized their arms. The boys who were behind us immediately ran forwards and fpoke to them, when they laid by their arms and received us as friends. They had been eating green berries and dried fifh. We had, indeed, fcarcely joined them, when a woman and a boy came from the river with water, which they very hofpitably gave us to drink. The people of this party had a very fickly appearance, which might have been the confequence of difeafe, or that indolence which is fo natural to them, or of both. One of the women had a tattooed line along the chin, of the fame length as her mouth.

The lads now informed me that they would go no further, but that
thefe

thefe men would take their places; and they parted from their families with as little apparent concern, as if they were entire ftrangers to each other.   One of them was very well underftood by my interpreter, and had refided among the natives of the fea coaft, whom he had left but a fhort time.   According to his information, we were approaching a river, which was neither large nor long, but whofe banks are inhabited; and that in the bay which the fea forms at the mouth of it, a great wooden canoe, with white people, arrives about the time when the leaves begin to grow: I prefume in the early part of May.

After we parted with the laft people, we came to an uneven, hilly, and fwampy country, through which our way was impeded by a con-fiderable number of fallen trees.   At five in the afternoon we were over-taken by a heavy fhower of rain and hail, and being at the fame time very much fatigued, we encamped for the night near a fmall creek.   Our courfe, till we came to the river, was about South-Weft ten miles, and then Weft, twelve or fourteen miles.   I thought it prudent, by way of fecurity, to fubmit to the fame inconveniences I have already defcribed, and fhared the beaver robe of one of my guides during the night.

Sunday 7.   I was fo bufily employed in collecting intelligence from our conduc-tors, that I laft night forgot to wind up my time-piece, and it was the only inftance of fuch an act of negligence fince I left Fort Chepewyan, on the 11th of laft October.   At five we quitted our ftation, and pro-ceeded acrofs two mountains, covered with fpruce, poplar, white birch, and other trees.   We then defcended into a level country, where we found a good road, through woods of cyprefs.   We then came to two

fmall

fmall lakes, at the diftance of about fourteen miles. Courfe about Weft. Through them the river paffes, and our road kept in a parallel line with it on a range of elevated ground. On obferving fome people before us, our guides haftened to meet them, and, on their approach, one of them ftepped forward with an axe in his hand. This party confifted only of a man, two women, and the fame number of children. The eldeft of the women, who probably was the man's mother, was engaged, when we joined them, in clearing a circular fpot, of about five feet in diameter, of the weeds that infefted it; nor did our arrival interrupt her employment, which was facred to the memory of the dead. The fpot to which her pious care was devoted, contained the grave of an hufband, and a fon, and whenever fhe paffed this way, fhe always ftopped to pay this tribute of affection.

As foon as we had taken our morning allowance, we fet forwards, and about three we perceived more people before us. After fome alarm we came up with them. They confifted of feven men, as many women, and feveral children. Here I was under the neceffity of procuring another guide, and we continued our route on the fame fide of the river, till fix in the evening, when we croffed it. It was knee deep, and about an hundred yards over. I wifhed now to ftop for the night, as we were all of us very much fatigued, but our guide recommended us to proceed onwards to a family of his friends, at a fmall diftance from thence, where we arrived at half paft feven. He had gone forward, and procured us a welcome and quiet reception. There being a net hanging to dry, I requefted the man to prepare and fet it in the water, which he did with great expedition, and then prefented me with a few fmall dried fifh. Our

courfe

courſe was South-Weſt about twelve miles, part of which was an exten-ſive ſwamp, that was ſeldom leſs than knee deep.   In the courſe of the afternoon we had ſeveral ſhowers of rain.   I had attempted to take an altitude, but it was paſt meridian.   The water of the river before the lodge was quite ſtill, and expanded itſelf into the form of a ſmall lake.   In many other places, indeed, it had aſſumed the ſame form.

It rained throughout the night, and it was ſeven in the morning be-fore the weather would allow us to proceed.   The guide brought me five ſmall boiled fiſh, in a platter made of bark; ſome of them were of the carp kind, and the reſt of a ſpecies for which I am not qualified to furniſh a name.   Having dried our clothes, we ſet off on our march about eight, and our guide very cheerfully continued to accompany us; but he was not altogether ſo intelligible as his predeceſſors in our ſervice. We learned from him, however, that this lake, through which the river paſſes, extends to the foot of the mountain, and that he expected to meet nine men, of a tribe which inhabits the North ſide of the river.

In this part of our journey we were ſurpriſed with the appearance of ſeveral regular baſons, ſome of them furniſhed with water, and the others empty; their ſlope from the edge to the bottom formed an angle of about forty-five degrees, and their perpendicular depth was about twelve feet. Thoſe that contained water, diſcovered gravel near their edges, while the empty ones were covered with graſs and herbs, among which we diſcovered muſtard, and mint.   There were alſo ſeveral places from whence the water appears to have retired, which are covered with the ſame ſoil and herbage.

We

We now proceeded along a very uneven country, the upper parts of which were covered with poplars, a little under-wood, and plenty of grafs: the intervening vallies were watered with rivulets. From thefe circumftances, and the general appearance of vegetation, I could not account for the apparent abfence of animals of every kind.

At two in the afternoon we arrived at the largeft river that we had feen, fince we left our canoe, and which forced its way between and over the huge ftones that oppofed its current. Our courfe was about South-South-Weft fixteen miles along the river, which might here juftify the title of a lake. The road was good, and our next courfe, which was Weft by South, brought us onward ten miles, where we encamped, fatigued and wet, it having rained three parts of the day. This river abounds with fifh, and muft fall into the great river, further down than we had extended our voyage.

A heavy and continued rain fell through great part of the night, and as we were in fome meafure expofed to it, time was required to dry our clothes; fo that it was half paft feven in the morning before we were ready to fet out. As we found the country fo deftitute of game, and forefeeing the difficulty of procuring provifions for our return, I thought it prudent to conceal half a bag of pemmican: having fent off the Indians, and all my people except two, we buried it under the fire-place, as we had done on a former occafion. We foon overtook our party, and continued our route along the river or lake. About twelve I had an altitude, but it was inaccurate from the cloudinefs of the weather. We continued our progrefs till five in the afternoon, when the water began to narrow,

and

and in about half an hour we came to a ferry, where we found a fmall raft. At this time it began to thunder, and torrents of rain foon followed, which terminated our journey for the day. Our courfe was about South, twenty-one miles from the lake already mentioned. We now difcovered the tops of mountains, covered with fnow, over very high intermediate land. We killed a whitehead and a grey eagle, and three grey partridges; we faw alfo two otters in the river, and feveral beaver lodges along it. When the rain ceafed, we caught a few fmall fifh, and repaired the raft for the fervice of the enfuing day.

Wednef. 10. At an early hour of this morning we prepared to crofs the water. The traverfe is about thirty yards, and it required five trips to get us all over. At a fhort diftance below, a fmall river falls in, that comes from the direction in which we were proceeding. It is a rapid for about three hundred yards, when it expands into a lake, along which our road conducted us, and beneath a range of beautiful hills, covered with verdure. At half paft eight we came to the termination of the lake, where there were two houfes that occupied a moft delightful fituation, and as they contained their neceffary furniture, it feemed probable that their owners intended fhortly to return. Near them were feveral graves or tombs, to which the natives are particularly attentive, and never fuffer any herbage to grow upon them. In about half an hour we reached a place where there were two temporary huts, that contained thirteen men, with whom we found our guide who had preceded us, in order to fecure a good reception. The buildings were detached from each other, and conveniently placed for fifhing in the lake. Their inhabitants called themfelves Sloua-cufs-Dinais, which denomination, as far as my interpreter,

preter could explain it to me, I underſtood to mean Red-fiſh Men. They were much more cleanly, healthy, and agreeable in their appearance, than any of the natives whom we had paſſed; neverthelefs, I have no doubt that they are the ſame people, from their name alone, which is of the Chepewyan language. My interpreters, however, underſtood very little of what they ſaid, ſo that I did not expect much information from them. Some of them ſaid it was a journey of four days to the ſea, and others were of opinion that it was ſix; and there were among them who extended it to eight; but they all uniformly declared that they had been to the coaſt. They did not entertain the ſmalleſt apprehenſion of danger from us, and, when we diſcharged our pieces, expreſſed no ſenſation but that of aſtoniſhment, which, as may be ſuppoſed, was proportionably encreaſed when one of the hunters ſhot an eagle, at a conſiderable diſtance. At twelve I obtained an altitude, which made our latitude 53. 4. 32. North, being not ſo far South as I expected.

I now went, accompanied by one of my men, an interpreter, and the guide, to viſit ſome huts at the diſtance of a mile. On our arrival the inhabitants preſented us with a diſh of boiled trout, of a ſmall kind. The fiſh would have been excellent if it had not taſted of the kettle, which was made of the bark of the white ſpruce, and of the dried graſs with which it was boiled. Beſides this kind of trout, red and white carp and jub, are the only fiſh I ſaw as the produce of theſe waters.

Theſe people appeared to live in a ſtate of comparative comfort: they take a greater ſhare in the labour of the women, than is common

among

among the favage tribes, and are, as I was informed, content with one wife. Though this circumftance may proceed rather from the difficulty of procuring fubfiftence, than any habitual averfion to polygamy.

My prefent guide now informed me, that he could not proceed any further, and I accordingly engaged two of thefe people to fucceed him in that office; but when they defired us to proceed on the beaten path without them, as they could not fet off till the following day, I determined to ftay that night, in order to accommodate myfelf to their convenience. I diftributed fome trifles among the wives and children of the men who were to be our future guides, and returned to my people. We came back by a different way, and paffed by two buildings, erected between four trees, and about fifteen feet from the ground, which appeared to me to be intended as magazines for winter provifions. At four in the afternoon, we proceeded with confiderable expedition, by the fide of the lake, till fix, when we came to the end of it: we then ftruck off through a much lefs beaten track, and at half paft feven ftopped for the night. Our courfe was about Weft-South-Weft thirteen miles, and Weft fix miles.

Thurfday 11.   I paffed a moft uncomfortable night: the firft part of it I was tormented with flies, and in the latter deluged with rain. In the morning the weather cleared, and as foon as our clothes were dried, we proceeded through a morafs. This part of the country had been laid wafte by fire, and the fallen trees added to the pain and perplexity of our way. An high, rocky ridge ftretched along our left. Though the rain returned, we continued our progrefs till noon, when our guides took to
some

some trees for shelter. We then spread our oil-cloth, and, with some difficulty, made a fire. About two the rain ceased, when we continued our journey through the same kind of country which we had hitherto passed. At half past three we came in sight of a lake; the land, at the same time gradually rising to a range of mountains whose tops were covered with snow. We soon after observed two fresh tracks, which seemed to surprise our guides, but they supposed them to have been made by the inhabitants of the country who were come into this part of it to fish. At five in the afternoon we were so wet and cold, (for it had at intervals continued to rain,) that we were compelled to stop for the night. We passed seven rivulets and a creek in this day's journey. As I had hitherto regulated our course by the sun, I could not form an accurate judgment of this route, as we had not been favoured with a sight of it during the day; but I imagine it to have been nearly in the same direction as that of yesterday. Our distance could not have been less than fifteen miles.

Our conductors now began to complain of our mode of travelling, and mentioned their intention of leaving us; and my interpreters, who were equally dissatisfied, added to our perplexity by their conduct. Besides, these circumstances, and the apprehension that the distance from the sea might be greater than I had imagined, it became a matter of real necessity that we should begin to diminish the consumption of our provisions, and to subsist upon two-thirds of our allowance; a proposition which was as unwelcome to my people, as it was necessary to be put into immediate practice.

At

At half paft five this morning we proceeded on our journey, with cloudy weather, and when we came to the end of the lake feveral tracks were vifible that led to the fide of the water; from which circumftance I concluded, that fome of the natives were fifhing along the banks of it. This lake is not more than three miles long, and about one broad. We then paffed four fmaller lakes, the two firft being on our right, and thofe which preceded on our left. A fmall river alfo flowed acrofs our way from the right, and we paffed it over a beaver-dam. A larger lake now appeared on our right, and the mountains on each fide of us were covered with fnow. We afterwards came to another lake on our right, and foon reached a river, which our guides informed us was the fame that we had paffed on a raft. They faid it was navigable for canoes from the great river, except two rapids, one of which we had feen. At this place it is upwards of twenty yards acrofs, and deep water. One of the guides fwam over to fetch a raft which was on the oppofite fide; and having encreafed its dimenfions, we croffed at two trips, except four of the men, who preferred fwimming.

Here our conductors renewed their menace of leaving us, and I was obliged to give them feveral articles, and promife more, in order to induce them to continue till we could procure other natives to fucceed them. At four in the afternoon we forded the fame river, and being with the guides at fome diftance before the reft of the people, I fat down to wait for them, and no fooner did they arrive, than the former fet off with fo much fpeed, that my attempt to follow them proved unfuccefs-ful. One of my Indians, however, who had no load, overtook them, when they excufed themfelves to him by declaring, that their fole

motive

motive for leaving us, was to prevent the people, whom they expected to find, from fhooting their arrows at us. At feven o'clock, however, we were fo fatigued, that we encamped without them : the mountains covered with fnow now appeared to be directly before us. As we were collecting wood for our fire, we difcovered a crofs road, where it appeared that people had paffed within feven or eight days. In fhort, our fituation was fuch as to afford a juft caufe of alarm, and that of the people with me was of a nature to defy immediate alleviation. It was neceffary, however, for me to attempt it; and I refted my principles of encouragement on a reprefentation of our paft perplexities and unexpected relief, and endeavoured to excite in them the hope of fimilar good fortune. I ftated to them, that we could not be at a great diftance from the fea, and that there were but few natives to pafs, till we fhould arrive among thofe, who being accuftomed to vifit the fea coaft, and, having feen white people, would be difpofed to treat us with kindnefs. Such was the general tenor of the reafoning I employed on the occafion, and I was happy to find that it was not offered in vain.

The weather had been cloudy till three in the afternoon, when the fun appeared; but furrounded, as we were, with fnow-clad mountains, the air became fo cold, that the violence of our exercife, was not fufficient to produce a comfortable degree of warmth. Our courfe to-day was from Weft to South, and at leaft thirty-fix miles. The land in general was very barren and ftony, and lay in ridges, with cyprefs trees fcattered over them. We paffed feveral fwamps, where we faw nothing to confole us but a few tracks of deer.

The

The weather this morning was clear but cold, and our ſcanty cover-ing was not ſufficient to proteƈt us from the ſeverity of the night. About five, after we had warmed ourſelves at a large fire, we pro-ceeded on our dubious journey.   In about àn hour we came to the edge of a wood, when we perceived an houſe, ſituated on a green ſpot, and by the ſide of a ſmall river.   The ſmoke that iſſued from it informed us that it was inhabited.   I immediately puſhed forward toward this man-ſion, while my people were in ſuch a ſtate of alarm, that they followed me with the utmoſt reluƈtance.   On looking back I perceived that we were in an Indian defile, of fifty yards in length.   I, however, was cloſe upon the houſe before the inhabitants perceived us, when the women and children uttered the moſt horrid ſhrieks, and the only man who ap-peared to be with them, eſcaped out of a back door, which I reached in time to prevent the women and children from following him.   The man fled with all his ſpeed into the wood, and I called in vain on my inter-preters to ſpeak to him, but they were ſo agitated with fear as to have loſt the power of utterance.   It is impoſſible to deſcribe the diſtreſs and alarm of theſe poor people, who believing that they were attacked by enemies, expeƈted an immediate maſſacre, which, among themſelves, never fails to follow ſuch an event.

Our priſoners conſiſted of three women, and ſeven children, which apparently compoſed three families.   At length, however, by our de-meanor, and our preſents, we contrived to diſſipate their apprehenſions. One of the women then informed us, that their people, with ſeveral others had left that place three nights before, on a trading journey to a tribe whom ſhe called Annah, which is the name the Chepewyans

give

give to the Knifteneaux, at the diftance of three days. She added alfo, that from the mountains before us, which were covered with fnow, the fea was vifible; and accompanied her information with a prefent of a couple of dried fifh. We now expreffed our defire that the man might be induced to return, and conduct us in the road to the fea. Indeed, it was not long before he difcovered himfelf in the wood, when he was affured, both by the women and our interpreters, that we had no hoftile defign againft him; but thefe affurances had no effect in quieting his apprehenfions. I then attempted to go to him alone, and fhewed him a knife, beads, &c. to induce him to come to me, but he, in return, made an hoftile difplay of his bow and arrows; and, having for a time exhibited a variety of ftrange antics, again difappeared. However, he foon prefented himfelf in another quarter, and after a fucceffion of parleys between us, he engaged to come and accompany us.

While thefe negotiations were proceeding, I propofed to vifit the fifhing machines, to which the women readily confented, and I found in them twenty fmall fifh, fuch as trout, carp, and jub, for which I gave her a large knife; a prefent that appeared to be equally unexpected and gratifying to her. Another man now came towards us, from an hill, talking aloud from the time he appeared till he reached us. The purport of his fpeech was, that he threw himfelf upon our mercy, and we might kill him, if it was our pleafure, but that from what he had heard, he looked rather for our friendfhip than our enmity. He was an elderly perfon, of a decent appearance, and I gave him fome articles to conciliate him to us. The firft man now followed with a lad along with him, both of whom were the fons of the old man, and, on his arrival

rival, he gave me feveral half-dried fifh, which I confidered as a peace-offering. After fome converfation with thefe people, refpecting the country, and our future progrefs through it, we retired to reft, with fenfations very different from thofe with which we had rifen in the morning. The weather had been generally cloudy throughout the day, and when the fun was obfcured, extremely cold for the feafon. At noon I obtained a meridian altitude, which gave 52. 58. 53. North latitude. I likewife took time in the afternoon.

Sunday 14.   This morning we had a bright fun, with an Eaft wind. Thefe people examined their fifhing machines, when they found in them a great number of fmall fifh, and we dreffed as many of them as we could eat. Thus was our departure retarded until feven, when we proceeded on our journey, accompanied by the man and his two fons. As I did not want the younger, and fhould be obliged to feed him, I requefted of his father to leave him, for the purpofe of fifhing for the women. He replied, that they were accuftomed to fifh for themfelves, and that I need not be apprehenfive of their encroaching upon my provifions, as they were ufed to fuftain themfelves in their journies on herbs, and the inner tegument of the bark of trees, for the ftripping of which he had a thin piece of bone, then hanging by his fide. The latter is of a glutinous quality, of a clammy, fweet tafte, and is generally confidered by the more interior Indians as a delicacy, rather than an article of common food. Our guide informed me that there is a fhort cut acrofs the mountains, but as there was no trace of a road, and it would fhorten our journey but one day, he fhould prefer the beaten way.

We

We accordingly proceeded along a lake, Weſt five miles. We then croſſed a ſmall river, and paſſed through a ſwamp, about South-Weſt, when we began gradually to aſcend for ſome time till we gained the ſummit of an hill, where we had an extenſive view to the South-Eaſt, from which direction a conſiderable river appeared to flow, at the diſtance of about three miles: it was repreſented to me as being navigable for canoes. The deſcent of this hill was more ſteep than its aſcent, and was ſucceeded by another, whoſe top, though not ſo elevated as the laſt, afforded a view of the range of mountains, covered with ſnow, which, according to the intelligence of our guide, terminates in the ocean. We now left a ſmall lake on our left, then croſſed a creek running out of it, and at one in the afternoon came to an houſe, of the ſame conſtruction and dimenſions as have already been mentioned, but the materials were much better prepared and finiſhed. The timber was ſquared on two ſides, and the bark taken off the two others; the ridge pole was alſo ſhaped in the ſame manner, extending about eight or ten feet beyond the gable end, and ſupporting a ſhed over the door: the end of it was carved into the ſimilitude of a ſnake's head. Several hieroglyphics and figures of a ſimilar workmanſhip, and painted with red earth, decorated the interior of the building. The inhabitants had left the houſe but a ſhort time, and there were ſeveral bags or bundles in it, which I did not ſuffer to be diſturbed. Near it were two tombs, ſurrounded in a neat manner with boards, and covered with bark. Beſide them ſeveral poles had been erected, one of which was ſquared, and all of them painted. From each of them were ſuſpended ſeveral rolls or parcels of bark, and our guide gave the following account of them; which, as far as we could judge from our imperfect knowledge of the language,

and

and the incidental errors of interpretation, appeared to involve two different modes of treating their dead; or it might be one and the fame
ceremony, which we did not diftinctly comprehend: at all events, it is
the practice of thefe people to burn the bodies of their dead, except the
larger bones, which are rolled up in bark and fufpended from poles, as I
have already defcribed. According to the other account, it appeared
that they actually bury their dead; and when another of the family
dies, the remains of the perfon who was laft interred are taken from the
grave and burned, as has been already mentioned; fo that the members
of a family are thus fucceffively buried and burned, to make room for
each other; and one tomb proves fufficient for a family through fucceeding generations. There is no houfe in this country without a tomb in
its vicinity. Our laft courfe extended about ten miles.

We continued our journey along the lake before the houfe, and, croffing a river that flowed out of it, came to a kind of bank, or weir, formed
by the natives, for the purpofe of placing their fifhing machines, many
of which, of different fizes, were lying on the fide of the river. Our
guide placed one of them, with the certain expectation that on his return
he fhould find plenty of fifh in it. We proceeded nine miles further, on
a good road, Weft-South-Weft, when we came to a fmall lake: we then
croffed a river that ran out of it, and our guides were in continual expectation of meeting with fome of the natives. To this place our courfe
was a mile and an half, in the fame direction as the laft. At nine at
night we croffed a river on rafts, our laft diftance being about four miles
South-Eaft, on a winding road, through a fwampy country, and along a
fucceffion of fmall lakes. We were now quite exhaufted, and it was

abfolutely

absolutely neceffary for us to ftop for the night. The weather being clear throughout the day, we had no reafon to complain of the cold. Our guides encouraged us with the hope that, in two days of fimilar exertion, we fhould arrive among the people of the other nation.

At five this morning we were again in motion, and paffing along a river, we at length forded it. This ftream was not more than knee deep, about thirty yards over, and with a ftony bottom. The old man went onward by himfelf, in the hope of falling in with the people, whom he expected to meet in the courfe of the day. At eleven we came up with him, and the natives whom he expected, confifting of five men, and part of their families. They received us with great kindnefs, and examined us with the moft minute attention. They muft, however, have been told that we were white, as our faces no longer indicated that diftinguifhing complexion. They called themfelves Neguia Dinais, and were come in a different direction from us, but were now going the fame way, to the Anah-yoe Teffe or River, and appeared to be very much fatisfied with our having joined them. They prefented us with fome fifh which they had juft taken in the adjoining lake.

Here I expected that our guides, like their predeceffors, would have quitted us, but, on the contrary, they expreffed themfelves to be fo happy in our company, and that of their friends, that they voluntarily, and with great cheerfulnefs proceeded to pafs another night with us. Our new acquaintance were people of a very pleafing afpect. The hair of the women was tied in large loofe knots over the ears, and plaited with great neatnefs from the divifion of the head, fo as to be included in the knots.

knots. Some of them had adorned their treffes with beads, with a very pretty effect. The men were clothed in leather, their hair was nicely combed, and their complexion was fairer, or perhaps it may be faid, with more propriety, that they were more cleanly, than any of the natives whom we had yet feen. Their eyes, though keen and fharp, are not of that dark colour, fo generally obfervable in the various tribes of Indians; they were, on the contrary, of a grey hue, with a tinge of red. There was one man amongft them of at leaft fix feet four inches in height; his manners were affable, and he had a more prepoffeffing appearance than any Indian I had met with in my journey; he was about twenty-eight years of age, and was treated with particular refpect by his party. Every man, woman, and child, carried a proportionate burden, confifting of beaver coating and parchment, as well as fkins of the otter, the marten, the bear, the lynx, and dreffed moofe-fkins. The laft they procure from the Rocky-Mountain Indians. According to their account, the people of the fea coaft prefer them to any other article. Several of their relations and friends, they faid, were already gone, as well provided as themfelves, to barter with the people of the coaft; who barter them in their turn, except the dreffed leather, with white people who, as they had been informed, arrive there in large canoes.

Such an efcort was the moft fortunate circumftance that could happen in our favour. They told us, that as the women and children could not travel faft, we fhould be three days in getting to the end of our journey; which muft be fuppofed to have been very agreeable information to people in our exhaufted condition.

In

In about half an hour after we had joined our new acquaintance, the signal for moving onwards was given by the leader of the party, who vociferated the words, Huy, Huy, when his people joined him and continued a clamorous converfation. We paffed along a winding road over hills, and through fwampy vallies, from South to Weft. We then croffed a deep, narrow river, which difcharges itfelf into a lake, on whofe fide we ftopped at five in the afternoon, for the night, though we had repofed feveral times fince twelve at noon; fo that our mode of travelling had undergone a very agreeable change. I compute the diftance of this day's journey at about twenty miles. In the middle of the day the weather was clear and fultry.

We all fat down on a very pleafant green fpot, and were no fooner feated, than our guide and one of the party prepared to engage in play. They had each a bundle of about fifty fmall fticks, neatly polifhed, of the fize of a quill, and five inches long: a certain number of thefe fticks had red lines round them; and as many of thefe as one of the players might find convenient were curioufly rolled up in dry grafs, and according to the judgment of his antagonift refpecting their number and, marks, he loft or won. Our friend was apparently the lofer, as he parted with his bow and arrows, and feveral articles which I had given him.

The weather of this morning was the fame as yefterday; but our fellow-travellers were in no hurry to proceed, and I was under the neceffity of preffing them into greater expedition, by reprefenting the almoft exhaufted ftate of our provifions. They, however, affured us, that after the next night's fleep we fhould arrive at the river where they were going,

going, and that we fhould there get fifh in great abundance. My young men, from an act of imprudence, deprived themfelves laft night of that reft which was fo neceffary to them. One of the ftrangers afking them feveral queftions refpecting us, and concerning their own country, one of them gave fuch anfwers as were not credited by the audience; whereupon he demanded, in a very angry tone, if they thought he was difpofed to tell lies, like the Rocky-Mountain Indians; and one of that tribe happening to be of the party, a quarrel enfued, which might have been attended with the moft ferious confequences, if it had not been fortunately prevented by the interference of thofe who were not interefted in the difpute.

Though our ftock of provifions was getting fo low, I determined neverthelefs, to hide about twenty pounds of pemmican, by way of providing againft our return. I therefore left two of the men behind, with directions to bury it, as ufual, under the place where we had made our fire.

Our courfe was about Weft-South-Weft by the fide of the lake, and in about two miles we came to the end of it. Here was a general halt, when my men overtook us. I was now informed, that fome people of another tribe were fent for, who wifhed very much to fee us, two of whom would accompany us over the mountains; that, as for themfelves, they had changed their mind, and intended to follow a fmall river which iffued out of the lake, and went in a direction very different from the line of our journey. This was a difappointment, which, though not uncommon to us, might have been followed by confiderable inconveniences.

It

It was my wifh to continue with them whatever way they went; but neither my promifes or entreaties would avail: thefe people were not to be turned from their purpofe; and when I reprefented the low ftate of our provifions, one of them anfwered, that if we would ftay with them all night, he would boil a kettle of fifh-roes for us. Accordingly, without receiving any anfwer, he began to make preparation to fulfil his engagement. He took the roes out of a bag, and having bruifed them between two ftones, put them in water to foak. His wife then took an handful of dry grafs in her hand, with which fhe fqueezed them through her fingers; in the mean time her hufband was employed in gathering wood to make a fire, for the purpofe of heating ftones. When fhe had finifhed her operation, fhe filled a watape kettle nearly full of water, and poured the roes into it. When the ftones were fufficiently heated, fome of them were put into the kettle, and others were thrown in from time to time, till the water was in a ftate of boiling; the woman alfo continued ftirring the contents of the kettle, till they were brought to a thick confiftency; the ftones were then taken out, and the whole was feafoned with about a pint of ftrong rancid oil. The fmell of this curious difh was fufficient to ficken me without tafting it, but the hunger of my people furmounted the naufeous meal. When unadulterated by the ftinking oil, thefe boiled roes are not unpalatable food.

In the mean time four of the people who had been expected, arrived, and, according to the account given of them, were of two tribes whom I had not yet known. After fome converfation, they propofed, that I fhould continue my route by their houfes; but the old guide, who was now preparing to leave us, informed me that it would lengthen my journey;

and

and by his advice I propofed to them to conduct us along the road which had been already marked out to us. This they undertook without the leaft hefitation; and, at the fame time, pointed out to me the pafs in the mountain, bearing South by Eaft by compafs. Here I had a meridian altitude, and took time.

At four in the afternoon we parted with our late fellow-travellers in a very friendly manner, and immediately forded the river. The wild parfnep, which luxuriates on the borders of the lakes and rivers, is a favourite food of the natives: they roaft the tops of this plant, in their tender ftate, over the fire, and taking off the outer rind, they are then a very palatable food.

We now entered the woods, and fome time after arrived on the banks of another river that flowed from the mountain, which we alfo forded. The country foon after we left the river was fwampy; and the fire having paffed through it, the number of trees, which had fallen, added to the toil of our journey. In a fhort time we began to afcend, and continued afcending till nine at night. We walked upwards of fourteen miles, according to my computation, in the courfe of the day, though the ftraight line of diftance might not be more than ten. Notwithstanding that we were furrounded by mountains covered with fnow, we were very much tormented with mufquitoes.

Wednef. 17.   Before the fun rofe, our guides fummoned us to proceed, when we defcended into a beautiful valley, watered by a fmall river. At eight we came to the termination of it, where we faw a great number of moles,

and

and began again to afcend. We now perceived many ground-hogs, and heard them whiftle in every direction. The Indians went in purfuit of them, and foon joined us with a female and her litter, almoft grown to their full fize. They ftripped off their fkins, and gave the carcafes to my people. They alfo pulled up a root, which appeared like a bunch of white berries of the fize of a pea; its fhape was that of a fig, while it had the colour and tafte of a potatoe.

We now gained the fummit of the mountain, and found ourfelves furrounded by fnow. But this circumftance is caufed rather by the quantity of fnow drifted in the pafs, than the real height of the fpot, as the furrounding mountains rife to a much higher degree of elevation. The fnow had become fo compact that our feet hardly made a perceptible impreffion on it. We obferved, however, the tracks of an herd of fmall deer which muft have paffed a fhort time before us, and the Indians and my hunters went immediately in purfuit of them. Our way was now nearly level, without the leaft fnow, and not a tree to be feen in any part of it. The grafs is very fhort, and the foil a reddifh clay, intermixed with fmall ftones. The face of the hills, where they are not enlivened with verdure, appears, at a diftance, as if fire had paffed over them. It now began to hail, fnow, and rain, nor could we find any fhelter but the leeward fide of an huge rock. The wind alfo rofe into a tempeft, and the weather was as diftreffing as any I had ever experienced. After an abfence of an hour and an half, our hunters brought a fmall doe of the rein-deer fpecies, which was all they had killed, though they fired twelve fhots at a large herd of them. Their ill

fuccefs

succefs they attributed to the weather. I propofed to leave half of the venifon in the fnow, but the men preferred carrying it, though their ftrength was very much exhaufted. We had been fo long fhivering with cold in this fituation that we were glad to renew our march. Here and there were fcattered a few crowberry bufhes and ftinted willows; the former of which had not yet bloffomed.

Before us appeared a ftupendous mountain, whofe fnow-clad fummit was loft in the clouds; between it and our immediate courfe, flowed the river to which we were going. The Indians informed us that it was at no great diftance. As foon as we could gather a fufficient quantity of wood, we ftopped to drefs fome of our venifon; and it is almoft fuperfluous to add, that we made an heartier meal than we had done for many a day before. To the comfort which I have juft mentioned, I added that of taking off my beard, as well as changing my linen, and my people followed the humanifing example. We then fet forwards, and came to a large pond, on whofe bank we found a tomb, but lately made, with a pole, as ufual, erefted befide it, on which two figures of birds were painted, and by them the guides diftinguifhed the tribe to which the deceafed perfon belonged. One of them, very unceremonioufly, opened the bark and fhewed us the bones which it contained, while the other threw down the pole, and having poffeffed himfelf of the feathers that were tied to it, fixed them on his own head. I therefore conjeftured, that thefe funeral memorials belonged to an individual of a tribe at enmity with them.

We continued our route with a confiderable degree of expedition, and as we proceeded the mountains appeared to withdraw from us. The country

country between them foon opened to our view, which apparently added to their awful elevation. We continued to defcend till we came to the brink of a precipice, from whence our guides difcovered the river to us, and a village on its banks. This precipice, or rather fucceffion of precipices, is covered with large timber, which confifts of the pine, the fpruce, the hemlock, the birch, and other trees. Our conductors informed us, that it abounded in animals, which, from their defcription, muft be wild goats. In about two hours we arrived at the bottom, where there is a conflux of two rivers, that iffue from the mountains. We croffed the one which was to the left. They are both very rapid, and continue fo till they unite their currents, forming a ftream of about twelve yards in breadth. Here the timber was alfo very large; but I could not learn from our conductors why the moft confiderable hemlock trees were ftripped of their bark to the tops of them. I concluded, indeed, at that time that the inhabitants tanned their leather with it. Here were alfo the largeft and loftieft elder and cedar trees that I had ever feen. We were now fenfible of an entire change in the climate, and the berries were quite ripe.

The fun was about to fet, when our conductors left us to follow them as well as we could. We were prevented, however, from going far aftray, for we were hemmed in on both fides and behind by fuch a barrier as nature never before prefented to my view. Our guides had the precaution to mark the road for us, by breaking the branches of trees as they paffed. This fmall river muft, at certain feafons, rife to an uncommon height and ftrength of current moft probably on the melting of the fnow; as we faw a large quantity of drift wood lying twelve feet above

the

the immediate level of the river. This circumftance impeded our progrefs, and the protruding rocks frequently forced us to pafs through the
water. It was now dark, without the leaft appearance of houfes, though
it would be impoffible to have feen them, if there had been any, at the
diftance of twenty yards, from the thicknefs of the woods. My men
were anxious to ftop for the night; indeed the fatigue they had fuffered
juftified the propofal, and I left them to their choice; but as the anxiety
of my mind impelled me forwards, they continued to follow me, till I
found myfelf at the edge of the woods; and, notwithftanding the remonftrances that were made, I proceeded, feeling rather than feeing my way,
till I arrived at an houfe, and foon difcovered feveral fires, in fmall huts,
with people bufily employed in cooking their fifh. I walked into one
of them without the leaft ceremony, threw down my burden, and, after
fhaking hands with fome of the people, fat down upon it. They received me without the leaft appearance of furprize, but foon made figns
for me to go up to the large houfe, which was erected, on upright pofts, at
fome diftance from the ground. A broad piece of timber with fteps cut in
it, led to the fcaffolding even with the floor, and by this curious kind of
ladder I entered the houfe at one end; and having paffed three fires, at
equal diftances in the middle of the building, I was received by feveral people, fitting upon a very wide board, at the upper end of it. I fhook hands
with them, and feated myfelf befide a man, the dignity of whofe countenance induced me to give him that preference. I foon difcovered one of my
guides feated a little above me, with a neat mat fpread before him, which
I fuppofed to be the place of honour, and appropriated to ftrangers. In
a fhort time my people arrived, and placed themfelves near me, when
the man by whom I fat, immediately rofe, and fetched, from behind a

plank

plank of about four feet wide, a quantity of roasted salmon. He then directed a mat to be placed before me and Mr. Mackay, who was now sitting by me. When this ceremony was performed, he brought a salmon for each of us, and half an one to each of my men. The same plank served also as a screen for the beds, whither the women and children were already retired; but whether that circumstance took place on our arrival, or was the natural consequence of the late hour of the night, I did not discover. The signs of our protector seemed to denote, that we might sleep in the house, but as we did not understand him with a sufficient degree of certainty, I thought it prudent, from the fear of giving offence, to order the men to make a fire without, that we might sleep by it. When he observed our design, he placed boards for us that we might not take our repose on the bare ground, and ordered a fire to be prepared for us. We had not been long seated round it, when we received a large dish of salmon roes, pounded fine and beat up with water so as to have the appearance of a cream. Nor was it without some kind of seasoning that gave it a bitter taste. Another dish soon followed, the principal article of which was also salmon-roes, with a large proportion of gooseberries, and an herb that appeared to be sorrel. Its acidity rendered it more agreeable to my taste than the former preparation. Having been regaled with these delicacies, for such they were considered by that hospitable spirit which provided them, we laid ourselves down to rest with no other canopy than the sky; but I never enjoyed a more sound and refreshing rest, though I had a board for my bed, and a billet for my pillow.

At five this morning I awoke, and found that the natives had lighted
a fire

a fire for us, and were fitting by it. My hofpitable friend immediately brought me fome berries and roafted falmon, and his companions foon followed his example. The former, which confifted among many others, of goofeberries, whirtleberries and rafpberries, were the fineft I ever faw or tafted, of their refpective kinds. They alfo brought the dried roes of fifh to eat with the berries.

Salmon is fo abundant in this river, that thefe people have a conftant and plentiful fupply of that excellent fifh. To take them with more facility, they had, with great labour, formed an embankment or weir acrofs the river for the purpofe of placing their fifhing machines, which they difpofed both above and below it. I expreffed my wifh to vifit this extraordinary work, but thefe people are fo fuperftitious, that they would not allow me a nearer examination than I could obtain by viewing it from the bank. The river is about fifty yards in breadth, and by obferving a man fifh with a dipping net, I judged it to be about ten feet deep at the foot of the fall. The weir is a work of great labour, and contrived with confiderable ingenuity. It was near four feet above the level of the water, at the time I faw it, and nearly the height of the bank on which I ftood to examine it. The ftream is ftopped nearly two thirds by it. It is conftructed by fixing fmall trees in the bed of the river in a flanting pofition (which could be practicable only when the water is much lower than I faw it) with the thick part downwards; over thefe is laid a bed of gravel, on which is placed a range of leffer trees, and fo on alternately till the work is brought to its proper height. Beneath it the machines are placed, into which the falmon fall when they attempt to leap over. On either fide there is a large

frame

frame of timber-work fix feet above the level of the upper water, in which paffages are left for the falmon leading directly into the machines, which are taken up at pleafure. At the foot of the fall dipping nets are alfo fuccefsfully employed.

The water of this river is of the colour of affes milk, which I attributed in part to the limeftone that in many places forms the bed of the river, but principally to the rivulets which fall from mountains of the fame material.

Thefe people indulge an extreme fuperftition refpecting their fifh, as it is apparently their only animal food. Flefh they never tafte, and one of their dogs having picked and fwallowed part of a bone which we had left, was beaten by his mafter till he difgorged it. One of my people alfo having thrown a bone of the deer into the river, a native, who had obferved the circumftance, immediately dived and brought it up, and, having configned it to the fire, inftantly proceeded to wafh his polluted hands.

As we were ftill at fome diftance from the fea, I made application to my friend to procure us a canoe or two, with people to conduct us thither. After he had made various excufes, I at length comprehended that his only objection was to the embarking venifon in a canoe on their river, as the fifh would inftantly fmell it and abandon them, fo that he, his friends, and relations, muft ftarve. I foon eafed his apprehenfions on that point, and defired to know what I muft do with the venifon that remained, when he told me to give it to one of the ftrangers whom he

pointed

pointed out to me, as being of a tribe that eat flesh. I now requested him to furnish me with some fresh salmon in its raw state ; but, instead of complying with my wish, he brought me a couple of them roasted, observing at the same time, that the current was very strong, and would bring us to the next village, where our wants would be abundantly supplied. In short, he requested that we would make haste to depart. This was rather unexpected after so much kindness and hospitality, but our ignorance of the language prevented us from being able to discover the cause.

At eight this morning, fifteen men armed, the friends and relations of these people, arrived by land, in consequence of notice sent them in the night, immediately after the appearance of our guides. They are more corpulent and of a better appearance than the inhabitants of the interior. Their language totally different from any I had heard; the Atnah and Chin tribe, as far as I can judge from the very little I saw of that people, bear the nearest resemblance to them. They appear to be of a quiet and peaceable character, and never make any hostile incursions into the lands of their neighbours.

Their dress consists of a single robe tied over the shoulders, falling down behind, to the heels, and before, a little below the knees, with a deep fringe round the bottom. It is generally made of the bark of the cedar tree, which they prepare as fine as hemp ; though some of these garments are interwoven with strips of the sea-otter skin, which give them the appearance of a fur on one side. Others have stripes of red and yellow threads fancifully introduced toward the borders, which have a very agreeable effect,

effect. The men have no other covering than that which I have defcribed, and they unceremonioufly lay it afide when they find it convenient. In addition to this robe, the women wear a clofe fringe hanging down before them about two feet in length, and half as wide. When they fit down they draw this between their thighs. They wear their hair fo fhort, that it requires little care or combing. The men have theirs in plaits, and being fmeared with oil and red earth, inftead of a comb they have a fmall ftick hanging by a ftring from one of the locks, which they employ to alleviate any itching or irritation in the head. The colour of the eye is grey with a tinge of red. They have all high cheek-bones, but the women are more remarkable for that feature than the men. Their houfes, arms, and utenfils I fhall defcribe hereafter.

I prefented my friend with feveral articles, and alfo diftributed fome among others of the natives who had been attentive to us. One of my guides had been very ferviceable in procuring canoes for us to proceed on our expedition; he appeared alfo to be very defirous of giving thefe people a favourable impreffion of us; and I was very much concerned that he fhould leave me as he did, without giving me the leaft notice of his departure, or receiving the prefents which I had prepared for him, and he fo well deferved. At noon I had an obfervation which gave 52. 28. 11. North longitude.

CHAP.

CHAPTER X.

Continue our journey.   Embark on a river.   Come to a weir.   Dexterity of the natives in paſſing it.   Arrive at a village.   Alarm occaſioned among the natives.   The ſubſequent favourable reception, accompanied with a banquet of ceremony.   Circumſtances of it.   Deſcription of a village, its houſes, and places of devotion.   Account of the cuſtoms, mode of living, and ſuperſtition of the inhabitants.   Deſcription of the chief's canoe.   Leave the place, and proceed on our voyage.

1793.
July.

AT one in the afternoon we embarked, with our ſmall baggage, in two canoes, accompanied by ſeven of the natives.   The ſtream was rapid, and ran upwards of ſix miles an hour.   We came to a weir, ſuch as I have already deſcribed, where the natives landed us, and ſhot over it without taking a drop of water.   They then received us on board again, and we continued our voyage, paſſing many canoes on the river, ſome with people in them, and others empty.   We proceeded at a very great rate for about two hours and an half, when we were informed that we muſt land, as the village was only at a ſhort diſtance.   I had imagined that the Canadians who accompanied me were the moſt expert canoe-men in the world, but they are very inferior to theſe people, as they themſelves acknowledged, in conducting thoſe veſſels.

Some

Some of the Indians ran before us, to announce our approach, when we took our bundles and followed. We had walked along a well-beaten path, through a kind of coppice, when we were informed of the arrival of our couriers at the houfes, by the loud and confufed talking of the inhabitants. As we approached the edge of the wood, and were almoft in fight of the houfes, the Indians who were before me made figns for me to take the lead, and that they would follow. The noife and con-fufion of the natives now feemed to encreafe, and when we came in fight of the village, we faw them running from houfe to houfe, fome armed with bows and arrows, others with fpears, and many with axes, as if in a ftate of great alarm. This very unpleafant and unexpected cir-cumftance, I attributed to our fudden arrival, and the very fhort notice of it which had been given them. At all events, I had but one line of conduct to purfue, which was to walk refolutely up to them, without manifefting any figns of apprehenfion at their hoftile appearance. This refolution produced the defired effect, for as we approached the houfes, the greater part of the people laid down their weapons, and came forward to meet us. I was, however, foon obliged to ftop from the number of them that furrounded me. I fhook hands, as ufual with fuch as were the neareft to me, when an elderly man broke through the crowd, and took me in his arms; another then came, who turned him away without the leaft ceremony, and paid me the fame compliment. The latter was followed by a young man, whom I underftood to be his fon. Thefe embraces, which at firft rather furprifed me, I foon found to be marks of regard and friendfhip. The crowd preffed with fo much violence and contention to get a view of us, that we could not move in any direction. An opening was at length made to allow a perfon to

approach

approach me, whom the old man made me underftand was another of his fons. I inftantly ftepped forward to meet him, and prefented my hand, whereupon he broke the ftring of a very handfome robe of fea-otter fkin, which he had on, and covered me with it. This was as flattering a reception as I could poffibly receive, efpecially as I confidered him to be the eldeft fon of the chief. Indeed it appeared to me that we had been detained here for the purpofe of giving him time to bring the robe with which he had prefented me.

The chief now made figns for us to follow him, and he conducted us through a narrow coppice, for feveral hundred yards, till we came to an houfe built on the ground, which was of larger dimenfions, and formed of better materials than any I had hitherto feen; it was his refidence. We were no fooner arrived there, than he directed mats to be fpread before it, on which we were told to take our feats, when the men of the village, who came to indulge their curiofity, were ordered to keep behind us. In our front other mats were placed, where the chief and his counfellors took their feats. In the intervening fpace, mats, which were very clean, and of a much neater workmanfhip than thofe on which we fat were alfo fpread, and a fmall roafted falmon placed before each of us. When we had fatisfied ourfelves with the fifh, one of the people who came with us from the laft village approached, with a kind of ladle in one hand, containing oil, and in the other fomething that refembled the inner rind of the cocoa-nut, but of a lighter colour; this he dipped in the oil, and, having eat it, indicated by his geftures how palatable he thought it. He then prefented me with a fmall piece of it, which I chofe to tafte in its dry ftate, though the oil was free from any unpleafant fmell. A fquare cake

of

of this was next produced, when a man took it to the water near the houſe, and having thoroughly ſoaked it, he returned, and, after he had pulled it to pieces like oakum, put it into a well-made trough, about three feet long, nine inches wide, and five deep; he then plentifully ſprinkled it with ſalmon oil, and manifeſted by his own example that we were to eat of it. I juſt taſted it, and found the oil perfectly ſweet, without which the other ingredient would have been very inſipid. The chief partook of it with great avidity, after it had received an additional quantity of oil. This diſh is conſidered by theſe people as a great delicacy; and on examination, I diſcovered it to conſiſt of the inner rind of the hemlock tree, taken off early in ſummer, and put into a frame, which ſhapes it into cakes of fifteen inches long, ten broad, and half an inch thick; and in this form I ſhould ſuppoſe it may be preſerved for a great length of time. This diſcovery ſatisfied me reſpecting the many hemlock trees which I had obſerved ſtripped of their bark.

In this ſituation we remained for upwards of three hours, and not one of the curious natives left us during all that time, except a party of ten or twelve of them, whom the chief ordered to go and catch fiſh, which they did in great abundance, with dipping nets, at the foot of the Weir.

At length we were relieved from the gazing crowd, and got a lodge erected, and covered in for our reception during the night. I now preſented the young chief with a blanket, in return for the robe with which he had favoured me, and ſeveral other articles, that appeared to be very gratifying to him. I alſo preſented ſome to his father, and amongſt them

was

was a pair of fciffars, whofe ufe I explained to him, for clipping his beard, which was of great length; and to that purpofe he immediately applied them. My diftribution of fimilar articles was alfo extended to others, who had been attentive to us. The communication, however, between us was awkward and inconvenient, for it was carried on entirely by figns, as there was not a perfon with me who was qualified for the office of an interpreter.

We were all of us very defirous to get fome frefh falmon, that we might drefs them in our own way, but could not by any means obtain that gratification, though there were thoufands of that fifh ftrung on cords, which were faftened to ftakes in the river. They were even averfe to our approaching the fpot where they clean and prepare them for their own eating. They had, indeed, taken our kettle from us, left we fhould employ it in getting water from the river; and they affigned as the reafon for this precaution, that the falmon diflike the fmell of iron. At the fame time they fupplied us with wooden boxes, which were capable of holding any fluid. Two of the men that went to fifh, in a canoe capable of containing ten people, returned with a full lading of falmon, that weighed from fix to forty pounds, though the far greater part of them were under twenty. They immediately ftrung the whole of them, as I have already mentioned, in the river.

I now made the tour of the village, which confifted of four elevated houfes, and feven built on the ground, befides a confiderable number of other buildings or fheds, which are ufed only as kitchens, and places for curing their fifh. The former are conftructed by fixing a certain

number

number of pofts in the earth, on fome of which are laid, and to others are faftened, the fupporters of the floor, at about twelve feet above the furface of the ground: their length is from an hundred to an hundred and twenty feet, and they are about forty feet in breadth. Along the centre are built three, four, or five hearths, for the two-fold purpofe of giving warmth, and dreffing their fifh. The whole length of the building on either fide is divided by cedar planks, into partitions or apartments of feven feet fquare, in the front of which there are boards, about three feet wide, over which, though they are not immovably fixed, the inmates of thefe receffes generally pafs, when they go to reft. The greater part of them are intended for that purpofe, and fuch are covered with boards, at the height of the wall of the houfe, which is about feven or eight feet, and reft upon beams that ftretch acrofs the building. On thofe alfo are placed the chefts which contain their provifions, utenfils, and whatever they poffefs. The intermediate fpace is fufficient for domeftic pur-pofes. On poles that run along the beams, hang roafted fifh, and the whole building is well covered with boards and bark, except within a few inches of the ridge pole; where open fpaces are left on each fide to let in light and emit the fmoke. At the end of the houfe that fronts the river, is a narrow fcaffolding, which is alfo afcended by a piece of timber, with fteps cut in it; and at each corner of this erection there are openings, for the inhabitants to eafe nature. As it does not appear to be a cuftom among them to remove thefe heaps of excremental filth, it may be fuppofed that the effluvia does not annoy them.

The houfes which reft on the ground are built of the fame materials, and on the fame plan. A floping ftage that rifes to a crofs piece of timber,

fupported

fupported by two forks, joins alfo to the main building, for thofe purpofes which need not be repeated.

When we were furrounded by the natives on our arrival, I counted
fixty-five men, and feveral of them may be fuppofed to have been abfent;
I cannot, therefore, calculate the inhabitants of this village at lefs than
two hundred fouls.

The people who accompanied us hither, from the other village,
had given the chief a very particular account of every thing they knew
concerning us: I was, therefore, requefted to produce my aftronomical
inftruments; nor could I have any objection to afford them this fatisfaction, as they would neceffarily add to our importance in their
opinion.

Near the houfe of the chief I obferved feveral oblong fquares, of
about twenty feet by eight. They were made of thick cedar boards,
which were joined with fo much neatnefs, that I at firft thought they
were one piece. They were painted with hieroglyphics, and figures
of different animals, and with a degree of correctnefs that was not to
be expected from fuch an uncultivated people. I could not learn
the ufe of them, but they appeared to be calculated for occafional
acts of devotion or facrifice, which all thefe tribes perform at leaft
twice in the year, at the fpring and fall. I was confirmed in this opinion
by a large building in the middle of the village, which I at firft took for
the half finifhed frame of an houfe. The ground-plot of it was fifty
feet by forty-five; each end is formed by four ftout pofts, fixed perpen-
dicularly

dicularly in the ground. The corner ones are plain, and fupport a beam of the whole length, having three intermediate props on each fide, but of a larger fize, and eight or nine feet in height. The two centre pofts, at each end, are two feet and an half in diameter, and carved into human figures, fupporting two ridge poles on their heads, at twelve feet from the ground. The figures at the upper part of this fquare reprefent two perfons, with their hands upon their knees, as if they fupported the weight with pain and difficulty: the others oppofite to them ftand at their eafe, with their hands refting on their hips. In the area of the building there were the remains of feveral fires. The pofts, poles, and figures, were pain ed red and black; but the fculpture of thefe people is fuperior to their painting.

Soon after I had retired to reft laft night, the chief paid me a vifit to infift on my going to his bed-companion, and taking my place himfelf; but, notwithftanding his repeated entreaties, I refifted this offering of his hofpitality.

At an early hour this morning I was again vifited by the chief, in company with his fon. The former complained of a pain in his breaft; to relieve his fuffering, I gave him a few drops of Turlington's Balfam on a piece of fugar; and I was rather furprifed to fee him take it without the leaft hefitation. When he had taken my medicine, he requefted me to follow him, and conducted me to a fhed, where feveral people were affembled round a fick man, who was another of his fons. They immediately uncovered him, and fhewed me a violent ulcer in the fmall of his back, in the fouleft ftate that can be imagined. One of his knees was alfo

afflicted

afflicted in the fame manner. This unhappy man was reduced to a skeleton, and, from his appearance, was drawing near to an end of his pains. They requested that I would touch him, and his father was very urgent with me to administer medicine; but he was in such a dangerous state, that I thought it prudent to yield no further to the importunities than to give the sick person a few drops of Turlington's balsam in some water. I therefore left them, but was soon called back by the loud lamentations of the women, and was rather apprehensive that some inconvenience might result from my compliance with the chief's request. On my return I found the native physicians busy in practising their skill and art on the patient. They blew on him, and then whistled; at times they pressed their extended fingers, with all their strength on his stomach; they also put their fore fingers doubled into his mouth, and spouted water from their own with great violence into his face. To support these operations the wretched sufferer was held up in a fitting posture; and when they were concluded, he was laid down and covered with a new robe made of the skin of a lynx. I had observed that his belly and breast were covered with scars, and I understood that they were caused by a custom prevalent among them, of applying pieces of lighted touch wood to their flesh, in order to relieve pain or demonstrate their courage. He was now placed on a broad plank, and carried by six men into the woods, where I was invited to accompany them. I could not conjecture what would be the end of this ceremony, particularly as I saw one man carry fire, another an axe, and a third dry wood. I was, indeed, disposed to suspect that, as it was their custom to burn the dead, they intended to relieve the poor man from his pain, and perform the last sad duty of surviving affection. When they had advanced a short

distance

diſtance into the wood, they laid him upon a clear ſpot, and kindled a fire againſt his back, when the phyſician began to ſcarify the ulcer with a very blunt inſtrument, the cruel pain of which operation the patient bore with incredible reſolution. The ſcene afflicted me and I left it.

On my return to our lodge, I obſerved before the door of the chief's reſidence, four heaps of ſalmon, each of which conſiſted of between three and four hundred fiſh. Sixteen women were employed in cleaning and preparing them. They firſt ſeparate the head from the body, the former of which they boil; they then cut the latter down the back on each ſide of the bone, leaving one third of the fiſh adhering to it, and afterwards take out the guts. The bone is roaſted for immediate uſe, and the other parts are dreſſed in the ſame manner, but with more attention, for future proviſion. While they are before the fire, troughs are placed under them to receive the oil. The roes are alſo carefully preſerved, and form a favourite article of their food.

After I had obſerved theſe culinary preparations, I paid a viſit to the chief, who preſented me with a roaſted ſalmon; he then opened one of his cheſts, and took out of it a garment of blue cloth, decorated with braſs buttons; and another of a flowered cotton, which I ſuppoſed were Spaniſh; it had been trimmed with leather fringe, after the faſhion of their own cloaks. Copper and braſs are in great eſtimation among them, and of the former they have great plenty: they point their arrows and ſpears with it, and work it up into perſonal ornaments; ſuch as collars, ear-rings, and bracelets, which they wear on their wriſts, arms, and legs. I preſume they find it the moſt advantageous article of trade with

the

the more inland tribes. They alfo abound in iron I faw fome of their twifted collars of that metal which weighed upwards of twelve pounds. It is generally beat into bars of fourteen inches in length, and one inch three quarters wide. The brafs is in thin fquares: their copper is in larger pieces, and fome of it appeared to be old ftills cut up. They have various trinkets; but their iron is manufactured only into poniards and daggers. Some of the former have very neat handles, with a filver coin of a quarter or eighth of a dollar fixed on the end of them. The blades of the latter are from ten to twelve inches in length, and about four inches broad at the top, from which they gradually leffen into a point.

When I produced my inftruments to take an altitude, I was defired not to make ufe of them. I could not then difcover the caufe of this requeft, but I experienced the good effect of the apprehenfion which they occafioned, as it was very effectual in haftening my departure. I had applied feveral times to the chief to prepare canoes and people to take me and my party to the fea, but very little attention had been paid to my application till noon; when I was informed that a canoe was properly equipped for my voyage, and that the young chief would accompany me. I now difcovered that they had entertained no perfonal fear of the inftruments, but were apprehenfive that the operation of them might frighten the falmon from that part of the river. The obfervation taken in this village gave me 52. 25. 52 North latitude.

In compliance with the chief's requeft I defired my people to take their bundles, and lay them down on the bank of the river. In the mean
time

time I went to take the dimenfions of his large canoe, in which, it was fignified to me, that about ten winters ago he went a confiderable diftance towards the mid-day fun, with forty of his people, when he faw two large veffels full of fuch men as myfelf, by whom he was kindly received: they were, he faid, the firft white people he had feen. They were probably the fhips commanded by Captain Cook. This canoe was built of cedar, forty-five feet long, four feet wide, and three feet and a half in depth. It was painted black and decorated with white figures of fifh of different kinds. The gunwale, fore and aft, was inlaid with the teeth of the fea-otter.*

When I returned to the river, the natives who were to accompany us, and my people, were already in the canoe. The latter, however, informed me, that one of our axes was miffing. I immediately applied to the chief, and requefted its reftoration; but he would not underftand me till I fat myfelf down on a ftone, with my arms in a ftate of preparation, and made it appear to him that I fhould not depart till the ftolen article was reftored. The village was immediately in a ftate of uproar, and fome danger was apprehended from the confufion that prevailed in it. The axe, however, which had been hidden under the chief's canoe, was foon returned. Though this inftrnment was not, in itfelf, of fufficient value to juftify a difpute with thefe people, I apprehended that the fuffering them to keep it, after we had declared its lofs,

---

* As Captain Cooke has mentioned, that the people of the fea-coaft adorned their canoes with human teeth, I was more particular in my inquiries; the refult of which was, the moft fatisfactory proof, that he was miftaken: but his miftake arofe from the very great refemblance there is between human teeth and thofe of the fea-otter.

might

might have occafioned the lofs of every thing we carried with us, and of our lives alfo. My people were diffatisfied with me at the moment; but I thought myfelf right then, and, I think now, that the circumftances in which we were involved, juftified the meafure which I adopted.

CHAP.

CHAPTER XI.

Renew our voyage. Circumstances of the river. Land at the house of a chief. Entertained by him. Carried down the river with great rapidity to another house. Received with kindness. Occupations of the inhabitants on its banks. Leave the canoe at a fall. Pass over land to another village. Some account of it. Obtain a view of an arm of the sea. Lose our dog. Procure another canoe. Arrive at the arm of the sea. Circumstances of it. One of our guides returns home. Coast along a bay. Some description of it. Meet with Indians. Our communication with them. Their suspicious conduct towards us. Pass onwards. Determine the latitude and longitude. Return to the river. Dangerous encounter with the Indians. Proceed on our journey.

<hr />

1793.
July.
Saturday 18.

A<small>T</small> one in the afternoon we renewed our voyage in a large canoe with four of the natives. We found the river almost one continued rapid, and in half an hour we came to an house, where, however, we did not land, though invited by the inhabitants. In about an hour we arrived at two houses, where we were, in some degree, obliged to go on shore, as we were informed that the owner of them was a person of consideration. He indeed received and regaled us in the same manner

as

as at the laſt village; and to increaſe his conſequence, he produced many European articles, and amongſt them were at leaſt forty pounds weight of old copper ſtills. We made our ſtay as ſhort as poſſible, and our hoſt embarked with us. In a very ſhort time we were carried by the rapidity of the current to another houſe of very large dimenſions, which was partitioned into different apartments, and whoſe doors were on the ſide. The inhabitants received us with great kindneſs; but inſtead of fiſh, they placed a long, clean, and well made trough before us full of berries. In addition to thoſe which we had already ſeen, there were ſome black, that were larger than the huckle berry, and of a richer flavour; and others white, which reſembled the blackberry in every thing but colour. Here we ſaw a woman with two pieces of copper in her under lip, as deſcribed by Captain Cook. I continued my uſual practice of making theſe people preſents in return for their friendly reception and entertainment.

The navigation of the river now became more difficult, from the nu-merous channels into which it was divided, without any ſenſible dimi-nution in the velocity of its current. We ſoon reached another houſe of the common ſize, where we were well received; but whether our guides had informed them that we were not in want of any thing, or that they were deficient in inclination, or perhaps the means, of being hoſpitable to us, they did not offer us any refreſhment. They were in a ſtate of buſy preparation. Some of the women were employed in beat-ing and preparing the inner rind of the cedar bark, to which they gave the appearance of flax. Others were ſpinning with a diſtaff and ſpindle. One of them was weaving a robe of it, intermixed with ſtripes of the ſea-

otter

otter skin, on a frame of adequate contrivance that was placed against the side of the house. The men were fishing on the river with drag-nets between two canoes. These nets are forced by poles to the bottom, the current driving them before it; by which means the salmon coming up the river are intercepted, and give notice of their being taken by the struggles they make in the bag or sleeve of the net. There are no weirs in this part of the river, as I suppose, from the numerous channels into which it is divided. The machines, therefore, are placed along the banks, and consequently these people are not so well supplied with fish as the village which has been already described, nor do they appear to possess the same industry. The inhabitants of the last house accompanied us in a large canoe. They recommended us to leave ours here, as the next village was but at a small distance from us, and the water more rapid than that which we had passed. They informed us also, that we were approaching a cascade. I directed them to shoot it, and proceeded myself to the foot thereof, where I re-imbarked, and we went on with great velocity, till we came to a fall, where we left our canoe, and carried our luggage along a road through a wood for some hundred yards, when we came to a village, consisting of six very large houses, erected on pallisades, rising twenty-five feet from the ground, which differed in no one circumstance from those already described, but the height of their elevation. They contained only four men and their families. The rest of the inhabitants were with us and in the small houses which we passed higher up the river.* These people do not seem to enjoy the abundance of their neighbours, as the men who returned

* Mr. Johnstone came to these houses the first day of the preceding month.

from

from fifhing had no more than five falmon; they refufed to fell one of them, but gave me one roafted of a very indifferent kind. In the houfes there were feveral chefts or boxes containing different articles that belonged to the people whom we had lately paffed. If I were to judge by the heaps of filth beneath thefe buildings, they muft have been erected at a more diftant period than any which we had paffed. From thefe houfes I could perceive the termination of the river, and its dif-charge into a narrow arm of the fea.

As it was now half paft fix in the evening, and the weather cloudy, I determined to remain here for the night, and for that purpofe we pof-feffed ourfelves of one of the unoccupied houfes. The remains of our laft meal, which we brought with us, ferved for our fupper, as we could not procure a fingle fifh from the natives. The courfe of the river is about Weft, and the diftance from the great village upwards of thirty-fix miles. There we had loft our dog, a circumftance of no fmall regret to me.

Saturday 20.   We rofe at a very early hour this morning, when I propofed to the Indians to run down our canoe, or procure another at this place. To both thefe propofals they turned a deaf ear, as they imagined that I fhould be fatisfied with having come in fight of the fea. Two of them peremptorily refufed to proceed; but the other two having confented to continue with us, we obtained a larger canoe than our former one, and though it was in a leaky ftate we were glad to poffefs it.

At about eight we got out of the river, which difcharges itfelf by

various

various channels into an arm of the fea. The tide was out, and had left a large fpace covered with fea-weed. The furrounding hills were involved in fog. The wind was at Weft, which was a-head of us, and very ftrong; the bay appearing to be from one to three miles in breadth. As we advanced along the land we faw a great number of fea-otters. We fired feveral fhots at them, but without any fuccefs from the rapidity with which they plunge under the water. We alfo faw many fmall porpoifes or divers. The white-headed eagle, which is common in the interior parts; fome fmall gulls, a dark bird which is inferior in fize to the gull, and a few fmall ducks, were all the birds which prefented themfelves to our view.

At two in the afternoon the fwell was fo high, and the wind, which was againft us, fo boifterous, that we could not proceed with our leaky veffel, we therefore landed in a fmall cove on the right fide of the bay. Oppofite to us appeared another fmall bay, in the mouth of which is an ifland, and where, according to the information of the Indians, a river difcharges itfelf that abounds in falmon.

Our young Indians now difcovered a very evident difpofition to leave us; and, in the evening, one of them made his efcape. Mr. Mackay, however, with the other, purfued and brought him back; but as it was by no means neceffary to detain him, particularly as provifions did not abound with us, I gave him a fmall portion, with a pair of fhoes, which were neceffary for his journey, and a filk handkerchief, telling him at the fame time, that he might go and inform his friends, that we fhould alfo

return

return in three nights.   He accordingly left us, and his companion, the young chief, went with him.

When we landed, the tide was going out, and at a quarter paft four it was ebb, the water having fallen in that fhort period eleven feet and an half.   Since we left the river, not a quarter of an hour had paffed in which we did not fee porpoifes and fea-otters.   Soon after ten it was high water, which rendered it neceffary that our baggage fhould be fhifted feveral times, though not till fome of the things had been wetted.

We were now reduced to the neceffity of looking out for frefh water, with which we were plentifully fupplied by the rills that ran down from the mountains.

When it was dark the young chief returned to us, bearing a large porcupine on his back.   He firft cut the animal open, and having dif-encumbered it of the entrails, threw them into the fea; he then finged its fkin, and boiled it in feparate pieces, as our kettle was not fufficiently capacious to contain the whole: nor did he go to reft, till, with the affiftance of two of my people who happened to be awake, every morfel of it was devoured.

I had flattered myfelf with the hope of getting a diftance of the moon and ftars, but the cloudy weather continually difappointed me, and I began to fear that I fhould fail in this important objeƐt; particularly as our provifions were at a very low ebb, and we had, as yet, no reafon to

expeƐt

expect any affiftance from the natives. Our ftock was, at this time, reduced to twenty pounds weight of pemmican, fifteen pounds of rice,
and fix pounds of flour, among ten half-ftarved men, in a leaky veffel,
and on a barbarous coaft. Our courfe from the river was about Weft-
South-Weft, diftance ten miles.

At forty minutes paft four this morning it was low water, which made
fifteen feet perpendicular height below the high-water mark of laft night.
Mr. Mackay collected a quantity of fmall mufcles which we boiled.
Our people did not partake of this regale, as they are wholly unac-
quainted with fea fhell-fifh. Our young chief being miffing, we imagined
that he had taken his flight, but, as we were preparing to depart, he fortunately made his appearance from the woods, where he had been to
take his reft after his feaft of laft night. At fix we were upon the water,
when we cleared the fmall bay, which we named Porcupine Cove, and
fteered Weft-South-Weft for feven miles, we then opened a channel
about two miles and an half wide at South-South-Weft, and had a view
of ten or twelve miles into it. As I could not afcertain the diftance from
the open fea, and being uncertain whether we were in a bay or among
inlets and channels of iflands, I confined my fearch to a proper place
for taking an obfervation. We fteered, therefore, along the land on the
left, Weft-North-Weft a mile and an half; then North-Weft one fourth
of a mile, and North three miles to an ifland; the land continuing to
run North-North-Weft, then along the ifland, South-South-Weft half a
mile, Weft a mile and an half, and from thence directly acrofs to the
land on the left, (where I had an altitude,) South-Weft three miles.*

* The Cape or Point Menzies of Vancouver.

From

From this pofition a channel, of which the ifland we left appeared to make a cheek, bears North by Eaft.

Under the land we met with three canoes, with fifteen men in them, and laden with their moveables, as if proceeding to a new fituation, or returning to a former one.   They manifefted no kind of miftruft or fear of us, but entered into converfation with our young man, as I fuppofed, to obtain fome information concerning us.   It did not appear that they were the fame people as thofe we had lately feen, as they fpoke the language of our young chief, with a different accent.   They then examined every thing we had in our canoe, with an air of indifference and difdain.   One of them in particular made me underftand, with an air of infolence, that a large canoe had lately been in this bay, with people in her like me, and that one of them, whom he called *Macubah*, had fired on him and his friends, and that *Benfins* had ftruck him on the back, with the flat part of his fword.   He alfo mentioned another name, the articulation of which I could not determine.   At the fame time he illuftrated thefe circumftances by the affiftance of my gun and fword; and I do not doubt but he well deferved the treatment which he defcribed. He alfo produced feveral European articles, which could not have been long in his poffeffion.   From his conduct and appearance, I wifhed very much to be rid of him, and flattered myfelf that he would profecute his voyage, which appeared to be in an oppofite direction to our courfe.   However, when I prepared to part from them, they turned their canoes about, and perfuaded my young man to leave me, which I could not prevent.

We

We coafted along the land* at about Weft-South-Weft for fix miles, and met a canoe with two boys in it, who were difpatched to fummon the people on that part of the coaft to join them. The troublefome fellow now forced himfelf into my canoe, and pointed out a narrow channel on the oppofite fhore, that led to his village, and requefted us to fteer towards it, which I accordingly ordered. His importunities now became very irkfome, and he wanted to fee every thing we had, particularly my inftruments, concerning which he muft have received information from my young man. He afked for my hat, my handker-chief, and, in fhort, every thing that he faw about me. At the fame time he frequently repeated the unpleafant intelligence that he had been fhot at by people of my colour. At fome diftance from the land a chan-nel opened to us, at South-Weft by Weft, and pointing that way, he made me underftand that *Macubah* came there with his large canoe. When we were in mid-channel, I perceived fome fheds, or the remains of old buildings, on the fhore; and as, from that circumftance, I thought it probable that fome Europeans might have been there, I directed my fteerfman to make for that fpot. The traverfe is upwards of three miles North-Weft.

We landed, and found the ruins of a village, in a fituation calculated for defence. The place itfelf was over grown with weeds, and in the centre of the houfes there was a temple, of the fame form and conftruc-tion as that which I defcribed at the large village. We were foon fol-lowed by ten canoes, each of which contained from three to fix men. They

---

* Named by Vancouver King's Ifland.

informed

informed us that we were expected at the village, where we fhould fee many of them. From their general deportment I was very apprehenfive that fome hoftile defign was meditated againft us, and for the firft time I acknowledged my apprehenfions to my people. I accordingly defired them to be very much upon their guard, and to be prepared if any violence was offered to defend themfelves to the laft.

We had no fooner landed, than we took poffeffion of a rock, where there was not fpace for more than twice our number, and which admitted of our defending ourfelves with advantage, in cafe we fhould be attacked. The people in the three firft canoes, were the moft troublefome, but, after doing their utmoft to irritate us, they went away. They were, however, no fooner gone, than an hat, an handkerchief, and feveral other articles, were miffing. The reft of our vifitors continued their preffing invitations to accompany them to their village, but finding our refolution, to decline them was not to be fhaken, they, about fun-fet relieved us from all further importunities, by their departure.

Another canoe, however, foon arrived, with feven ftout, well-looking men. They brought a box, which contained a very fine fea-otter fkin, and a goat fkin, that was beautifully white. For the former they demanded my hanger, which, as may well be fuppofed, could not be fpared in our prefent fituation, and they actually refufed to take a yard and an half of common broad cloth, with fome other articles, for the fkin, which proves the unreflecting improvidence of our European traders. The goat-fkin was fo bulky that I did not offer to purchafe it. Thefe men alfo told me that *Macubah* had been there, and left his fhip behind a

point

point of land in the channel, South-Weſt from us; from whence he had come to their village in boats, which theſe people repreſented by imitating our manner of rowing. When I offered them what they did not chooſe to accept for the otter-ſkin, they ſhook their heads, and very diſtinctly anſwered " No, no." And to mark their refuſal of any thing we aſked from them, they emphatically employed the ſame Britiſh monoſyllable. In one of the canoes which had left us, there was a ſeal, that I wiſhed to purchaſe, but could not perſuade the natives to part with it. They had alſo a fiſh, which I now ſaw for the firſt time. It was about eighteen inches in length, of the ſhape and appearance of a trout, with ſtrong, ſharp teeth. We ſaw great numbers of the animals which we had taken for ſea otters, but I was now diſpoſed to think that a great part of them, at leaſt, muſt have been ſeals.

The natives having left us, we made a fire to warm ourſelves, and as for ſupper, there was but little of that, for our whole daily allowance did not amount to what was ſufficient for a ſingle meal. The weather was clear throughout the day, which was ſucceeded by a fine moon-light night. I directed the people to keep watch by two in turn, and laid myſelf down in my cloak.

This morning the weather was clear and pleaſant; nor had any thing occurred to diſturb us throughout the night. One ſolitary Indian, indeed, came to us with about half a pound of boiled ſeal's fleſh, and the head of a ſmall ſalmon, for which he aſked an handkerchief, but afterwards accepted a few beads. As this man came alone, I concluded that no general plan had been formed among the natives to annoy us, but this opinion did not altogether calm the apprehenſions of my people.

Soon

Soon after eight in the morning, I took five altitudes for time, and the mean of them was 36° 48' at fix in the afternoon, 58. 34. time, by the watch, which makes the achrometer flow apparent time 1ʰ 21ᵐ 44ˢ.

Two canoes now arrived from the fame quarter as the reft, with feveral men, and our young Indian along with them. They brought a very few fmall fea-otter fkins, out of feafon, with fome pieces of raw feal's flefh. The former were of no value, but hunger compelled fome of my people to take the latter, at an extravagant price. Mr. Mackay lighted a bit of touch wood with a burning-glafs, in the cover of his tobacco-box, which fo furprifed the natives, that they exchanged the beft of their otter fkins for it. The young man was now very anxious to perfuade our people to depart, as the natives, he faid, were as numerous as mufquitoes, and of very malignant character. This information produced fome very earneft remonftrances to me to haften our departure, but as I was determined not to leave this place, except I was abfolutely compelled to it, till I had afcertained its fituation, thefe folicitations were not repeated.

While I was taking a meridian, two canoes, of a larger fize, and well manned, appeared from the main South-Weft channel. They feemed to be the fore-runners of others, who were coming to co-operate with the people of the village, in confequence of the meffage fent by the two boys, which has been already mentioned; and our young Indian, who underftood them, renewed his entreaties for our departure, as they would foon come to fhoot their arrows, and hurl their fpears at us. In relating our danger, his agitation was fo violent that he foamed at the mouth. Though I was not altogether free from apprehenfions on the occafion, it

was

was neceffary for me to difguife them, as my people were panic ftruck, and fome of them afked if it was my determination to remain there to be facrificed? My reply was the fame as their former importunities had received, that I would not ftir till I had accomplifhed my object; at the fame time, to humour their fears, I confented that they fhould put every thing into the canoe, that we might be in a ftate of preparation to de-part. The two canoes now approached the fhore, and in a fhort time five men, with their families, landed very quietly from them. My inftruments being expofed, they examined them with much apparent admiration and aftonifhment. My altitude, by an artificial horizon, gave 52° 21' 33"; that by the natural horizon was 52° 20' 48" North latitude.*

Thefe Indians were of a different tribe from thofe which I had already feen, as our guide did not underftand their language. I now mixed up fome vermilion in melted greafe, and infcribed, in large characters, on the South-Eaft face of the rock on which we had flept laft night, this brief memorial—" Alexander Mackenzie, from Canada, by land, the twenty-fecond of July, one thoufand feven hundred and ninety-three."

As I thought that we were too near the village, I confented to leave this place, and accordingly proceeded North-Eaft three miles, when we landed on a point, in a fmall cove, where we fhould not be readily feen, and could not be attacked except in our front.

Among other articles that had been ftolen from us, at our laft ftation,

* This I found to be the cheek of Vancouver's Cafcade Canal.

was

was a founding-line, which I intended to have employed in this bay, though I fhould not probably have found the bottom, at any diftance from the fhore, as the appearance both of the water and land indicated a great depth. The latter difplayed a folid rock, rifing, as it appeared to me, from three to feven hundred feet above high water mark. Where any foil was fcattered about, there were cedars, fpruce-firs, white birch, and other trees of large growth. From its precipices iffued ftreams of fine water, as cold as ice.

The two canoes which we had left at our laft ftation, followed us hither, and when they were preparing to depart, our young chief embarked with them. I was determined, however, to prevent his efcape, and compelled him, by actual force, to come on fhore, for I thought it much better to incur his difpleafure, than to fuffer him to expofe himfelf to any untoward accident among ftrangers, or to return to his father before us. The men in the canoe made figns for him to go over the hill, and that they would take him on board at the other fide of it. As I was neceffarily engaged in other matters, I defired my people to take care that he fhould not run away; but they peremptorily refufed to be employed in keeping him againft his will. I was, therefore, reduced to the neceffity of watching him myfelf.

I took five altitudes, and the mean of them was 29. 23. 48. at 3. 5. 53. in the afternoon, by the watch, which makes it flow apparent

time	1ᵐ	22ʰ	38ˢ		
In the forenoon it was .	1	21	44	2 44 22	
Mean of both .				1 22 11	
Difference nine hours going of the time-piece flow				8	
				1 22 19	

I obferved

I obferved an emerfion of Jupiter's third fatellite, which gave 8° 32' 21" difference of longitude. I then obferved an emerfion of Jupiter's firft fatellite, which gave 8. 31. 48. The mean of thefe obfervations is 8° 32' 2" which is equal to 128. 2. Weft of Greenwich.

I had now determined my fituation, which is the moft fortunate circumftance of my long, painful, and perilous journey, as a few cloudy days would have prevented me from afcertaining the final longitude of it.*

At twelve it was high water, but the tide did not come within a foot and an half of the high water mark of laft night. As foon as I had completed my obfervations, we left this place: it was then ten o'clock in the afternoon. We returned the fame way that we came, and though the tide was running out very ftrong, by keeping clofe in with the rocks, we proceeded at a confiderable rate, as my people were very anxious to get out of the reach of the inhabitants of this coaft.

During our courfe we faw feveral fires on the land to the Southward, and after the day dawned, their fmokes were vifible. At half paft four this morning we arrived at our encampment of the night of the 21ft, which had been named Porcupine Cove. The tide was out, and confiderably lower than we found it when we were here before; the high-

Tuefday 23.

---

* Mr. Meares was undoubtedly wrong in the idea, fo pofitively infifted on by him in his voyage, that there was a North-Weft paffage to the Southward of fixty-nine degrees and an half c f latitude, as I flatter myfelf has been proved by my former voyage. Nor can I refrain from expreffing my furprife at his affertion, that there was an inland fea or archipelago of great extent between the iflands of Nootka and the main, about the latitude where I was at this time. Indeed I have been informed that Captain Grey, who commanded an American veffel, and on whofe authority he ventured this opinion, denies that he had given Mr. Meares any fuch information. Befides, the contrary is indubitably proved by Captain Vancouver's furvey, from which no appeal can be made.

water

water mark being above the place where we had made our fire. This fluctuation muſt be occaſioned by the action of the wind upon the water, in thoſe narrow channels.

As we continued onwards, towards the river, we ſaw a canoe, well manned, which at firſt made from us with great expedition, but afterwards waited, as if to reconnoitre us; however, it kept out of our way, and allowed us to paſs. The tide being much lower than when we were here before, we were under the neceſſity of landing a mile below the village. We obſerved that ſtakes were fixed in the ground along the bay, and in ſome places machines were faſtened to them, as I afterwards learned, to intercept the ſeals and otters. Theſe works are very extenſive, and muſt have been erected with no common labour. The only bird we ſaw to-day was the white-headed eagle.*

Our guide directed us to draw the canoe out of the reach of the tide and to leave it. He would not wait, however, till this operation was performed, and I did not wiſh to let him go alone. I therefore followed him through a bad road encumbered with underwood. When we had quitted the wood, and were in ſight of the houſes, the young man being about fifteen or twenty paces before me, I was ſurpriſed to ſee two men running down towards me from one of the houſes, with daggers in their hands and fury in their aſpect. From their hoſtile appearance, I could not doubt of their purpoſe. I therefore ſtopped ſhort, threw down my cloak, and put myſelf in a poſture of defence, with my gun preſented

* This bay was now named Mackenzie's Outlet.

towards

towards them. Fortunately for me, they knew the effect of fire-arms, and inftantly dropped their daggers, which were faftened by a ftring to their wrifts, and had before been held in a menacing attitude. I let my gun alfo fall into my left hand, and drew my hanger. Several others foon joined them, who were armed in the fame manner; and among them I recognifed the man whom I have already mentioned as being fo troublefome to us, and who now repeated the names of Macubah and Benzins, fignifying at the fame time by his action, as on a former oc-cafion, that he had been fhot at by them. Until I faw him my mind was undifturbed; but the moment he appeared, conceiving that he was the caufe of my prefent perilous fituation, my refentment predominated, and, if he had come within my reach, I verily believe, that I fhould have terminated his infolence for ever.

The reft now approached fo near, that one of them contrived to get behind me, and grafped me in his arms. I foon difengaged myfelf from him; and, that he did not avail himfelf of the opportunity which he had of plunging his dagger into me, I cannot conjecture. They cer-tainly might have overpowered me, and though I fhould probably have killed one or two of them, I muft have fallen at laft.

One of my people now came out of the wood. On his appearance they inftantly took to flight, and with the utmoft fpeed fought fhelter in the houfes from whence they had iffued. It was, however, upwards of ten minutes before all my people joined me; and as they came one after the other, thefe people might have fucceffively difpatched every

one

one of us. If they had killed me, in the firſt inſtance, this conſequence would certainly have followed, and not one of us would have returned home to tell the horrid fate of his companions.

After having ſtated the danger I had encountered, I told my people that I was determined to make theſe natives feel the impropriety of their conduct toward us, and compel them to return my hat and cloak which they had taken in the ſcuffle, as well as the articles previouſly purloined from us ; for moſt of the men who were in the three canoes that we firſt ſaw, were now in the village. I therefore told my men to prime their pieces afreſh, and prepare themſelves for an active uſe of them, if the occaſion ſhould require it.

We now drew up before the houſe, and made ſigns for ſome one to come down to us. At length our young chief appeared, and told us that the men belonging to the canoes had not only informed his friends, that we had treated him very ill, but that we had killed four of their companions whom we had met in the bay. When I had explained to them as well as it was in my power, the falſehood of ſuch a ſtory, I inſiſted on the reſtoration of every thing that had been taken from us, as well as a neceſſary ſupply of fiſh, as the conditions of my departure ; accordingly the things were reſtored, and a few dried fiſh along with them. A reconciliation now took place, but our guide or young chief was ſo much terrified that he would remain no longer with us, and requeſted us to follow with his father's canoe, or miſchief would follow. I determined, however, before my departure, to take an obſervation, and at noon got

a meridian

a meridian altitude, making this place, which I named Rafcal's Village, 52. 23. 43. North latitude.

On my informing the natives that we wanted fomething more to eat, they brought us two falmons; and when we fignified that we had no poles to fet the canoe againft the current, they were furnifhed with equal alacrity, fo anxious were they for our departure. I paid, however, for every thing which we had received, and did not forget the loan of the canoe.

CHAP.

CHAPTER XII.

Return up the river. Slow progreſs of the canoe, from the ſtrength of the current. The hoſtile party of the natives precede us. Impetuous con-duĉt of my people. Continue our very tedious voyage. Come to ſome houſes; received with great kindneſs. Arrive at the principal, or Salmon Village. Our preſent reception very different from that we experienced on our former viſit. Continue our journey. Circumſtances of it. Find our dog. Arrive at the Upper, or Friendly Village. Meet with a very kind reception. Some further account of the manners and cuſtoms of its inhabitants. Brief vocabulary of their language.

————

1793.
July.

THE current of the river was ſo ſtrong, that I ſhould have complied with the wiſhes of my people, and gone by land, but one of my Indians was ſo weak, that it was impoſſible for him to perform the journey. He had been ill ſome time; and, indeed, we had been all of us more or leſs afflicted with colds on the ſea coaſt. Four of the people therefore ſet off with the canoe, and it employed them an hour to get half a mile. In the mean time the native, who has been already mentioned as having treated us with ſo much inſolence, and four of his companions, went up the river in a canoe, which they had above the rapid, with as many boxes as men

in

in her. This circumstance was the cause of fresh alarm, as it was generally concluded that they would produce the same mischief and danger
in the villages above, as they had in that below. Nor was it forgotten
that the young chief had left us in a manner which would not be inter-
preted in our favour by his father and friends.

At length the canoe arrived, and the people declared in the most un-
reserved terms, that they would proceed no further in her; but when
they were made acquainted with the circumstances which have just been
described, their violence increased, and the greater part of the men an-
nounced their determination to attempt the mountains, and endeavour,
by passing over them, to gain the road by which we came to the first
village. So resolved were they to pursue this plan, that they threw
every thing which they had into the river, except their blankets. I
was all this time sitting patiently on a stone, and indulging the hope
that, when their frantic terror had subsided, their returning reason
would have disposed them to perceive the rashness of their project; but when I observed that they persisted in it, I no longer remained a silent listener to their passionate declarations, but proceeded
to employ such arguments as I trusted would turn them from their
senseless and impracticable purpose. After reproving my young Indian
in very severe terms, for encouraging the rest to follow their mad design of passing the mountains, I addressed myself generally to them,
stating the difficulty of ascending the mountains, the eternal snows with
which they were covered, our small stock of provisions, which two days
would exhaust, and the consequent probability that we should perish with
cold and hunger. I urged the folly of being affected by the alarm of
                                                                danger

danger which might not exift, and if it did, I encouraged them with the means we poffeffed of furmounting it. Nor did I forget to urge the inhumanity and injuftice of leaving the poor fick Indian to languifh and die. I alfo added, that as my particular objeft had been accomplifhed, I had now no other but our common fafety; that the fole wifh of my heart was to employ the beft means in my power, and to purfue the beft method which my underftanding could fuggeft, to fecure them and myfelf from every danger that might impede our return.

My fteerfman, who had been with me for five years in that capacity, inftantly replied that he was ready to follow me wherever I fhould go, but that he would never again enter that canoe, as he had folemnly fworn he would not, while he was in the rapid. His example was followed by all the reft, except two, who embarked with Mr. Mackay,* myfelf, and the fick Indian. The current, however, was fo ftrong, that we dragged up the greateft part of the way, by the branches of trees. Our p ogrefs, as may be imagined, was very tedious, and attended with uncommon labour; the party who went by land being continually obliged to wait for us. Mr. Mackay's gun was carried out of the canoe and loft, at a time when we appeared to ftand in very great need of it, as two canoes, with fixteen or eighteen men, were coming down the ftream; and the apprehenfions which they occafioned did not fubfide till they fhot by us with great rapidity.

At length we came in fight of the houfe, when we faw our young Indian

---

* It is but common juftice to him, to mention in this place that I had every reafon to be fatisfied with his conduft.

with

with fix others, in a canoe coming to meet us. This was a very encouraging circumſtance, as it ſatisfied us that the natives who had preceded, and whoſe malignant deſigns we had every reaſon to ſuſpeƈt, had not been ab e to prejudice the people againſt us. We, therefore, landed at the houſe, where we were received in a friendly manner, and having procured ſome fiſh, we proceeded on our journey.

It was almoſt dark when we arrived at the next houſe, and the firſt perſons who preſented themſelves to our obſervation were the turbulent Indian and his four companions. They were not very agreeable objeƈts; but we were neverthelefs well received by the inhabitants, who preſented us with fiſh and berries. The Indians who had cauſed us ſo much alarm, we now diſcovered to be inhabitants of the iſlands, and traders in various articles, ſuch as cedar-bark, prepared to be wove into mats, fiſh-ſpawn, copper, iron, and beads, the latter of which they get on their own coaſt. For theſe they receive in exchange roaſted ſalmon, hemlock-bark cakes, and the other kind made of ſalmon roes, ſorrel, and bitter berries. Having procured as much fiſh as would ſerve us for our ſupper, and the meals of the next day, all my people went to reſt except one, with whom I kept the firſt watch.

After twelve laſt night, I called up Mr. Mackay, and one of the men, to relieve us, but as a general tranquillity appeared to prevail in the place, I recommended them to return to their reſt. I was the firſt awake the morning, and ſent Mr. Mackay to ſee if our canoe remained where we left it; but he returned to inform me that the Iſlanders had loaded it with their articles of traffic, and were ready to depart. On this intelligence

ligence I hurried to the water fide, and feizing the canoe by the ftem, I
fhould certainly have overfet it, and turned the three men that were in it,
with all their merchandife, into the river, had not one of the people of
the houfe, who had been very kind to us, informed me that this was their
own canoe, and that my guide had gone off with ours.   At the fame moment the other two Indians who belonged to the party, jumped nimbly
into it, and pufhed off with all the hafte and hurry that their fears may be
fuppofed to dictate.

We now found ourfelves once more without a guide or a canoe.   We
were, however, fo fortunate as to engage, without much difficulty, two
of thefe people to accompany us; as, from the ftrength of the current,
it would not have been poffible for us to have proceeded by water without their affiftance.   As the houfe was upon an ifland, we ferried over
the pedeftrian party to the main bank of the river, and continued our
courfe till our conductors came to their fifhing ground, when they propofed to land us, and our fmall portion of baggage; but as our companions were on the oppofite fhore, we could not acquiefce, and after
fome time perfuaded them to proceed further with us.   Soon after we
met the chief, who had regaled us in our voyage down the river.   He
was feining between two canoes, and had taken a confiderable quantity
of falmon.   He took us on board with him, and proceeded upwards with
great expedition.   Thefe people are furprifingly fkilful and active in
fetting againft a ftrong current.   In the rougheft part they almoft filled
the canoe with water, by way of a fportive alarm to us.

We landed at the houfe of the chief, and he immediately placed a fifh
before

before me. Our people now appeared on the oppofite bank, when a canoe was fent for them. As foon as they had made their meal of fifh, they proceeded on their route, and we followed them, the chief and one of the natives having undertaken to conduct us.

At five in the afternoon we came to two houfes, which we had not feen in going down. They were upon an ifland, and I was obliged to fend for the walking party, as our conductors, from the latenefs of the hour, refufed to proceed any further with us till the next day. One of our men, being at a fmall diftance before the others, had been attacked by a female bear, with two cubs, but another of them arrived to his refcue, and fhot her. Their fears probably prevented them from killing the two young ones. They brought a part of the meat, but it was very indifferent. We were informed that our former guide, or young chief, had paffed this place, at a very early hour of the morning, on foot.

Thefe people take plenty of another fifh, befides falmon, which weigh from fifteen to forty pounds. This fifh is broader than the falmon, of a greyifh colour, and with an hunch on its back; the flefh is white, but neither rich nor well flavoured. Its jaw and teeth are like thofe of a dog, and the latter are larger and ftronger than any I had ever feen in a fifh of equal fize: thofe in front bend inwards, like the claws of a bird of prey. It delights in fhallow water, and its native name is Dilly.

We received as many fifh and berries from thefe people as completely fatisfied our appetites. The latter excelled any of the kind that we

had

had feen. I faw, alfo, three kinds of goofeberries, which, as we paffed through the woods, we found in great abundance.

Thurfday 25.   I arofe before the fun, and the weather was very fine. The men who were to accompany us went to vifit their machines, and brought back plenty of fifh, which they ftrung on a rope, and left them in the river. We now embarked thirteen in a canoe, and landed my men on the South bank, as it would have been impracticable to have ftemmed the tide with fuch a load. The under-wood was fo thick that it was with great diffi- culty they could pafs through it. At nine we were under the neceffity of waiting to ferry them over a river from the South, which is not ford- able. After fome time we came to two deferted houfes, at the foot of a rapid, beyond which our boatmen abfolutely refufed to conduct us by water. Here was a road which led oppofite to the village. We had, however, the curiofity to vifit the houfes, which were erected upon pofts; and we fuffered very feverely for the indulgence of it; for the floors were covered with fleas, and we were immediately in the fame condition, for which we had no remedy but to take to the water. There was not a fpot round the houfes, free from grafs, that was not alive, as it were, with this vermin.

Our guides propofed to conduct us on our way, and we followed them on a well-beaten track. They, however, went fo faft, that we could not all of us keep up with them, particularly our fick Indian, whofe fituation was very embarraffing to us, and at length they contrived to efcape. I very much wifhed for thefe men to have accompanied us to the village, in order to do away any ill impreffions which might have arifen from the

young

young chief's report to his father, which we were naturally led to expect would not be in our favour.

This road conducted us through the fineft wood of cedar trees that I
had ever feen. I meafured feveral of them that were twenty-four feet
in the girth, and of a proportionate height. The alder trees are alfo of
an uncommon fize; feveral of them were feven feet and an half in circumference, and rofe to forty feet without a branch; but my men declared
that they had, in their progrefs, feen much larger of both kinds. The
other wood was hemlock, white birch, two fpecies of fpruce-firs, willows, &c. Many of the large cedars appeared to have been examined,
as I fuppofe by the natives, for the purpofe of making canoes, but finding
them hollow at heart, they were fuffered to ftand. There was but little
underwood, and the foil was a black rich mould, which would well reward the trouble of cultivation. From the remains of bones on certain
fpots, it is probable that the natives may have occafionally burned their
dead in this wood.

As it was uncertain what our reception might be at the village, I examined every man's arms and ammunition, and gave Mr. Mackay, who
had unfortunately loft his gun, one of my piftols. Our late conductors
had informed us that the man whom we left in a dying ftate, and to
whom I had adminiftered fome Turlington's balfam, was dead; and it
was by no means improbable that I might be fufpected of haftening
his end.

At one in the afternoon we came to the bank of the river, which was
oppofite

oppofite to the village, which appeared to be in a ftate of perfect tranquillity.   Several of the natives were fifhing above and below the weir,
and they very readily took us over in their canoes.   The people now
hurried down to the water fide, but I perceived none of the chief's family
among them.   They made figns to me to go to his houfe; I fignified to
them not to crowd about us, and indeed drew a line, beyond which I
made them underftand they muft not pafs.   I now directed Mr. Mackay,
and the men to remain there, with their arms in readinefs, and to keep
the natives at a diftance, as I was determined to go alone to the chief's
houfe; and if they fhould hear the report of my piftols, they were ordered
to make the beft of their way from thefe people, as it would then be equally
fruitlefs and dangerous to attempt the giving me any affiftance, as it
would be only in the laft extremity, and when I was certain of their intention to deftroy me, that I fhould difcharge my piftols.   My gun I gave
to Mr. Mackay, when, with my loaded piftols in my belt, and a poniard in
my hand, I proceeded to the abode of the chief.   I had a wood to pafs
in my way thither, which was interfected by various paths, and I took
one that led to the back inftead of the front of the houfe; and as the
whole had been very much altered fince I was here before, I concluded
that I had loft my way.   But I continued to proceed, and foon met
with the chief's wife, who informed me, that he was at the next houfe.
On my going round it, I perceived that they had thrown open the gable
ends, and added two wings, nearly as long as the body, both of which
were hung round with falmon as clofe as they could be placed.   As
I could difcover none of the men, I fat down upon a large ftone near
fome women who were fupping on falmon roes and berries.   They invited me to partake of their fare, and I was about to accept their invitation,

when

when Mr. Mackay joined me, as both himself and all my party were alarmed at my being alone. Nor was his alarm leffened by an old man whom he met in the wood, and who made ufe of figns to perfuade him to return. As he came without his gun, I gave him one of my piftols. When I faw the women continue their employment without paying the leaft attention to us, I could not imagine that any hoftile defign was preparing againft us. Though the non-appearance of the men awakened fome degree of fufpicion that I fhould not be received with the fame welcome as on my former vifit. At length the chief appeared, and his fon, who had been our guide, following him: difpleafure was painted in the old man's countenance, and he held in his hand a bead tobacco pouch which belonged to Mr. Mackay, and the young chief had purloined from him. When he had approached within three or four yards of me, he threw it at me with great indignation, and walked away. I followed him, however, until he had paffed his fon, whom I took by the hand, but he did not make any very cordial return to my falutation; at the fame time he made figns for me to difcharge my piftol, and give him my hanger which Mr. Mackay had brought me, but I did not pay the leaft attention to either of his demands.

We now joined the chief, who explained to me that he was in a ftate of deep diftrefs for the lofs of his fon, and made me underftand that he had cut off his hair and blackened his face on the melancholy occafion. He alfo reprefented the alarm which he had fuffered refpecting his fon who had accompanied us; as he apprehended we had killed him, or had all of us perifhed together. When he had finifhed his narrative, I took him and his fon by their hands, and requefted them to come with me to

the

the place where I had left my people, who were rejoiced to fee us return, having been in a ftate of great anxiety from our long abfence. I immediately remunerated the young chief for his company and affiftance in our voyage to the fea, as well as his father, for his former attentions. I gave them cloth and knives, and, indeed, a portion of every thing which now remained to us. The prefents had the defired effect of reftoring us to their favour; but thefe people are of fo changeable a nature, that there is no fecurity with them. I procured three robes and two otter-fkins, and if I could have given fuch articles in exchange as they preferred, I fhould probably have obtained more. I now reprefented the length of the way which I had to go, and requefted fome fifh to fupport us on our journey, when he defired us to follow him to the houfe, where mats were immediately arranged and a fifh placed before each of us.

We were now informed, that our dog, whom we had loft, had been howling about the village ever fince we left it, and that they had reafon to believe he left the woods at night to eat the fifh he could find about the houfes. I immediately difpatched Mr. Mackay, and a man, in fearch of the animal, but they returned without him.

When I manifefted my intention to proceed on my journey, the chief voluntarily fent for ten roafted falmon, and having attended us with his fon, and a great number of his people, to the laft houfe in the village, we took our leave. It was then half paft three in the afternoon.

I directed Mr. Mackay to take the lead, and the others to follow him

in

in Indian files, at a long and fteady pace, as I determined to bring up the rear. I adopted this meafure from a confufion that was obfervable among the natives which I did not comprehend. I was not without my fufpicions that fome mifchief was in agitation, and they were increafed from the confufed noife we heard in the village. At the fame time a confiderable number came running after us; fome of them making figns for us to ftop, and others rufhing by me. I perceived alfo, that thofe who followed us were the ftrangers who live among thefe people, and are kept by them in a ftate of awe and fubjection; and one of them made figns to me that we were taking a wrong road. I immediately called out to Mr. Mackay to ftop. This was naturally enough taken for an alarm, and threw my people into great diforder. When, however, I was underftood, and we had muftered again, our Indian informed us, that the noife we heard was occafioned by a debate among the natives, whether they fhould ftop us or not. When, therefore, we had got into the right road, I made fuch arrangements as might be neceffary for our defence, if we fhould have an experimental proof that our late and fickle friends were converted into enemies.

Our way was through a foreft of ftately cedars, beneath a range of lofty hills, covered with rocks, and without any view of the river. The path was well beaten, but rendered incommodious by the large ftones which lay along it.

As we were continuing our route, we all felt the fenfation of having found a loft friend at the fight of our dog; but he appeared, in a great degree, to have loft his former fagacity. He ran in a wild way backwards and forwards; and though he kept our road, I could not induce

him

him to acknowledge his master. Sometimes he seemed disposed to approach as if he knew us; and then, on a sudden, he would turn away, as if alarmed at our appearance. The poor animal was reduced almost to a skeleton, and we occasionally dropped something to support him, and by degrees he recovered his former sagacity.

When the night came on we stopped at a small distance from the river, but did not venture to make a fire. Every man took his tree, and laid down in his clothes, and with his arms, beneath the shade of its branches. We had removed to a short distance from the path; no centinel was now appointed, and every one was left to watch for his own safety.

Friday 26.

After a very restless, though undisturbed night, we set forward as soon as day appeared, and walked on with all possible expedition, till we got to the upper, which we now called Friendly Village, and was the first we visited on our outward journey.

It was eight in the morning of a very fine day when we arrived, and found a very material alteration in the place since we left it. Five additional houses had been erected and were filled with salmon: the increase of inhabitants was in the same proportion. We were received with great kindness, and a messenger was dispatched to inform the chief, whose name was Soocomlick, and who was then at his fishing-weir, of our arrival. He immediately returned to the village to confirm the cordial reception of his people; and having conducted us to his house, entertained us with the most respectful hospitality. In short, he behaved to us with so much attention and kindness, that I did not withhold any thing in my

power

power to give, which might afford him fatisfaction. I prefented him with two yards of blue cloth, an axe, knives, and various other articles. He gave me in return a large fhell which refembled the under fhell of a Guernfey oyfter, but fomewhat larger. Where they procure them I could not difcover, but they cut and polifh them for bracelets, ear-rings, and other perfonal ornaments. He regretted that he had no fea-otter fkins to give me, but engaged to provide abundance of them whenever either my friends or myfelf fhould return by fea ; an expectation which I thought it right to encourage among thefe people. He alfo earneftly requefted me to bring him a gun and ammunition. I might have procured many curious articles at this place, but was prevented by the confideration that we muft have carried them on our backs upwards of three hundred miles through a mountainous country. The young chief, to his other acts of kindnefs, added as large a fupply of fifh as we chofe to take.

Our vifit did not occafion any particular interruption of the ordinary occupation of the people ; efpecially of the women, who were employed in boiling forrel, and different kinds of berries, with falmon-roes, in large fquare kettles of cedar wood. This pottage, when it attained a certain confiftency, they took out with ladles, and poured it into frames of about twelve inches fquare and one deep, the bottom being covered with a large leaf, which were then expofed to the fun till their contents became fo many dried cakes. The roes that are mixed up with the bitter berries, are prepared in the fame way. From the quantity of this kind of provifion, it muft be a principal article of food, and probably of traffic. Thefe people have alfo portable chefts of cedar, in which they pack them, as

well

well as their salmon, both dried and roasted. It appeared to me, that they eat no flesh, except such as the sea may afford them, as that of the sea-otter and the seal. The only instance we observed to the contrary, was in the young Indian who accompanied us among the islands, and has been already mentioned as feasting on the flesh of a porcupine: whether this be their custom throughout the year, or only during the season of the salmon fishery; or, whether there were any casts of them, as in India, I cannot pretend to determine. It is certain, however, that they are not hunters, and I have already mentioned the abhorrence they expressed at some venison which we brought to their village. During our former visit to these people, they requested us not to discharge our fire-arms, lest the report should frighten away the salmon, but now they expressed a wish that I should explain the use and management of them. Though their demeanour to us was of the most friendly nature, and they appeared without any arms, except a few who accidentally had their daggers, I did not think it altogether prudent to discharge our pieces; I therefore fired one of my pistols at a tree marked for the purpose, when I put four out of five buck shot, with which it was loaded, into the circle, to their extreme astonishment and admiration.

These people were in general of the middle stature, well-set, and better clothed with flesh than any of the natives of the interior country. Their faces are round, with high cheek bones, and their complexion between the olive and the copper. They have small grey eyes with a tinge of red; they have wedge heads, and their hair is of a dark brown colour, inclining to black. Some wear it long, keep it well combed, and let it hang loose over their shoulders, while they divide and tie it in knots over

the

the temples. Others arrange its plaits, and bedawb it with brown earth, so as to render it impervious to the comb; they, therefore, carry a bodkin about them to eafe the frequent irritation, which may be fuppofed to proceed from fuch a ftate of the head. The women are inclined to be fat, wear their hair fhort, and appear to be very fubject to fwelled legs, a malady that, probably, proceeds from the pofture in which they are always fitting: as they are chiefly employed in the domeftic engagements of fpinning, weaving, preparing the fifh, and nurfing their children, which did not appear to be numerous. Their cradle differed from any that I had feen; it confifted of a frame fixed round a board of fufficient length, in which the child, after it has been fwathed, is placed on a bed of mofs, and a conductor contrived to carry off the urinary difcharge. They are flung over one fhoulder by means of a cord faftened under the other, fo that the infant is always in a pofition to be readily applied to the breaft, when it requires nourifhment I faw feveral whofe heads were inclofed in boards covered with leather, till they attain the form of a wedge. The women wear no clothing but the robe, either loofe or tied round the middle with a girdle, as the occafion may require, with the addition of a fringed apron, already mentioned, and a cape, in the form of an inverted bowl or difh. To the robe and cap, the men add, when it rains, a circular mat with an opening in the middle fufficient to admit the head, which extending over the fhoulders, throws off the wet. They alfo occafionally wear fhoes of dreffed moofefkin, for which they are indebted to their neighbours. Thofe parts, which among all civilized nations are covered from familiar view, are here openly expofed.

They

They are altogether dependent on the fea and rivers for their fuſte-nance, fo that they may be confidered as a ſtationary people; hence it is that the men engage in thoſe toilſome employments, which the tribes who ſupport themſelves by the chaſe, leave entirely to the women. Polygamy is permitted among them, though, according to my obſerva-tion, moſt of the men were ſatisfied with one wife, with whom, how-ever, chaſtity is not confidered as a neceſſary virtue. I faw but one woman whoſe under lip was fplit and disfigured with an appendant ornament. The men frequently bathe, and the boys are continually in the water. They have nets and lines of various kinds and ſizes, which are made of cedar bark, and would not be known from thoſe made of hemp. Their hooks confiſt of two pieces of wood or bone, forming when fixed together, an obtuſe angle.

Their fpears or darts are from four to ſixteen feet in length; the barb or point being fixed in a focket, which, when the animal is ſtruck, flips from it: thus the barb being faſtened by a ſtring to the handle, remains as a buoy; or enables the aquatic hunter to tire and take his prey. They are employed againſt fea-otters, feals, and large fiſh.

Their hatchets are made principally of about fourteen inches of bar-iron, fixed into a wooden handle, as I have already deſcribed them; though they have fome of bone or horn: with theſe, a mallet and wooden wedge, they hew their timbers and form their planks. They muſt alfo have other tools with which they complete and poliſh their work, but my ſtay was fo ſhort, my anxiety fo great, and my ſituation fo critical, that many circumſtances may be ſuppoſed to have efcaped me.

Their

Their canoes are made out of the cedar tree, and will carry from eight to fifty perfons.

Their warlike weapons, which, as far as I could judge, they very feldom have occafion to employ, are bows and arrows, fpears, and daggers. The arrows are fuch as have been already defcribed, but rather of a flighter make. The bows are not more than two feet and an half in length; they are formed of a flip of red cedar; the grain being on one fide untouched with any tool, while the other is fecured with finews attached to it by a kind of glue. Though this weapon has a very flender appearance, it throws an arrow with great force, and to a confiderable diftance. Their fpears are about ten feet long, and pointed with iron. Their daggers are of various kinds, being of Britifh, Spanifh, and American manufacture.

Their houfehold furniture confifts of boxes, troughs, and difhes formed of wood, with different veffels made of watape. Thefe are employed, according to their feveral applications, to contain their valuables and provifions, as well as for culinary purpofes, and to carry water. The women make ufe of mufcle-fhells to fplit and clean their fifh, and which are very well adapted to that purpofe.

Their ornaments are necklaces, collars, bracelets for the arms, wrifts, and legs, with ear-rings, &c.

They burn their dead, and difplay their mourning, by cutting their hair fhort, and blackening their faces. Though I faw feveral places where

bodies

bodies had been burned, I was furprifed at not feeing any tomb or memorial of the dead, particularly when their neighbours are fo fuperftitioufly
attentive to the erection and prefervation of them.

From the number of their canoes, as well as the quantity of their
chefts and boxes, to contain their moveables, as well as the infufficiency
of their houfes, to guard againft the rigours of a fevere winter, and the
appearance of the ground around their habitations, it is evident that
thefe people refide here only during the fummer or falmon feafon, which
does not probably laft more than three months. It may be reafonably
inferred, therefore, that they have villages on the fea-coaft, which they
inhabit during the reft of the year. There it may be fuppofed they leave
the fick, the infirm, and the aged; and thither they may bear the afhes of
thofe who die at the place of their fummer refidence.

Of their religion I can fay but little, as my means of obfervation were
very contracted. I could difcover, however, that they believed in a
good and an evil fpirit: and that they have fome forms of worfhip to conciliate the protection of one, and perhaps to avert the enmity of the
other, is apparent from the temples which I have defcribed; and where,
at ftated periods, it may be prefumed they hold the feafts, and perform
the facrifices, which their religion, whatever it may be, has inftituted as
the ceremonials of their public worfhip.

From the very little I could difcover of their government, it is altogether different from any political regulation which had been remarked
by

by me among the favage tribes. It is on this river alone that one man appears to have an exclufive and hereditary right to what was neceffary to the exiftence of thofe who are affociated with him. I allude to the falmon weir, or fifhing place, the fole right to which confers on the chief an arbitrary power. Thofe embankments could not have been formed without a very great and affociated labour; and, as might be fuppofed, on the condition that thofe who affifted in conftructing it fhould enjoy a participating right in the advantages to be derived from it. Neverthelefs, it evidently appeared to me, that the chief's power over it, and the people, was unlimited, and without control. No one could fifh without his permiffion, or carry home a larger portion of what he had caught, than was fet apart for him. No one could build an houfe without his confent; and all his commands appeared to be followed with implicit obedience. The people at large feemed to be on a perfect equality, while the ftrangers among them were obliged to obey the commands of the natives in general, or quit the village. They appear to be of a friendly difpofition, but they are fubject to fudden gufts of paffion, which are as quickly compofed; and the tranfition is inftantaneous, from violent irritation to the moft tranquil demeanor. Of the many tribes of favage people whom I have feen, thefe appear to be the moft fufceptible of civilization. They might foon be brought to cultivate the little ground about them which is capable of it. There is a narrow border of a rich black foil, on either fide of the river, over a bed of gravel, which would yield any grain or fruit, that are common to fimilar latitudes in Europe.

The

The very few words which I collected of their language, are as follow:—

Zimilk,	Salmon.
Dilly,	A fish of the size of a salmon, with canine teeth.
Sepnas,	Hair of the head.
Kietis,	An axe.
Clougus,	Eyes.
Itzas,	Teeth.
Ma-acza,	Nose.
Ich-yeh,	Leg.
Shous-shey,	Hand.
Watts,	Dog.
Zla-achle,	House.
Zimnez,	Bark mat robe.
Couloun,	Beaver or otter ditto.
Dichts,	Stone.
Neach,	Fire
Ulkan,	Water.
Gits com,	A mat.
Shiggimia,	Thread.
Till-kewan,	Chest or box.
Thlogatt,	Cedar bark.
Achimoul,	Beads got upon their coast.
Il-caiette,	A bonnet.
Couny,	A clam shell.
Nochasky,	A dish composed of berries and salmon roes.
Caiffre,	What ?

CHAP.

CHAPTER XIII.

Leave the Friendly Village. Attentions of the natives at our departure. Stop to divide our provisions. Begin to ascend the mountains. Circumcumstances of the ascent. Journey continued. Arrive at the place from whence we set out by land. Meet with Indians there. Find the canoe, and all the other articles in a state of perfect security and preservation. Means employed to compel the restoration of articles which were afterwards stolen. Proceed on our homeward-bound voyage. Some account of the natives on the river. The canoe is run on a rock, &c. Circumstances of the voyage. Enter the Peace River. Statement of courses. Continue our route. Circumstances of it. Proceed onwards in a small canoe, with an Indian, to the lower fort, leaving the rest of the people to follow me. Arrive at Fort Chepewyan. The voyage concluded.

———————

1793. July.

AT eleven in the morning we left this place, which I called Friendly Village, accompanied by every man belonging to it, who attended us about a mile, when we took a cordial leave of them; and if we might judge from appearances, they parted from us with regret.

In a short time we halted, to make a division of our fish, and each man had about twenty pounds weight of it, except Mr. Mackay and myself, who were content with shorter allowance, that we might have less weight

to

to carry. We had alfo a little flour, and fome pemmican. Having com-pleted this arrangement with all poffible expedition, we proceeded on-wards, the ground rifing gradually, as we continued our route. When we were clear of the wood, we faw the mountain towering above, and ap-parently of impracticable afcent. We foon came to the fork of the river, which was at the foot of the precipice, where the ford was three feet deep, and very rapid. Our young Indian, though much recovered, was ftill too weak to crofs the water, and with fome difficulty I carried him over on my back.

It was now one in the afternoon, and we had to afcend the fummit of the firft mountain before night came on, in order to look for water. I left the fick Indian, with his companion and one of my men, to fol-low us, as his ftrength would permit him. The fatigue of afcending thefe precipices I fhall not attempt to defcribe, and it was paft five when we arrived at a fpot where we could get water, and in fuch an ex-tremity of wearinefs, that it was with great pain any of us could crawl about to gather wood for the neceffary purpofe of making a fire. To relieve our anxiety, which began to increafe every moment for the fitua-tion of the Indian, about feven he and his companions arrived; when we confoled ourfelves by fitting round a blazing fire, talking of paft dan-gers, and indulging the delightful reflection that we were thus far ad-vanced on our homeward journey. Nor was it poffible to be in this fituation without contemplating the wonders of it. Such was the depth of the precipices below, and the height of the mountains above, with the rude and wild magnificence of the fcenery around, that I fhall not attempt to defcribe fuch an aftonifhing and awful combination of objects; of which, indeed, no defcription can convey an adequate idea.

Even

Even at this place, which is only, as it were, the firſt ſtep towards gaining the ſummit of the mountains, the climate was very ſenſibly changed. The air that fanned the village which we left at noon, was mild and cheering; the graſs was verdant, and the wild fruits ripe around it. But here the ſnow was not yet diſſolved, the ground was ſtill bound by the froſt, the herbage had ſcarce begun to ſpring, and the crowberry buſhes were juſt beginning to bloſſom.

So great was our fatigue of yeſterday, that it was late before we proceeded to return over the mountains, by the ſame route which we had followed in our outward journey. There was little or no change in the appearance of the mountains ſince we paſſed them, though the weather was very fine. Saturday 27.

At nine this morning we arrived at the ſpot, where we ſlept with the natives on the 16th inſtant, and found our pemmican in good condition where we had buried it. Sunday 28.

The latitude of this place, by obſervation, when I paſſed, I found to be 52. 46. 32. I now took time, and the diſtance between ſun and moon. I had alſo an azimuth, to aſcertain the variation.

We continued our route with fine weather, and without meeting a ſingle perſon on our way, the natives being all gone, as we ſuppoſed, to the Great River. We recovered all our hidden ſtores of proviſions, and arrived about two in the afternoon of Sunday, Auguſt the 4th, at the place which we had left a month before.

A conſiderable number of Indians were encamped on the oppoſite ſide

of

of the ſmall river, and in conſequence of the weather, confined to their lodges: as they muſt have heard of, if not ſeen, us, and our arms being out of order from the rain, I was not ſatisfied with our ſituation; but did not wiſh to create an alarm. We, therefore, kept in the edge of the wood, and called to them, when they turned out like ſo many furies, with their arms in their hands, and threatening deſtruction if we dared to approach their habitations. We remained in our ſtation till their paſſion and apprehenſions had ſubſided, when our interpreter gave them the neceſſary information reſpecting us. They proved to be ſtrangers to us, but were the relations of thoſe whom we had already ſeen here, and who, as they told us, were upon an iſland at ſome diſtance up the river. A meſſenger was accordingly ſent to inform them of our arrival.

On examining the canoe, and our property, which we had left behind, we found it in perfect ſafety; nor was there the print of a foot near the ſpot. We now pitched our tent, and made a blazing fire, and I treated myſelf, as well as the people, with a dram; but we had been ſo long without taſting any ſpirituous liquor, that we had loſt all reliſh for it. The Indians now arrived from above, and were rewarded for the care they had taken of our property with ſuch articles as were acceptable to them.

Monday 5.

At nine this morning I ſent five men in the canoe, for the various articles we had left below, and they ſoon returned with them, and except ſome bale goods, which had got wet, they were in good order, particularly the proviſions, of which we were now in great need.

Many of the natives arrived both from the upper and lower parts of
the

the river, each of whom was dreffed in a beaver robe. I purchafed fifteen of them; and they preferred large knives in exchange. It is an extraordinary circumftance, that thefe people, who might have taken all the property we left behind us, without the leaft fear of detection, fhould leave that untouched, and purloin any of our utenfils, which our confidence in their honefty gave them a ready opportunity of taking. In fact, feveral articles were miffing, and as I was very anxious to avoid a quarrel with the natives, in this ftage of our journey, I told thofe who remained near us, without any appearance of anger, that their relations who were gone, had no idea of the mifchief that would refult to them from taking our property. I gravely added, that the falmon, which was not only their favourite food, but abfolutely neceffary to their exiftence, came from the fea which belonged to us white men; and that as, at the entrance of the river, we could prevent thofe fifh from coming up it, we poffeffed the power to ftarve them and their children. To avert our anger, therefore, they muft return all the articles that had been ftolen from us. This fineffe fucceeded. Meffengers were difpatched to order the reftoration of every thing that had been taken. We purchafed feveral large falmon of them and enjoyed the delicious meal which they afforded.

At noon this day, which I allotted for repofe, I got a meridian altitude, o. 1. 11. which gave 53. 24. 10. I alfo took time. The weather had been cloudy at intervals.

Every neceffary preparation had been made yefterday for us to con- Tuefday 6 tinue our route to day; but before our departure, fome of the natives

arrived

arrived with part of the ſtolen articles; the reſt, they ſaid, had been taken by people down the river, who would be here in the courſe of the morning, and recommended their children to our commiſeration, and themſelves to our forgiveneſs.

The morning was cloudy, with ſmall rain, neverthelefs I ordered the men to load the canoe, and we proceeded in high ſpirits on finding ourſelves once more ſo comfortably together in it. We landed at an houſe on the firſt iſland, where we procured a few ſalmon, and four fine beaver ſkins. There had been much more rain in theſe parts than in the country above, as the water was pouring down the hills in torrents. The river conſequently roſe with great rapidity, and very much impeded our progreſs.

The people on this river are generally of the middle ſize, though I ſaw many tall men among them. In the cleanlineſs of their perſons they reſemble rather the Beaver Indians than the Chepewyans. They are ignorant of the uſe of fire arms, and their only weapons are bows and arrows, and ſpears. They catch the larger animals in ſnares, but though their country abounds in them, and the rivers and lakes produce plenty of fiſh, they find a difficulty in ſupporting themſelves, and are never to be ſeen but in ſmall bands of two or three families. There is no regular government among them; nor do they appear to have a ſufficient communication or underſtanding with each other, to defend themſelves againſt an invading enemy, to whom they fall an eaſy prey. They have all the animals common on the Weſt ſide of the mountains, except the buffalo and the wolf; at leaſt we ſaw none of the latter, and there being none of the former, it is evident that their progrefs is from the South-Eaft. The fame language is fpoken, with very little exception from the extent of my travels down this river, and in a direct line from the North-Eaft head of it in the latitude 53° or 54° to Hudfon's Bay; fo that a Chepewyan, from which tribe they have all fprung, might leave Churchill River, and proceeding in every direction to the North-Weft of this line without knowing any language except his own, would underftand them all: I except the natives of the fea coaft, who are altogether a different people. As to the people to the Eaftward of this river, I am not qualified to fpeak of them.

At twelve we ran our canoe upon a rock, fo that we were obliged to land in order to repair the injury fhe had received; and as the rain came on with great violence, we remained here for the night. The falmon were now driving up the current in fuch large fhoals, that the water feemed, as it were, to be covered with the fins of them.

About nine this morning the weather cleared, and we embarked. Wednef 7 The fhoals of falmon continued as yefterday. There were frequent fhowers throughout the day, and every brook was deluged into a river. The water had rifen at leaft one foot and an half perpendicular in the laft twenty-four hours. In the dufk of the evening we landed for the night.

The water continued rifing during the night; fo that we were dif- Thurfday 8. turbed twice in the courfe of it, to remove our baggage. At fix in the morning we were on our way, and proceeded with continual and laborious

rious exertion, from the increaſed rapidity of the current.   After having paſſed the two carrying places of Rocky Point, and the Long Portage, we encamped for the night.

Friday 9.

We ſet off at five, after a rainy night, and in a foggy morning.   The water ſtill retained its height.   The ſun, however, ſoon beamed upon us ; and our clothes and baggage were in ſuch a ſtate that we landed to dry them.   After ſome time we re-embarked, and arrived at our firſt en-campment on this river about ſeven in the evening.   The water fell con-ſiderably in the courſe of the day.

Saturday 10.

The weather was cloudy with ſlight ſhowers, and at five this morn-ing we embarked, the water falling as faſt as it had riſen.   This circum-ſtance ariſes from the mountainous ſtate of the country on either ſide of the river, from whence the water ruſhes down almoſt as faſt as it falls from the heavens, with the addition of the ſnow it melts in its way.   At eight in the evening we ſtopped for the night.

Sunday 11.

At five this morning we proceeded with clear weather.   At ten we came to the foot of the long rapid, which we aſcended with poles much eaſier than we expected.   The rapids that were ſo ſtrong, and violent in our paſſage downwards, were now ſo reduced, that we could hardly be-lieve them to be the ſame.   At ſun-ſet we landed and encamped.

Monday 12.

The weather was the ſame as yeſterday, and we were on the water at a very early hour.   At nine we came to a part of the river where there was little or no current.   At noon we landed to gum the canoe, when I

took

took a meridian altitude, which gave 54. 11. 36. North latitude. We continued our route nearly Eaft, and at three in the afternoon approached the fork, when I took time, and the diftance between the fun and moon. At four in the afternoon we left the main branch. The current was quite flack, as the water had fallen fix feet, which muft have been in the courfe of three days. At fun-fet we landed and took our ftation for the night.

There was a very heavy rain in the night, and the morning was cloudy; we renewed our voyage, however, at a very early hour, and came to the narrow gut between the mountains of rock, which was a paffage of fome rifk; but fortunately the ftate of the water was fuch, that we got up without any difficulty, and had more time to examine thefe extraordinary rocks than in our outward paffage. They are as perpendicular as a wall, and give the idea of a fucceffion of enormous Gothic churches. We were now clofely hemmed in by the mountains, which have loft much of their fnow fince our former paffage by them. We encamped at a late hour, cold, wet, and hungry: for fuch was the ftate of our provifions, that our neceffary allowance did not anfwer to the active cravings of our appetites.

The weather was cold and raw, with fmall rain, but our neceffities would not fuffer us to wait for a favourable change of it, and at half paft five we arrived at the fwampy carrying-place, between this branch and the fmall river. At three in the afternoon the cold was extreme, and the men could not keep themfelves warm even by their violent exertions which our fituation required; and I now gave them the remainder

of

of our rum to fortify and fupport them. The canoe was fo heavy that the lives of two of them were endangered in this horrible carrying place. At the fame time it muft be obferved, that from the fatiguing circumftances of our journey, and the inadequate ftate of our provifions, the natural ftrength of the men had been greatly diminifhed. We encamped on the banks of the bad river.

Thurfday 15.   The weather was now clear, and the fun fhone upon us. The water was much lower than in the downward paffage, but as cold as ice, and, unfortunately, the men were obliged to be continually in it to drag on the canoe. There were many embarras, through which a paffage might have been made, but we were under the neceffity of carrying both the canoe and baggage.

About fun-fet we arrived at our encampment of the 13th of June, where fome of us had nearly taken our eternal voyage. The legs and feet of the men were fo benumbed, that I was very apprehenfive of the confequences. The water being low, we made a fearch for our bag of ball, but without fuccefs. The river was full of falmon, and another fifh like the black bafs.

Friday 16.   The weather continued to be the fame as yefterday, and at two in the afternoon we came to the carrying-place which leads to the firft fmall lake; but it was fo filled with drift wood, that a confiderable portion of time was employed in making our way through it. We now reached the high land which feparates the fource of the Tacoutche Teffe, or Columbia River, and Unjigah, or Peace River: the latter of which, after receiving
many

many tributary ſtreams, paſſes through the great Slave Lake, and diſembogues itſelf in the Frozen Ocean, in latitude 69½ North, longitude
135. Weſt from Greenwich; while the former, confined by the immenſe
mountains that run nearly parallel with the Pacific Ocean, and keep it
in a Southern courſe, empties itſelf in 46. 20. North latitude and longitude 124. Weſt from Greenwich.

If I could have ſpared the time, and had been able to exert myſelf,
for I was now afflicted with a ſwelling in my ancles, ſo that I could not
even walk, but with great pain and difficulty, it was my intention to
have taken ſome ſalmon alive, and coloniſed them in the Peace River,
though it is very doubtful whether that fiſh would live in waters that
have not a communication with the ſea.

Some of the inhabitants had been here ſince we paſſed; and I apprehend, that on ſeeing our road through their country, they miſtook us
for enemies, and had therefore deſerted the place, which is a moſt convenient ſtation; as on one ſide, there is great plenty of white fiſh, and
trout, jub, carp, &c. and on the other, abundance of ſalmon, and probably other fiſh. Several things that I had left here in exchange for
articles of which I had poſſeſſed myſelf, as objects of curioſity, were
taken away. The whirtle berries were now ripe, and very fine of their
kind.

The morning was cloudy, and at five we renewed our progreſs. We
were compelled to carry from the lake to the Peace River, the paſſage,

Saturday 17.

from

from the falling of the water, being wholly obſtruĉt d by drift-wood. The meadow through which we paſſed was entirely inundated; and from the ſtate of my foot and ancle, I was obliged, though with great reluctance, to ſubmit to be carried over it.

At half paſt ſeven we began to glide along with the current of the Peace River; and almoſt at every canoe's length we perceived Beaver roads to and from the river. At two in the afternoon, an objeĉt attracted our notice at the entrance of a ſmall river, which proved to be the four beaver ſkins, already mentioned to have been preſented to me by a native, and left in his poſſeſſion to receive them on my return. I imagine, therefore, that being under the neceſſity of leaving the river, or, perhaps, fearing to meet us again, he had taken this method to reſtore them to me; and to reward his honeſty, I left three times the value of the ſkins in their place. The ſnow appeared in patches on the mountains. At four in the afternoon we paſſed the place where we found the firſt natives, and landed for the night at a late hour. In the courſe of the day we caught nine outards, or Canddo geeſe, but they were as yet without their feathers.

Sunday 18.   As ſoon as it was light we proceeded on our voyage, and drove on before the current, which was very much diminiſhed in its ſtrength, ſince we came up it. The water indeed was ſo low, that in many parts it expoſed a gravelly beach. At eleven we landed at our encampment of the ſeventh of June, to gum the canoe and dry our clothes: we then re-embarked, and at half paſt five arrived at the place, where I loſt my

book

book of memorandums, on the fourth of June, in which were certain courſes and diſtances between that day and the twenty ſixth of May, which I had now an opportunity to ſupply. They were as follow:

North-North-Weſt half a mile, Eaſt by North half a mile, North by Eaſt a quarter of a mile, North-Weſt by Weſt a quarter of a mile, Weſt-South-Weſt half a mile, North-Weſt a mile and a quarter, North-North Weſt three quarters of a mile, North by Eaſt half a mile, North-Weſt three quarters of a mile, Weſt half a mile, North-Weſt three quarters of a mile, Weſt-North-Weſt one mile and a quarter, North three quarters of a mile, Weſt by North one quarter of a mile, North-Weſt one mile and an half, Weſt-North-Weſt half a mile, North-North-Weſt three quarters of a mile, Weſt one quarter of a mile, North-North-Eaſt half a mile, North-North-Weſt two miles, and North-Weſt four miles.

We were ſeven days in going up that part of the river which we came down to-day; and it now ſwarmed, as it were, with beavers and wild fowl. There was rain in the afternoon, and about ſun-ſet we took our ſtation for the night.

We had ſome ſmall rain throughout the night. Our courſe to-day was South-South-Weſt three quarters of a mile, Weſt-North-Weſt half a mile, North half a mile, North-Weſt by Weſt three quarters of a mile, North by Weſt half a mile; a ſmall river to the left, South-Weſt by Weſt three quarters of a mile, Weſt-North-Weſt a mile and an half, North-Weſt by North four miles, a rivulet on the right, Weſt-North-Weſt three quarters of a mile; a conſiderable river from the left, North-North-Weſt

two

two miles, North half a mile, Weft-North-Weft one mile and an half; a rivulet on the right, North-Weft by Weft one mile and a quarter, Weft-North-Weft one mile, Weft-South-Weft a quarter of a mile, North-North-Weft half a mile, North-Weft half a mile, Weft-South-Weft three quarters of a mile, North-Weft by Weft three miles, Weft-South-Weft three quarters of a mile, North-Weft by Weft one mile; a fmall river on the right, South-Weft a quarter of a mile, Weft-North-Weft, iflands, four miles and an half, a river on the left, North half a mile, Weft a quarter of a mile, North a quarter of a mile, North-Weft by Weft three quarters of a mile, North-North-Eaft three quarters of a mile, North-Weft by North half a mile, Weft-North-Weft a mile and an half, and North-Weft by North half a mile. The mountains were covered with frefh fnow, whofe fhowers had diffolved in rain before they reached us. North-Weft three quarters of a mile, South-Weft a quarter of a mile, North a mile and three quarters, Weft-North-Weft a mile and a quarter, North-Weft a mile and an half, North-North-Weft half a mile, Weft-North-Weft a quarter of a mile, North half a mile; here the current was flack: North-Weft by North half a mile, North-Weft by Weft a quarter of a mile, North-North-Weft a quarter of a mile, North-Weft by Weft one mile and a quarter, North half a mile, North-Eaft by North one mile and three quarters, South-Weft one mile and a quarter, with an ifland, North by Eaft one mile, North-Weft. Here the other branch opened to us, at the diftance of three quarters of a mile.

I expected from the flacknefs of the current in this branch, that the Weftern one would be high, but I found it equally low. I had every reafon to believe that from the upper part of this branch, the diftance

could

could not be great to the country through which I paffed when I left the Great River; but it has fince been determined otherwife by Mr. J. Finlay, who was fent to explore it, and found its navigation foon terminated by falls and rapids.

The branches are about two hundred yards in breadth, and the water was fix feet lower than on our upward paffage. Our courfe, after the junction, was North-North-Weft one mile, the rapid North-Eaft down it three quarters of a mile, North by Weft one mile and a quarter, North by Eaft one mile and an half, Eaft by South one mile, North-Eaft two miles and an half, Eaft-North-Eaft a quarter of a mile; a rivulet; Eaft by South one mile and an half, North-Eaft two miles, Eaft-North-Eaft one mile, North-North-Eaft a quarter of a mile, North-Eaft by Eaft half a mile, Eaft-South-Eaft a quarter of a mile, Eaft-North-Eaft half a mile, North-Eaft two miles, North-Eaft by Eaft two miles and a quarter, South-Eaft by Eaft a quarter of a mile; a rivulet from the left; Eaft by North a mile and an half, Eaft by South one mile, Eaft-North-Eaft one mile and three quarters; a river on the right; North-North-Eaft three quarters of a mile, North-Eaft a mile and an half, North-Eaft by Eaft a mile and a quarter, Eaft-North-Eaft half a mile, and North-Eaft by North half a mile. Here we landed at our encampment of the 27th of June, from whence I difpatched a letter in an empty keg, as was mentioned in that period of my journal, which fet forth our exifting ftate, progrefs, and expectation.

Though the weather was clear, we could not embark this morning before five, as there was a rapid very near us, which required day-light to run it, that we might not break our canoe on the rocks. The baggage

gage we were obliged to carry. Our courſe was North by Eaſt a mile and an half, North-North-Eaſt a mile and an half down another rapid on the Weſt ſide; it requires great care to keep directly between the eddy current, and that which was driving down with ſo much impetuoſity. We then proceeded North-North-Weſt, a river from the right; a mile and a quarter, North-North-Eaſt a mile and an half, a river from the left; North one mile and three quarters, North-Eaſt two miles, North-Eaſt by Eaſt two miles and a quarter, Eaſt by North one mile, North-Eaſt by Eaſt four miles, a river from the left, and Eaſt by South a mile and an half. Here was our encampment on the 26th of May, beyond which it would be altogether ſuperfluous for me to take the courſes, as they are inſerted in their proper places.

As we continued our voyage, our attention was attracted by the ap-pearance of an Indian encampment. We accordingly landed, and found there had been five fires, and within that number of days, ſo that there muſt have been ſome inhabitants in the neighbourhood, though we were not ſo fortunate as to ſee them. It appeared that they had killed a num-ber of animals, and fled in a ſtate of alarm, as three of their canoes were left careleſsly on the beach, and their paddles laying about in diſorder. We ſoon after came to the carrying-place called the Portage de la Mon-tagne de Roche. Here I had a meridian altitude, which made the lati-tude 56. 3. 51. North.

The water, as I have already obſerved, was much lower than when we came up it, though at the ſame time, the current appeared to be ſtronger from this place to the forks; the navigation, however, would now be attended with greater facility, as there is a ſtony beech all tho way, ſo

that

that poles, or the towing line, may be employed with the beſt effect, where the current overpowers the uſe of paddles.

We were now reduced to a very ſhort allowance; the diſappointment, therefore, at not ſeeing any animals was proportioned to our exigences, as we did not poſſeſs at this time more than was ſufficient to ſerve us for two meals. I now diſpatched Mr. Mackay and the Indians to proceed to the foot of the rapids, and endeavour in their way to procure ſome proviſions, while I prepared to employ the utmoſt expedition in getting there; having determined, notwithſtanding the diſinclination of my people, from the recollection of what they had ſuffered in coming that way, to return by the ſame route. I had obſerved, indeed, that the water which had fallen fifteen feet perpendicular, at the narrow paſs below us, had loſt much of its former turbulence.

As diſpatch was eſſential in procuring a ſupply of proviſions, we did not delay a moment in making preparation to renew our progreſs. Five of the men began to carry the baggage, while the ſixth and myſelf took the canoe aſunder, to cleanſe her of the dirt, and expoſe her lining and timbers to the air, which would render her much lighter. About ſun-ſet Mr. Mackay and our hunters returned with heavy burdens of the fleſh of a buffalo: though not very tender, it was very acceptable, and was the only animal that they had ſeen, though the country was covered with tracks of them, as well as of the mooſe-deer and the elk. The former had done rutting, and the latter were beginning to run. Our people returned, having left their loads mid-way on the carrying place. My companion and myſelf completed our

under-

undertaking, and the canoe was ready to be carried in the morning. An hearty meal concluded the day, and every fear of future want was removed.

Wedneſ. 21.   When the morning dawned we ſet forwards, but as a fire had paſſed through the portage, it was with difficulty we could trace our road in many parts; and with all the exertion of which we were capable, we did not arrive at the river till four in the afternoon.   We found almoſt as much difficulty in carrying our canoe down the mountain as we had in getting it up; the men being not ſo ſtrong as on the former occaſion, though they were in better ſpirits; and I was now enabled to aſſiſt them, my ancle being almoſt well.   We could not, however, proceed any further till the following day, as we had the canoe to gum, with ſeveral great and ſmall poles to prepare; thoſe we had left here having been carried away by the water, though we had left them in a poſition from fifteen to twenty feet above the water-mark, at that time. Theſe occupations employed us till a very late hour.

Thurſd. 22.   The night was cold, and though the morning was fine and clear, it was ſeven before we were in a ſtate of preparation to leave this place, ſometimes driving with the current, and at other times ſhooting the rapids.   The latter had loſt much of their former ſtrength; but we, nevertheleſs, thought it neceſſary to land very frequently, in order to examine the rapids before we could venture to run them.   However, the canoe being light, we very fortunately paſſed them all, and at noon arrived at the place where I appointed to meet Mr. Mackay and the hunters: there we found them, with plenty of excellent fat meat,
ready

ready roafted, as they had killed two elks within a few hundred yards of the fpot where we then were. When the men had fatisfied their appetites, I fent them for as much of the meat as they could carry. In coming hither, Mr. Mackay informed me, that he and the hunters kept along the high land, and did not fee or crofs the Indian path. At the fame time, there can be no doubt but the road from this place to the upper part of the rapids is to be preferred to that which we came, both for expedition and fafety.

After ftaying here about an hour and an half, we proceeded with the ftream, and landed where I had forgotten my pipe-tomahawk and feal, on the eighteenth of May. The former of them I now recovered.

On leaving the mountains we faw animals grazing in every direction. In paffing along an ifland, we fired at an elk, and broke its leg; and, as it was now time to encamp, we landed; when the hunters purfued the wounded animal, which had croffed over to the main land, but could not get up the bank. We went after it, therefore, in the canoe, and killed it. To give fome notion of our appetites, I fhall ftate the elk, or at leaft the carcafe of it, which we brought away, to have weighed two hundred and fifty pounds; and as we had taken a very hearty meal at one o'clock, it might naturally be fuppofed that we fhould not be very voracious at fupper; neverthelefs, a kettle full of the elk flefh was boiled and eaten, and that veffel replenifhed and put on the fire. All that remained, with the bones, &c. was placed, after the Indian fafhion, round the fire to roaft,

and

and at ten next morning the whole was confumed by ten perfons and a large dog, who was allowed his fhare of the banquet. This is no exaggeration; nor did any inconvenience refult from what may be confidered as an inordinate indulgence.

Friday 23.   We were on the water before day-light; and when the fun rofe a beautiful country appeared around us, enriched and animated by large herds of wild cattle. The weather was now fo warm, that to us, who had not of late been accuftomed to heat, it was overwhelming and oppreffive. In the courfe of this day we killed a buffalo and a bear; but we were now in the midft of abundance, and they were not fufficiently fat to fatisfy our faftidious appetites, fo we left them where they fell. We landed for the night, and prepared ourfelves for arriving at the Fort on the following day.

Saturday 24.   The weather was the fame as yefterday, and the country increafing in beauty; though as we approached the Fort, the cattle appeared proportionably to diminifh. We now landed at two lodges of Indians, who were as aftonifhed to fee us, as if we had been the firft white men whom they had ever beheld. When we had paffed thefe people not an animal was to be feen on the borders of the river.

At length, as we rounded a point, and came in view of the Fort, we threw out our flag, and accompanied it with a general difcharge of our fire-arms; while the men were in fuch fpirits, and made fuch an active ufe of their paddles, that we arrived before the two men whom we

left

left here in the ſpring, could recover their ſenſes to anſwer us. Thus we landed at four in the afternoon, at the place which we left on the ninth of May.———Here my voyages of diſcovery terminate. Their toils and their dangers, their ſolicitudes and ſufferings, have not been exaggerated in my deſcription. On the contrary, in many inſtances, language has failed me in the attempt to deſcribe them. I received, however, the reward of my labours, for they were crowned with ſucceſs.

As I have now reſumed the character of a trader, I ſhall not trouble my readers with any ſubſequent concern, but content myſelf with the cloſing information, that after an abſence of eleven months, I arrived at Fort Chepewyan, where I remained, for the purpoſes of trade, during the ſucceeding winter.

———

THE following general, but ſhort, geographical view of the country may not be improper to cloſe this work, as well as ſome remarks on the probable advantages that may be derived from advancing the trade of it, under proper regulations, and by the ſpirit of commercial enterprize.

By ſuppoſing a line from the Atlantic, Eaſt, to the Pacific, Weſt, in the parallel of forty-five degrees of North latitude, it will, I think, nearly deſcribe the Britiſh territories in North America. For I am of opinion, that the extent of the country to the South of this line, which we have a right to claim, is equal to that to the North of it, which may be claimed by other powers.

The

The outline of what I fhall call the firft divifion, is along that track of country which runs from the head of James-Bay, in about latitude 51. North, along the Eaftern coaft, as far North as to, and through, Hudfon's Straits, round by Labrador; continuing on the Atlantic coaft, on the out-fide of the great iflands, in the gulf of St. Laurence, to the river St. Croix, by which it takes its courfe, to the height of land that divides the waters emptying themfelves into the Atlantic, from thofe difcharged into the river St. Laurence.   Then following thefe heights, as the boundary between the Britifh poffeffions, and thofe of the American States, it makes an angle Wefterly until it ftrikes the difcharge of Lake Champlain, in latitude 45. North, when it keeps a direct Weft line till it ftrikes the river St. Lau-rence, above Lake St. Francis, where it divides the Indian village St. Rigeft; from whence it follows the centre of the waters of the great river St. Laurence: it then proceeds through Lake Ontario, the connection between it and Lake Erie; through the latter, and its chain of connec-tion, by the river Detroit, as far South as latitude 42. North, and then through the lake and river St. Clair, as alfo Lake Huron, through which it continues to the ftrait of St. Mary, latitude $46\frac{1}{2}$. North; from which we will fuppofe the line to ftrike to the Eaft of North, to the head of James-Bay, in the latitude already mentioned.

Of this great tract, more than half is reprefented as barren and broken, difplaying a furface of rock and frefh water lakes, with a very fcattered and fcanty proportion of foil.   Such is the whole coaft of Labrador, and the land, called Eaft Main to the Weft of the heights, which divide the waters running into the river and gulf of St. Laurence, from thofe flowing into Hudfon's Bay.   It is confequently inhabited only by

a few

a few favages, whofe numbers are proportioned to the fcantinefs of the foil; nor is it probable, from the fame caufe, that they will encreafe. The frefh and falt waters, with a fmall quantity of game, which the few, ftinted woods afford, fupply the wants of nature: from whence, to that of the line of the American boundary, and the Atlantic ocean, the foil, wherever cultivation has been attempted, has yielded abundance; particularly on the river St. Laurence, from Quebec upwards, to the line of boundary already mentioned; but a very inconfiderable proportion of it has been broken by the plough-fhare.

The line of the fecond divifion may be traced from that of the firft at St. Mary's, from which alfo the line of American boundary runs, and is faid to continue through Lake Superior, (and through a lake called the Long Lake which has no exiftence), to the Lake of the Woods, in latitude 49. 37. North, from whence it is alfo faid to run Weft to the Miffiffipi, which it may do, by giving it a good deal of Southing, but not otherwife; as the fource of that river does not extend further North than latitude 47. 38. North, where it is no more than a fmall brook; confequently, if Great-Britain retains the right of entering it along the line of divifion, it muft be in a lower latitude, and wherever that may be, the line muft be continued Weft, till it terminates in the Pacific Ocean, to the South of the Columbia. This divifion is then bounded by the Pacific Ocean on the Weft, the Frozen Sea and Hudfon's Bay on the North and Eaft. The Ruffians, indeed, may claim with juftice, the iflands and coaft from Behring's Straits to Cook's Entry.

The

The whole of this country will long continue in the poffeffion of its prefent inhabitants, as they will remain contented with the produce of the woods and waters for their fupport, leaving the earth, from various caufes, in its virgin ftate.   The proportion of it that is fit for cultivation is very fmall, and is ftill lefs in the interior parts : it is alfo very difficult of accefs; and whilft any land remains uncultivated to the South of it, there will be no temptation to fettle it.   Befides, its climate is not in general fufficiently genial to bring the fruits of the earth to maturity. It will alfo be an afylum for the defcendants of the original inhabitants of the country to the South, who prefer the modes of life of their forefathers, to the improvements of civilifation.   Of this difpofition there is a recent inftance.   A fmall colony of Iroquois emigrated to the banks of the Safkatchiwine, in 1799, who had been brought up from their infancy under the Romifh miffionaries, and inftructed by them at a village within nine miles of Montreal.

A further divifion of this country is marked by a ridge of high land, rifing, as it were, from the coaft of Labrador, and running nearly South-Weft to the fource of the Utawas River, dividing the waters going either way to the river and gulf of St. Laurence and Hudfon's Bay, as before obferved.   From thence it ftretches to the North of Weft, to the Northward of Lake Superior, to latitude 50. North, and longitude 89. Weft, when it forks from the laft courfe at about South-Weft, and continues the fame divifion of waters until it paffes North of the fource of the Miffiffipi.   The former courfe runs, as has been obferved, in a North-Weft direction, until it ftrikes the river Nelfon, feparating the waters that difcharge themfelves into Lake Winipic, which forms part

of

of the faid river, and thofe that alfo empty themfelves into Hudfon's Bay, by the Albany, Severn, and Hay's or Hill's Rivers. From thence it keeps a courfe of about Weft-North-Weft, till it forms the banks of the Miffinipi or Churchill River, at Portage de Traite, latitude 55. 25. North. It now continues in a Weftern direction, between the Safkatchiwine and the fource of the Miffinipi, or Beaver River, which it leaves behind, and divides the Safkatchiwine from the Elk River; when, leaving thofe alfo behind, and purfuing the fame direction it leads to the high land that lies between the Unjigah and Tacoutche rivers, from whence it may be fuppofed to be the fame ridge. From the head of the Beaver River, on the Weft, the fame kind of high ground runs to the Eaft of North, between the waters of the Elk River and the Miffinipi forming the Portage la Loche, and continuing on to the latitude 57¼. North, dividing the waters that run to Hudfon's Bay from thofe going to the North Sea: from thence its courfe is nearly North, when an angle runs from it to the North of the Slave Lake, till it ftrikes Mackenzie's River.

The laft, but by no means the leaft, is the immenfe ridge, or fucceffion of ridges of ftony mountains, whofe Northern extremity dips in the North Sea, in latitude 70. North, and longitude 135. Weft, running nearly South-Eaft, and begins to be parallel with the coaft of the Pacific Ocean, from Cook's entry, and fo onwards to the Columbia. From thence it appears to quit the coaft, but ftill continuing, with lefs elevation, to divide the waters of the Atlantic from thofe which run into the Pacific. In thofe fnow-clad mountains rifes the Miffiffippi, if we admit the Miffifouri to be its fource,

which

which flows into the Gulph of Mexico; the River Nelfon, which is loft
in Hudfon's Bay; Mackenzie's River, that difcharges itfelf into the
North Sea; and the Columbia emptying itfelf into the Pacific Ocean.
The great River St. Laurence and Churchill River, with many leffer
ones, derive their fources far fhort of thefe mountains. It is, indeed, the
extenfion of thefe mountains fo far South on the fea-coaft, that prevents
the Columbia from finding a more direct courfe to the fea, as it runs
obliquely with the coaft upwards of eight degrees of latitude before it
mingles with the ocean.

It is further to be obferved, that thefe mountains, from Cook's entry
to the Columbia, extend from fix to eight degrees in breadth Eafterly;
and that along their Eaftern fkirts is a narrow ftrip of very marfhy, boggy,
and uneven ground, the outer edge of which produces coal and bitumen:
thefe I faw on the banks of Mackenzie's River, as far North as latitude 66. I alfo difcovered them in my fecond journey, at the commencement of the rocky mountains in 56. North latitude, and 120. Weft longitude; and the fame was obferved by Mr. Fidler, one of the fervants of the
Hudfon's-Bay Company, at the fource of the South branch of the Safkatchiwine, in about latitude 52. North, and longitude $112\frac{1}{2}$. Weft.* Next
to this narrow belt are immenfe plains, or meadows, commencing in a
point at about the junction of the River of the Mountain with Mackenzie's River, widening as they continue Eaft and South, till they reach
the Red River at its confluence with the Affiniboin River, from whence

* Bitumen is alfo found on the coaft of the Slave Lake, in latitude 60. North, near its difcharge by Mackenzie's River; and alfo near the forks of the Elk River.

they

they take a more Southern direction, along the Mississippi towards Mexico. Adjoining to these plains is a broken country, composed of lakes, rocks, and soil.

From the banks of the rivers running through the plains, there appeared to ooze a saline fluid, concreting into a thin, scurf on the grass. Near that part of the Slave River where it first loses the name of Peace River, and along the extreme edge of these plains, are very strong salt springs, which in the summer concrete and crystallize in great quantities. About the Lake Dauphin, on the South-West side of Lake Winipic, are also many salt ponds, but it requires a regular process to form salt from them. Along the West banks of the former is to be seen, at intervals, and traced in the line of the direction of the plains, a soft rock of lime-stone, in thin and nearly horizontal stratas, particularly on the Beaver, Cedar, Winipic, and Superior lakes, as also in the beds of the rivers crossing that line. It is also remarkable that, at the narrowest part of Lake Winipic, where it is not more than two miles in breadth, the West side is faced with rocks of this stone thirty feet perpendicular; while, on the East side, the rocks are more elevated, and of a dark-grey granite.

The latter is to be found throughout the whole extent North of this country, to the coast of Hudson's Bay, and as I have been informed, from that coast, onwards to the coast of Labrador; and it may be further observed, that between these extensive ranges of granite and lime-stone are found all the great lakes of this country.

There

There is another very large diſtrict which muſt not be forgotten; and behind all the others in ſituation as well as in ſoil, produce, and climate. This comprehends the tract called the Barren Grounds, which is to the North of a line drawn from Churchill, along the North border of the Rein-Deer Lake, to the North of the Lake of the Hills and Slave Lake, and along the North ſide of the latter to the rocky mountains, which terminate in the North Sea, latitude 70. North, and longitude 135. Weſt; in the whole extent of which no trees are viſible, except a few ſtinted ones, ſcattered along its rivers, and with ſcarce any thing of ſurface that can be called earth; yet, this inhoſpitable region is inhabited by a people who are accuſtomed to the life it requires. Nor has bountiful Nature withheld the means of ſubſiſtence; the rein deer, which ſupply both food and clothing, are ſatisfied with the produce of the hills, though they bear nothing but a ſhort curling moſs, on a ſpecies of which, that grows on the rocks, the people themſelves ſubſiſt when famine invades them. Their ſmall lakes are not furniſhed with a great variety of fiſh, but ſuch as they produce are excellent, which, with hares and partridges, form a proportion of their food.

The climate muſt neceſſarily be ſevere in ſuch a country as we have deſcribed, and which diſplays ſo large a ſurface of freſh water. Its ſeverity is extreme on the coaſt of Hudſon's Bay, and proceeds from its immediate expoſure to the North-Weſt winds that blow off the Frozen Ocean.

Theſe winds, in croſſing directly from the bay over Canada and the

Britiſh

Britifh dominions on the Atlantic, as well as over the Eaftern States of North America to that ocean, (where they give to thofe countries a length of winter aftonifhing to the inhabitants of the fame latitudes in Europe), continue to retain a great degree of force and cold in their paffage, even over the Atlantic, particularly at the time when the fun is in its Southern declination. The fame winds which come from the Frozen Ocean, over the barren grounds, and acrofs frozen lakes and fnowy plains, bounded by the rocky mountains, lofe their frigid influence, as they travel in a Southern direction, till they get to the Atlantic Ocean, where they clofe their progrefs. Is not this a fufficient caufe for the difference between the climate in America, and that of the fame latitude in Europe?

It has been frequently advanced, that the difference of clearing away the wood has had an aftonifhing influence in meliorating the climate in the former: but I am not difpofed to affent to that opinion in the extent which it propofes to eftablifh, when I confider the very trifling proportion of the country cleared, compared with the whole. The employment of the axe may have had fome inconfiderable effect; but I look to other caufes. I myfelf obferved in a country, which was in an abfolute ftate of nature, that the climate is improving; and this circumftance was confirmed to me by the native inhabitants of it. Such a change, therefore, muft proceed from fome predominating operation in the fyftem of the globe which is beyond my conjecture, and, indeed, above my comprehenfion, and may, probably, in the courfe of time, give to America the climate of Europe. It is well known, indeed, that the waters are decreafing there, and that many lakes are draining and filling up by the earth

which

which is carried into them from the higher lands by the rivers: and this may have fome partial effect.

The climate on the Weft coaft of America affimilates much more to that of Europe in the fame latitudes: I think very little difference will be found, except fuch as proceeds from the vicinity of high mountains covered with fnow. This is an additional proof that the difference in the temperature of the air proceeds from the caufe already mentioned.

Much has been faid, and much more ftill remains to be faid on the peopling of America. On this fubject I fhall confine myfelf to one or two obfervations, and leave my readers to draw their inferences from them.

The progrefs of the inhabitants of the country immediately under our obfervation, which is comprifed within the line of latitude 45. North, is as follows: that of the Efquimaux, who poffefs the fea coaft from the Atlantic through Hudfon's Straits and Bay, round to Mackenzie's River, (and I believe further) is known to be weftward: they never quit the coaft, and agree in appearance, manners, language, and habits with the inhabitants of Greenland. The different tribes whom I defcribe under the name of Algonquins and Knifteneaux, but originally the fame people, were the inhabitants of the Atlantic coaft, and the banks of the river St. Laurence and adjacent countries: their progrefs is Wefterly, and they are even found Weft and North as far

as

as Athabafca. On the contrary, the Chepewyans, and the numerous tribes who fpeak their language, occupy the whole fpace between the Knifteneaux country and that of the Efquimaux, ftretching behind the natives of the coaft of the Pacific, to latitude 52. North, on the river Columbia. Their progrefs is Eafterly; and, according to their own traditions, they came from Siberia; agreeing in drefs and manner with the people now found upon the coaft of Afia.

Of the inhabitants of the coaft of the Pacific Ocean we know little more than that they are ftationary there. The Nadowafis or Affiniboins, as well as the different tribes not particularly defcribed, inhabiting the plains on and about the fource and banks of the Safkatchiwine and Affiniboin rivers, are from the Southward, and their progrefs is North-Weft.

––––––––––––

The difcovery of a paffage by fea, North-Eaft or North-Weft from the Atlantic to the Pacific Ocean, has for many years excited the attention of governments, and encouraged the enterprifing fpirit of individuals. The non-exiftence, however, of any fuch practical paffage being at length determined, the practicability of a paffage through the continents of Afia and America becomes an object of confideration. The Ruffians, who firft difcovered that, along the coafts of Afia no ufeful or regular navigation exifted, opened an interior communication by rivers, &c.

and

through that long and wide-extended continent, to the ſtrait that ſepa-rates Aſia from America, over which they paſſed to the adjacent iſlands and continent of the latter. Our ſituation, at length, is in ſome degree ſimilar to theirs: the non-exiſtence of a practicable paſſage by ſea, and the exiſtence of one through the continent, are clearly proved; and it requires only the countenance and ſupport of the Britiſh Govern-ment, to increaſe in a very ample proportion this national advantage, and ſecure the trade of that country to its ſubjects.

Experience, however, has proved, that this trade, from its very nature cannot be carried on by individuals. A very large capital, or credit, or indeed both, is neceſſary, and conſequently an aſſociation of men of wealth to direct, with men of enterpriſe to act, in one common intereſt, muſt be formed on ſuch principles, as that in due time the latter may ſucceed the former, in continual and progreſſive ſucceſſion. Such was the equitable and ſucceſsful mode adopted by the merchants from Ca-nada, which has been already deſcribed.

The junction of ſuch a commercial aſſociation with the Hudſon's-Bay Company, is the important meaſure which I would propoſe, and the trade might then be carried on with a very ſuperior degree of advan-tage, both private and public, under the privilege of their charter, and would prove, in fact, the complete fulfilment of the conditions, on which it was firſt granted.

It would be an equal injuſtice to either party to be excluded from the
option

option of such an undertaking; for if the one has a right by charter, has not the other a right by prior possession, as being successors to the subjects of France, who were exclusively possessed of all the then known parts of this country, before Canada was ceded to Great-Britain, except the coast of Hudson's Bay, and having themselves been the discoverers of a vast extent of country since added to his Majesty's territories, even to the Hyperborean and the Pacific Oceans?

If, therefore, that company should decline, or be averse to engage in, such an extensive, and perhaps hazardous, undertaking, it would not, surely, be an unreasonable proposal to them, from government, to give up a right which they refuse to exercise, on allowing them a just and reasonable indemnification for their stock, regulated by the average dividends of a certain number of years, or the actual price at which they transfer their stock.

By enjoying the privilege of the company's charter, though but for a limited period, there are adventurers who would be willing, as they are able, to engage in, and carry on the proposed commercial undertaking, as well as to give the most ample and satisfactory security to government for the fulfilment of its contract with the company. It would, at the same time, be equally necessary to add a similar privilege of trade on the Columbia River, and its tributary waters.

If however, it should appear that the Hudson's-Bay Company have an exclusive right to carry on their trade as they think proper, and continue it on the narrow scale, and with so little benefit to the public as they now do; if they should refuse to enter into a co-operative junction with

others,

others, what reasonable cause can they assign to government for denying the navigation of the bay to Nelson's River; and, by its waters, a passage to and from the interior country, for the use of the adventurers, and for the sole purpose of transport, under the most severe and binding restrictions not to interfere with their trade on the coast, and the country between it and the actual establishments of the Canadian traders*.

By these waters that discharge themselves into Hudson's Bay at Port Nelson, it is proposed to carry on the trade to their source, at the head of the Saskatchiwine River, which rises in the Rocky Mountains, not eight degrees of longitude from the Pacific Ocean. The Tacoutche or Columbia river flows also from the same mountains, and discharges itself likewise in the Pacific, in latitude 46. 20. Both of them are capable of receiving ships at their mouths, and are navigable throughout for boats.

The distance between these waters is only known from the report of the Indians. If, however, this communication should prove inaccessible, the route I pursued, though longer, in consequence of the great

---

* Independent of the prosecution of this great object, I conceive that the merchants from Canada are entitled to such an indulgence, (even if they should be considered as not possessing a rightful claim,) in order that they might be enabled to extend their trade beyond their present limits, and have it in their power to supply the natives with a larger quantity of useful articles; the enhanced value of which, and the present difficulty of transporting them, will be fully comprehended when I relate, that the tract of transport occupies an extent of from three to four thousand miles, through upwards of sixty large lakes, and numerous rivers; and that the means of transport are slight bark canoes. It must also be observed, that those waters are intercepted by more than two hundred rapids, along which the articles of merchandise are chiefly carried on men's backs, and over an hundred and thirty carrying-places, from twenty-five paces to thirteen miles in length, where the canoes and cargoes proceed by the same toilsome and perilous operations.

angle

angle it makes to the North, will anfwer every neceffary purpofe. But whatever courfe may be taken from the Atlantic, the Columbia is the line of communication from the Pacific Ocean, pointed out by nature, as it is the only navigable river in the whole extent of Vancouver's minute furvey of that coaft: its banks alfo form the firft level country in all the Southern extent of continental coaft from Cook's entry, and, confequently, the moft Northern fituation fit for colonization, and fuitable to the refidence of a civilized people. By opening this intercourfe between the Atlantic and Pacific Oceans, and forming regular eftablifhments through the interior, and at both extremes, as well as along the coafts and iflands, the entire command of the fur trade of North America might be obtained, from latitude 48. North to the pole, except that portion of it which the Ruffians have in the Pacific. To this may be added the fifhing in both feas, and the markets of the four quarters of the globe. Such would be the field for commercial enterprife, and incalculable would be the produce of it, when fupported by the operations of that credit and capital which Great Britain fo pre-eminently poffeffes. Then would this country begin to be remunerated for the expences it has fuftained in difcovering and furveying the coaft of the Pacific Ocean, which is at prefent left to American adventurers, who without regularity or capital, or the defire of conciliating future confidence, look altogether to the intereft of the moment. They, therefore, colle&t all the fkins they can procure, and in any manner that fuits them, and having exchanged them at Canton for the produce of China, return to their own country. Such adventurers, and many of them, as I have been informed, have been very fuccefsful, would inftantly difappear from before a well-regulated trade.

It

It would be very unbecoming in me to ſuppoſe for a moment, that the Eaſt India Company would heſitate to allow thoſe privileges to their fellow-ſubjects which are permitted to foreigners, in a trade that is ſo much out of the line of their own commerce, and therefore cannot be injurious to it.

Many political reaſons, which it is not neceſſary here to enumerate, muſt preſent themſelves to the mind of every man acquainted with the enlarged ſyſtem and capacities of Britiſh commerce, in ſupport of the meaſure which I have very briefly ſuggeſted, as promiſing the moſt important advantages to the trade of the united kingdoms.

THE END.

R. Noble,
Old Bailey.

ERRATA.

─────────

The Reader is particularly requested to attend to the following Errata, as they are essential to the sense of the passages to which they apply.

PRELIMINARY ACCOUNT OF THE FUR TRADE.

Page 12,   Line 2, *for* Croix *read* Crosse.
             18, *for* thirty *read* forty.
   15,   16, *for* Mississooric *read* Missisouri.
   17,   11, *dele* Portage.
   21,   9, *for* and Montreal, where they received stores *read* and at Montreal, where they received, stored, &c.
   27,   17, *for* others *read* winterers.
   28,   28, *for* four *read* eight.
             12, *for* this *read* the.
   31,   24, *for* over *read* to.
   32,   14, *for* at *read* to.
   33,   7, *for* Portage *read* décharge.
             11, *instead of* but a very short distance from Lake Coulonge *read* at a very short distance from the Décharge.
   34,   8, *for* the latter comes in *read* the latter river comes from.
             26, *after the word* paces *add* next to this is mauvais de Musique, where, &c.
   35,   3, *instead of* take its source from the first vase to the great river *read* at the first vase, from whence the great river.
             5, *for* the whole distance *read* the distance of this Portage.
   36,   5, *for* in every lake and river *read* along every great river.
   39,   22, *dele* the whole of.
   40,   8, *for* St. Mary's *read* St. Mary's coastways.
   43,   22, *for* clear *read* is cleared of wood.
   46,   14, *for* about *read* in.
   50,   4, *for* Perche *read* Peche.
             16, *for* they *read* we.
   51,   4, *for* which leads through *read* which conducts these waters through the succeeding lakes and rivers, till they discharge themselves.
             11, *for* ends *read* runs.
             12, *dele* falling into a lake-pond.
   52,   4, *for* la Roche *read* le Roché.
   53,   6, *for* lake Pascau, &c. *read* Passeau Minac Sagaigan, or lake of Dry Berries.
   54,   4, *for* portage *read* pointe.
   55,   21, *after* an half, *place a period;* after water, *a comma.*
   56,   2, *for* land *read* lake.
   60,   3, *for* that enters lake Winipic, *read* which enters that lake.
   63,   15, *dele* off.
   73,   4, *for* pounds *read* shillings.
             5, *for* which *read* of which.
             21, *dele* of the lake.
   80,   20, *for* Croisé *read* Crosse.
   83,   17, *dele* and a.
   101,   4, *for* beech-tree *read* birch-tree.
   106,   18, *for* considerable *read* inconsiderable.

JOURNALS

ERRATA.

JOURNALS OF THE VOYAGES, &c.

Page 8,   Line 20,   *for* 1785 *read* 1786.

14,   in the second note, *for* fish *read* flesh.

18,   7,   *for* Frenchmen *read* Canadians.

23,   12,   *for* evening *read* morning.

27,   10,   *for* army *read* arms.

48,   10,   *for* curve *read* groove.

88,   10,   *for* whirtle-berries *read* hurtle-berries.

104,   12,   *for* them *read* it.

105,   8,   *for* obtained *read* completed.

109,   10,   *dele* five geese.

133,   9,   *for* these people *read* my people.

138,   14,   *for* the *read* his.

141,   3,   *for* the hunter *read* our hunter.

157,   20,   *dele* where.

        21,   *for* island several *read* where several.

184,   9,   *for* according *read* accordingly.

211,   16,   *for* East by East *read* East-South-East.

216,   date omitted.

       17,   *read* Wednesday 12.

257,   9,   *for* Chin Indians *read* Carrier Indians, and *vice versâ*.

288,   20,   *for* struck *read* stuck.

297,   date wanting.

322,   14,   *for* and *read* or.

332,   14,   *for* skin of a lynx *read* skins of the lynx.

334,   3,   *for* beat into bars *read* in bars.

335,   6,   *for* their iron is manufactured only into *read* their manufactured iron consists only of.

351,   1,   in the note, *for* positively *read* earnestly.

        2,   *for* passage *read* practicable passage.

381,   22,   *dele* 0. 1. 11.

388,   17,   *for* Cando *read* Canada.

403,   22,   *for* from *read* along.

404,   13,   *dele* difference of.

410,   11,   *for* and Columbia rivers flow *read* or Columbia River flows.

      12,   *for* themselves *read* itself.

       7,   in the note, *for* large lakes *read* large fresh water lakes.

It is to be observed, that the Courses *throughout the Journals are taken by* Compass, *and that the* Variation *must be considered.*